A volume in the
DOUGLASS SERIES IN EDUCATION,
edited by HARL R. DOUGLASS, Ph.D.,
DIRECTOR OF THE COLLEGE OF EDUCATION,
UNIVERSITY OF COLORADO

SCHOOL FINANCE

Its Theory and Practice

WILLIAM EVERETT ROSENSTENGEL
PROFESSOR OF EDUCATION
UNIVERSITY OF NORTH CAROLINA

and

JEFFERSON N. EASTMOND
ASSOCIATE PROFESSOR OF EDUCATION
BRIGHAM YOUNG UNIVERSITY

THE RONALD PRESS COMPANY > NEW YORK

3

Library of Congress Catalog Card Number: 57–6813

PRINTED IN THE UNITED STATES OF AMERICA

To

FREDA and ALBERTA

for their understanding

and direct and indirect

assistance

PREFACE

The purpose of this book is to provide a thorough discussion of the theory and practice of public school finance. Rapid social changes since World War II have produced in the public schools an enrollment which is much larger than would have been expected a generation ago. Likewise, the economic level achieved by the American people since the war has been most unusual. These factors, together with the changing value of the dollar, have brought forth more acutely some of the old as well as many new financial problems. The understanding of these problems and the formulation of sound solutions have become important to the success of school administration. This volume presents facts and principles which should prove helpful in the financial management of the public schools.

The book is divided into four parts: Part One discusses the principles which are important in understanding public school finance, with emphasis on their background and development. Part Two deals with the methods of financing public education and the structural and operational features of a satisfactory state program. The leadership function of the state and the need for participation by the federal government in the financing of public education are presented. Part Three treats the management of school funds on the local level. The local educational leader must have the knowledges and skills necessary for budgeting—and for the management of income, indebtedness, and expenditures—in order that he may advise the board of education on the operation of the public schools. Part Four discusses special problems which the administrator must face in connection with the financial management of the public schools, such as payroll procedures, insurance, and transportation.

This book is designed to serve as a text for colleges and university students who are preparing to become school administrators and as a day-by-day guide for superintendents, principals, and business managers. Carefully phrased topics for study and discussion are included with each chapter to provide the student with further applications of the principles and to direct him in more detailed exploration of the many areas of school finance.

The authors are grateful to many writers and publishers for the privilege of quoting their materials. Gratitude is also expressed to the school administrators who generously responded to requests for information and forms used in this book. To Professor Harl R. Douglass, editor of the series of which this volume is a part, the authors express thanks for counsel, criticism, and encouragement.

William Everett Rosenstengel
Jefferson N. Eastmond

January, 1957

CONTENTS

PART I

IMPORTANCE, DEVELOPMENT, AND PRINCIPLES OF SCHOOL FINANCE

1

THE CRITICAL NEEDS AND IMPORTANCE
OF SCHOOL FINANCE

ONE AXIOM evolved from human history is that public education is a democratic necessity. This was recognized by many of our great leaders in early American history. President Thomas Jefferson reflected the awareness when he said, "If a nation expects to be ignorant and free in a state of civilization, it expects what never was and what never will be." Universal free public education was invented by the United States to safeguard freedom and preserve its democratic institutions.

Through America's experience and the experience of other countries has grown the realization that the free public school is society's prime instrument for human progress. America's greatness today is recognized by our contemporary historians as largely a result of the success of the United States experiment with universal free public education. Commager has commented on the public school contribution to American democracy in this manner:

No other people has demanded so much of education as has the American. None other was ever served so well by its schools and educators.

From the beginning education has had very special, and very heavy, tasks to perform. Democracy could not work without an enlightened electorate. The various states and regions could not achieve unity without a sentiment of nationalism. The nation could not absorb tens of millions of immigrants from all parts of the globe without rapid and effective Americanization. Economic and social distinctions and privileges, severe enough to corrode democracy itself, had to be fought. To our schools went the momentous responsibility of inspiring a people to pledge and hold allegiance to these historic principles of democracy, nationalism, Americanism and egalitarianism.

3

Because we are a "new" nation we sometimes forget how very old are some of our institutions and practices. The United States—today the oldest democracy in the world and the oldest republic—also has the oldest public school system in the world.[1]

There are many ways in which public education affects America's success and well-being. Not only has it provided an environment wherein children of all classes have "rubbed elbows," but America's public school has been a tremendous force in erasing artificial class barriers, developing common understandings, and instilling a high degree of social cooperation among the American people. Furthermore, since the major policy decisions in our country must be made by the citizenry and since sound decisions are more apt to be made by a reasonably well-educated people, good schools are essential to the satisfactory functioning of our democratic form of government. No other institution or aspect of American life relates more directly or more basically to our local and national well-being. The effective intelligence and character of the American citizenry will determine the strength and character of our nation.

To perpetuate our democracy and national strength, the schools must build into the American people "the knowledges and skills which will make them industrially, socially, and personally competent." It is for this reason that public education in the United States is fundamentally a duty to be imposed on each citizen. The American people, however, have come to hold a point of view that public education is more than a necessity for the protection and preservation of the state. A satisfactory public education is regarded as the right of every individual. President Eisenhower voiced this conviction in his speech to the American people when he said:

It is the inalienable right of every person from childhood on to have access to knowledge. In our form of society this right of the individual takes on a special meaning, for the education of all our citizens is imperative to the maintenance and invigoration of America's free institutions.[2]

There have been twentieth-century developments of education throughout the world that have had some terrifying results. The world has witnessed how totalitarian nations have used education, not as an instrument of human progress, but as a tool in building a nationalistic, warlike people who have threatened the entire free world and endangered civilization. Some of our world leaders have seen this newly recognized, miraculous power of education as ranking

[1] Henry Steele Commager, "Our Schools Have Kept Us Free," *Life*, XXVIII (October 16, 1950), 46–47.

[2] President Dwight D. Eisenhower's State of the Union message delivered June 6, 1955.

with atomic energy as the two great insights of our century. This does not lessen the emphasis on universal education as a democratic necessity, but it focuses on the need to give more emphasis to our system of education if America is to meet the great challenges it faces in fulfilling its responsibility of world leadership.

I. SCHOOL FINANCE, BACKBONE OF THE EDUCATIONAL PROGRAM

Recognizing the importance of good public education to American society is one thing; achieving it is quite another. Adequate support is basic to the effective functioning of every aspect of the school program. It is an adequate financial arrangement that undergirds the entire school program. Money pays teachers' salaries, obtains instructional supplies and equipment, and is a factor in class size and teacher load. It is the financial foundation that determines the adequacy and modernity of school buildings, furniture, supervision, transportation, and the quality of the curriculum. All of these facets of the educational program are a function of the adequacy of school support. School finance is truly the backbone of the educational program.

Although generous financial support alone will not insure satisfactory schools, "good schools are not likely to be provided unless adequate financial support is available." Some of the characteristics of a really good school are now firmly established. Many of our schools, however, fall far short of these commonly accepted standards. The basic reason for not having good schools throughout America today is primarily the lack of allocating adequate funds for educational purposes.

Some of the persistent problems of American education are revealed in an inventory that was taken some years ago concerning school conditions.

Americans take too much for granted. We are all comfortably aware of the fact that our nation as a whole has the highest standard of living in the world and one of the finest, freest and most liberal educational systems. How many of us, however, are aware that there are 10 million adults with so little schooling that they are virtually illiterate, that there are nearly 2 million children, age 6 to 15, not in school, and that 5 million out of 17 million men examined in the (World War II) draft were rejected for educational, mental, and physical deficiencies which might have been prevented to some extent by good education?[3]

In view of the slowness of the American schools to accept change, the continued teacher shortage, the prolonged inflationary domestic

[3] John K. Norton and Eugene S. Lawler, *Unfinished Business in American Education* (Washington, D.C.: The American Council on Education, 1946), p. i.

conditions, and the role America has played in a world in conflict and tension since this inventory, there is little reason to suppose the scene has changed radically in the ensuing years. These same problems are with us today. The essence of this kind of a summary of educational needs in the United States, however, is difficult to reconcile in view of the fundamental faith of the American people in education and in view of the basic recognition of universal education as a democratic necessity and as an inalienable right of each citizen.

A strong relationship exists between adequate monies for education and the quality of the school program that is offered. It is therefore apparent that state fiscal policies for schools need continuous attention and re-examination by citizens to insure strong educational systems. Certainly Americans must give more attention to the financial adequacy of their schools if the United States is to meet the many challenges presented in the second half of the twentieth century.

Glibly mouthing support for education is one thing; providing good, efficient schools is quite another. America's experience with public education reveals that financial support is not, by itself, adequate for the provision of good schools. Citizen interest and participation in school affairs is also absolutely essential for a high quality of education. Each citizen must realize his part in molding the strength of America by assuming his responsibility to maintain good schools in his local community. He must give his support both financially and in other ways.

In our present governmental structure there are few public services which reflect citizen feelings as directly as does public education. It therefore becomes important for each citizen to become convinced that his personal, his community, his state, his national educational expenditures represent sound investments. He must come to realize that in the final analysis it is the moral, physical, and intellectual strength of the people that determines a nation's greatness and that the results of good schools are reflected in the economic well-being of a nation. With reference to this conclusion, reliable research efforts are accumulating evidence that may be summed up as follows:

The schools are not economic parasites draining off national income into some non-productive enterprise. On the contrary, education (a) provides the intelligence and skill essential to modern industry, (b) contributes to health and safety, (c) results in better conservation of natural resources, (d) leads to personal thrift and the development of capital resources, (e) is the basis of efficiency in business management, (f) increases the volume and lifts the level of consumer demand, (g) improves the earning power and spending power of the people, and (h) through the purchase of buildings, equipment and materials and through the salaries of its employees turns its expenditures quite directly back into the economic life stream of the nation.[4]

It can readily be shown that the intelligence and efficiency of workers and management vitally affect production of American business and industry. It can also be shown that the level of education of the American citizen is closely related to the extent and quality of his participation in civic and community affairs. The U.S. Chamber of Commerce and other groups have long supported studies showing that there is almost no phase of a community's political, social, or economic life which is not in one way or another affected by the quality of its schools.

2. TRENDS AND IMPENDING NEEDS IN SCHOOL FINANCE

Any attempt to predict or project into the future is usually aided by an understanding of the past. Since this is particularly true in the area of school finance, it is appropriate to examine here some of the important trends that have a direct bearing on school support.

The problems of school finance in the American elementary and secondary schools pivot principally upon three important and interrelated factors. These are (1) the number of children to be educated, (2) the national economy, and (3) the amount of money spent for education. In order to give an accurate notion of the status and needs of school finance in the future, we shall examine the current and past status of these three factors and attempt to project them into the future.

The number of children to be educated

During the first half of the twentieth century, the total population of America doubled, to a 1950 figure of more than 151 million (see Table 1). This increase has, of course, been reflected in school enrollment. While the elementary schools have quite consistently enrolled about two-thirds of the total school-age population (5 to 17 years), the high schools have shown a remarkable increase in the percentage of the population enrolled during this fifty-year period. Beginning with an enrollment of some 519,000 at the turn of the century, high school enrollments doubled every decade until 1930 and reached a high of more than 6.6 million in 1940, and then after a slight decline reached approximately this same enrollment figure in 1955 (see Table 1). The long upward trend in secondary school enrollments reflects the growing emphasis the American people have come to place on

[4] American Association of School Administrators, *The Expanding Role of Education*, 26th Yearbook (Washington, D.C.: The Association, 1948), pp. 281–82.

TABLE 1. Historical summary and projections of statistical data related to school finance

(Thousands)

Item	1900	1910	1920	1930	1940	1950	1955	1960	1965
Total U.S. population	75,603	91,972	105,711	122,775	131,892	151,240	165,000[a]	177,000[a]	190,000[a]
Total population ages 5-17 years	21,404	24,240	27,729	31,571	29,805	30,788	37,300[a]	44,400[a]	48,100[a]
Elementary enrollment (K-8)									
Public	14,984	16,899	19,378	21,279	18,833	19,405	24,210[d]	29,390[d]	31,548[c]
Non-public	1,278			2,235	2,153	2,663	3,530[d]	4,260[d]	4,111[c]
Total	16,262	18,529	20,964	23,514	20,986	22,068	27,740[d]	33,650[d]	35,659[b]
Secondary enrollment (9-12)									
Public	519	915	2,200	4,399	6,601	5,707	6,620[d]	8,180[d]	10,565[c]
Non-public	180			341	458	626	800[d]	990[d]	1,325[c]
Total	699			4,740	7,059	6,333	7,420[d]	9,170[d]	11,890[b]
Total school enrollment (K-12)	16,961			28,254	28,045	28,401	35,160	42,820	47,549[b]

SOURCES: Basic Data, *Biennial Survey of Education in the U.S.*, 1950-52.
a. National Citizens Commission for the Public Schools, *Financing Public Education in the Decade Ahead* (New York: The Commission, 1954). p. 42.
b. U.S. Office of Education, "40 Million In School," *School Life*, XXXVIII (October, 1955), pp. 5-6.
c. Authors' estimate.
d. Emery M. Foster and Carol J. Hobson, "Vital Statistics of American Education: 1954-1960," *School Life*, XXXVII (October, 1954), pp. 6-7.

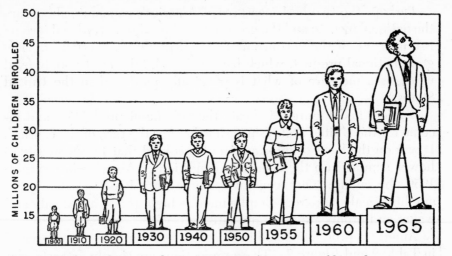

Fig. 1. Total school-age population, 1900–1965. (For sources of basic data, projection, and estimates, see Table 1.)

the value of education. The fluctuations in this trend are results of changes in the fertility of the American people or of economic conditions.

Table 1 also contains population and enrollment projections to the year 1965. By that year the estimated total U.S. population will be about 190 million and the number of school-age children (5 to 17 years) is estimated to be more than 48 million.

By 1965, as illustrated in Figure 1, public high school enrollments may be expected to reach an all-time high. These enrollment figures with their accompanying demands for facilities, supplies, and teachers give some notion of the increased burden that must be supported by public school finance during the next few years. It is estimated that some 950,000 new classrooms will be needed to house American school children by the end of 1965. Figuring building costs in terms of present-day dollar values, this alone will require more than $30 billion.

The national economy

Analyzing the needs of education is only a part of the problem to be considered in the financing of schools. The amount of money for these and other purposes is also an important consideration. How adequately the financial needs of education are met is obviously dependent on the general prosperity or economic ability of the nation.

Perhaps the two best measures of America's economic ability are the national income and the gross national product. National income is a measure of the net income from all productive activities. The gross national product, which has come to be the most widely used index, is a measure of what is physically produced in the United States.[5]

Table 2 and Figure 2 indicate the volume of production and income for the United States since shortly after the turn of the century. It was on the basis of information of this kind that President Eisenhower summed up the economic condition of America in the mid-1950's by saying: "Our economy today is marvelously prosperous by any historical standard. Employment is high, prices are steady and wages and profits are generally satisfactory."[6]

America's production and income for the future are also presented in Table 2 and Figure 2. These projections are simply extensions of the existing trends, but may be assumed to be reasonably accurate for a number of reasons. First, the total labor force can be quite accurately predicted over a decade since all people who will be over 14 years of age are now living and mortality rates can be predicted within close limits. Second, there is little chance of making more than a slight error in estimating the number of working hours per year that will be put in by the average employed person. Third, fairly accurate forecasts of productivity are possible because for a long time the average annual rate of increase in "output per manhour" has been relatively constant.

Based on present price levels, tax rates, and levels of employment, the gross national product is estimated to be at least $525 billion by 1965. This is more than double that of 1949, and it represents a higher standard of living and an expansion of the "enormous margin of luxury" which America enjoys and has available for supporting vitally needed services such as public education.

[5] The gross national product is a concept designed to measure the continuing flow of goods and services into consumption and use. It is a measure of *output* and represents the gross value of all goods and services produced by business enterprises (including farmers, professional persons, and other self-employed individuals) and by governmental agencies. The term thus measures the market value of the nation's total annual output of goods and services. This is a gross figure because although it excludes the value of raw material and semifinished goods—products "consumed" in the production process—it does not exclude the value of the physical capital used up or worn out in that process.

[6] From President Dwight D. Eisenhower's "Economic Report of the President," delivered to Congress on January 28, 1954.

TABLE 2. General indicators of U.S. economy, 1920–1975

(in Billions of Current Dollars)

Year	National income	Gross national product
1920	$ 60.0[a]	
1925	76.0[a]	
1930	75.7	$ 91.1
1935	57.1	72.5
1940	81.6	100.6
1945	181.2	213.6
1950	240.0	285.1
1955	307.0[b]	368.0[b]
1960		425.0[c]
1970		
1975		574.0[e]

Basic data from U.S. Department of Commerce, 1955 Biennial Edition (Washington, D.C.: U.S. Government Printing Office, 1955), pp. 2-3. No series of indicators is readily available in terms of constant purchasing power; therefore these sums are reported in current dollars.

a. Estimates, not exactly comparable, from Carl S. Shoup, *Principles of National Income Analysis* (New York: Houghton Mifflin Co., 1947), pp. 81 and 371.
b. Authors' estimates from latest reported data in *Survey of Current Business*.
c. Gerhard Colm, *The American Economy in 1960* (Washington, D. C.: National Planning Association, Staff Report No. 81, 1952), p. 22.
d. National Citizens Commission for the Public Schools, *Financing Public Education in the Decade Ahead* (New York: The Commission, 1954), p. 49.
e. Estimate of the President's Materials Policy Commission as reported in The Tax Foundation, Inc., *Government Finances in 1965* (New York: The Foundation, 1955), p. 10.

Historical expenditure trends

An analysis of trends in school expenditures over a long period of time reveals some important insights into the progress of American education.

Simply comparing school costs over any given period is generally quite inadequate since there are many additional considerations to be made in obtaining an accurate perspective to the basic problems of school finance. Caution must also be exercised in any attempt to apply to local or state school systems any generalizations that may be true for the nation as a whole. For example, when consideration is made of the changes in school population in relation to school expenditures, it is possible that while the total number of pupils in America may be rapidly increasing, in certain states or communities

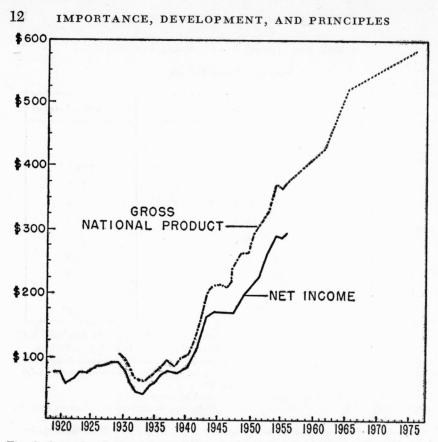

Fig. 2. General indicators of U.S. economy, 1919–1975, in billions of current dollars. (For sources of basic data, projections, and estimates, see notes to Table 2.)

there may actually be a sharply declining school population because of migrations or other reasons.

Some additional major factors such as (1) cost of living, (2) number of pupils enrolled, (3) length of school day, and (4) salaries must be considered in comparing school expenditures. Because of the significance of the period, comparisons of school expenditures over the first half of the twentieth century are made. See Table 3 for the basic historical data for this analysis.

The total annual school expenditures in the United States increased from $215 million in 1900 to $5.8 billion in 1950. This means that America spent twenty-seven times as much on its schools during the final year than it spent during the initial year of this period. There are, however, a number of inescapable reasons for this tremendous rise in school costs.

With an increasing total U.S. population during this half-century

TABLE 3. Historical summary of public school statistics, 1900–1950

Item	1900	1910	1920	1930	1940	1950	Per cent increase 1900–1950
Total school expenditures (millions)	$215.0	$426.2	$1,036.2	$2,316.8	$2,344.1	$5,837.6	2,615
Cost-of-living index[a]	31.0[b]	41.8[c]	85.7	71.4	81.6	102.8	232
Total number of pupils enrolled (millions)	15.5	17.8	21.6	25.7	25.4	25.1	62
Per cent of school-aged population enrolled	72.4	73.5	77.8	81.3	85.3	81.6	11
Per cent of enrolled pupils in daily attendance	68.6	72.1	74.8	82.8	86.7	88.7	23
Average length of school term in days	144.3	157.5	161.9	172.7	175.0	167.9	16
Total expenditures per pupil in ADA[a]	$ 20.21	$ 33.23	$ 64.16	$ 108.49	$ 105.74	$ 258.85	1,181
Pupil-teacher ratio	36.7	34.1	31.8	30.1	29.0	27.5	−25
Average teacher salary[a]	$325	$485	$ 871	$1,420	$1,441	$3,010	826

Basic data from U.S. Office of Education, *Biennial Survey of Education in the United States, 1950-52* (Washington, D.C.: Department of Health, Education, and Welfare, 1955), pp. 25-26.

a. Cost-of-Living Index derived from U.S. Department of Commerce, *Statistical Abstracts of the United States, 1955* (Washington, D.C.: U.S. Government Printing Office, 1955), p. 317.

b. Estimated from National Citizens Commission for the Public Schools, *How Do We Pay for Our Schools?* (New York: The Commission, 1954), p. 15.

c. Estimated from Arvid J. Burke, *Financing Public Schools in the United States* (New York: Harper & Bros., 1951), p. 42.

there were, of course, a great many more children of school age to be educated. Accompanying this increase were the extensions of educational opportunity upward to include high schools for all those pupils desiring such an education and downward to make kindergartens available to a great number of America's children.

These factors of population and extension, together with attendance laws and an increased appreciation of the value of education, have meant that 62 per cent or some 10 million more students had to be educated in 1950 than were served by the schools of 1900.

In addition to this increase in total school membership, the percentage of enrolled pupils in daily school attendance increased from 69 per cent in 1900 to nearly 90 per cent in 1950. And the school term was gradually lengthened during this period from an initial 144 days up to 168 days by mid-century.

If all these pupil attendance factors are taken into consideration, the increases in educational expenditures, although high, do not appear to be quite so phenomenal. On an expenditure-per-pupil-in-attendance basis, school costs over this period increased from $20 to $259, which means that America spent only thirteen times as much on each pupil in 1950 as it did in 1900.

This ratio of expenditures per pupil of 1 to 13, however, is still an incomplete and inaccurate comparison because it fails to take cognizance of an increase in the cost of living during this half-century. Since the value of the dollar in 1950 was only about 30 cents, in comparison with the cost of living at the beginning of the century, a more reasonable and accurate comparison of school costs would be a ratio of 1 to 4 instead of 1 to 13.

The conclusion that the schools of 1950 were spending four times as many constant dollars on each pupil in attendance as were the schools of 1900 still warrants some explanation of such an increase in educational costs. Since most of these increased costs must be defended as an improved quality and quantity of school services, some facts should be given consideration.

One fact is that the curriculum and other school services have expanded greatly and these expansions have been expensive. Shops, laboratories, kitchens, multipurpose rooms, and a large variety of instructional materials and equipment reveal not only some of the improved facilities but provide some idea of how the 1950 school curriculum was beyond even the imagination of most people living 50 years earlier. In addition, costly services have been provided for pupil transportation, student health, and children's hot lunches.

A second fact is that over the years fewer pupils have been assigned to each teacher. In 1900 the pupil-teacher ratio in America's schools was about 37 to 1. By 1950 this had diminished 25 per cent to a ratio of approximately 28 to 1. Even though the smaller class size is more costly, it is certainly more consistent with recognized professional standards and more adequate as far as providing for individual differences within classrooms is concerned.

A third fact is that a substantial increase in the professional training and qualifications of teachers, together with a nation-wide increase in the cost of all types of labor and professional services, has markedly increased teachers' salaries. Even though the average salary of teachers rose from $325 in 1900 to $3,010 at the mid-century point, the 1950 level of pay for teaching was considered low by many. This opinion was held in view of the amount of professional training required for certification and the status of teachers' salaries in relation to the earnings of other professions as well as the earnings of skilled and unskilled workers in America.

Recent trends and projections of school expenditures

School expenditures since 1940 are of particular interest to students of school finance. The United States, having just recovered from a great depression, was plunged into war in the early 1940's. During World War II school costs rose slowly and school enrollments declined, but education faced a financial crisis in nearly every state. There was a great exodus of teachers from the classrooms across the nation to take better paying positions in business and industry or join the military services. Legislatures in many of the states were compelled to enact emergency appropriations in order to maintain existing school services, and school building programs were curtailed because of critical shortages of strategic materials.

School costs and enrollments began to climb rapidly after the end of the war in 1945 (see Table 4). Federal price controls, however, were relaxed in the postwar period and the cost-of-living index rose sharply. School expenditures failed to keep pace with this rise in prices, and America's schools were plagued with a continuing and acute teacher shortage in the face of swelling enrollments and an immense backlog of school building needs. In attempts to solve these problems, school expenditures have continued to increase with particularly heavy capital outlay costs for facilities.

On the basis of children already born and the present fertility rate of the American people, it is possible to project school enrollments into the future and thus make some reliable estimates of future expenditures for education. Projected enrollments and expenditures to the year 1965 are presented in Table 4.

TABLE 4. Actual and projected U.S. school expenditures and enrollments in the elementary and secondary schools, 1940–1965[a]

Item	School year ending										
	1940	1942	1944	1946	1948	1950	1952	1954	A 1960	A 1965	B 1965
Current (operating) expenditures[b]	$ 1.94	$ 2.07	$ 2.29	$ 2.71	$ 3.79	$ 4.65	$ 5.72	$ 6.54			
Capital outlay, interest, etc.[b]	$ .39	$ .26	$ .16	$ .20	$ .51	$ 1.15	$ 1.62	$ 2.10			
Total public school expenditures[b]	$ 2.34	$ 2.32	$ 2.45	$ 2.91	$ 4.31	$ 5.84	$ 7.34	$ 8.64	$ 10.8	$ 12.1	$ 17.2
Per pupil enrolled (single dollars)	$92	$95	$105	$125	$180	$232	$287	$288	$288	$288	$410
Total private and parochial school expenditures[b]			$ .3[c]	$ .3[c]	$ .5[c]	$ .7[c]	$ .9[c]	$ 1.1[c]	$ 1.4	$ 1.4	$ 2.2
Per pupil enrolled (single dollars)				$78	$164	$213	$236	$260	$260	$260	$410
Total expenditures, all school systems[b]			$ 2.8	$ 3.2	$ 4.8	$ 6.5	$ 8.2	$ 9.7	$ 12.2	$ 13.5[d]	$ 19.4
Total public school enrollment (thousands)	25,434	24,562	23,267	23,300	23,945	25,111	25,562	29,998	37,570	42,113	
Total private school enrollment (thousands)	2,611	2,617		3,825	3,054	3,288	3,809	4,235	5,250	5,436	

a. Sources of basic data, U.S. Office of Education; see sources cited in Tables 1 and 3.

b. In billions of dollars.

c. National Citizens Commission for the Public Schools, *Financing Public Education in the Decade Ahead* (New York: The Commission, 1954), p. 51.

d. This estimate coincides with that made by the National Citizens Commission, although computed on different bases, *Ibid.*, p. 52.

A is a projection that assumes the same cost per pupil in 1965 as was spent in 1954.

B is a projection that assumes a minimum defensible school program that meets this criterion of the adaptability test. Since, with a modest allowance for capital outlay and interest, New York State has a foundation program that meets this criterion, this projection takes New York's current expenditures for 1954 of $356 per pupil in average daily attendance and adds 15 per cent for capital outlay costs for a total cost of $410 per pupil. See Chapter 6.

Assuming no increase in the per pupil costs, it is seen that by 1960 America will be spending some $10.8 billion on its public schools and almost $1.4 billion on private schools for a total of $12.2 billion for education in its elementary and secondary schools. This represents an increase of 26 per cent over the 1954 expenditures.

By 1965, again assuming no increase in per pupil costs, public school expenditures will amount to $12.1 billion and private schools will be spending more than $1.4 billion for a total cost of $13.5 billion. This represents an increase of almost 40 per cent over the 1954 expenditures for schools.

It is unlikely that per pupil costs will not increase between the years 1954 and 1965. As a matter of considered judgment, it is expected that per pupil costs will rise in order to provide an improved quality of education for the children of America. Assuming that per pupil costs rise nationally to $410 per pupil, which approximates the amount spent in 1954 in New York State and which approaches an efficient level of expenditures,[7] total school costs will rise to $19.4 billion. This means that $17.2 billion would be expended for public schools and $2.2 billion spent by private schools and represents about 100 per cent increase over the total expenditures for schools in 1954.

Trends in public school revenues

Over an extended period of time an analysis of the sources of funds for public education can give some penetrating insights into the problems of school finance. It is these trends in revenue sources that give some concern to individuals who are sensitive to the problems of school control. This is particularly true of those persons who believe that in education, as in private business, the extent of control by any level of government is inevitably proportional to the amount of funds supplied. This is an unwarranted and dangerous belief,[8] but an examination of the trends in school revenues as given in Table 5 reveals why such people become alarmed.

The past quarter of a century has witnessed a substantial rise in the amounts of money supplied by local governmental sources. Local revenue sources in 1930 supplied $1.7 billion; but by 1954 these same sources furnished $4.5 billion. Despite this 165 per cent increase in the amount of local money supplied, it should be noted that percentage-wise the local sources showed a gradual decrease over this period. Local funds in 1930 supplied 83 per cent of all public ele-

[7] See Chap. 6.
[8] See Chap. 3 for a discussion of this particularly troublesome problem of support and control.

TABLE 5. Public school revenue receipts by governmental source, 1930–1945

School year ending	Total revenue receipts[a] (millions)	Source (millions)			Percentage distribution		
		Local	State	Federal	Local	State	Federal
1930	2,088.6	$1,727.6	$ 353.7	$ 7.3	82.7	16.9	.4
1932	2,068.0	1,649.2	410.6	8.3	79.7	19.9	.4
1934	1,810.7	1,365.9	423.2	21.5	75.4	23.4	1.2
1936	1,971.4	1,383.2	578.4	9.8	70.2	29.3	.5
1938	2,222.9	1,540.4	656.0	26.5	69.3	29.5	1.2
1940	2,260.5	1,536.4	684.4	39.8	68.0	30.3	1.7
1942	2,416.6	1,622.3	760.0	34.3	67.1	31.4	1.4
1944	2,604.3	1,709.3	859.2	35.9	65.6	33.0	1.4
1946	3,059.8	1,956.4	1,062.1	41.4	63.9	34.7	1.4
1948	4,311.5	2,514.9	1,676.4	120.3	58.3	38.9	2.8
1950	5,437.0	3,115.5	2,165.7	155.8	57.3	39.8	2.9
1952	6,423.8	3,716.4	2,478.6	227.7	57.8	38.6	3.5
1954	7,862.7[b]	4,542.5	2,930.6	368.5	57.9[b]	37.4[b]	4.7[b]

*Basic Source: U.S. Office of Education, *Statistics of State School Systems*, 1951-52, Biennial Survey of Education in the United States, 1950-52 (Washington, D. C.: Government Printing Office, 1955), p. 14.

a. Detail will not necessarily add to totals because of rounding.

b. U. S. Office of Education, "Biennial Survey of Education," *School Life*, XXXVIII (November, 1955), p. 9.

mentary and secondary school revenues. By 1954, this same source furnished only 58 per cent of the money spent by these schools.

Although the proportion of local funds was decreasing between 1930 and 1954, the proportion and amount of state funds were increasing. State sources rose from $354 million, or 17 per cent of the school revenues, in 1930 up to $2.9 billion, or 37 per cent of the school revenues, by 1954. Furthermore, although constituting but a small portion of the total, federal governmental sources showed the most significant increases during this period. School revenues from federal sources rose from some $7 million, or less than .5 per cent of the total, in 1930 up to an all-time high in 1954 of $368 million, or nearly 5 per cent of the total amount of school revenue.

For some persons these revenue trends seem alarming. To these people it seems apparent that the financial control of the local school systems is slipping away from the locality, *where it belongs*, to the state and federal governments where it neither belongs nor functions effectively.

Other persons, particularly those who are well informed about the problems and issues in public school finance, view these same trends as wholesome. Although recognizing the dangers of shifting the control away from the localities, these people do not believe that any such shifting is either necessary or inevitable simply because the pattern of revenue sources changes. Instead, the issue of control is held to be separate and apart from that of support in the realm of public services such as education. With this viewpoint, the major trends in school revenues are recognized as being in the best interests of public education because: (1) they provide a more equitable distribution of the burden among the various governmental units, and (2) they make possible an increased level of financial support that would be impossible if schools were forced to subsist almost solely on local sources.

3. SCHOOL SUPPORT IS A PROBLEM OF POLICIES, NOT RESOURCES

After looking at the revenue and expenditure trends for schools and the projected enrollments, the costs of schools together with the increasing costs of other public services may appear frightening to some. The question arises as to whether or not these increasing costs will ever stop, and the answer must be that they probably will not diminish for many years to come unless the American people sharply revise their concept of the public service responsibilities of government in the United States. In the best interests of all America, it is continually necessary to discriminate carefully as to which public services must be expanded, which can be feasibly held at the present level, and which can be curtailed or eliminated. Along with this discrimination among services, however, must go a realistic appraisal of our nation's ability to afford public services and public education particularly. An intelligent perspective toward the cost of public education is given by consideration of at least the following three concepts.

The first concept to be recognized is that America enjoys a great prosperity. The national income has increased tremendously during the past twenty-five years. Allowing for both inflation and higher taxes, the disposable income of the average American is higher today than ever before. The per-capita income of the American people has increased more than 40 per cent during the past twenty-five years in actual purchasing power, or constant dollars after paying personal taxes.[9] Some economists estimate that such an increase actually means a four-fold rise in discretionary spending power, or the amount of income over and above that needed to supply the 1940 per capita level of such necessities as food, clothing, and shelter. This reveals that there is an unprecedented margin of luxury in the United States at the present time.

A second concept to be considered is that America is now spending relatively little for public education in relationship to what it spends for other goods and services. As long as America is spending less for education than for alcoholic beverages or nonessential transportation or recreation, there is little danger of expanding education at the expense of other essential activities. In terms of money spent, it is surprising how little the public thinks of education. For example, in 1952, $8.9 billion was spent for alcoholic beverages, $5.1 billion for tobacco, $6.7 billion for education, $8.3 billion for new cars, $9.6 billion for medical care and insurance, $2.5 billion for beauty culture, preparations, and service.[10] This was the pattern of expenditures at a time when the United States was in a recognized struggle for its very existence in a divided world of tension. Part of the problem lies in the difficulty of marshaling demand for public education in competition with the amount of advertising carried on to create consumer demand for material goods. The fact that schools must be largely paid for in a direct tax which is felt heavily and annually by the tax-

[9] The per-capita personal income, adjusted for cost-of-living differences, rose from $1,045 in 1930 to $1,496 in 1953, an increase of 43 per cent. This is reported in the *Survey of Current Business*, July, 1953, p. 175.

[10] Fredrick Dewhurst and Associates, *America's Needs and Resources, a New Survey* (New York: Twentieth Century Fund, Inc., 1955), Appendix.

TABLE 6. The relationship of the gross national product and the national income to expenditures for elementary and secondary schools in the U.S., 1930–1965[a]

Item	1930	1936	1940	1946	1950	1954	1960	1965	1965
Gross national product (billions)	$91.1	$82.7	$100.6	$209.2	$285.1	$360.5	$425	$525	$525
National income (billions)	75.7	64.9	81.6	179.6	240.0	299.7			
Total school expenditures (billions)	2.3[b]	2.0[b]	2.3[b]	3.2	6.5	9.7	12.2[c]	13.5[c]	19.4[d]
Per cent school expenditures are of G.N.P.	2.5	2.4	2.3	1.5	2.3	2.7	2.9	2.6	3.7
Per cent school expenditures are of national income	3.0	3.1	2.8	1.8	2.7	3.2			

a. For sources of information see Tables 2 and 3.
b. Excludes expenditures for private schools.
c. This expenditure estimate assumes no increase in the 1954 per-pupil cost. See Table 4.
d. This expenditure estimate assumes an increase in per-pupil costs to $410 per student in average daily attendance. See Table 4.

payer militates against the increasing of school expenditures in proportion to the expenditures of some of the above-mentioned items.

A third concept to be considered is that a small amount is spent for public education in view of the total income or production of our nation. In 1930, America was spending only about 3 per cent of its national income on elementary and secondary education and although this percentage declined to a mere 1.8 per cent in 1946, it had risen again to 3.2 per cent by 1954 (see Table 6). An almost parallel trend is revealed when school expenditures are seen to be but 2.5 per cent of the gross national product of 1930, and although this percentage dipped to only 1.5 per cent in 1946, it rose again to 2.7 per cent by 1954. It is also shown in Table 6 that the projection of school enrollments and future school costs to the year 1965 reveals that school expenditures may take from 2.6 to 3.7 per cent of the gross national product in that year. Such expenditure estimates for our swelling school enrollments are certainly consistent with the proportion of America's wealth that has been expended on education in the past, although they will continue to be only modest amounts in terms of the American economy. Certainly there is no reason to believe that the increasing school costs will interfere with other expenditures for goods and services required by an expanding population nor infringe on other public expenditures for such services as hospitals and highways. This conclusion is identical to the one reached in 1954 by the National Citizens Commission for the Public Schools.[11]

If the three preceding concepts are taken into consideration, one is afforded a realistic perspective of America's wealth and the amount of money required for education in the United States. It thus becomes increasingly clear that the problems of school finance in meeting school costs currently and in future years are problems of public policy and not of resources.

4. BETTER PUBLIC UNDERSTANDING FOR BETTER PUBLIC POLICIES

Public education thrives best in a climate of intelligent, well-informed public understanding of schools and school problems. By its very nature, public education in America is intimately associated with the public in the local communities. To the people of the local district is delegated the power for shaping the destinies of their schools. It is the enlightened exercise of this power that best serves the purposes of American education.

[11] National Citizens Commission for the Public Schools, *Financing Public Education in the Decade Ahead* (New York: The Commission, 1954), p. 8.

Control of government by an enlightened citizenry is one of the basic tenets of our democratic way of life. Control of government by an uninformed citizenry is a farce—a sham—a prostitution of the basic principle upon which the nation has been built. Public education is a form or branch of government and, like other democratic government, its successful functioning requires a citizenry that understands the significance of such things as property assessment and public debt, curricular objectives and philosophies, and professional services and governmental controls on all levels. It is with the active participation of such an informed public that schools are invigorated and rise above a level of mediocrity.

Various research studies have scientifically substantiated this position in showing that the level of citizen understanding in a community is closely related to measures of educational quality that can be taken in its schools.[12]

The need, however, is for lay understanding that is reflected not only in local educational policies but also in the public policies developed in the legislatures and state governing boards. Although it is true that legislatures in their deliberations listen to the voices of the communities, the complexities of state government and the existence of lobbying and pressure groups call for an aggressive program of promoting public understanding of education on a state and federal level. Along with adequately meeting school costs, the great need is to retain and enhance the faith and confidence of the American people in their system of public education.

The question then arises as to how public understanding of school matters can be promoted and achieved. The answer, of course, is that it must come over a period of time and as a result of deliberately varied and continuous attempts at its achievement. Such a task is a great challenge to American educators and it consists of many activities and considerations. It requires the involvement of lay citizens in the genuine solution of school problems. It calls for a vitalization of legally required hearings on budgetary and other school matters. It demands accurate, attractive, and simplified reporting of school information so that in their participation the lay citizens can intelligently make important judgments and decisions on school matters. It also requires a high degree of cooperative effort and action among school boards, professional groups, and citizen committees in order to bring information and influence to bear on the formulation of progressively better public policies that affect education.

[12] Truman M. Pierce, *Controllable Community Characteristics Related to the Quality of Education* (New York: Bureau of Publications, Teachers College, Columbia University, 1947), pp. 29–39.

TOPICS FOR STUDY AND DISCUSSION

1. Make an analysis of trends in your state and in your school district, and then answer the following questions:
   (a) During the past 25 years, what changes have occurred in the total population, the school-age population, and the total school enrollment in your state and school district? Compare these figures with those in Table 1.
   (b) To what extent has the amount expended for education in your state changed during the past 25 years? How does this change compare with changes in your district and with changes in the nation? (See Tables 3 and 4.)
   (c) During the past quarter of a century, what proportion of the money spent for education came from local sources? State sources? Federal sources? How do these proportions compare with those of the nation? (See Table 5.)
   (d) Based on present per-pupil costs, how much money will it take in 1964/65 to educate the children of your state? Of your school district?
2. In analyzing comparative costs over a period of years, what are the cautions to be observed? What considerations tend to make such comparisons more realistic?
3. Estimate the total national expenditures for elementary and secondary schools in 1965 if educational costs were to rise to $400 per pupil.
4. Make a list of arguments as to why America should be spending more money for education.
5. The quotation cited from *Unfinished Business in American Education* focuses on some of the problems with which the United States must cope. Bring the elements within this quotation up to date by citing recent figures on illiteracy, the number of youngsters not in school, and the percentage of military rejections during the Korean conflict.
6. What specific actions would you recommend in order to alleviate some of the problems cited in question 5?

SELECTED REFERENCES

American Association of School Administrators. *The Expanding Role of Education,* 26th Yearbook. Washington, D.C.: The Association, 1948.

BURKE, ARVID J. *Financing Public Schools in the United States.* New York: Harper & Bros., 1951, chaps. II, III, and IV.

CHASE, FRANCIS S. and EDGAR L. MORPHET. *The Forty-eight State School Systems.* Chicago: Council of State Governments, 1949.

COLM, GERHARD. *The American Economy in 1960.* National Planning Association, Staff Report No. 81, 1952.

COMMAGER, HENRY STEELE. "Our Schools Have Kept Us Free." *Life,* XXVIII (October 16, 1950), 46–47.

DEWHURST, FREDRICK, and ASSOCIATES. *America's Needs and Resources: a New Survey.* New York: Twentieth Century Fund Inc., 1955.

National Citizens Commission for the Public Schools. *Financing Public Education in the Decade Ahead.* New York: The Commission, 1954.

National Citizens Commission for the Public Schools. *How Do We Pay for Our Schools?* New York: The Commission, 1954.

NORTON, JOHN K. and PAUL R. MORT. *Still Unfinished Business.* Washington, D.C.: National Education Association, 1948.

U.S. Office of Education. *Biennial Survey of Education in the United States, 1950–1952* Washington, D.C.: Department of Health, Education, and Welfare, 1955.

2

THE HISTORICAL DEVELOPMENT OF
SCHOOL FINANCE

THE DEVELOPMENT of the free public school in the United States is a significant part of the history of our American democracy. It is recognized that a nation's vital problems, beliefs, and ideals are accurately mirrored in its schools. This makes America's pioneering struggle to establish tax-supported, publicly-controlled schools one of the precious parts of the heritage of all the free peoples of the world. Few other historical developments provide such an insight into America's character and moral strength.

How America's schools were to be financed and controlled is undoubtedly one of the most momentous decisions ever made. And it was not made easily. At times the struggle became so bitter that church and party ties were broken, father and son were alienated and took different sides of the issue, and neighborhoods, communities, and states were vigorously involved in the turmoil. Some recognition of the impact of this issue is given by Cubberley. He refers to it as "the battle for free state schools" and says:

> Excepting the battle for the abolition of slavery perhaps no question has ever been before the American people for settlement which caused so much feeling or aroused such bitter antagonisms. Old friends and business associates parted company over the question, lodges were forced to taboo the subject to avoid disruption, ministers and their congregations often quarreled over the question of free schools, and politicians avoided the issue. The friends of free schools were at first regarded as fanatics, dangerous to the State, and the opponents of free schools were considered by them as old-time conservatives or as selfish members of society.[1]

[1] Ellwood P. Cubberley, *Public Education in the United States* (rev. ed.; New York: Houghton Mifflin Co., 1934), p. 164.

America's heated battle for free schools was generally confined to the second quarter of the nineteenth century. However, this was only one stage in the development of public school finance in the United States. This chapter attempts to outline the significant historical aspects of school finance from colonial times.

I. COLONIAL BEGINNINGS

The early settlers of America brought with them the ideals and traditions of their mother countries. The many countries and varied backgrounds represented by the new colonists account for the great diversity in methods and efforts made for the training of children in colonial America. The prevailing attitudes of the colonists held that whatever provisions were made for the education of children and youth were to be made by the family or the church. In the New England colonies, however, a different attitude seemed to prevail.

The early laws of Massachusetts

The early development of America's system of public school finance began in the colony of Massachusetts. It was here that a homogeneous group of English Puritans established the embryonic forms of school support and control that were eventually to be adopted by all the states. Some of the early laws of the church-state form of Massachusetts government are the very seeds or prototypes of our present American practices.

The Massachusetts laws of 1634 and 1638 provided for the taxation of all property for town and colony benefits. This is the very principle that underlies our present-day taxation for school support. Equally significant was this colony's law of 1642 which ordered that *all* children should be taught "to read and understand the principles of religion and the capital laws of the country." This distinctively Calvinistic law enacted by a legislative body represents the first of its kind to be made anywhere in the English-speaking world.[2]

Another, and more important, early Massachusetts law without English precedents was the one passed in 1647. This famous law ordered the establishment and maintenance of a school system to serve all the children, and it provided for its support by the equalized and compulsory tax of all "householders." It also provided a penalty for the towns that failed to comply with the law's minimum requirements.

Taken together, these distinctively American laws of colonial Massachusetts provided for compulsory education at public expense with

[2] *Ibid.*, p. 17.

the state asserting the right to set and enforce standards. It thus becomes apparent that these laws provide the foundation for the present system of finance and control of the American school systems.

These Massachusetts laws served as a basis for similar and contemporary legislation in other New England colonies. However, it was only after many long hard struggles that their basic principles were enacted into law by state legislatures in other parts of the United States.

Early methods of school finance

Asking for voluntary contributions each Sunday was the earliest method of raising funds for school support in New England. But the shortcomings and inadequacies of this method led Massachusetts to move toward compulsory contributions and later to pass the law of 1647 which called for a town rate—the forerunner of the district tax.

Funds from the town rate were never completely adequate in colonial New England and therefore had to be supplemented by other revenue. One of the common sources for supplementary funds was the fuel or wood tax. This required each parent to haul a specified amount of firewood to the schoolhouse. He could pay someone else to do it for him, otherwise he was assessed a certain amount of money. This tax was small, troublesome, and more difficult to collect than the more widely-used rate bill.

The rate bill was collected as an ordinary tax, but it was assessed against households on a pro rata basis in terms of the number of children the parents sent to school. The rate bill was an early New England pattern of school support that was brought from England. With the passage of time, other states began to use this means to supplement other available funds. Even though the rate bill charge was small, the experience of the states was that it kept many indigent children away from schools. This method of support seemed to be a difficult one to eliminate after it had once been adopted.

Other sources of school funds for colonial, and later national, schools were tuition fees, land endowments, a variety of license taxes, local appropriations, occupational taxes, organized lotteries, bank taxes, fines and penalties, insurance premium taxes, and state appropriations.

2. EARLY GLIMMERS OF STATE RESPONSIBILITY

Except for the New England area all elementary education during the colonial period was left to private initiative or to religious or philanthropic motives. It is only the colonial developments in New

England that are important in tracing the development of school finance. Evolving practices in New England during these early times eventually provided the design for currently prevailing practices throughout America.

Between the time of the establishment of the early "town schools" in colonial New England (1647) and the launching of our national and state governments, a very fundamental and significant change took place among the New England people. Essentially, the change meant a dwindling of the old religious motives and interests with a parallel decline and breakdown in the unity of the old New England town.

For the schools this period was marked by a weakening of the "town schools," the innovation of the "moving town school," and the eventual emergence of the district system. In this process an important pattern of school finance emerged. It was one in which the revenue collected by the town from the general taxation of all property was apportioned back to all the parishes (school districts). Each parish received from the town that amount it had paid in taxes, and with this money it was to maintain its own school.[3]

Along with the development of the district system of schools came a gradual separation of church and civil affairs. In the early New England period of the 1640's the religious town and civil town were coterminous and inseparable. However, because of their public service nature and tax support feature, when the schools were established they were placed by the colony legislature under the civil town rather than under the religious town. In time, school affairs were discussed in the town hall instead of in the "Meeting-house," and the taxes for school purposes became town taxes instead of church taxes. Cubberley sums up this transition by saying:

Thus gradually but certainly did the earlier religious school pass out from under the control of the Church and become a state school. When our national government and the different state governments were established, the States were ready to accept, in principle at least, the theory gradually worked out in New England that schools are state institutions and should be under the control of the State.[4]

The profound implications of these early developments in the New England schools can be appreciated when one sees how they determined the design of public education in the very early state laws. For example, Georgia's Constitution, which is somewhat typical of the early provisions for education by the state, provided in 1777 that

[3] *Ibid.*, pp. 68–73.
[4] *Ibid.*, pp. 74–75.

"Schools shall be erected in each county, and supported at the general expense of the State, as the Legislature shall hereafter point out."[5]

3. EARLY EFFORTS OF THE FEDERAL AND STATE GOVERNMENTS

After the Revolutionary War the formation of the new American government gave rise to some problems concerning the claims of some states to western lands. These were solved by 1786 when the states relinquished their claims to the Continental Congress with the understanding that these lands were to be opened to settlement and ultimately admitted to the Union as new states.

Although some evidence exists that the basic motive was to stimulate western migration rather than to promote education, the Congress in 1787 passed the famous Northwest Ordinance. This law provided that the sixteenth section of every township in the western lands was to be reserved for the maintenance of schools. It also contained the following statement of purpose which has come to be regarded as a kind of charter for public education in the United States: "Religion, morality, and knowledge being necessary to good government and the happiness of mankind, schools and the means of education shall be forever encouraged."[6]

These federal land grants began with the admission of Ohio to statehood in 1802 and they stimulated a new interest in schools. Following the lead of Ohio, new western states dedicated to schools all income from the sale or use of these sections of land.

For a time there seems to have been a widespread notion that the income from these land grants and permanent endowment funds would eventually support all necessary schools. These permanent school funds and lands, however, were handled differently in each state, and through their use and misuse an important principle of school finance emerged. Perhaps this principle is best illustrated through the experience of Connecticut.

Connecticut was one of the sixteen states older than Ohio that did not receive any of the federal land grants. But like other older states it had taken some early action to build up a permanent school fund of its own. In 1795 Connecticut sold its vast "Western Reserve" of 3,800,000 acres for about thirty cents an acre and thereby added some

---

[5] This and other early constitutional provisions for public schools appear in Edgar W. Knight, *Readings in Educational Administration* (New York: Henry Holt & Co., Inc., 1953), pp. 2–8.

[6] Arthur B. Moehlman, *School Administration* (2d ed.; New York: Houghton Mifflin Co., 1951), p. 24.

$1,200,000 to its permanent school fund. With such a large amount of money all taxes for education were eliminated, and for a time the state assumed the complete support of its meager schools. The result was almost disastrous. The people of Connecticut virtually forgot about their schools. An attitude of contempt followed this woeful neglect of education, and as revenue once again became needed for schools, the pernicious rate-bill was used. The state lapsed into a kind of "educational coma," and the prodigious efforts and statesmanship of Henry Barnard and others were required to get the citizens again to assume their educational responsibility of providing schools for all Connecticut children. Connecticut's experience pointed out an axiom of school finance. This principle or axiom holds that only when people make some kind of financial sacrifice for their schools do they take an active and wholesome interest in education.[7]

The erroneous notion that permanent school funds could serve as a panacea to school finance problems was gradually abandoned. The dissolution of this idea was hastened by a rapidly increasing population in the United States as well as the eventual realization of how little in yearly income was really produced by these funds.

By the end of the first third of the nineteenth century it was pretty well recognized by alert citizens that the general and direct taxation of property was the only wise and stable method for support of a state system of public schools. It was also apparent that all the northern states were then involved in a struggle for direct, local, county, and state taxation for education. The slogan of those destined to win this battle was: "The wealth of the State must educate the children of the State."[8] This slogan later emerged as an established principle of public school finance in the United States.

4. THE FREE SCHOOL CONCEPT

The introduction to this chapter pointed out the general nature of America's struggle to achieve free state schools. It has also been shown that the free, tax-supported, state school system was an early development in the early Calvinistic New England colonies, and that it was this pattern that was destined to form the basis for the design of public education throughout America. The great free-school controversies of the second quarter of the nineteenth century were mostly confined to the northern states. Outside of New England the pre-

[7] H. G. Good, *A History of Western Education* (New York: The Macmillan Co., 1947), p. 422.
[8] Cubberley, *op. cit.*, p. 180.

vailing educational ideals and institutions were still those transplanted from Europe during the colonial period.

Conditioning elements for free schools

In addition to a growing spirit of democracy everywhere in America, there were a number of well-timed movements that accustomed people to think of free secular education for all.

One of these influencing developments was the Sunday school movement. Although this was brought to the United States from England in the last part of the eighteenth century, it rendered its greatest service to American education during the first two decades following 1800. This movement was not at first organized as a church institution but rather to educate the ignorant poor. Before it came exclusively under church control, the Sunday school became an institution for *all* children, not just the poor, and was an important influence in conditioning people to think of secular education for all.[9]

Another valuable influence was that of the Lancastrian system of monitorial teaching which was introduced in America about 1806 and was almost completely discarded by 1835. So insignificant and meager were the funds available for free education that some means of cheap instruction was absolutely essential in order to introduce any system of public schools. The Lancastrian system was the answer to this problem. Its compelling feature was that it was cheap. In New York City, for example, under this system the cost per pupil in 1822 was $1.22 per year.[10] Even with rising prices and reduced classes Philadelphia as late as 1834 provided one teacher to 218 pupils, and the cost per pupil was less than $5 per year.[11] The cheapness of this system convinced many that the cost of universal education need not be prohibitive. Its cheapness also had a great influence in obtaining legislative appropriations for schools.

Contemporary with the introduction of the Lancastrian system was the initiation of the federal land grants. In addition to stimulating interest in schools, these land grants represented a form of indirect taxation, and the income from the funds accumulated went for school support and thereby relieved taxation for education.

Other kinds of prevalent, indirect taxes, ranging from lotteries to bank taxes were important in conditioning people to the idea of public schools without seeming to tax the citizenry for school support.

[9] Stephen Duggan, *A Student's Textbook in the History of Education* (3d ed.; New York: Appleton-Century-Crofts, Inc., 1948), p. 391.
[10] Good, *op. cit.*, p. 405.
[11] Duggan, *op. cit.*, p. 391.

General features of the struggle for free schools

In the campaigns and controversies over free schools, each state's experience was unique. However, there were some common elements in this segment of each state's history.

In general the legislatures granted communities permission to organize school districts and levy taxes on all property within the boundaries of the district. The citizens of the district had the right to vote whether or not a tax would be levied on the property. At first, state aid was given from permanent endowment funds. Later, many states proffered aid that was derived from tax sources.

Another common element in each state's "battle" was that the campaign in each state seemed to center around some outstanding person. In Pennsylvania this was Thaddeus Stevens; in Ohio, Samuel Galloway; in Illinois, Ninian Edwards; in Kentucky, Robert Breckinridge. Other, less renowned leaders arose in other states as the "battle" was carried forward.

5. FIXING AND EXTENDING THE STATE SYSTEM

Winning the struggle for free state schools was an important event in the history of public school finance. There were, however, two other steps to be taken. One of these was to firmly establish the concept through exercising it. There had been laws enacted before that had served only as "dead letters." The other step to be taken was to extend the scope and extent of the common schools.

Establishing the state school system

The actual establishment of a state school system came, not with the enactment of a law, but when the state was able to enforce educational requirements or standards in the local districts and communities. This power of enforcement came when the state began to grant a substantial amount of aid to schools. The withholding of state funds served as an effective means of compelling a district to conform to state requirements.

A mandatory local tax for schools was one of the first requirements made by the various states. Although the specific nature of this requirement differed among the states, the typical demand was that the district match with local tax money any state-aid funds received. The next requirement was generally that of compelling districts to hold school for some specified minimum amount of time. Other requirements followed these.

It was a real achievement for a state to attain the position where it could tax for school support and compel local districts to do the same. Being able to require districts to meet certain standards that were deemed to be in the best interests of all the people of the state was another creditable accomplishment. After these controls had been achieved, further progress was only a matter of improving the adequacy and methods of school finance and of upgrading and extending the system.

Extending the state school system

The establishment of free, tax-supported schools that had occurred by about the middle of the nineteenth century included only the elementary or common schools. Education beyond the common schools at that time was carried on in private or semiprivate academies and colleges. Another important development in school finance came with the upward extension of the free schools to include the high school in one common system of public schools.

In this extension, Massachusetts again took the lead in 1827 by requiring that a high school be maintained in every town having more than 500 families.[12] New York followed the lead of Massachusetts, but progress was slow in both states. The development of high schools in America lagged primarily because their support had to come entirely from increased local taxation. Another retarding factor was that all legislation concerning high schools was of a permissive type, except in Massachusetts where it was mandatory.

Legislative provisions for high schools were difficult to obtain and were frequently attacked in the courts. The most famous case of this kind came in Michigan in 1872 and is referred to as the Kalamazoo case. This court decision influenced virtually all subsequent judicial opinions in matters pertaining to the establishment of tax-supported high schools. It is for this reason that the Kalamazoo case is considered a landmark in the upward extension of the public school system.

In the Kalamazoo decision, Justice Cooley first succinctly stated the views of the opponents of the tax-supported high school by stating:

It is, as [the court] understand [s the contention], that there is no authority in this state to make the high schools free by taxation levied on the people at large. The argument is that while there may be no constitutional provision expressly prohibiting such taxation, the general course of legislation in the state and the general understanding of the people have been as to require us to regard the

[12] Cubberley, *op. cit.*, p. 257.

instruction in the classics and in living modern languages in these schools as in the nature not of practical and therefore necessary instruction for the benefit of the people at large, but rather as accomplishments for the few, to be sought after in the main by those best able to pay for them, and to be paid for by those who seek them, and not by general tax. And not only has this been the general state policy, but this higher learning of itself, when supplied by the state, is so far a matter of private concern to those who receive it that the courts ought to declare it incompetent to supply it wholly at public expense.

Then Justice Cooley declared the decision of the court by stating, in part:

The instrument submitted by the [Constitutional] convention to the people and adopted by them provided for the establishment of free schools in every school district for at least three months of every year, and for the university. By the aid of these we have every reason to believe the people expected a complete collegiate education might be obtained . . . . The inference seems irresistible that the people expected the tendency towards the establishment of high schools in the primary school districts would continue until every locality capable of supporting one was supplied. . . .

If these facts do not demonstrate clearly and conclusively a general state policy . . . in the direction of free schools in which education, and at their option the elements of classical education, might be brought within the reach of all the children of the state, then, as it seems to us, nothing can demonstrate it. We might follow the subject further, and show that the subsequent legislation has all concurred with this policy, but it would be a waste of time and labor. We content ourselves with the statement that neither in our state policy, in our constitution, or in our laws, do we find the primary school districts restricted in the branches of knowledge which their officers may cause to be taught, or the grade of instruction that may be given, if their voters consent in regular form to bear the expense and raise the taxes for the purpose.[13]

6. THE SEARCH FOR STATE-SUPPORT PATTERNS

The result of the struggle for free schools was essentially the determination that the community rather than the family should have the responsibility for financing schools. There was also some recognition of the state's financial responsibility for education.

At the time these issues were basically settled, school costs were low and wealth was fairly well distributed. Consequently, there were few complications in having communities or school districts support education almost wholly by local taxation. After the middle of the nineteenth century, however, America began to change from an agrarian society to an industrial one. With this change came a gradual concentration of wealth in limited areas. This was due to the development of natural resources and with the emergence of new industries such as railroads and utilities. These developments

[13] Knight, *op. cit.*, pp. 245–52.

brought sweeping social and political as well as economic changes throughout the United States.

All of these changes in America had some vexing counterparts from the point of view of school finance. Within all the states, wide differences arose in tax resources of the various school districts and great inequalities in educational opportunity began to appear. Increasing demands on the schools together with the establishment of more and more high schools made educational costs rise. All of these factors accentuated the need for a rational and more adequate system of state support for schools. Attempts at meeting these demands by the various states brought forth a wide variety of state-support patterns. These efforts were characterized by trial-and-error procedures in seeking some satisfactory means of supporting the public schools.

Early patterns of apportionment

One of the earliest ways of apportioning state funds for education was a distribution based on "taxes-where-paid." This method of allocating monies in proportion to taxes paid was eventually discarded since it failed to "pool costs . . . , equalize burdens or advantages, or . . . stimulate to educational activity."[14] Another early method closely akin to this was the apportioning of school funds on the basis of property valuation.

In the gradual evolution of improved practices in the apportionment of school funds, the following bases were used: total population, school census, actual school enrollment, average membership (average—number—belonging), average daily attendance, aggregate days attendance, teachers employed, teacher quotas (such as 70 census children, or 35 children in average daily attendance, etc.), and effort and need.[15] In many instances, combinations of the foregoing bases were used.

Attempts to define satisfactory methods of apportionment

Prior to the twentieth century, one or both of the two basic principles of "equalization" and "reward for effort" seemed to underlie all state-aid programs. There appears to have been little conscious recognition of these two principles, however, until after the pioneer study of Cubberley[16] in 1905. This study analyzed the methods of

---

[14] Ellwood P. Cubberley, *State School Administration* (New York: Houghton Mifflin Co., 1927), p. 348.

[15] Each of these bases is discussed in detail in Cubberley, *ibid.*, pp. 452–77.

[16] Ellwood P. Cubberley, *School Funds and Their Apportionment* (New York: Bureau of Publications, Teachers College, Columbia University, 1905), p. 348.

apportionment of state school funds and pointed out the need for state aid to equalize as well as stimulate educational opportunities.

Following Cubberley's initial study, several efforts were made to analyze practices and principles of state school-fund apportionments. State-aid programs during the first quarter of the century continued to be meager and in the nature of relief or charity grants. During this period some monumental studies in school finance were completed by such men as Swift[17] and Updegraff and King.[18] The crowning effort of this period, however, was the thirteen-volumed Educational Finance Inquiry which was sponsored by the American Council on Education and completed during the years 1921–24.

Undoubtedly the most influential study of the Educational Finance Inquiry was the Strayer and Haig[19] report on financing education in New York State. In their report Strayer and Haig contended that the principle of equalization demanded that the state assume the responsibility of providing an acceptable minimum program of education in every district. In addition, they held that such a program should be provided after an equivalent tax effort had been made in all local districts and that solely through local initiative might the district exceed the state's minimum program.

This foundation program concept, as defined by Strayer and Haig, lacked any specific devices or techniques for its implementation. These, however, were soon provided by Mort[20] in his studies on the measurement of educational need. The resultant conceptual design of school support, as defined by Strayer and Haig and implemented through the studies of Mort,[21] had had a widespread and significant affect on practices of state school-support in America.

The Educational Finance Inquiry stimulated a great deal of research in the decade following its publication. Most of this effort, however, was aimed at refining technical details of the foundation program and working out its application to individual states. The next monumental work on school finance was published in 1933 under grants from the U.S. Office of Education and the American Council

[17] Fletcher H. Swift, *A History of the Public Permanent Common School Funds in the United States, 1795–1905* (New York: Henry Holt & Co., Inc., 1911).

[18] Harlan Updegraff and L. A. King, *Survey of the Fiscal Policies of the State of Pennsylvania in the Field of Education,* Part II (Harrisburg: Report of Citizens' Committee on the Finances of Pennsylvania, 1922).

[19] George D. Strayer and Robert M. Haig, *The Financing of Education in the State of New York,* A Report of the Education Finance Inquiry Commission (New York: The Macmillan Co., 1924).

[20] Paul R. Mort, *The Measurement of Educational Need* (New York: Bureau of Publications, Teachers College, Columbia University, 1924).

[21] Paul R. Mort, *State Support for Public Schools* (New York: Bureau of Publications, Teachers College, Columbia University, 1926).

on Education. This was the National Survey of School Finance and was completed under the direction of Cooper and Mort.[22] It was an analysis of the "sources and apportionment of school revenues and their expenditures."

A large amount of research has been done in school finance since the 1930's. In addition to some significant surveys, these efforts have involved further refinements of techniques and applications of the foundation program. As far as efforts to basically change patterns of state school-support are concerned, however, the most promising studies to date seem to be the adaptability studies[23] carried out by Mort, his students, his colleagues, and others. Fundamentally, these studies support the notion that in addition to equalizing educational opportunity at a relatively high level, state aid funds should be channeled to local districts in a way that encourages schools to adapt or take on change to successfully meet new or perennial needs.

TOPICS FOR STUDY AND DISCUSSION

1. If there had been no essential difference in the religion of the colonists of Massachusetts and those of Virginia, are there some economic or climatic factors that might yet explain why different attitudes toward government and education developed? Explain.
2. Explain what is meant by: "The wealth of the State must educate the children of the State."
3. How do you explain the intense bitterness that developed over the question of free, tax-supported schools?
4. Make an analysis of the arguments proposed against the tax support of high schools. Do you think Judge Cooley's decision adequately refutes these arguments? Explain.
5. Restate the principle that has been drawn from the "educational coma" that developed in Connecticut after this state sold its "Western Reserve" lands. What are the implications of this principle as related to a modern state-support program?
6. Why was the Lancastrian system of teaching so inexpensive? Why do you think the system was discarded?
7. Trace the development of free public schools in your home state. Give a report on the man in the state who appeared to be the great protagonist for free schools.
8. Explain how the power of enforcement of educational standards within the local districts came to a state only after a substantial amount of state aid was given to the local school districts.

[22] William J. Cooper and Paul R. Mort, *The National Survey of School Finance* (New York: Bureau of Publications, Teachers College, Columbia University, 1933).
[23] Donald H. Ross, ed. *Administration for Adaptability* (New York: Metropolitan School Study Council, Teachers College, Columbia University, 1951).

9. Give a report on the contribution of one of the twentieth century leaders in school finance, such as: Ellwood P. Cubberley, Fletcher H. Swift, Harlan Updegraff, Paul R. Mort, George D. Strayer, etc.

SELECTED REFERENCES

COOPER, WILLIAM J. and PAUL R. MORT. *The National Survey of School Finance.* New York: Bureau of Publications, Teachers College, Columbia University, 1933.

DUGGAN, STEPHEN. *A Student's Textbook in the History of Education,* 3d ed. New York: Appleton-Century-Crofts, Inc., 1948.

GOOD, H. G. *A History of Western Education.* New York: The Macmillan Co., 1947.

KNIGHT, EDGAR W. *Readings in Educational Administration.* New York: Henry Holt & Co., Inc., 1953.

MOEHLMAN, ARTHUR B. *School Administration,* 2d ed. New York: Houghton Mifflin Co., 1951.

ROSS, DONALD H. (ed.). *Administration for Adaptability.* New York: Metropolitan School Study Council, Teachers College, Columbia University, 1951.

STRAYER, GEORGE D. and ROBERT M. HAIG. *The Financing of Education in the State of New York,* A Report of the Educational Finance Inquiry Commission. New York: The Macmillan Co., 1924.

SWIFT, FLETCHER H. *A History of the Public Permanent Common School Funds in the United States, 1795–1905.* New York: Henry Holt & Co., Inc., 1911.

UPDEGRAFF, HARLAN and L. A. KING. *Survey of the Fiscal Policies of the State of Pennsylvania in the Field of Education,* Part II. Harrisburg: Report of Citizens' Committee on the Finances of Pennsylvania, 1922.

3

BASIC CONCEPTS AND PRINCIPLES OF SCHOOL FINANCE

WITH THE rising costs of public expenditures in recent years have come some accompanying attempts to effect economy in government. Some politicians have capitalized upon the growing awareness of increased governmental costs to attempt to effect crippling curtailments of funds for education. In their attempts to reduce or limit governmental expenditures, however, these persons have encountered unusual resistance in behalf of education.

In terms of other divisions of government, these crusades in the name of economy have found the schools to be singularly immune to their onslaughts. This has been enlightening to many, frustrating to some. It has evoked some blistering accusations of the schools and those controlling them. Education has been cited by some demagogues as being "an insidious fourth branch of government." Others in their opposition toward expanding education have accused the schools of being completely free from any supervision on the part of the duly elected political representatives of the people.

The furor raised from these attacks and the refutations made by educators have frequently created some public confusion and suspicion of education. They have, however, focused attention on the need for a better public and professional understanding and appreciation of the basic principles and the structural design of public education in America. This chapter will attempt to: (1) identify the fundamental values or principles in the American culture that have molded and continue to shape the laws, practices, and procedures of public school finance; (2) cite the sources that define the structure of

American public education and thereby determine the form of school finance provisions; and (3) examine the most significant concepts in the structural design of American public education.

I. THE FUNDAMENTAL PRINCIPLES OF SCHOOL FINANCE

An understanding of school finance involves the mastery of two facets of the topic. One of these concerns the theory or the rationale that underlies this important aspect of school administration. The other is concerned with application, or the specific practices and techniques used by the "practical" administrator. Both of these facets of school finance are important and the authors of this book have attempted to give them equal emphasis.

Whenever something is accomplished, it is done in some specific way. However, there are many ways of accomplishing the same thing. In the area of school finance, for example, there are several ways of making up a budget, or paying for a school building, or designing a state's school finance program. The specific ways of doing things are called techniques.

The "practical" school administrator is always anxious to know how to get things done. He is more interested in the specific, prescriptive directions for performing a given task than he is in the basic principles or rationale that lie behind the technique itself. He doesn't realize that the mere application of a series of a standardized technique is akin to quackery.

The professional school administrator, on the other hand, analyzes his problems in terms of basic principles—those general rules, concepts, or values that serve as guides for creative action. Operating on the level of principles, instead of standardized practices or techniques, gives an administrator a tremendous range and versatility in attacking and solving school problems. In addition, he is enabled to discover new techniques and to continually evaluate and refine the practices he frequently uses.

Let us now examine some of these fundamental principles or values that should guide the policies and practices of the professional school administrator in his work in school finance.

Of the several principles of school administration that Mort has brought into clear focus and definition,[1] the most important for school finance purposes are those of democracy, prudence, equality of opportunity, and adaptability.

[1] Paul R. Mort, *Principles of School Administration* (New York: McGraw-Hill Book Co., Inc., 1946).

The principle of democracy

The basic or central value in our American culture is the respect for the individual. This means that our society holds a high regard for the worth of the common man, despite his religion, color, occupation, political views, or social position.[2] This faith implies that each individual should be enabled to develop to his fullest capacity. And it is further implied that the individual should not be used as a means to the ends desired by others, but should "share in the formulation and fulfillment of the policies and programs under which he shall live and work." The principle of democracy holds that each individual has a right to participate in the making of decisions that stand to affect him.

The whole purpose and design of American education is, and should be, an expression of this principle. The local, representative, nonpartisan boards of education have been created in order that the voice of the people might be directly reflected into the molding of local educational policies. And it is critically important to America's future that these local boards continue to maintain a large amount of autonomy. Local self-government is the best device now known to protect the rights of the individual. In addition it helps preserve popular government on the state and national levels and has been held by some to be "the great political university" for the training of citizens to better assume their civic responsibilities.

There is always the ever-present and dangerous tendency to let some of the governmental machinery for local control fall into disuse and rust with public indifference and lethargy. As an attempt to safeguard against this, the school finance laws of virtually every state provide for some procedures that demand public assent or a vote of all of the people concerned. These common provisions, which are actually legislative expressions of the democracy principle, include such requirements as voting on school bond issues, holding annual budget hearings, and making local elections mandatory for school tax levies that exceed certain legislatively defined levels.

All of these legislative provisions, however, assure only a *minimum* of democracy in the operation of schools. In order to reasonably fulfill the demands of the principle of democracy, administrative procedure and decision-making must continually involve the public, the pupils, and the members of the school staff. Although this democratic procedure is generally left to the disposition of the administrative officers, it is wise to insure it through the policies of a governing board

---

[2] B. Othanel Smith, William O. Stanley, and J. Harlan Shores, *Fundamentals of Curriculum Development* (Yonkers-on-Hudson, New York: World Book Co., 1950), pp. 105–9.

of education. There are numerous opportunities for following the democracy principle in the area of school finance. These opportunities range from sound procedures in formulating the budget to the defining of salary schedules.

There is one other dimension of the democracy principle that has important and far-reaching implications for public school finance. This is the concept that presupposes a capacity to participate in decision-making. Leaving the making of important decisions in the hands of incompetent persons or groups and defending this practice as democratic is a farce and an abuse of the term.

This idea of capacity to participate has some important meanings concerning the information to which citizens are entitled in order to make wise decisions about their schools. It also has some direct bearing on the problem of local district organization—one of the most critical problems in school finance. It thus becomes apparent that it is utterly futile and undemocratic to allow residents of small, poorly organized districts to make important educational decisions. Decisions on educational matters, even when made in very small districts, are the concern of all of the people in the state. Those persons residing in very small school districts seldom grasp the significance of their decisions concerning schools. These districts are almost universally lacking in the necessary professional and lay leadership. Such leadership is essential to supply the information and understanding so necessary in making sound educational decisions.

The principle of democracy, which stems directly from the basic cultural value that holds the worth of man in high esteem, demands that each person have the right and the opportunity to be a participant in any decisions that will affect him. The exercise of this principle must, of course, be tempered by consideration of the demands of other important principles and by a capacity and readiness on the part of those persons concerned. As these considerations are made, the clearest expression of this principle in school operation is to provide a legal structure that assures enlightened and vigorous local self-government.

The principle of equality of opportunity

This principle is akin to the principle of democracy since it stems from the same basic value, the high regard for the worth of the individual.[3] It deserves special attention, however, because it plays such

[3] Mort has identified four distinct principles that are rooted in this same basic value. For a more complete treatment of the principle of equality of opportunity and for a discussion of the other related principles, see Paul R. Mort, *Principles of School Administration, op. cit.,* Part II.

a prominent role in the design of state programs of school support.

The principle of equality of opportunity demands the offsetting of those factors beyond the control of the individual that keep him from having that minimum standard of opportunities which society considers essential for all its citizens.

This principle with its implications for school finance was first expressed in 1923 by Strayer and Haig.[4] It is at the very heart of the foundation-program concept, which is considered as being the one most valuable instrument in clarifying the state-local relationship for financing public schools.

It should be made clear that the principle of equality of opportunity does not imply the enforcement of a universal standard, a uniformity or identity—a complete lack of discrimination. On the contrary, this principle calls only for aiding those individuals who, because of some barriers or handicaps, are prevented from enjoying those benefits or advantages accessible to the normal or average individuals in the society.

There is no interpretation of this principle that would imply a retardation or denial of opportunity to the favored in order that they might not exceed the normal. The school finance laws of many states are replete with expressions of this principle of equality of opportunity. It is embodied in state-aid provisions which assist the poorer districts more than the abler districts. These provisions may cover many elements such as transportation, school building construction, supervision, or just general support, unspecified for any particular use.

Expressions of this principle can likewise be found in local board of education policies that tend to compensate for handicaps of individuals or communities within the district. These compensating features often take the form of special facilities or needed assistance because of depressed neighborhoods, sparsely settled localities, or acquired or innate deficiencies.

The principle of prudence

Prudence implies caution and wisdom. It demands a check on hasty or expensive actions or decisions, and it guards against complex or poorly administered policies or activities. Prudence is the common-sense, unimpassioned regulation of everyday affairs that reflects experience and maturity.

It is this principle, according to a thesaurus at hand, that counsels

---

[4] George Strayer and Robert M. Haig, *The Financing of Education in the State of New York,* The Education Finance Inquiry Commission (New York: The Macmillan Co., 1924), p. 173.

to "be cautious, take care, . . . be on one's guard, think twice, look before one leaps, count the cost, feel one's way, see how the land lies. . . ."

The prudential principle finds extensive expression in our society. It is continually and broadly employed in private and public enterprise and in every other facet of our lives. Our governmental systems on every level are replete with vigilant safeguards, checks and balances, and other manifestations of this principle. And, of course, school government is literally flooded with prudential provisions. This is particularly true in the area of school finance in order to insure control and account for and prevent any waste or misuse of public monies.

The principle of adaptability

Adaptability means the capacity to take on change or to adjust. When this concept is applied to schools and school systems, it becomes apparent that these institutions, as others, must be able to take on change and make modifications. For a school system, adaptability means the ability to conform to new demands, to fulfill new needs, or to better meet old or perennial needs. It implies change by adopting new features, practices, or policies. It also suggests change by the discarding or the sloughing-off of these same elements as they become old, obsolete, or outmoded.

The critical need for a high degree of adaptability in our schools becomes apparent as one considers the functions of American public education. The rapid, almost breath-taking changes in the social, economic, and political dimensions of the world and of our society put great demands on the schools to keep abreast in its training of citizens in this age of jet airplanes and atomic bombs. It would, of course, be disastrous if schools should stand still amid the swift and sweeping changes of our time.

There is another compelling reason for schools to be adaptable. To see this reason one need only to reflect on the tremendous amount of twentieth-century research in the behavioral sciences and some of the far-reaching insights gleaned from these efforts. Viewing the educational implications of these findings means becoming aware of the acute need for continual change of methods, services, procedures, and facilities in order to bring educational practice more nearly in line with research-derived reality and fact.

Focusing attention on the local district level brings out still another reason for a high degree of adaptability in schools. In addition to adapting to the changes in our society and to the new insights of research, the American school in its local setting will function most effectively only as it modifies its program to fit the unique needs and desires of the community in which it resides.   Communities change, and the schools must change with them, or else fail to effectively fulfill their functions.

Since the early part of this century, adaptability has been implicitly recognized in the financing of schools.   It was this motive that justified the granting of taxing power to local districts in order that the required state program might be supplemented.   Early patterns of state aid for stimulation purposes were also expressions of the adaptability principle.

Mort and Cornell,[5] however, were the first persons to isolate and define this principle.   Their initial analysis of adaptability and their subsequent study of it in Pennsylvania[6] has provided a basis for dozens of subsequent adaptability investigations by others.[7]

The principle of adaptability demands that schools be encouraged to take on needed and desirable changes.   It suggests that the administrative mechanism include specific provisions to enhance and assure a high degree of adaptability.   Today, manifestations of the principle of adaptability are numerous in the financial structure and operation of schools.   It is this principle that provides the motive for maintaining pilot, or lighthouse, schools and school districts, for granting local leeway in taxation and minimum programs, for retaining a decentralized pattern of school district organization, and for most of the permissive school legislation enacted within the states.   In addition, it is the adaptability studies that currently provide the basis for the most significant efforts to define a defensible level of school support.[8]

2. SOURCES OF THE STRUCTURAL DESIGN OF EDUCATION

Since the Federal Constitution makes no mention of education, it is regarded as one of those Tenth Amendment functions "reserved to the States respectively or to the people."   This fact makes it necessary to go to the constitutions of the various states in order to find the cornerstones and foundations of American public education.

[5] Paul R. Mort and Francis G. Cornell, *Adaptability of Public School Systems* (New York: Bureau of Publications, Teachers College, Columbia University, 1938).

[6] Paul R. Mort and Francis G. Cornell, *American Schools in Transition* (New York: Bureau of Publications Teachers College, Columbia University, 1941).

[7] Donald H. Ross, ed. *Administration for Adaptability*, Vol. II (New York: Metropolitan School Study Council, Teachers College, Columbia University, 1951).

[8] See Chap. 6.

State constitutional provisions

Initially, some of the oldest states made no constitutional provisions for education. Making such provisions became increasingly prevalent, however, as the Union expanded. During the latter part of the nineteenth century, Congress insisted that such provisions be essential in a state's enabling legislation.

Today, all states have some constitutional provision for education. The number and kinds of provisions concerning education vary widely among the states. Some are very lengthy; others are short. Some are full of encumbering details; others are rather general in nature.

The primary purpose of these state constitutional provisions is to insure the establishment and maintenance of a system of public schools. It is generally recognized that these provisions serve their purpose best when they are free from details and simply implement the essential agencies for general control and require the legislature to establish and maintain a system of free public schools. When a state constitution is complicated with many details, it is inevitable that it will provide a serious block to educational progress. Needs and conditions are constantly changing in our society, and specific constitutional provisions become obsolete. It is extremely difficult in some states to make the needed constitutional amendments to effect desirable changes in schools.

The inclusion of educational arrangements in a state's constitution has given education an important status. This status is enhanced when the constitution establishes the key administrative and policy-making agencies for education. An example of this status is stated in a recent lower court decision in the State of Utah:

> We may take notice of the fact that no legislative enaction does, or can receive the careful draftsmanship, nor the long and careful consideration in finding its way into the statutes, that was given the provisions of the Constitution. We also note that the Constitution is the supreme law of the land. It and the State are Siamese twins, created by the same act, at the same time by the people of Utah, and are inseparable unless both shall die. The Constitution is often erroneously referred to as the 'framework of the Government.' It is the Government in writing; it created the state. Without a constitution there would be no state. The political machinery, mechanism, and officials are not the government of the State. They are merely the implements, means, agencies, and rubber stamps through which the people of Utah seek to realize the objectives, purposes, principles and ideals which led to the adoption of the constitution and the creation of the state.[9]

[9] *University of Utah, etc.* v. *Board of Examiners of the State of Utah, et al.* (Third District Court, State of Utah, Case No. 92438, 1954).

Statutory provisions

In all states the most important educational policy-making body is the legislature. Its educational authority stems from the state constitution. The current educational laws or statutes of a state that are made by the legislature are generally compiled with the constitutional provisions in a volume called the *school code*.

The *school code* thus represents all the statutes governing education and represents the "ways and means for the conduct of the education function."

Besides actually creating school districts, the legislature must determine the nature and extent of control to be exercised by those who are to operate the schools of the state. The schools are thus the responsibility of the state legislatures, even though they delegate the operation of the schools to the local communities.

The recognized role of the legislature, then, is to provide by law a framework within which the state and local administrative bodies can operate effectively. The laws are generally classified as mandatory or permissive. Mandatory laws are those requiring compliance and these form the minimum program within a state. Permissive laws, on the other hand, are broad delegations of power which allow the various school units to experiment with education and to make better adaptations of instruction to peculiar local needs and interests.

Judicial review

In addition to state constitutional provisions and the statutes enacted by the various state legislatures, the courts in America define the legal framework within which schools operate. The whole of the legal structure of education, therefore, "is subject to the interpretation of the courts."

School codes represent the legislative interpretations of the education function given to the legislature by the state constitution. Actually, the statutes in these codes have "no ultimate finality until they have been reviewed by the courts." The courts become operative when some controversy arises about the interpretation or application of a law. The state courts review the statutes in their relationship to the state constitution and the general powers reserved to the state. The United States Supreme Court, however, has become the final authority in certain areas of educational dispute within the states, because of the elasticity in the limits involved in depriving "any person of life, liberty, or property, without due process of law" or in the impairment of contractual obligations.

It is virtually impossible for the legislature to anticipate all situations that may arise under a particular statute. It is necessary, therefore, that the statute be so stated as to at least "convey the principal ideas intended by the legislature." The function of the courts, then, is to render the interpretation of the statutes in terms of the specific situations that arise.

The extent of influence of court decisions will of course vary greatly and depend upon the nature of the case. One decision may have a far-reaching effect on education. Another may be concerned with some minor technicality and be of only slight importance.

The significant feature of court decisions concerning education, however, is their cumulative influence. Since most decisions are reached through some reference to an inherited common law and previous decisions made by other courts, there is a general consistency or integrity in court decisions. This is not always the case since entirely new situations may arise or a fundamental change in public values may gradually come about. It is this general consistency of court decisions, however, that allows judicial actions to delineate the legal framework within which schools operate.

Recognizing the law to be whatever the courts decide it should be might prove dangerous if the courts could render decisions on their own initiative. The protection against the misuse of this great freedom of the courts comes through the fact that no decision can be rendered unless some aggrieved person or agency takes an issue to the courts for a judgment. This greatly limits the range of decision-making on the part of the courts.

Other sources of legal definition

There are three other sources of legal definitions which determine the framework within which the schools function. These are (a) the opinions of the attorney general, (b) the rules and regulations of the board of education, and (c) the opinions of the commissioner of education, or state superintendent of public instruction.

Rather than taking an issue to the courts, the state superintendent or the attorney general may be asked for an opinion on the meaning of some law in relation to some action or proposed action. These opinions, some of which may be included in a state's *school code,* serve to define the legal setting for education.

The rules and regulations of a board of education, whether state or local, also define the legal framework within which the schools operate. The courts have consistently held that such rules and regulations have the force and effect of law, unless they are in conflict with express statutory provisions.[10]

Recognizing the foregoing sources as those from which education obtains its legal structural design, let us now look at the structural design itself.

3. THE STRUCTURAL DESIGN OF AMERICAN EDUCATION

An over-all view of American education reveals not one system, but 48 different systems. These are "supplemented by direct federal control of schools in territories subject to federal jurisdiction."

Although there exists wide diversity among the states in the specific aspects of the educational systems, there are some common, unifying characteristics. It is from these common factors that one is able to portray the structural design of American education. Only those major characteristics of the structural design that have a direct and important bearing on school finance are discussed.

Education is a state function

The early history of American education reveals how custom, tradition, and early state and federal ordinances helped to establish education as a state function. Today, constitutional provisions of the several states place the responsibility on the legislatures for establishing and maintaining a system of free public education. Other collateral evidence can be found in practice and in court decisions to demonstrate that "essentially and intrinsically, the schools are matters of state and not local jurisdiction."

Every state, with the exception of some southern states during the Civil War and part of the Reconstruction period, has provided education without interruption.[11] As a result of the United States Supreme Court ruling against segregated public schools, this practice may now change since some southern states have taken the necessary legal action enabling them to circumvent the decision by abolishing some aspects of their public school systems. This, however, only tends to substantiate the present legal concept that education is a function of the various states.

If there were any doubt about this legal concept, the courts would be the ultimate and final authority. Whenever the issue has been involved, the judicial interpretations of the various state supreme courts

[10] Newton Edwards, *The Courts and the Public Schools* (Chicago: The University of Chicago Press, 1933), pp. 155–56.

[11] Arthur B. Moehlman, *School Administration* (New York: Houghton Mifflin Co., 1951), p. 26.

and the United States Supreme Court have, without exception, up-held the concept that *education is a state function*.[12]

There are some important implications for school finance in this concept. One of these pertains to the freedom of the legislature to determine methods of school support. It is well established that the powers of the legislature over schools are plenary, provided, of course, that its actions do not conflict with its state or the federal constitutions. Relatively few cases that have challenged this power have gone before the courts, and in those instances the issues have involved either the legislature's encroachment on constitutional limitations or the use of some device for withholding state aid as a way of enforcing a state's regulations or laws.[13] The following decision made by the Supreme Court of Indiana is somewhat typical in describing the broad powers of the legislature over education:

Essentially and intrinsically the schools in which are educated and trained the children who are to become the rulers of the commonwealth are matters of state, and not of local jurisdiction. In such matters the state is the unit and the Legislature the source of power. The authority over schools and school affairs is not necessarily a distributive one to be exercised by local instrumentalities, but, on the contrary, it is a central power residing in the Legislature of the state. It is for the law making power to determine whether the authority shall be exercised by a State Board of Education, or distributed to county, township, or city organization throughout the state. . . .[14]

As to the specific implications of these legislative powers for taxation purposes, the following decision is enlightening:

The public school system is a matter of state, and not local concern, and the establishment, maintenance, and control of the public schools is a legislative function. To promote the public schools, the state, through the Legislature, may levy taxes directly, or the state, having, as it does, full control over its agencies, the counties, may authorize them to levy a tax, or may by statute require them to levy a tax for the establishment and maintenance of public schools. . . .

The exercise of the taxing power to promote a system of public schools for all the counties does not infringe upon the right of local self-government, because a public school system, like a highway system, a penal system, or a matter of public health is not of purely local, but of state concern. The state is a unit, and the Legislature is the state's source of legislative power, from which flows the mandate of the state.[15]

Although it is implied in the foregoing decision, it should be noted that a district may be compelled to maintain schools of a given stand-

---

[12] *Ibid.*, p. 27.

[13] Robert R. Hamilton and Paul R. Mort, *The Law and Public Education* (Chicago: The Foundation Press, Inc., 1941), p. 144.

[14] *State v. Harworth*, 122 Ind. 462, 23 N. E. 946, 7 L. R. A. 240.

[15] *State v. Meador*, 284 Tenn. S. W. 890. Case cited by Edwards, *op. cit.*, p. 8.

ard; and the courts have consistently held that there is no inherent or implied right in school districts' levying taxes.[16] The power to tax is a special power that must be specifically granted either by constitutional mandate or legislative provision.

A second implication that flows from the concept of education as a state function is the supremecy of school matters over city home-rule charters. In most states there are instances where the boundaries of a municipal corporation are coterminous with those of a school district. Even though these two corporate entities are superimposed on the same territory, they have different functions to perform and are legally considered as separate as if they were located in different parts of the state.[17] The following decision gives the general view of the courts in this matter:

> If the field of legislation upon the subject of education belongs to the state, it belongs to it in its entirety. If the cause of education is not a subject of municipal regulation, the municipality cannot touch it or interfere with it in the slightest degree. School buildings are an essential agency in the state's educational scheme, and to allow muncipalities a voice in the construction, repair, control, or management of the school buildings within their borders is to yield to them the power to frustrate the state's plan in promoting education throughout the state. If power be granted to interfere in this respect, there would be no logical limitation to municipal interference with the district schools . . .
>
> These considerations lead irresistibly to the conclusion that although the boundaries of a school district may be coterminous with the boundaries of a city, there is no merger of the school district affairs with city affairs. They remain separate and distinct units of government for the purpose of exercising separate and distinct powers and for the accomplishment of separate and distinct purposes.[18]

This separateness of municipalities and school districts remains even when there may be an apparent merger because of the delegation of some school administrative functions to municipal officers. In such cases the status of these municipal officers has been held to be not that of representing the city, but rather as ex-officio officers representing the state and serving in an advisory capacity to the board of education.[19] This issue is discussed further in Chapter 4 under the caption of fiscal independence.

A third implication of the state responsibility for education is concerned with the legality of apportioning locally collected tax money in a manner designed to equalize educational opportunity within a

[16] Hamilton and Mort, op. cit., pp. 144–45.

[17] Edwards, op. cit., p. 71.

[18] State v. Mayor, etc. of City of Milwaukee, 189 Wis. 84, 206 N.W. 210. Case cited by Edwards, op. cit., p. 77.

[19] Edwards, op. cit., pp. 71–72.

state. This contention goes to the very heart of the school finance laws of many states.

It is a well-established point of law that taxpayers of one municipality cannot be compelled to contribute to the local and municipal purposes of another.[20] If public education were a local or municipal function, monies raised in one school district could not be used in another district. However, education is a state function, and school taxes are not considered as local or municipal taxes even though levied and collected by these agencies. As a court in Kentucky has ruled:

> When a municipal body, or a county, or a school district levies taxes for school purposes, the tax so levied is a State and not a municipal, county or district tax, although it may be levied and collected by municipal or county or district officers. The fact that the tax is levied and collected for the State by the agencies of the State appointed for that purpose does not deprive it of its character as a State tax.[21]

The fact that school taxes are state and not local taxes has given an entirely different concept as to the use of school tax money outside the district in which it is collected. The decision of the Supreme Court of Maine illustrates the reasoning of the courts on this matter:

> The Legislature has the right under the constitution to impose an equal rate of taxation upon all property in the State, including the property in unorganized townships, for the purpose of distributing the proceeds thereof among the cities, towns and plantations for common school purposes, and the mere fact that the tax is assessed upon the property in four municipal subdivisions and distributed among three, is not in itself fatal . . .
>
> The fundamental question is this, is the purpose for which the tax is assessed a public purpose, not whether any portion of it may find its way back again to the pocket of the taxpayer or to the direct advantage of himself or family. . . . In order that taxation may be equal and uniform in the constitutional sense, it is not necessary that the benefits arising therefrom should be enjoyed by all the people in equal degree nor that each one of the people should participate in each particular benefit . . .[22]

Education is a unique form of government

Even though education is a state function, it is typically the responsibility of the local community. The state legislature simply delegates to the local school districts, which it has created, the major portion of the task of running the schools. Thus, the local school system may appear to be just another form of local government. Local

---

[20] *Ibid.*, pp. 245–46.

[21] *City of Louisville* v. *Board of Education*, 154 Ky. 316, 157 S. W. 379. Case cited by Edwards, *op. cit.*, p. 228.

[22] *Sawyer* v. *Gilmore*, 109 Me. 169, 83 Atl. 673. Case cited by Edwards, *op. cit.*, p. 247.

representatives serve as school board members. Local taxes for schools are levied and collected locally. Local citizens can apparently modify their schools as they like to best fit their peculiar educational needs.

Because of this seemingly local nature of school government, many students of public government have advocated in the name of simplicity that the schools be made an integral part of the other local government. Educators have vigorously resisted any such move, and have pointed out that school government is not local government. The local school tax, they have cited, may appear to be just another local tax but is actually a state tax and has been legally defined many times as such. Likewise, the local school officer may appear to be just another local officer, but he is actually a state officer and has been consistently so defined by the courts. Thus, education resists any attempt to be merged at the local level since it is really a form of state government and therefore is held to be unique and different from any other local government. Educators have held that school government is, and must remain, separate and apart from other local government.

In consideration of education as a form of state government, this same resistance of education toward merger with other forms of state government becomes apparent. Here again, education is held to be unique and parallel with all other state government. In order to emphasize this separateness, education has frequently been given status commensurate with the legislative, executive, and judicial branches of government and referred to as a fourth branch of government.[23]

In summary, it becomes apparent that, generally speaking, a special status has been given to education in the various states in order to assure its nonpartisan, nonsectarian, free, and classless character. It is a unique form of government that is "separate but parallel with all other local and state government."

Education's operational pattern

The third critical concept in the structural design of education is the basic operational pattern for schools. Administrative machinery is provided in the school laws of each state for carrying out the state education function. Although the machinery varies in many details among the various states, the pattern is essentially the same.

Since school districts are simply creations of the state in order that it may more effectively administer its educational policies, they possess no inherent rights except those specifically granted by the legis-

[23] Moehlman, op. cit., p. 35.

lature or the state constitution. School districts may, therefore, be abolished or made larger or smaller. The legislature may determine the types of school to be established, the means of their support, the character of their administration, the content of their curricula, and the qualifications of their teachers. All of these matters may be prescribed without regard to the wishes of the local districts. There is, therefore, no inherent right of local self-government in education.

Because of their lack of any inherent powers, school districts have only such lawful authority as is conferred upon them by statute. The powers of school boards are, therefore, restricted. However, in determining the functions of school boards, one must be careful not to confuse the exercise of power or jurisdiction with the exercise of discretion. It is the discretion that local boards may exercise in carrying out their stated and implied powers that gives them the great range of authority and control.

Statutes conferring powers on school districts must necessarily be phrased in rather general terms. It is obviously impossible to foresee and embody in a law all of the specific acts which school boards may legitimately wish to carry out. The result is that a great deal of discretion or judgment is left to the local board in carrying out its functions as specified or implied in the laws.

In every state the local school boards must, of course, operate within the structure or general framework that is set up by the state laws. However, because of their general nature, these laws permit a much larger amount of local board authority than is generally supposed. In addition, there appears to be an American tradition that favors maintaining and strengthening local control over the schools. This tradition is called a "home rule" tradition by Mort and Reusser and seems operative even though it is not specified in our legal structure or theory.[24]

The American tradition seems to be that state laws provide but a framework or a bare minimum of what should constitute the school program. Within these laws, it is the responsibility of the local school board to provide the flexibility and enrichment necessary to best serve the educational needs of the community.

4. BASIC CONCEPTS OF SUPPORT AND CONTROL

One of the outstanding trends in public school finance during the 20th century has been the steady increase in state support. This, of course, has been the inevitable result of some of the vast social, political, and economic changes in our nation. The expanding of tax

[24] Mort and Reusser, *op. cit.*, p. 33.

sources available and used for governmental purposes has been an important factor in the increase in state support for schools.

Coupled with this trend of increasing central support has been a trend toward the extension and multiplication of central control. To some, this accompanying trend in control is logical and inevitable. To these people, the statement that "control follows the dollar" is a basic principle in any private or public enterprise. To others, including the authors, this "pseudo-principle" is erroneous and alarming and the trend of increasing central control is a dangerous one.

The faulty notion that control and support are inextricably bound together is one that threatens the very core of our free, democratic form of government. This is particularly true when the concept degenerates so far that some so-called experts in government and public finance can proclaim that those who cannot afford to pay their own way are not entitled to govern themselves.

Let us analyze this concept and its implications. The basic fallacy is that of trying to apply this private enterprise idea to the realm of democratic public government. It simply has no place, and this can be illustrated on any level of government. Suppose we should examine the implications of this as it might be applied on a community level. The "control follows the dollar" idea may be appropriate in the local bank or other corporate business where the wealthy Mr. Doe, a large property owner, holds most of the stock, therefore supplies most of the money, and in turn exercises most of the control. On the other hand, let us examine the pattern of control and support for the schools in the same community. When the school tax is levied, it is probable that Mr. Doe (or some business or utility) is also the largest taxpayer. It is even conceded that he (or some company) pays up to 40, 50, or even 60 per cent of the total amount of local taxes for school support. To reason, however, that Mr. Doe should have any more than a single vote—the same as the most meager taxpayer in the community—is erroneous, and repugnant to our democratic form of government.

It is this same "control follows the dollar" reasoning that suggests that if a certain percentage of the money for schools comes from a certain level of government, then that level of government is entitled to that proportional amount of control. Thus, if the state supplies 75 per cent of the funds in a financially poor district, then the state agency is entitled to three fourths of the control of the schools. This concept is also dangerous and inconsistent with our democratic form of government.

It is the people who pay the tax money and it is the people who establish the agencies to collect it. It may be more convenient for a state agency to collect certain kinds of tax money while the local agency may be in the best position to collect other taxes. In any event, it is the people who establish the agencies and it is they who should decide which agencies or levels of government can best collect which revenues. The people, however, may use one agency to collect taxes and a different agency to spend them. In other words, the people may decide that the state agency is in the best position to collect most of the revenue for schools from sales, income, and other taxes. But the people may believe that the local agency (school board) is in the best position to determine how school money is to be spent. Or, they may believe that the state and local agencies should share the responsibility of controlling expenditures. In any event, it should be the people who decide which agencies should collect tax money and which agencies should spend it, and there is no necessary relationship between who collects and who expends public money. As far as schools are concerned, this means that there is no inherent right for any level of government to control school expenditures simply because it happens to collect the funds on which schools are supported.

Some states have been able to provide a large proportion of the money for school support and yet leave the control of schools in the local district. Other states have exercised considerable central control even with very little state support.[25] Thus, experience reveals the practicality of separating the fund-raising or support function from the expending or control function.

There is a rule that should govern the decisions made in connection with this problem. It is that the exercise or operation of a function should be placed where, in the long run, the most benefits can accrue to all the people.

TOPICS FOR STUDY AND DISCUSSION

1. Give a report on the several principles of school administration identified by Mort in *Principles of School Administration*.
2. After examining a court decision, a set of rules and regulations of a school board, or a section of your state's *school code*, list some practices or policies that can be identified as specific expressions of the principles of democracy, equality of opportunity, prudence, and adaptability.
3. Draw a chart that shows the relationships of all of the elements of government that have some affect on education in the elementary and secondary schools of your state. Who controls the expenditures made by these various elements of government?

[25] Arvid J. Burke, *Financing Public Schools in the United States* (New York: Harper & Bros., 1951), p. 288.

4. Examine the provisions made for education in the constitution of your state. Is it complicated with specific details that can become obsolete in a relatively short time? What are the specific procedures that need to be followed to amend your state's constitution?
5. Examine the constitutional provisions for education in an annotated edition of your state code. Notice the various court cases that have involved some aspect of the constitution. Select one of these cases and make a report on it after reading it in its entirety in your State Supreme Court Reports or in the legal report for your region.

SELECTED REFERENCES

BURKE, ARVID J. *Financing Public Schools in the United States.* New York: Harper & Bros., 1951.

EDWARD, NEWTON. *The Courts and the Public Schools.* Chicago: University of Chicago Press, 1933.

HAMILTON, ROBERT R. and PAUL R. MORT. *The Law and Public Education.* Chicago: Foundation Press, Inc., 1941.

MOEHLMAN, ARTHUR B. *School Administration.* New York: Houghton Mifflin Co., 1951.

MORT, PAUL R. *Principles of School Administration.* New York: McGraw-Hill Book Co., Inc., 1946.

MORT, PAUL R. and FRANCIS G. CORNELL. *Adaptability of Public School Systems.* New York: Bureau of Publications, Teachers College, Columbia University, 1938.

SMITH, B. OTHANEL, WILLIAM O. STANLEY, and J. HARLAN SHORES. *Fundamentals of Curriculum Development.* Yonkers-on-the-Hudson, N.Y.: World Book Co., 1950.

ROSS, DONALD H. (ed.). *Administration for Adaptability*, Vol. 2. New York: Metropolitan School Study Council, Teachers College, Columbia University, 1951.

PART II

METHODS OF FINANCING PUBLIC EDUCATION

4

STRUCTURAL FEATURES OF A SATISFACTORY STATE-SUPPORT PROGRAM

IN THE previous chapter it was shown that the various states have the legal responsibility for education in America. Just what are the financial implications of defining education as a state function? The states themselves provide the answer to this question. There is no set of specific answers. All of the states have assumed some active responsibility for the financial support of schools. However, there is a great range in the extent and methods of this support.

Some states have seen fit to provide only very limited state funds for education. These states have empowered the school districts to obtain local tax money for education and then let the locality carry almost all of the responsibility for school support. The assumption has been that the districts would make the necessary effort to provide a satisfactory school program. Because of a lack of interest in schools in some communities, not all districts have made sufficient effort. The major difficulty these plans have encountered, however, has been the great difference in the basic financial ability, or wealth per student, of the various school districts. The tremendous range in ability among the districts in many states has often been a result of an inadequate pattern of school district organization. States with small school administrative units may have some districts that are several hundred times as able to provide schools as are others. Even in the larger unit states, those with county or semicounty school districts, this range in financial ability is typically so great that some of the less

61

able districts cannot provide an acceptable program on local resources alone, even if tax levies are set so high as to be confiscatory in nature.

The inescapable fact is that there are no states wherein a satisfactory educational program can be assured in all local school districts solely by means of local taxes.   There is, then, a need for some state support in every state, and such support has been defended by a widely accepted principle of school finance which holds that "all of the wealth of a state should be taxed for the education of all of the children of a state."

Some few states have assumed the entire responsibility for providing a rather complete educational program in each locality.   In these cases, the schools have been supported almost entirely with state funds.   In theory, some persons may see this as an acceptable solution to the problem of guaranteeing a satisfactory school program to every child in the state.   In practice, however, this definitely does not appear to be the answer.   Under such a pattern of support, school programs tend to become prescriptive, sterile, and lose their adaptability.   Citizen interest in schools appears to dwindle and financial support tends to be low and foster a low level of mediocrity in education.

Experience has shown that the best schools can be developed when the local people take a keen interest in and assume a reasonable degree of responsibility for the development of the local school programs.   In those states which have tried to finance the major portion of the school program and leave the gaps to be filled in by the people, education has suffered.   The people soon develop a belief that the state should do everything for the school and fail to maintain the interest that motivates citizens to exert the necessary effort to build strong and vigorous educational programs.

Salaries of teachers tend to lag, thereby not attracting young, bright people to the teaching profession.   The low salaries and scarcity of teachers often make it necessary for local administrators to hire teachers who are not only the less desirable persons from the standpoint of ability but those who do not have adequate preparation in the subjects they are to teach.

Educational offerings in the schools are often curtailed instead of being broadened to meet the needs of youth in a changing world. The programs of study in the different schools tend to be the bare minimum required by the state for high school graduates. Supplies and equipment necessary for a good educational program are often very meager. This is not only true for such courses as science and for vocational subjects, which require rather expensive equipment and supplies, but it is also true for the so-called academic subjects and the elementary grades. In these cases local administrators are forced to resort to the practice of charging the students fees so that more adequate material may be obtained. Such practice puts a hardship upon the individuals who may not be financially able to support the program and leaves those with wealth not paying their just part.

Many of the pupil services—such as guidance, health, recreational facilities, and others which are generally provided in a modern school —are often omitted in those schools operated in part by the state. The state fails to make financial provisions for such and the citizens of the local communities do not feel that they should pay out money through local taxes to provide those services which the state has not thought essential in its program. All in all, the educational program of the state tends to become one that may have been fairly adequate for the past generation but one that does not meet the needs of youth in the modern world.

What then is the answer? How should a state provide for the financing of its schools so that in the long run they will be operated in the best interests of all the people of the state? The answers to these questions are complicated, but they are available and quite firmly established. There are certain features of a satisfactory state-support program that have been distilled from the experiences of many states, each of which has been trying in its own way to fulfill its educational responsibilities.

One of the conclusions to be drawn from this wealth of experience is that the manner in which the state supports schools is equally as important as the amount of money it spends for education. A state-support program that is not based on sound principles of school finance may defeat the very purposes it has been set up to accomplish. It may thwart initiative, reward inefficiency, and provide a meager and inadequate school program.

I. A SATISFACTORY PATTERN OF SCHOOL DISTRICT ORGANIZATION

Although not technically a part of a state school-support program, the basic organization of school districts in a state is so critically important that it must be given special attention. Experts in school finance have long recognized the inseparable relationship of the problems of school finance and school district organization. They have repeatedly pointed out the necessity of appraising a state's fiscal policies in terms of (1) established principles of school finance and (2) the impact of these policies on local organizational structures.

Attempting to superimpose an adequate school-support plan in a state without recognition of its faulty district organizational structure is akin to building a house on the quicksands of a swamp. Such a plan is inefficient, inordinately expensive, and because of lack of a firm foundation is continually fraught with the danger of being badly warped or falling apart.

The following discussion covers the major reasons for correcting the organizational structure and gives some general suggestions on how this can and must be rectified in order to have a sound state-support program.

Poorly organized districts are a violation of the principle of democracy

In the very large school districts there appears to be a danger of seriously violating the principle of democracy because of an accompanying loss of close public participation and interest in educational affairs. This atrophy of popular participation and interest seems to be almost inescapable in extremely large county units and in large city systems. It may be that some devices can eventually be used within these systems to bring about more "participation in decision-making" on important school matters. However, this has not yet been accomplished. Some sociologists have even raised the question as to whether or not the schools, as they are presently operated in the large cities, have to a great extent lost their function as instruments of community integration.[1]

Mort and Reusser recognize the existence of large county districts and city systems of more than 100,000 population as being possibly too large for effective local autonomy.[2] They suggest some possible solutions to the problem and consider it as being quite as serious and of about the same magnitude as the problem America faces in eliminating unsatisfactorily small districts.

The existence of very small districts with local autonomy is also a violation of the principle of democracy. As ironic as this may at first seem, some considered thought will reveal that self-government presupposes an ability or capacity to fulfill the function itself. This capacity is typically lacking in very small districts.

---

[1] Baker Brownell, *The Human Community* (New York: Harper & Bros., 1950), Part VI.

[2] Paul R. Mort and Walter C. Reusser, *Public School Finance* (2d ed.; New York: McGraw-Hill Book Co., Inc., 1951), pp. 92–93.

Studies of small school districts reveal that they frequently lack adequate professional and lay leadership. This means that they do not have the capacity for local self-control, and since education is legally recognized as being of interest to all of the people in the state, very small districts are generally incapable of making decisions in the best interests of the state as a whole.

Even the most ardent advocates of "home rule" have recognized that decentralized authority can be maintained only when local units are sufficiently strong to secure competent leadership and capably perform the functions required of them. The continued existence of very small districts means that the state must recognize these limitations of lay and professional leadership. The district must then either be abolished or else prudential state controls must be superimposed with the consequent loss of whatever local initiative might have initially been there.

Some investigations have attempted to point out to citizens who fear losing control of their schools that the only sure means for regaining some of their lost educational controls is through adequate reorganization. This is particularly true in those districts where children must attend some schools as tuition-paying students in a neighboring school district.

The state legislature has the responsibility for creating the kind of local districts that can effectively exercise local initiative and local control.

Poorly organized districts are a violation of the principle of equality of educational opportunity

Under the same minimum or foundation program there exists a wide difference in educational opportunity between districts that are satisfactorily organized and those that are poorly organized. Thus, one of the basic purposes of the foundation program—the equalization of educational opportunity—may be frustrated because of a poor organizational structure.

The central problem in this whole matter is size. The close relationship between the size of school districts and the character and scope of their educational programs and facilities has long been known. The fact that very small districts have extremely meager programs is so well established that Chisholm and Cushman,[3] in reviewing the specific research on this topic, pointed out that little new research had been done on the problem since 1945.

[3] National Conference of Professors of Educational Administration, *Problems and Issues in Public School Finance* (New York: Bureau of Publications, Teachers College, Columbia University, 1952), p. 80.

The size of the individual school is to some degree dependent upon the size and geographic outlay of the administrative unit. There is some evidence showing that at the same median expenditure levels elementary schools with fewer than one hundred pupils provide only about one-third as many special services as do schools with twice this number of pupils or more.[4] This same condition is found in the secondary schools also, where size seems to be an even more important factor. Matched on expenditure levels, those high schools with fewer than one hundred pupils in attendance provide relatively few special services. As size increases up to five hundred pupils, the number of services goes up. And those high schools with more than five hundred students typically have the most enriched programs.[5]

In secondary schools the quality of the educational program seems to be related to the class size, the number of subjects taught by teachers, and the number of different teachers from whom the average student receives instruction. Because of these factors, small schools tend to have a much more restrictive program than do larger ones, and it is generally conceded that high schools with an enrollment of fewer than three hundred students cannot usually offer a strong program in more than one or two fields.

These deficiencies of small schools are naturally reflected in the administrative units. Small administrative units are almost universally plagued with narrow educational offerings, poor laboratory and library facilities, and teachers with substandard professional preparation. In addition, these small units are generally lacking in administrative leadership and supervision for the continuous improvement of instruction. The cost of employing a competent superintendent of schools is almost prohibitive, and the challenge of efficiently utilizing his services is a great one in districts employing fewer than forty teachers.

Various conferences and commissions have from time to time prescribed minimum standards for school district structure. As far as size is concerned, these recommendations have ranged from an absolute minimum of 1,000 up to 1,500 pupils in attendance in a twelve-grade program of instruction.[6] There is abundant evidence to show that administrative units smaller than this are almost universally deficient in their educational programs. And the smaller they are, the

[4] Arvid J. Burke, *A Postwar Program of State Aid for Schools* (Albany, N.Y.: New York State Teachers Association, 1946), Chap. 3.

[5] *Loc. cit.*

[6] Chisholm and Cushman, *op. cit.*, pp. 67–69. See also National Commission on School District Reorganization, *Your School District* (Washington, D. C.: National Education Association, 1948).

greater their deficiency. Even those districts of approximately 1,500 pupils must ordinarily secure supplementary administrative and supervisory services in order to provide a really adequate educational program.

Small school districts simply cannot make available, without prohibitive cost, those educational opportunities that satisfy the needs, aptitudes, capacities, and interests of students. It thus becomes apparent that the provision of state aid to guarantee a minimum level of expenditure in all school districts does not provide for a basic equality of educational opportunity if poorly organized units continue to exist within the state.

Poorly organized districts are a violation of the prudential principle

One of the facets of the prudential principle demands the wise use of money in order that public funds are not wasted. The continued existence of exceedingly small districts really constitutes a waste of money, hence a violation of this principle.

Research reveals that up to a certain size there is a very direct relationship between the cost of education and the size of the school unit. Generally equivalent educational programs cost less per pupil as the size of the district increases. Thus, the smaller the school the higher the per-pupil cost. This means that in states that have poor organization of school administrative units, either substantial money can be saved or else great improvements in educational programs can be brought about by a sensible program of district reorganization. In some states these savings may amount to millions of dollars annually.[7]

Excessive costs are typically found in districts where the elementary schools have less than one teacher per grade and where high schools have less than ten teachers. Studies have also compared high school size with a measure of the cost per-pupil unit of educational opportunity, and a significant negative relationship has been found to exist up to a school size of about 500 pupils.[8] In studies of these small high schools, the general conclusion has been that the per-pupil cost in schools with less than 100 pupils is approximately twice the cost of those with more than 200 pupils.

[7] For a summary of studies pointing out financial savings through district reorganization in various states see Chisholm and Cushman, *ibid.*, p. 73.

[8] William J. Woodham, *The Relationship Between the Size of Secondary Schools, the Per-Pupil Cost and the Breadth of Educational Opportunity* (Gainesville, Fla.: University of Florida, doctoral dissertation, 1951), p. 185.

Studies have also shown that it is financially efficient to have districts organized to maintain both high schools and elementary schools rather than to have them organized for either elementary or high school purposes only.[9]

Poorly organized districts violate the principle of adaptability

Studies of adaptability are those that investigate how school systems take on change or how modern or up-to-date are schools and their educational programs. These studies have been conducted in school districts of various size and type and they tend to reinforce the currently accepted standards of satisfactorily organized school systems.

As far as the inadequacy of small districts is concerned, Mort and Cornell in a study of a broad sampling of Pennsylvania schools found size to be significantly related to adaptability.[10] That is, the larger the district the more modern or adaptable it was. When desirable changes needed to be made, it was generally the larger districts, those with more than 86 classroom units, that first made the change. And those with more than 30 classroom units were much more adaptable than the smaller ones.

Other studies of adaptability have given some insight into the problem of districts being organized that are too large or otherwise unsatisfactory. The clue that has led investigators to believe that large cities are unsatisfactorily organized has been the presence of highly adaptable schools in satellite communities just outside the great cities. The evidence suggests that if the limits of the great cities were extended to include these satellite communities, a large proportion of America's high expenditure and most adaptable schools would be eliminated.[11]

The conclusion has thus been drawn that close popular control coupled with a high degree of ability, or wealth, are two basic factors necessary in the provision for highly adaptable schools. To include in the city system those very able communities that lie around the fringes of the great city would not only shift the actual control but also shift the interest from the local school unit where it is focused and effective to the larger school system where it is diffused and ineffective.

[9] Kenneth E. McIntyre, "The School Redistricting Problem in Nebraska," *The American School Board Journal*, CXIX (December, 1949), 15–16.

[10] Paul R. Mort and Francis G. Cornell, *American Schools in Transition* (New York: Bureau of Publications, Teachers College, Columbia University, 1941), pp. 137–38.

[11] Mort and Reusser, *op. cit.*, p. 93.

This same reasoning applies to the organization of large county units. In this case it is quite possible that the most able communities with the most adaptable, or potentially adaptable, schools are eclipsed in a school district that encompasses a large area and has an over-all low ability for providing outstanding schools.

The pattern of school district organization adopted by a state should take cognizance of the principle of adaptability and thereby assure close public participation and interest in educational affairs.

Poorly organized districts must be encouraged to reorganize by the state-support program

The organizational structure of school districts in any state is vital to educational efficiency and effectiveness. Yet, in most parts of America, school district structure has antedated some of the great social and economic changes in our country as well as the significant development of state support for public education. Difficulties naturally arise when attempts are made to set up on an obsolete district structure some kind of school finance program that can be considered adequate by modern concepts of educational opportunity.

How a state's support program influences this structure, therefore, is an important consideration to be made in assessing or analyzing a state's fiscal policies. The very key to effecting a more satisfactory organization of administrative units within a state may lie in the state's school finance program.

Some states have been highly successful in effecting a complete reorganization of their inadequate districts. And this has frequently been done primarily through carefully designing the school finance laws so that desirable reorganization was encouraged. To the districts concerned, this kind of encouragement may entail substantial state aid in operating schools, in transporting pupils, and in building new school buildings. These laws should also provide the means for distributing or disposing of the assets and liabilities of districts that reorganize.

On the other hand, there are many examples of states that have enacted school finance laws that have unintentionally frustrated any kind of needed reorganization of school districts. Contrary to their original purposes, such laws actually perpetuate inefficient systems and thereby limit educational opportunity.

State support programs sometimes operate in very subtle ways to handicap or block district reorganization. For example, a state with a very liberal state aid program may distribute these funds in such a way that weak and inefficient districts are given no incentive to reorganize. There are instances where the obviously needed reorganization of some districts has been retarded because it meant a substantial loss of many thousands of dollars of state aid annually for the total area concerned.

Sometimes the barrier to reorganization may be primarily because of a very meager program of state support or because of a laxness on the part of the state to require districts to share in the cost of education according to their ability to pay. In the latter case, this may result in such a wide difference in local support that some citizens are reluctant to support an otherwise desirable program of reorganization.

The bonded indebtedness of some districts has sometimes served as the effective deterrent of reorganization. This has been particularly true when no state support has been in sight for needed schoolhouse construction or where the legal debt limitation for districts has been unrealistic.

From the point of view of state support, the problem usually amounts to one of providing differential treatment to those districts that are badly in need of reorganization. One possible device is to limit the amount of state aid available to these districts. Although this scheme provides some incentive for needed reorganization, there is no assurance that this will be effected immediately. In the meantime, it is the children in the district that are punished by being denied adequate educational opportunity.

An alternate and more sensible solution is to place the punishment on the local taxpayers of the poorly organized district. This can be done by making available the district's fair share of state aid funds, and requiring a much greater local tax effort in order for these unsatisfactory districts to participate in the state's foundation program.[12]

2. AN ADEQUATE FOUNDATION PROGRAM

How much effort citizens in the local school district should make and how extensive should be the state's participation in providing for educational opportunity in the public schools have been difficult questions. Because of the research carried on during the past 35 years, however, the answers can now be rather simply determined within each state. This is because of the development of a concept commonly termed the *foundation program*. This same concept is sometimes referred to as the equalization program or the minimum school program.

The minimum foundation program concept has been "the most valuable single tool for clarifying the financial relationships between

12 Mort and Reusser, *op. cit.*, pp. 582–86.

state government and school districts." It is a simple concept and has been used successfully by more and more states during the past few years.

The foundation program concept resolves the questions of state or local support by holding that the state and the local districts must share as partners the financial responsibility of providing a basic school program for each child. The extent of the state's participation will be on a sliding scale that will vary with each school district, according to the district's financial ability to provide schools for its resident children. But every citizen is to be taxed equitably in order to provide this basic or foundation program.

Defining the foundation program

The foundation program must be defined in terms that describe the kind of a school program desired as well as in terms of expenditure level. The kind of educational program could be the minimum standards set by the state, or it could be the kind of education the people have developed through the past years, or it could be the kind of a program that the people, after careful deliberation, think is required at any given time to meet the needs of all the people of the state. In determining the educational program, consideration should be given to the quantity and quality of education guaranteed to all the children of the state. Some of the factors which determine quantity and quality of education are:

1. Upper and lower limits of the program
2. Length of school term
3. Curricular offerings
4. Cocurricular opportunities
5. Teacher preparation
6. Teacher load
7. Instructional aids and services

The educational program must be translated into costs or expenditure levels.

The expenditure level may be defined as the amount the people of the state agree upon that can be justified for every school of the state. This may be expressed in so many dollars per pupil or per classroom unit. The various provisions of the definition must be incorporated in the state laws.

Usually the foundation program funds have provided for current expenses. However, some states have found it desirable to include in

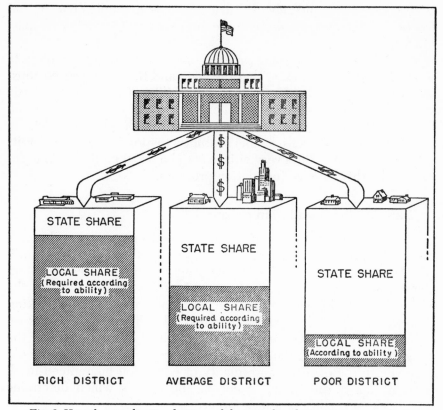

STATE SHARE

LOCAL SHARE
(Required according to ability)

RICH DISTRICT

STATE SHARE

LOCAL SHARE
(Required according to ability)

AVERAGE DISTRICT

STATE SHARE

LOCAL SHARE
(According to ability)

POOR DISTRICT

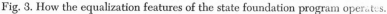

Fig. 3. How the equalization features of the state foundation program operates.

the program money for capital outlay and debt service.[13]   How the equalization feature of the foundation program operates in different districts of a state is illustrated in Figure 3.

The foundation program is, therefore, a state guaranteed program. It is a support program in which all districts may participate, provided each district has raised its proportionate amount according to its ability to pay and has met whatever additional requirements the state may deem necessary in order to qualify for state aid.

In practice, a number of states have set the level of the foundation program so low and made the availability of state aid contingent upon so many factors that only the most impoverished districts participate.   This is a violation of the foundation program concept since its fundamental principle is that of equality of educational opportunity.   The concept holds that every child in the state should be provided with equal and acceptable educational opportunity up to

[13] See Chapter 5 for more detailed discussion on calculating transportation and building costs as part of the foundation program.

some prescribed minimum. The definition of an acceptable program will, of course, differ in each state.

The foundation program is more than a device for apportioning state aid to local school districts. It is, in reality, the quality and quantity of educational experiences to be provided to all the boys and girls throughout the state. And it is this educational program, translated into dollars and cents, that the state guarantees.

In a legal sense, the state should design a program that considers *quality of education* as a prime factor. It is realized that the state must also consider the ability of the state and local districts to finance the educational program. "Each state must develop its own standards for school support. The objective measurement of local needs and local fiscal capacity and the degree to which districts should be required to support education are factors affecting the amount of state support which would be required."[14]

What are the services to be provided for in a satisfactory foundation program? No clear-cut answer is given by the experience of the states. Some states have used it only for providing transportation. Others have seen fit to use it only in the area of construction of school buildings. Still others have limited its use to that of a special-purpose fund for equalizing teachers' salaries. All of these uses are, of course, compromises or warped and stilted uses of the concept. Its true meaning holds that the foundation program should include *all* the services and facilities that a state desires to assure to every community, and that some acceptable minimum level or extent of these services and facilities be guaranteed.

An important problem that arises with the use of the foundation program is that of earmarking funds within the program itself. The argument for such a practice stems from the definition of the foundation program. A logical way of guaranteeing that the elements of the program are adequately provided in the local districts is for the state to designate that certain amounts of money must be spent for particular features or specific services.

Authorities in school finance are generally opposed to earmarking. It is their contention that research and experience have shown the practice to be undesirable since it "thwarts local initiative and diminishes desirable local control." Ideally, no part of the foundation program funds should be earmarked or consigned for specific use. Local units should be given a maximum degree of responsibility whenever there is reasonable possibility that wise judgment will be exercised. Local boards of education should determine the nature of expendi-

[14] Calvin Grieder and William E. Rosenstengel, *Public School Administration* (New York: The Ronald Press Co., 1954), p. 418.

tures locally. With the advisory leadership of the state department, it is the local board that can best determine which aspects of the program are to be expanded or given less emphasis in terms of local needs and resources. Earmarking has the affect of restricting local discretion on the basis of cost, as determined by average practice or estimate. It does not give local school districts the encouragement nor the power to carry out educational programs that are responsive to the varying needs and desires of their communities. Expanding some of the desirable aspects of the foundation program should be left to the exercise of effective state department of education leadership rather than attempting to earmark funds for this purpose.

3. FEATURES THAT ENCOURAGE VIGOROUS LOCAL INITIATIVE

A keen citizen interest in school affairs accompanies the kind of active local support that keeps school programs responsive to local needs and aspirations. It is this vital interest and support that is known as local initiative.

Factors effecting local initiative

Local initiative on the part of a community is dependent on many factors. It is related to the public's understanding about schools. It is known to have some relationship to the social, economic, and demographic characteristics of the district's population. It may be enhanced or cultivated by effective district administration of a sound public relations program. And most important of all, it is closely related to the design and operation of the state's school support program. It is this last mentioned influence that is of most interest to students of public school finance.

The principle of state responsibility for education has an important bearing on local initiative. It is the solemn duty of the state legislature in its establishment and maintenance of public schools to adopt whatever design or devices are necessary to serve the best interests of all the people in the state. In dealing with school legislation, this means that a sensitive balance must be maintained in control and jurisdiction between the state's central educational agencies and those that operate locally.

The existence of considerable local control has been found to be crucial in maintaining a high degree of local initiative. Therefore, whenever changes are made in the school finance structure, they should be examined and weighed carefully in terms of shifts of control that may occur. Frequently these shifts of control are very subtle and may unintentionally take place without immediate recognition. There is an increasing and dangerous tendency to shift control away from the local units, and educators as well as other citizens must be continually alert to these shifts since they decidedly affect local initiative, a vital element in operating good schools.

Required local effort

The amount of local effort, as expressed by the local tax levy on property, is considered as one index of local initiative. The support of schools should require sufficient sacrifice on the part of the citizens in every district so that a genuine interest is maintained in the educational program and how school monies are spent. This has some important connotations for state requirements for district participation in the foundation program.

On the other hand, it is also important that the less wealthy districts are not required to tax themselves too heavily in order to provide some kind of acceptable foundation program. If local effort has to be strained or overburdened in an attempt to provide a skimpy or truncated education program, then for all practical purposes there is no local control. Effective local autonomy is present only to the degree that the people in the local district have the direct authority and the means of determining the characteristics of the educational program. This means that they must have the power to obtain the necessary funds without review by some central agency. Control by the local unit must, however, be definitely limited as far as it concerns the denial of minimum educational opportunities. According to the foundation program concept, the local district, with state help if necessary, must provide a basic minimum program which is deemed adequate in the best interests of all the people in the state.

Fiscal independence

Whenever a school administrative unit is coterminous with a civil unit, such as a county or a city, it is frequently necessary to clarify their administrative and financial relationships.[15] School government represents a form of government that is "separate but parallel" to other forms of government and yet extends with special protection from the individual community up into the state constitution. Within this concept the consistency of court decisions was cited[16] as estab-

---

[15] Closely related to these clarifications is the concept established in Chapter 3 that, structurally, education is a unique form of government that resists classification as being either state or local in its character.
[16] See Chapter 3.

lishing the separateness and supremacy of school matters over municipal governmental matters. There appears to be some exception to this in about half of America's large cities where the control of schools seems to be in a state of uncertainty and transition.

Fiscal independence refers to an arrangement where, within the limits prescribed by the state, the board of education has full authority to determine how much money the schools need for effective operation and to see that the necessary taxes are levied to raise this money.

Where school boards do not have this authority, the schools are said to be fiscally dependent. In such a case, the schools in a city or county are financed as a subordinate division of the general city or county government.

Two factors seem to effectively exert pressure in bringing about fiscally dependent schools. One of these factors has been an over-all tax limit that a state has imposed on the governmental unit. Under such a tax limit, the schools and the local government must share in the revenue of whatever tax is levied. The other factor has been the notion held by students of political science and government. They have viewed the schools as just another phase of local government. From this viewpoint they have insisted that the arguments of simplicity and economy compel schools to be organized and financed as a subordinate department in the same manner as the police department, the fire department, or the garbage and sanitation department. This point of view is obviously in flagrant opposition to that held by educators and is also a direct contradiction of a long series of court decisions on the status of school districts as "arms of state government."

Educators hold that fiscal dependence complicates rather than simplifies governmental structure because it attempts to subsume a legally recognized state function, education, under a purely local government. School boards are state agents and should not be required to share responsibility for determining school fiscal affairs with representatives of other local governmental agencies. School authorities also argue that the interest of the schools can be best served when the control is given to a single board that has its full attention devoted to one major activity. They further point out that as far as the research and experience on this problem is concerned, investigations made in terms of economy and efficiency generally tend to favor fiscal independence.

The problem of fiscal independence, however, is not solely confined to cities. It can become a very serious matter when local school boards become fiscally dependent upon politically elected county officials or when state boards of education become dependent upon political committees or agencies. For all intents and purposes this dependence shifts at least a part of the control of the schools to the political agencies or officials rather than leaving it to the presumably nonpartisan school board where it belongs.

TOPICS FOR STUDY AND DISCUSSION

1. Explain what is meant by the statement that "the manner in which the state supports schools is equally as important as the amount of money it spends for education."
2. Discuss the position that holds that the problem of reorganizing school districts in America that are "too large" is of equal magnitude as that of reorganizing districts that are "too small."
3. Make a comparison of per-pupil costs of the schools in your district. Do you see any relationship between these costs and the size of the school units? Explain.
4. From a biennial or annual report of your state department of education, compare the per-pupil costs of the very small districts of your state with those of districts of an acceptable size (1,500 or more pupils). What can you infer as to the quality of education in these comparison districts?
5. Check your inference in #4, above, by analyzing in the comparison districts such factors as the level of professional preparation of the school staff, the per cent of turnover in the professional staff, etc.
6. What are the greatest needs in your state as far as school district reorganization is concerned? What are the major blocks in the improvement of the structural organization in your state? What specific steps would you suggest to remedy the situation?
7. Suppose you are a local superintendent in the state of "New Oceola." The level of the state's foundation program has been defined at $5,000 per classroom unit. The qualifying, uniform levy for all districts is 10 mills. What will be the amount of state aid your district will receive if:
   (a) the assessed valuation of your district is $25 million and your district can report 100 classroom units of educational need?
   (b) the assessed valuation of your district is $40 million and your district can report 80 classroom units of educational need?
   (c) the assessed valuation of your district is $32.5 million and your district can report 105 classroom units?
8. What is the level of the foundation program in your state? What is the qualifying, minimum levy for districts in your state to participate in the state aid program? What is the assessed valuation of your district? What proportion of the school funds expended last year in your district were from state sources?

SELECTED REFERENCES

BURKE, ARVID J. *Financing Public Schools in the United States.* New York: Harper & Bros., 1951.

GRIEDER, CALVIN, and WILLIAM E. ROSENSTENGEL. *Public School Administration.* New York: The Ronald Press Co., 1954, chap. XVIII.

HUTCHINS, CLAYTON D., and ALBERT R. MUNSE, *Expenditures for Education at the Midcentury.* (U.S. Office of Education, Misc. No. 18.) Washington, D.C.: Government Printing Office, 1953.

————. *Public School Finance Programs of the United States.* (U.S. Office of Education, Misc. No. 22 [no date]) Washington, D.C.: Government Printing Office.

McINTYRE, KENNETH E. "The Schools Redistricting Problem in Nebraska," *American School Board Journal,* CXII (December, 1949), 15–16.

MORT, PAUL R., and FRANCIS G. CORNELL. *American Schools in Transition.* New York: Bureau of Publications, Teachers College, Columbia University, 1941. pp. 137–38.

MORT, PAUL R., and WALTER C. REUSSER. *Public School Finance* (2d ed.). New York: McGraw-Hill Book Co., Inc., 1951, chap. XVII.

National Conference of Professors of Educational Administration and National Citizens Commission for the Public Schools. *Problems and Issues in Public School Finance.* New York: Bureau of Publication, Teachers College, Columbia University, 1952, chap. III.

National Education Association, Research Division. "School Finance Goals," *Research Bulletin,* XXIV (October, 1946), 87–127.

OPERATIONAL FEATURES OF A SATIS-
FACTORY STATE-SUPPORT PROGRAM

IN ADDITION to the basic design or structure of a state's plan of school support, there are certain features that enhance the plan's operation. It is these operational features that simplify the equitable apportionment of state funds and assure the provision for collateral but essential aspects of educational opportunity. These features also delineate the control and leadership functions of local school districts and of central agencies. They provide for the essential experimentation and adaptability of a state's system of public schools.

1. MEASURES OF EDUCATIONAL NEED FOR
APPORTIONING STATE AID

The basis on which state funds are apportioned to local school districts is obviously an important feature of any plan of state school support. In the effective operation of a state-support plan, particularly of the type that capitalizes on the concept of the foundation program, one of the basic problems to be solved is the determination of how much need for state support exists in each district.

Requiring a uniform levy in each district is only part of the answer. This uniform, local levy will obviously raise different amounts of revenue in each school district. The amount will depend, of course, on the valuation of taxable property within the district. However, the amount of money raised from a uniform tax has little or no relationship to the educational need that exists. The amount of revenue thus available may be only remotely related to the number of children to be educated or transported, or the number of teachers to be employed, or the required amount of supervision and special services necessary to provide an acceptable level of educational opportunity throughout the district.

How should this need be determined for each individual school district? One occasionally proposed method is to leave the determination of need to the state department of education. This office could then apportion state aid funds on the basis of need to each district. Such a plan, however, is repugnant to the concept of public education in America since it shifts a substantial amount of control of the schools to this central agency.

Another suggested way may be to let the local boards of education determine how much state support is needed. For example, the law might be written so that the local district is reimbursed for 60 per cent of whatever is spent. This is also wholly unsatisfactory since it unwisely provides for far too broad a leeway for local districts in determining the amount of state money to come to the locality.

What then is a satisfactory solution to this problem of determining educational need? The logical and most obvious answer is that some kind of objective index must be used. This index should be applicable to all districts and should be embodied in the state's school finance laws. Besides simplifying the laws, the use of an objective index of educational need makes it possible to avoid any unnecessary statutory prescriptions. These include the tendency to earmark funds for specific aspects of the school program or to meticulously specify the discretionary powers of state school officers, measures which are restrictive on wholesome local autonomy and initiative.

The concept of the foundation program with its underlying principle of equality of educational opportunity gives a useful perspective to many indexes that may be suggested for use in the distribution of state funds. Weighed in the balance of equality of opportunity, previously acceptable measures of educational need may be found to be quite inadequate. Some measures of need with their accompanying strengths and shortcomings are now briefly presented.

The school census and attendance

The laws of a state generally determine the meaning of "school-age children," and the age limits of the children included in this definition vary among the states. The apportionment of state funds has frequently been made on the basis of the number of school-age children residing in the various school districts.

Apportioning state aid on this basis has some serious weaknesses.

As an index of educational need, the census is fraught with inaccuracies. It does not take cognizance of the amount of private-school attendance, poor attendance, or attendance by resident children to schools outside the district. Actually, it discourages the careful enforcement of attendance laws. It fails to recognize the movement of pupils into or out of the districts during the school year. Varying lengths of school terms and differences in staff adequacy or pupil-teacher ratios are also overlooked. It is frequently inaccurate even in its determination of the pupils actually serviced by the schools since the specified legal age limits may include some pupils who have already completed their schooling or exclude some who are still in regular attendance.

If all of these weaknesses in the census could be corrected, it would still be unsound as a basis for distributing school funds. School costs are only roughly related to the number of children educated. This becomes evident by contrasting urban with sparsely settled rural school districts where some obvious cost variables are apparent. These differences are revealed in pupil-teacher ratios, transportation costs, the expense of adequate supervision, and the cost of retaining teachers with comparable professional training and experience. Even more important, however, is the fact that the distribution of school funds on a per census-child basis generally favors the densely populated urban districts that typically have the highest local taxpaying ability. Sparsely populated, rural districts, on the other hand, tend to be penalized, and normally these districts are the ones with the lowest local taxpaying ability. This is obviously in conflict with the equalization principle embodied in the concept of the foundation program.

It should be apparent that the distribution of state funds solely on the basis of actual attendance or actual enrollment is subject to most of the same weaknesses as those cited in the use of the census. This is essentially true even though these measures may not be subject to inaccuracies of the census and the fact that they may promote the strict enforcement of attendance laws.

The number of teachers

Another means of distributing state aid uses the number of teachers employed as the basis for apportionments. Although this index of need has some advantages over the use of raw census, attendance, or enrollment figures, it is also subject to some of the same criticisms.

Using the number of teachers as the basis for determining a district's share of state aid may be helpful to the sparsely populated rural areas where it is difficult to maintain a reasonable pupil-teacher ratio. However, in contrasting its impact on urban or similarly populated districts that differ markedly in wealth, the result is quite the opposite of equalization. The more able districts that can afford smaller class sizes and more adequate staffs are favored under such a state aid program.

Teachers' salaries

Some states have attempted to tie the method of apportioning state aid to the implementation of a state minimum salary schedule based on training and experience. Under such a plan the state typically recognizes the cost of the school program as being the cost of the state salary schedule plus an additional percentage for nonsalary costs.

The intent of such provisions is undoubtedly good in aiming to provide adequately trained teachers for all communities. In practice, however, there are some pitfalls, particularly if the level of the support program is not sufficient to allow the least financially able districts to obtain the highest caliber of teachers recognized on the schedule. The result of this kind of plan is that the wealthier districts, because of their greater local tax ability to exceed the state's minimum schedule, will generally staff their schools with the highest caliber personnel. The poorer districts are unable to compete on this basis and as a result are forced to employ those teachers that have been "picked over." These teachers that are the least wanted are typically those with the least professional training and experience. These deficiencies are of course reflected in the salary schedule and are thus the cause of a diminished amount of state aid going to the districts that have the greatest need.

Abstract, standard cost units

The most satisfactory measures of educational need are those representing standard units of cost based on extensive experience and research. The definition of these standard units may include a few or several actual cost items in the operation of schools. Each of the items included can be appropriately weighted in order to give a more accurate measure of the educational load to be supported in all school districts within a state.

The most frequently used measures of educational need of this standard unit cost type are the weighted classroom unit and the weighted elementary pupil unit. Both of these measures represent identical approaches to the problem and can therefore be roughly equated. The difference is only in the basic unit chosen. Describing the difference in these two measures is analogous to citing the difference in using an egg or a dozen eggs as the unit in measuring egg shipments. A crate of eggs can be described as containing 360 eggs or it can be described as containing 30 dozens of eggs. Both descriptions are accurate and equivalent even though the basic units employed are different.

To illustrate how these units are standardized and weighted, let us examine a weighted classroom unit as it might be legislatively defined. Such a definition could provide that each of the following were the equivalent to one classroom unit: 20 kindergarten pupils in average daily attendance (ADA); 20 high school pupils in ADA; 24 elementary pupils in ADA; 3 vocational, agriculture, or home economics teachers employed on a 12-month contract; one superintendent of schools; 2 full-time, fully certificated principals, supervisors, librarians, or counselors.

In such a definition of a classroom unit it can be seen that different amounts of recognition can be given to the various elements that comprise the total educational load. Wherever possible, the amount of recognition given to the various elements should reflect the experience of the state concerned.

Attention is called to the fact that the elements used in computing the total number of classroom units for a district refer not to individual pupils or teachers or administrators personally, but only in the *abstract*. Thus there is no intent at specifying how much money should be spent by local boards for these items. Instead, the classroom unit is simply a device used to describe objectively the educational need of a given community or school district.

The weighting of the elementary pupil unit is also to be made on the basis of the expenditure experience of the state, and research. This is generally done by assigning a weight to some of the elements considered. For example, each high school pupil in ADA may be defined as the equivalent of 1.3 elementary pupil units.

The efforts of Mort and some of his students have been focused on having the one weighted unit serve completely in a state-support program. To do this they have refined some corrections to take care of the additional cost of operating small schools in rural areas and also provide for transportation needs. These have been called sparsity corrections.[1] They are determined by plotting a two-way distribution of the number of teachers employed (or some other factors that reflect increased costs) and the number of pupils in average daily at-

[1] Paul R. Mort and Walter C. Reusser, *Public School Finance* (2d ed.; New York: McGraw-Hill Book Co., Inc., 1951), pp. 601–14.

tendance (or some other measure of the pupil population density). From drawing in lines of best fit and devising the formula for each of these lines, it is then possible to compute from the appropriate formula the increased amount of educational need of any school district, regardless of its size or the density of its population. These sparsity corrections become an integral part of the state's method of determining educational need, and thus are used in apportioning state funds.

In addition to measuring educational need, standard cost units are useful in setting the level of the foundation program. This is generally done by stating that the expenditure of a specified amount per classroom unit (or per weighted elementary pupil unit) constitutes the foundation program. Therefore, simply by multiplying this stated amount by the total number of classroom units to which a district is entitled, the total cost of its foundation program is determined. Subtracting from this total cost the revenue raised by the district, based upon its ability to pay, will give the amount of state aid to which the district is entitled.

2. MEASUREMENT OF LOCAL FINANCIAL ABILITY

A foundation program combining state and local support, if it is to attain any degree of equality in the tax burden of the school units of the state, involves some measure of taxpaying ability of the local district. The assessed valuation of property is probably the oldest method used for measuring the ability of a district to support education. Today there are, however, other means of finding the real ability of a district to support education.

Assessed valuation of property

Local revenue for schools is usually obtained from the general property tax.[2] The amount of tax is determined by multiplying the assessed valuation of the taxable property by the approved tax rate. The assessed valuation of property is extremely inequitable. The inequity among assessed values is largely due to the methods used in assessing property. The methods range from listing the value of the property as given by the owner to scientific procedures. Even within a state different methods are used to obtain the assessed valuation of property. In one county the property may be assessed at 20 per cent of the true value while in another the property may be assessed at 80 per cent. Within counties or districts one will find about as much

---

[2] General property taxes provide more than 50 per cent of the school revenues in the United States. In 24 states it is the source of more than 60 per cent of the school funds.

variation in assessment values because certain influences such as friendship—economic or social—are prevalent. There does not seem to be an agreement even among the tax authorities on the method of determining the true value of property for taxing purposes.

If the state has an effective means of assuring that all property throughout the state is uniformly assessed, the local contribution can be specified simply by requiring a local tax of so many mills per dollar of assessed valuation. This is the way it is expressed in the preceding formula.

Careful consideration of the functioning of this feature of requiring a specified uniform local levy will reveal, however, that it encourages the local district to lower its valuation of property and thereby receive more state aid. Some state attempts at equalization have been frustrated because of the "competitive underassessment" of property that has taken place among the various school districts.

Obviously, if assessment ratios vary among the districts, the state cannot equitably require a fixed tax rate for providing the local contribution to the cost of the foundation program. To do so would mean that the districts with the higher assessment ratios would be penalized since they contribute more in terms of their ability to pay than do those districts with lower assessment ratios. Some other scheme for determining the local contribution must therefore be made if assessment ratios are allowed to vary.

One of the ways some states (e.g., Washington) cope with the problem of varying assessments is to authorize some state agency to determine these ratios for each district and thus vary the required tax rate in terms of the existing assessment ratio. Those districts having low assessment ratios then have the option of levying proportionately higher tax rates or raising their assessment ratios to conform with those of the other districts.

State equalization of assessments and state supervision of local assessments have been used in a number of states. Although either of these methods is much more satisfactory than local assessment, there remains much to be desired before assessment of property for tax purposes may be used satisfactorily for combining state and local effort to support schools.

An index of taxpaying ability

As a means of avoiding the injustices arising from unsatisfactory methods of assessing property for taxpaying purposes, a few states[3]

[3] At the present time there are seven states which have used indexes of taxpaying ability to measure local taxpaying ability: Alabama, Florida, Kentucky, Texas, West Virginia, Arkansas, and Georgia. Tennessee uses an index figure, based upon two

have adopted an index of taxpaying ability to determine the amount the local district must raise to share in the state foundation program. The measurement of taxpaying ability of the local school unit is an important factor if the state is going to equalize the financing of public education.

To meet the problem of varying assessment ratios, a state may bypass completely or partially property assessments and resort to the use of economic indexes of taxpaying ability for each district. Whereas property assessments are "notoriously inexact, unscientific, and inequitable," the use of economic indexes is perhaps the most scientific approach to this whole problem and holds promise for widespread use in the future. It should be stressed, however, that the use of economic indexes is not intended to replace good property-tax administration. They can, nevertheless, serve a real need in those states in which determination of assessment ratios is not practical.

The procedure followed in developing an index of taxpaying ability for each district is to determine on a number of selected items the ratio between the district total and the state total. These items might include measures of such things as the amount of automobile license tax paid, the value of farm products, the amount of retail sales, the value added by manufacture, the income tax paid, payrolls, etc. For a simplified example, suppose a given school district has 3 per cent of the state's total motor vehicle registrations, pays 2 per cent of the state's total income tax payments, and pays 4 per cent of the total retail sales tax collected by the state. If these were the only three measures that were to be used in computing ability indexes, and if they were all found to be of equal importance, then they might be simply averaged together to give an ability index of 3 per cent for this school district. To use this ability index in determining the amount of local contribution that this district is to make is the next step. This is done by first determining what the total amount of local contributions of all school districts is to be in order to supplement state sources in financing the foundation program throughout the state. This total local contribution will be a fixed amount of money, e.g., $40 million of the total cost of the state's foundation program which will be $100 million. In order to determine the local contribution to be made by the school district used in this example, its ability index, 3 per cent, is multiplied by the total amount to be

factors: (1) ratio of assessed valuation of county to the total assessed valuation of state, and (2) ratio that the estimated true value of property of the country is to the estimated true value of the property of the state. For an analysis of these, see Francis G. Cornell, *The Index of Local Economic Ability in State School Finance Programs* (Washington, D.C.: National Education Association, Committee on Tax Education and School Finance, 1953).

contributed by all local districts, $40 million, and the resultant amount of $1.2 million, would be this district's local contribution. In this instance, each district's local contribution is computed similarly by multiplying its ability index times $40 million.

If properly developed, the use of ability indexes will give approximately the same results as would be obtained through the careful, uniform assessment of all property within the state and then requiring a fixed tax rate to be levied in every district. The use of ability indexes is facilitated in those states with a county-unit pattern of district organization since the data needed for determining these indexes are ordinarily available by counties. In those states wherein school districts are smaller than the county, assessment standards can be made uniform throughout the county and the total county-wide cost can then be divided equitably by allocating it among the districts in proportion to the amount of the county's assessed valuation that is in the local school district.

3. PROVISIONS THAT ENCOURAGE LEADERSHIP AND EXPERIMENTATION

The studies of adaptability of school systems, done principally by Mort and his students, have focused attention on the necessity for a state's support program to provide for educational experimentation, tryout, and leadership within any given state. To make such provisions is to recognize the fact that schools must continually change and improve in order to keep abreast of new and better educational practice and in order to keep pace with the changes that continually occur in the communities served by the schools.

If schools are to be continually changing in order to perform their functions most efficiently, then there must be some means provided that will give intelligent direction to these changes. There must be some assurance that the adaptations made are the kind that most efficiently fulfill the identified needs.

Making changes in schools is expensive in terms of the time, money, and effort involved. It means the discarding and replacing of expensive equipment that has become obsolete. It means the changing of curricula. It means upgrading, inspiring, and changing the behavior of teachers and administrators. Indeed, making needed changes in schools is costly. Not making these changes, however, is even more costly in terms of the quality of education the pupils receive.

To bring about desirable changes in schools with a minimum of cost and a maximum of effectiveness requires leadership and experimentation. School systems more readily adapt new practices to meet local needs after these practices have been tried out and found to be satisfactory. Schools change more readily if they can imitate rather than invent improved educational practice.[4] A state's school-support program, therefore, must recognize the necessity for invention and tryout as well as encourage the diffusion or imitation of desirable educational practice.

Good educational practice is encouraged by supporting an adequate foundation program and a system of communication among districts. An acute need for the invention phase of this process still exists. There are two different ways for a state to provide the needed leadership and experimentation and thus assure some degree of adaptability in its schools. A state should use both methods, making provisions for pilot schools and making provisions for widespread local research and implementation.

Encouraging pilot school districts

When we permit change to take place in schools without a conscious and deliberate effort to stimulate it and provide leadership for it, the results are disheartening. Unless these efforts are made, schools tend to lag far behind acceptable school practice.

One of the ways to provide this leadership, and thus enhance the adaptability of all schools, is to encourage some of the most able districts within a state to greatly exceed the foundation program. These relatively high-expenditure districts, called pilot or lighthouse districts, can pioneer in finding new educational practices that will better solve some of the current needs and problems faced by all schools. By initiating practices through an enriched program, these districts point the way for others to make wholesome and tested changes. In this way pilot schools give intelligent direction to the adaptability of other school systems.

In addition to their leadership and experimentation function, pilot schools provide a "show-window" for the state to see the quality and variety of educational experiences that can be obtained through relatively high expenditures for education. This may serve as a means for obtaining a better expenditure level for all the schools of the state.

The encouragement of pilot districts calls for modification in a state's school finance laws. The simplest way to provide this encouragement is to provide a substantial amount of state aid to all districts in the form of a flat grant. This, of course, is in addition to state funds

[4] Mort and Cornell, *op. cit.*, pp. 79–80.

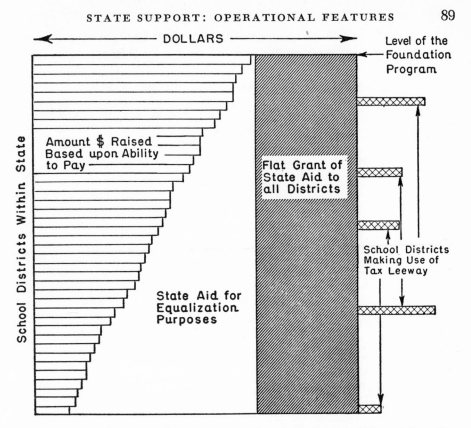

Fig. 4. A state aid program that encourages pilot school districts. (Adapted from New York State Educational Conference Board, *Fiscal Policy for Public Education in the State of New York* [Albany: The Board, 1947], p. 69.)

supplied for purely equalization purposes. Such a pattern of support is illustrated in Figure 4.

In essence, this change in the state's method of financing schools is simply a device for redetermining the level of the foundation program or how it is to be financed. It does, however, grant substantial funds to the wealthiest districts, which straight equalization does not do. The effect of this flat grant is to further relieve the property tax in the local districts. With a lightly taxed and thus responsive source of school revenue, the most able districts can capitalize on this opportunity to provide educational programs that far exceed anything they could otherwise afford.

The flat grant pattern of state aid may be defended by more than just the argument for pilot schools. It is a means for broadening the tax base for school support. It is a desirable way of returning to localities the revenue from equitable taxes that because of their nature cannot be efficiently administered on the local level.

Encouraging widespread research and experimentation

Another means of providing direction and leadership for the improvement of schools is to encourage a program of research and experimentation in all school districts. Such a program has been almost nonexistent in American school systems. In those few districts that have had some budgetary allowance for research, this activity has been typically confined to the tabulation of attendance data or the computation of local norms of tests. Certainly, school districts have accomplished little that can be considered as significant, fundamental research in education.

Local districts can and should search for needed innovations and try out promising practices developed locally. Indeed, it is becoming more and more apparent that the implementation of improved practice is hastened by the participation of individuals and faculties in the process of defining the desired innovations. There appears to be great promise in the emerging concept of "action research," or the kind of research that involves many persons and primarily seeks to improve existing educational practice.

From the point of view of a district-wide attack on this problem, it is appropriate to adopt the pilot school concept for local use. Within a local district a certain school (or schools) can function as a laboratory for discovering and validating improved educational practice. Such a program can successfully complement whatever pilot school provisions are made by the state. And, in the absence of pilot districts, these local provisions may be extremely beneficial.

4. TRANSPORTATION PROVISIONS

Over the past quarter of a century, transportation has become an increasingly important consideration in state-support programs. While only a very few states made any state aid provisions for transportation during the first decade of this century, today there are only a few that do not provide at least some support for this essential service.

The principle of equality of educational opportunity calls for a program of state support that assures the adequate provision of all essential services and facilities. Because of this, it is now generally recommended that transportation allowances be one aspect of a state's foundation program. One of the major difficulties encountered in fulfilling this recommendation has been in determining the most equitable basis for apportioning state funds for essential transportation services. A variety of methods have been used. There appears, however, to be no unanimity on which method is best.

Some states use a special formula for calculating the transportation needs of each district. These formulas represent varying degrees of complexity and are typically based on a few or several of the following items: the number of elementary pupils transported, the number of secondary pupils transported, the number and size of buses or the number of bus drivers, the length of the routes, the condition of equipment, the road conditions, and the number of schools to which pupils are transported.

A few states consider transportation costs as being directly related to the population density and have included these and other costs in a set of standard sparsity corrections used in the computation of educational need.[5]

Other states furnish state aid for an allowable percentage of the total amount spent for transportation. To encourage economy and efficiency under such arrangements, states frequently set some qualifying specifications or standards to be adhered to by the local district. These may include such items as: the maintenance of various standards of safety, adequacy, and efficiency; a certain amount of local support for transportation; certain limits on the total amount of aid for transportation that any district may receive.

Research on state support for transportation has been focused on the refinement of various indexes of transportation need.[6] Authorities are agreed that this essential service should be given adequate recognition in a state-support program. These people seem to favor the determination of transportation need on the basis of the area density of the pupil population and the number of pupils transported, with certain corrections made for unusual road conditions.[7]

5. CAPITAL OUTLAY AND DEBT SERVICE PROVISIONS

Since the beginning of the twentieth century there has been a trend toward an increasing state responsibility for capital outlay and debt service of school districts. This has paralleled a similar trend in state control over schoolhouse construction. Control has come through the enforcement of minimum standards and the establishment of

---

[5] Francis G. Cornell and William P. McClure, *Financing Education in Efficient School Districts* (Urbana, Ill.: College of Education, University of Illinois Press, 1949), pp. 152–53.

[6] National Conference of Professors of Educational Administration, *Problems and Issues in Public School Finance* (New York: Bureau of Publications, Teachers College, Columbia University, 1952), pp. 210–11.

[7] *Ibid.*, pp. 176–77.

prudential checks regulating indebtedness and other aspects of providing school plant facilities.

Trends of state to finance capital outlay and debt service

Despite some early state support, it has only been since the 1940's that more than a few instances have existed where any substantial aid has been apportioned to school districts for capital outlay purposes. Currently, about one half of the states recognize the need for some support for school plant programs. In most cases, however, this support is so limited that it is of little consequence or it is specifically designated as being of an emergency nature only. Nevertheless, it does represent a trend toward a greater acceptance of the implications of the principle of equality of opportunity. An increasing number of states are accepting the responsibility for assuring an adequacy of all essential services and facilities.

As the various states have begun to assume this responsibility, the problem of control and local initiative has arisen. This same problem of minimizing central control is the one that has been so successfully solved with the foundation program concept.

There is nothing within the concept of the foundation program that would limit its scope to include only current expenditures. Historically, however, provisions for capital outlay and debt service have generally been absent when foundation programs have been implemented. Some authorities have explained this as evidence of a fundamental reluctance of the states in making such funds available. Others have viewed this as reflecting the need for simplification of a program that was only being tried out and not yet established within the states. These people hold that the inclusion of provisions for capital outlay would have served only to unduly complicate and thereby possibly delay the acceptance of the foundation program.

Since the time of adoption of the foundation program in many states, there has developed a more intense need for state support of capital outlay and debt service for local school districts. A tremendous backlog of school building needs was caused by the neglect of construction during the depressed thirties, the inability to build during the wartime forties, and the procrastination of the postwar period when local boards looked longingly for a decline in the continued spiraling of building costs. The need became critical. Emergency action was taken by several states. There were still some definite problems in getting capital outlay provisions smoothly integrated into an existing foundation program or, for that matter, into any other type of school finance program.

Developing an index of need

Making capital outlay a part of the foundation program calls for the development of an index of need, an objective basis upon which state aid can be distributed equitably. This is no mean task. It is complicated by such factors as debt limits, the wide range of existing indebtedness among the districts of a state, and the variance of building costs in different regions and at different times when indebtedness may occur.

Research has suggested several solutions to this problem of defining an objective measure of school plant need.[8] One has been the allocation to the local district of an amount equal to some fixed percentage of the annual current expenditures of the district. This amount is designated for capital outlay and debt service use, and over a period of time will take care of school building needs.[9] Other research suggestions have proposed separate equalization formulas based on the depreciation of existing school facilities or on standard units of housing computed from average practice and from attendance data.[10]

The procedure varies widely among the states granting support for capital outlay and debt service. Furthermore, it typically reflects little of the research efforts made on this problem. A few states make such support an integral part of the foundation program, and this method appears to be gaining more and more acceptance. Other states confine to special aids any capital outlay and debt service support. These may be distributed on some kind of equalization basis, on a matching basis, or on some other basis where only those districts with emergency conditions receive any state support. A few states have not loaned any state money to districts for capital outlay purposes. Another approach to this problem has been made by having some central agency issue the bonds and then rent the facilities to the local district. Allowing the local district to pay this rent out of current revenues is one way of circumventing any debt limit laws.[11]

[8] *Ibid.*, pp. 211–14

[9] Foster E. Grossnickle, *Capital Outlay in Relation to a State's Minimum Program* (New York: Bureau of Publications, Teachers College, Columbia University, 1931). See also Paul R. Mort, *The Financing of School Buildings* (Providence R. I.: State Board of Education, 1955).

[10] Arvid J. Burke, *Financing Public Schools in the United States* (New York: Harper & Bros., 1951), p. 319.

[11] Francis G. Cornell and Eugene P. McLoone, "Finance and Material Management," *Review of Educational Research*, XXV (October, 1955), 355.

Out of the limited but diversified experience with state support of capital outlay and debt service, most authorities would agree with the following conclusions: (1) The state support plan of every state should provide for adequately financing capital outlay and debt service. (2) On the basis of objective, unit measures of school building need, this phase of support should be incorporated into the foundation program. This is the most favored plan, but if such support is limited to special aid or separate emergency appropriations, need and ability should provide the basis for apportionment. (3) Any program of state support for capital outlay and debt service should have its emphasis on long-range needs. It should, therefore, be restricted only for use in satisfactorily organized districts. (4) Any plan should allow for emergency conditions and recognize the effect of sparse population on the need and cost of plant facilities. (5) The meeting of state building standards and other qualifying conditions for state aid should minimize state control and encourage local initiative by allowing districts the freedom to exceed, at their own expense, such standards in order to better meet local desires and needs.

6. STATE LEADERSHIP WITH LOCAL CONTROL

The foundation program concept provides an insight into how central agencies concerned with education should function for maximum effectiveness. Since this design for state support is aimed at assuring adequate educational opportunities throughout the entire state, it logically follows that the administration of the state program be the responsibility of the state education agency. This agency is usually defined as the state board of education whose policies are carried out by a state department of education under the leadership of a state superintendent.[12]

The efforts and services provided by the state department of education should be only supplementary to those of the local school districts. The department's operations should be confined to persuasive leadership of an advisory nature. Its services should be of a technical, specialized type, administered in a way that encourages maximum local initiative and control.

Controls operated by the state department should be confined to those that a reasonable amount of evidence indicates cannot, in the best interests of all the people of the state, function locally.

Another focus of state department efforts can legitimately be to keep the actions and policies of local boards in line with the considered judgment of all the people in the district. A defensible kind

[12] See Chapter 8 for a more detailed discussion on this subject.

of central control, then, is the kind that establishes local procedures which give the assurance that the most important school board decisions reflect the thinking of the district's population.

The sole exception to the general policy of limited central control is in those districts that are so small and poorly organized that local leadership is insufficient to exercise local autonomy in school affairs.

Powers of central agencies must be continuously re-examined. Any controls granted to these agencies because of unsatisfactory district organization must be withdrawn after reorganization has taken place. It is imperative that central controls be minimized as far as they affect tax limits, local budgets, audits with the right of challenge, or aspects of the local education program. Such controls when held centrally tend to set up a vicious cycle since they emasculate local government, and this in turn calls for further central control. Such a pattern is an unwholesome one since the sensible solution lies in strengthening the local structure, revenue system, and administration of school districts in order to enhance and invigorate local control and initiative.

7. A SUMMARY OF CHARACTERISTICS OF A FOUNDATION PROGRAM

There are many features which must be incorporated into the operational features of a satisfactory state-supported educational program. A summary of these follows:

1. The state finance plan should have as its objective the guaranteeing of equality of educational opportunities in the foundation program for all children of the state. In order to achieve this objective the plan should at least:
   (a) Encourage efficiency and economy in organization and administration of all the schools within its boundaries.
   (b) Provide adequate support for all essential elements of school costs included in the basic program.
   (c) Provide as comprehensive a foundation program as the ability of the state permits.
   (d) Require each local administrative unit to make a minimum effort in proportion to its ability to pay in order to participate in the foundation program.
   (e) Encourage local administrative units to supplement the minimum effort required to participate in the program.
2. The foundation program should include all items of cost necessary to operate a sound educational program. This will include not only current expense but also capital outlay and debt service. In some states which operate a state system of transportation it might

be feasible to continue such a plan and not delegate the program to the local units. However, the total cost would be an item of expenditure in the basic foundation program.

3. The cost of a foundation program to be financed jointly from state and local sources should be based on a standard measure, such as the classroom unit. Classroom units should be so defined that different amounts of recognition can be given to the several elements that comprise the total educational load—regular classroom teachers, vocational teachers, special education teachers, administrative and supervisory officers, librarians, and so forth.

4. The cost of the foundation program to be financed jointly from state and local sources should take into consideration the sparsity factor. There are areas where schools must operate at a cost out of all proportion to the average.

5. The percentage of the foundation program to be provided by the state should be determined by the legislative body. The difference between the total foundation program and the amount the state provides will be the amount to be raised by the local administrative units.

6. In the absence of good property tax administration, the local effort required of each district should be determined by an objective index of taxpaying ability. The index of each district would show the proportion of wealth in the county to the total wealth in the state. The total amount required of each county should be determined by multiplying its index by the total amount required of all counties in the state.

7. The foundation program should provide for maximum state leadership and minimum controls.

8. The amount of state money apportioned to a district may be stated by the following formula:

The Amount of State Aid to Each District = Total Number of Classroom Units in the District Times the Amount per Classroom Defined by the State as the Foundation Program − Amount of money Raised Locally Based Upon Ability to Pay

TOPICS FOR STUDY AND DISCUSSION

1. What is the basic measure of educational need used by your state? What suggestions would you make for its improvement?

2. Suppose your state uses the classroom unit as its basic measure of educational need and defines one classroom unit as being equivalent to: (1) 30 kindergarten pupils in ADA; (2) 25 elementary pupils in ADA; (3) 20 high school pupils in ADA; (4) a full-time, certified

superintendent of schools; and (5) every two additional full-time, certified nonteaching personnel.   Compute the total number of classroom units (C.R.U.) for a district that has:

> 240 kindergarten children in ADA
> 1,500 elementary pupils in ADA
> 640 Junior high school pupils in ADA
> 550 High school pupils in ADA
> 1 Superintendent, 2 supervisors
> 5 full-time principals and 2 teaching
>   principals that are allowed half-time
>   for administrative duties.

3. What will be the minimum amount of money to be spent in the operation of schools in the above district if the level of the state's foundation program is set at $7,500 per classroom unit?
4. Suppose a state uses "weighted-elementary-pupil units" as its basic measure of educational need, and it defines one W.E.P.U. as equal to 1 elementary pupil in ADA.   Each high school pupil in ADA is equal to 1.3 W.E.P.U.'s.   Compute the total number of W.E.P.U.'s for which the district in topic #2 above could qualify.   What would be the minimum operational expenditure in this district if the state defined its foundation program level at $320 per W.E.P.U.?
5. What might be some of the objections to distributing state aid on an equalization and flat-grant basis as is shown in the figure in this chapter? Summarize the advantages of such a plan.

SELECTED REFERENCES

BURKE, ARVID J. *Financing Public Schools in the United States.* New York: Harper & Bros., 1951, chaps. XII and XIII.

CORNELL, FRANCIS G. and WILLIAM P. McCLURE.   *Financing Education in Efficient School Districts.*   Urbana, Ill.: College of Education, University of Illinois Press, 1949.

CORNELL, FRANCIS G. and EUGENE P. McLOONE, "Finance and Material Management," *Review of Educational Research,* XXV (October, 1955), 355.

GROSSNICKLE, FOSTER E.   *Capital Outlay in Relation to a State's Minimum Program.*   New York: Bureau of Publications, Teachers College, Columbia University, 1931.

HUTCHINS, CLAYTON D. and ALBERT R. MUNSE.   *Public School Finance Programs in the United States.*   (U.S. Office of Education, Misc. No. 22.) Washington, D.C.: Government Printing Office, 1955.

MORT, PAUL R.   *The Financing of School Buildings.*   Providence, R.I.: State Board of Education, 1955.

MORT, PAUL R. and FRANCIS G. CORNELL.   *American Schools in Transition.* New York: Bureau of Publications, Teachers College, Columbia University, 1941.

MORT, PAUL R. and WALTER C. REUSSER.   *Public School Finance,* 2d ed.   New York: McGraw-Hill Book Co., Inc., 1951, chap. XX.

National Conference of Professors of Educational Administration and National

Citizens Commission for the Public Schools. *Problems and Issues in Public School Finance.* New York: Bureau of Publications, Teachers College, Columbia University, 1952, chaps. V, VI, and VII.

National Education Association, Committee on Tax Education and School Finance. *The Index of Local Economic Ability in State School Finance Programs.* Washington, D.C.: The Association, 1953.

6

STATE AND LOCAL SCHOOL
EXPENDITURES

As AN INTEGRAL part of determining the design of the school finance program, the question of adequacy arises. This is true on a state basis in the development of the foundation program and in the stimulation of lighthouse or pilot school districts. It is also true on the district level in determining the character of the local educational program.

The question of adequacy of education is a critical problem. Although the problem must be frequently solved in every state and in every local school district, it is surprising to find how indefensible most solutions are. It seems obvious that any decision on this matter should be grounded in reliable information and basic research. Establishing the adequacy of a school program on the basis of facts and sound research, however, is the exception. Typically, the state-level decisions made in fixing the amount of school support are made under political pressures and are based on flimsy evidence as far as actual educational implications are concerned.

The fact that levels of support are fixed "by guess and by golly" is unfortunate and unnecessary. It does, however, point up the critical need for a continuous program of educational research, an area of activity that has been sadly neglected in the past. Furthermore, it highlights a lag in the dissemination of research findings and concepts in public school finance. Reliable research studies have solidly established the close relationship between educational cost and school quality. This cost-quality concept for schools is relatively new.

Mort and Reusser have described this important affinity between expenditure and educational quality as being one of the most firmly

99

established of all known relationships in the operation of schools. And they point out that the relationship is so strong that a community, a state, or a nation can confidently give vigorous support to its schools and expect to receive sound and greatly increased educational returns.[1]

In order to show this relationship between the cost and character of education it is necessary to examine the various methods currently used in determining how much is to be spent for school purposes.

I. DETERMINING THE EXPENDITURE LEVEL OF THE STATE'S EDUCATIONAL PROGRAM

There are a number of methods employed by the several states in setting the level of the state program—the foundation program. The following analysis represents not only current and past practice but also points out promising methods to be used in future years.

Arithmetic and politics

The method that emphasizes arithmetic and politics is the most commonly used and yet is the least defensible. By this method the level (cost per unit of educational need) is determined solely on the basis of what is politically expedient. The resultant expenditure figure that is set has no relationship to the character of the school program. Indeed, there is no pretense that it does. A typical illustration of this method is where a state legislature is beset by pressures and demands for more money for schools. The cry goes out for retaining teachers and maintaining existing services. In the face of these pressures and the unencumbered revenue sources available, the legislature increases the current, arbitrarily set level by some arithmetical proportion, say 33 per cent. The resultant expenditure figure is still quite arbitrary and nebulous in relationship to the educational program in the state. However, it has given temporary respite from some political responsibilities and is arithmetically simple in its relationship to the previous state school program. This is the manner in which most school finance laws are enacted and accounts for the extended "starvation" school programs found in many state systems.

Comparisons as a basis for determining expenditure levels

Many states and many communities decide on a level of financial support for their schools almost solely on the basis of what other comparable states or communities are spending. This is by far the most

---

[1] Paul R. Mort and Walter C. Reusser, *Public School Finance* (2d ed.; New York: McGraw-Hill Book Co., Inc., 1951), p. 140.

popular method used in reports by legislative councils or survey commissions. Such documents are replete with comparative tables showing regional states' or national levels of expenditures, measures of ability, indexes of effort, population growth, economic expansion, and trends in taxation.

This type of report is interesting and helpful, but to use only this kind of information to determine the level of a foundation program or what a community need spend for schools has some serious shortcomings. It is nothing more than a "keeping up with the Joneses" kind of reasoning for determining what is to be spent. No attempt is made to examine the school program. No attempt is made to analyze what specific improvements or additional services are to be obtained. Instead, the appeal is almost entirely one of modifying the present level of expenditures in order to make a more favorable comparison with other states or with other communities.

Occasionally these surveys include comparisons of services or descriptions of programs offered at various expenditure levels.[2] Even though such reports are relatively rare, they certainly make a more defensible appeal and offer a more usable guide for making decisions than does the type that compares expenditures with no analysis of the programs offered.

Expenditure implications of laws or standards

The idea has occurred to many that a satisfactory method of determining how much should be spent for schools is to analyze the financial implications of state laws or recognized standards set by state boards or accrediting associations. In practice, however, this method has not been successful. Its weaknesses become readily apparent when one examines the laws or standards themselves and then attempts to affix price tags on them.

Even though some schools at considerable cost will fulfill the requirements of the law in the spirit intended by those enacting it, others will find ways of meeting the letter of the law in a very meager and inadequate way with relatively small expenditures. The laws or standards themselves are almost always too broad or flexible to assure a universal translation into closely comparable school costs. For example, a school district with adequate financial resources may conscientiously fulfill the statutory requirements for, let us say, health education. In meeting these requirements the school provides for

2 Paul R. Mort, *Reconstruction of the System of Public School Support in the State of New Jersey*, Report of the Governor's School Commission (Trenton, N.J.: The Commission, 1933), Vol. II, pp. 27–29.

regular instruction to classes of reasonable size under the direction of a professionally competent teacher in well-equipped classrooms and laboratories. Another school district that lacks interest or resources may fulfill these same statutory requirements with very meager provisions. It may have health education given very irregularly in ill-equipped classrooms to physical education classes of excessive size. These classes may be taught by a poorly-prepared athletic coach on stormy days where the limited indoor gymnasium facilities preclude an activity period for all students.

Both of these districts meet the state law requirements for providing instruction in health. In the first case there is a considerable cost involved. In the second case the school meets the letter of the law without additional cost. This same illustration could apply to virtually any subject or activity requirement found in state mandates. It is for this reason that this method has been considered impractical or unrealistic and is used very little. The notion should thus be rejected that an adequate foundation program can be assured through state laws and regulations that give no clue as to the costs involved.

Some states have attempted to legislate minimum salary requirements in their attempts to set the level of a defensible foundation program. Even these regulations may be subverted, however, unless districts are prevented from diluting the intended program by such things as maintaining inordinately large classes or causing excessive staff turnover by consistently employing only those teachers with minimal training and experience.

The average, well-organized districts

In some instances the level of the foundation program has been set through determining the amount spent for schools in properly organized districts of average wealth. In essence, this method implies that citizens throughout the state would spend for schools approximately what the citizens of these average districts spend if the wealth of the state were distributed equally among the various districts and all districts were satisfactorily organized.

Specifically, this method is carried out as follows: Within a given state those districts are selected that approximate the state average in the amount of taxable resources available per pupil to be educated. Eliminated from this group of districts are all of those that are atypical or poorly organized, such as the large cities or the districts that employ only a few teachers because of the small number of people served. Of those districts yet remaining in the group, the median of their unit expenditures (expenditures per pupil or per classroom unit) is determined. It is this figure that is then used as the unit cost of the state's foundation program.

This method of determining the level of a state's foundation program has at least two serious defects. In the first place, this method is simply one of measuring consumer demand in districts where expenditure levels may reflect a lack of educational leadership, a lag in property assessments, or a tradition in tax levies or tax limits. It assumes an informed public that knows enough about its schools to make competent decisions about how much should be spent. It does not focus on the adequacy of the school program itself.

In the second place, this method makes the erroneous assumption that the taxable wealth available to the district is the same as that available to the state. The state has available for taxation a great many more sources of revenue than the local district has. Taxes for local use are almost exclusively limited to real property. In addition to property, however, the state has vast taxable resources that are not readily accessible to the district. Taxes on motor fuels, incomes, sales, inheritances, and natural resources are illustrative of some of the means used by states to get at resources that are for all practical purposes restricted from use on the local level. If these resources were readily available for local district taxation, it is quite probable that the citizens in these average districts would be willing to spend more on the education of their children. This consideration is overlooked, however, in this method as it has been generally used.

The adaptability method

To adapt means to change, to suit, or to adjust. To measure the adaptability of a school system one would have to determine its capacity to take on changes or to adjust its program to cope with the needs of the community served. School systems vary widely in their ability to modify their programs and policies in order to meet new societal or community needs and demands or to better fulfill some of the persistent ones. The determination of a school system's adaptability is most commonly made by an appraisal of how up-to-date or how modern its educational program is. This is accomplished by looking for certain elements or practices in the curriculum and school policies. The presence or absence of these elements reflects the extent to which the school system has modified its program in recognition of the great economic, social, and psychological insights for education that have been gained during the past half-century. Of the instruments developed for measuring the adaptability of school systems, perhaps the most widely used are the *Guide for Self-appraisal of School Systems*[3] and *The Growing Edge*.[4]

The first significant attempt to set the level of expenditure for a foundation program by this method was the result of a study conducted during the late 1930's on the adaptability of schools in Pennsylvania.[5]   The amount of money spent for education was one of the factors found to be closely related to the adaptability of a school system.   One of the conclusions of the Pennsylvania study was that school systems spending more than a specified amount ($2,000 per weighted-classroom unit, 1935 dollar values) were quite generally found to have a reasonable amount of adaptability—to be above the "danger zone."   The argument, therefore, became that of a state's assuring all schools of an expenditure level above this specified amount in order to insure a reasonable degree of adaptability or up-to-dateness in the schools' programs.

Following this pioneering attempt in Pennsylvania, a very successful attempt was made to establish the level of the foundation program in New York State on the basis of the assured adaptability of its schools.   This action was rooted in a 1943 study in which an adaptability measuring instrument was applied to one hundred villages, cities, and rural school systems in the state of New York.   The results of this study were summarized on a chart.[6]   This chart was very effective in helping the New York state legislature determine the expenditure levels in a school finance law passed during the late 1940's.   The chart, with its school costs adjusted to reflect the changes in costs of living since 1942, is given in Figure 5.[7]

This chart is a dramatic illustration of some of the kinds of returns that can be expected from spending additional money on schools. The captions on the chart reveal that the criteria used in the observations were expressions of some of the insights of the past half-century into the effectiveness and the basic functions of schools.   The observations were sensitive to teaching that capitalized on the use of interest and variety, the use of realistic situations, the recognition of individual

[3] Paul R. Mort and Francis G. Cornell, *Guide for Self-appraisal of School Systems* (New York: Bureau of Publications, Teachers College, Columbia University, 1937).

[4] Paul R. Mort, William S. Vincent, and Clarence A. Newell, *The Growing Edge* (New York: Metropolitan School Study Council, 1946).

[5] Paul R. Mort and Francis G. Cornell, *American Schools in Transition* (New York: Teachers College, Columbia University, 1941), p. 193.

[6] New York Educational Conference Board, *What Education Our Money Buys* (Albany, N.Y.: The Board, 1943).

[7] Figure 5 is presented through the courtesy of the New York Educational Conference Board.   See *Fiscal Policy for the State of New York* (Albany, N.Y.: The Board, 1947), pp. 24–25.

differences and needs of children, and the inclusion of pupils in program planning. The observers were also alert to other hallmarks of adaptability such as the recognition of a wider range of skills than the 3-R's, an expanded concept of the role of the school in such areas as health, safety, and vocational preparation, and the school as a kind of laboratory wherein pupils practice good citizenship and discover and develop their own special aptitudes and talents.

An examination of the three different columns in Figure 5 will reveal the extent to which the various practices had spread through the schools operating at three different levels of expenditure. The chart reveals how few of these newer educational patterns are found in the $130 per pupil expenditure schools. Schools spending $200 per pupil, those represented in the middle column, have most of these modern practices to some degree, but in no single instance to a complete degree. The right-hand column in the chart reveals how extensively these practices are found in the highest expenditure schools.

With reference to the chart in Figure 5, the action taken by the New York legislature in the late 1940's was to adopt the $200 per weight pupil cost as the level of the state's foundation program. This gave some assurance to the legislators that a reasonable degree of modernness and adaptability would be possessed by every school in the state. Thus, even the poorer districts could be alert to new developments in the rapidly developing field of education.

Using the adaptability method to determine expenditure levels has the positive feature of focusing attention on the educational program itself. It also has the advantage of basing decisions on research findings and of providing a rational explanation of what returns are available for various amounts of money spent on schools. This is obviously a better method than one that relies principally on a traditional willingness or ability or on what others are doing as a defensible basis for school expenditures.

The frontal attack with research

The research that undergirds the adaptability method represents the most recent approach toward the establishment of cost-quality relationships in education. Nevertheless, it should be apparent that these studies represent an oblique approach to the problem. While they provide certain points along the expenditure scale below which certain patterns of educational practice are not likely to be found, they lack strength in the basic theory behind the studies themselves. Why will these practices not be found in schools operating below certain expenditure levels? Because, according to the rationale of

I. READING, WRITING, ARITHMETIC

School Cost Levels°		
1 $130	$200	$260°°
2 $115	$175	$225
3 $ 75	$115	$150

1. Are reading, writing, arithmetic taught so as to make them useful?

2. Is it just 3-R's, or many extra skills that pupils need to master?

3. Are methods efficient for improving the low spots of individuals?

4. Is there a plan for teaching pupils how to study?

II. BASIC KNOWLEDGE FOR AMERICANS

1. Is knowledge taught realistically with up-to-date materials?

2. Are new revised courses continually being added to the best of the old?

3. Do teachers know enough: can they do it as well as teach it?

III. LEARNING TO THINK

1. Are there realistic enterprises in the school that require pupils to think them out to make them work?

2. Does the school give pupils the chance to think about whatever they do, rather than following always what someone else has decided?

3. Do teachers know enough about thinking to help pupils learn to do their own thinking?

IV. EXPLORING PUPILS' ABILITIES

School Cost Levels°		
1 $130	$200	$260°°
2 $115	$175	$225
3 $ 75	$115	$150

1. Does school have a wide number of activities to explore each pupil's talents?

2. Are the interests of pupils used to enrich their studies in school?

V. GROWTH OF CHARACTER

1. Does the school operate like a real society where character develops through practice and action?

2. Are there activities set up in the school definitely planned to develop character?

3. Are the interest and attention of each teacher focused positively upon each pupil?

VI. HEALTH AND SAFETY

1. What medical attention assures sound bodies?

2. Are there sports for everybody?

3. Are buildings and grounds completely healthful and safe?

4. Is healthful living a part of all instruction?

= no; none   = Little   = Some

° This refers to costs in grade K-6, assuming approximately 1.3 times this amount for grades 7 and above.

1 (1947)   2 (1945)   3 (1942)

Fig. 5. The Character of Education at Three Expenditure Levels (Adapted from What

(NOTE: The expenditure level for 1956

VII. HOMES FOR AMERICA

	School Cost Levels°		
1	$130	$200	$260°°
2	$115	$175	$225
3	$ 75	$115	$150

1. Does practical experience predominate in training homemakers?

2. Is book information related to real problems of living?

3. Do teachers know enough about their pupils to help them get along with others and make the most of themselves?

VIII. THE WORLD OF WORK

1. Is practical vocational experience the mainstay of job training?

2. Is developing talents for the world of work a part of every teacher's plans?

3. Is book information related to real problems in the world of work?

4. Is there individual help in preparing for and getting a job?

IX. MAKING CITIZENS

1. Is the school a place where pupils get plenty of practice in good citizenship?

2. Is book information related to real problems of practical citizenship?

3. Is citizenship training a part of every teacher's plans?

X. REGARD FOR THE INDIVIDUAL

	School Cost Levels°		
1	$130	$200	$260°°
2	$115	$175	$225
3	$ 75	$115	$150

1. Do teachers use scientific methods to help them understand their pupils?

2. Does every youngster get his chance to do what he can do?

XI. THE SCHOOL AND THE COMMUNITY

1. Does the public know what good schools can do?

2. Do staff, public, and pupils work together to make the school better?

3. Is the school a center of many community activities?

XII. THE TEACHER AND THE SCHOOL

1. Do teachers have poise, personality, scholarship, background, experience, and skill?

2. Are there staff members with special training to help solve exceptional problems?

3. Are teachers continually planning, redesigning courses of study, or doing advanced study?

4. Are equipment, supplies, and materials adequate?

5. Is the executive a school leader, an educational statesman?

 = much

 = very much

°° This represents from $250 upwards—some almost twice as much.

1 (1947)   2 (1945)   3 (1942)

Education Our Money Buys. New York State Educational Conference Board, 1943).
is over $300 per weighted pupil.)

these studies, the school system itself is unable to take on changes as rapidly as it should below certain expenditure levels.

It is difficult to understand, or explain, how pouring additional money into a given school system of low adaptability will immediately and automatically change methods and behavior of teachers and administrators; and make for vibrant and rich experiences in classrooms that heretofore have provided static and sterile educational programs. Even though this is the implication of the chart in Figure 5, in reality this is not the case, even from the point of view of the adaptability studies themselves. These studies show that change in schools comes about slowly and is closely tied to community characteristics and the composition of the professional staff. The amount of money spent for schools is but one item of many, and there is little evidence in these studies to indicate that it has a major causal relationship to the adaptability of school systems.

Adaptability studies have shown that changes in schools take place slowly. It is true that they can be speeded up, but this entails changes in the community, in the faculty, and in the administration. Spending more money does not automatically do this.

The question arises as to whether there might not be a more direct and fruitful approach to this problem of determining just what educational returns are obtained at various expenditure levels. Certainly the adaptability studies are a great contribution, and their major strength lies in the fact that they have developed from empirical observations in schools of various expenditure levels. Similarly, successful studies can undoubtedly be carried out by research that seeks specifically the quality of education to be bought for what amounts of money, instead of the adaptability approach which shows that below certain levels of expenditure, certain educational practices are not likely to be found.

No state has yet made a direct consideration of what a foundation program should be in terms of the economic, social, and personal needs of its citizens and in the light of what is now known of the possibilities and power of education. A continuing program of research is needed to help provide the kinds of answers to problems that are raised when wise citizens make important decisions about the kind of schools needed to best serve their particular state and their own community.

The common-sense approach

The common-sense method used in determining how much should be spent for schools is to consider first the basic experiences from which an acceptable school program is derived and then to translate them into dollars and cents. The process includes a group discussion of school programs, the problems and costs involved, and, if possible, resultant agreement on the quality and scope of the educational opportunities to be provided.

The group or groups involved in this process should be composed of both lay citizens and professional educators. If the decisions to be made concern an entire state, then there should be state-wide participation, study, and discussion. The ideal procedure would mean that conferences, study groups, and open meetings be held in every community throughout a state. These efforts should culminate in the work of a state committee whose work will genuinely reflect the recommendations from the various communities. The findings of this state committee should serve as a guide to the legislature.

This kind of approach involves broad participation and results in decisions that are made after extensive study and deliberation. The primary focus throughout the whole process is directly on the character of the educational program desired.

This method of determining the level of expenditures actually utilizes the positive elements of all those previously mentioned. The decisions made should reflect a consideration of the finest research available, including the adaptability studies. Comparisons of ability and practice among other states or other communities are to be considered in the process. Some cognizance must be taken of the implications of present laws. And some consideration must be given to the political aspects of the entire procedure as far as public policy is concerned.

In working through this common-sense approach, the logical place to begin is with the philosophy and stated objectives of the schools concerned. Consistent with these, the process itself is a continuous attempt to reach agreement on just what constitutes a good school program in the light of available resources. It requires thought, discussion, and eventual unanimity on definitions and descriptions of services and facilities. Such things as class size, teacher qualifications, essential supervision, special services, and school plant adequacy must all come within the province of these discussions.

After agreement has been reached on the essential nature and extent of the facilities and services involved, it must be reached on the translation of these into realistic costs. These decisions will represent average practice and not an earmarking of funds. It is in the process of reaching agreements on these matters that research findings and new perspectives must be integrated into the decision-making processes. The resultant conclusions will be assured of an adequacy and a balance not otherwise obtainable.

2. DETERMINING HOW MUCH TO SPEND FOR A SPECIFIC SCHOOL PROGRAM

Local school boards or communities must frequently determine the amount to be spent for the schools within their jurisdiction. These decisions are, of course, limited or colored by the laws of the state, but the opportunity typically exists for a district to exceed the prescribed foundation program. Within this leeway granted to local boards of education the decisions must be made that determine how much is to be spent. It is here that the greatest demands are made upon the leadership and statesmanship of the local professional head of the school system. The adequacy of the expenditures above the state's program is directly a function of how well the local superintendent can size up local needs and translate the findings of educational research into meaningful terms that can be understood by the lay citizen and school board member.

An educational leader must interpret research and point out its implications for the local community.

What is the meaning of the research available as far as local school expenditures are concerned? An analysis of Figure 5 reveals that in terms of school efficiency it is possible to spend too little on schools. A school system may not get an efficient educational return for the money spent if it does not spend an adequate amount. Perhaps the best way to envision our schools from the point of view of efficiency is to draw the analogy of a large generator that is hooked up with a series of light bulbs. In terms of energy put into the generator, it takes a certain amount to simply overcome friction and get the machine turning. It is only after sufficient energy is put into the generator to overcome friction and turn the machine at a reasonably good speed that the bulbs begin to light up. It is the same with schools. It takes a certain amount of money just to heat the buildings, just to provide a minimum of materials, and just to hire people to keep school. This is simply overcoming friction (Column 1 of Figure 5). It is the amount expended above this minimum that begins to bring substantial returns for the money spent by schools (Columns 2 and 3 of Figure 5).

Another analogy can be drawn from this same research. From the best available information we now have as to how schools are run on a sound financial basis, we can look at how other enterprises are operated. Let's look at farming, for example. The results of operating a farm over a long period of time on marginal expenditures are obvious. Low crop yield, dilapidated buildings, and a poor financial investment are the results of not spending enough on a farm over a period of time. The evidence in Figure 5 reveals a similar story for school expenditures. Too many of our schools are run on marginal expenditures or on a basis where they face one financial crisis after another. In these communities the school boards have to make valiant efforts just to keep teachers and maintain existing services in the face of public apathy, shrinking dollar values, lagging assessments on property, and legal tax limitations.

What can happen to revive a school system in these straits? The same thing that must happen to revive a farm. A little more money than just the bare minimum must be spent over an extended period of time, and spent wisely. Tremendously increased educational returns accrue through the expenditure of relatively little additional money (see Figure 5). A dairy farm that has been run on marginal expenditures over an extended period of time will typically yield about 250 pounds of butterfat per animal. As demonstrated many, many times, by spending a little more money than the very minimum on this herd—that is, by culling, keeping records, improving the nutritious diet of the animals—the same dairy farm can be made to yield more than 425 pounds of butterfat per animal. As far as educational returns in school are concerned, this same proportion of increased efficiency is possible through wise expenditures and prudent educational investments.

There is, however, one important difference between the returns on expenditures for schools in contrast with the returns on other enterprises. This difference is tied to the phenomenon of diminishing returns. In the illustrations used there is obviously some point at which any additional energy put into the generator will not make the lights burn brighter since the lights will have reached their maximum brightness. More energy input beyond this point is a waste. Similarly, in a dairy herd there is a maximum production figure for a cow. Increased expenditures and effort beyond this point are wasted.

The question logically arises as to when increased expenditures for a school arrive at the point of diminishing returns. Just where is the point beyond which the spending of more money for schools will not continue to bring about more educational returns? The answer to this question has been revealed in a study of educational returns in high expenditure school systems made by Woollatt.[8] His study revealed that as far as teaching the skills and areas of knowledge, the discovery and developing of special aptitudes, and the development of gross behavior patterns (like thinking and citizenship) is concerned, there is no point of diminishing returns in education.

[8] Lorne H. Woollatt, *The Cost-Quality Relationship on the Growing Edge* (New York: Teachers College, Columbia University, 1949).

At least the American public schools have never spent enough money to reach such a point, if such a point does exist. Woollatt found that the general picture was one of increasing educational quality accompanying increasing expenditure. He concluded that "spending more to get more is established as an axiom in preparing school budgets."

TOPICS FOR STUDY AND DISCUSSION

1. What is the guaranteed level of school expenditure in your state? Is this figure defensible in terms of research efforts related to the quality of education provided? On what basis was this figure accepted?
2. Notice that the chart in Figure 5 has been corrected for changes in price levels since it was originally made. By finding the most recent "retail sales index,"[9] make additional corrections in the various expenditure level columns so that the chart will reflect current costs.
3. Using the chart in Figure 5 as a basis, outline a brief speech on "School Costs and Educational Returns" that you might deliver to some group of laymen in your community in order to obtain support for a higher level of expenditure for schools.
4. What might be some of the beneficial results of establishing a nation-wide foundation program of more than $200 per weighted pupil? What are some of the prudential considerations you would recommend to accompany the implementation of such a program?

SELECTED REFERENCES

Mort, Paul R. and Francis G. Cornell. *American Schools in Transition.* New York: Teachers College, Columbia University, 1941.

Mort, Paul R. and Francis G. Cornell. *Guide for Self-appraisal of School Systems.* New York: Bureau of Publications, Teachers College, Columbia University, 1937.

Mort, Paul R. and Walter C. Reusser. *Public School Finance,* 2d ed. New York: McGraw-Hill Book Co., Inc., 1951.

Mort, Paul R., William S. Vincent, and Clarence A. Newell. *The Growing Edge.* New York: Metropolitan School Study Council, 1946.

New York Educational Conference Board. *What Education Our Money Buys.* Albany, N.Y.: The Board, 1943.

New York Educational Conference Board. *Fiscal Policy for the State of New York.* Albany, N.Y.: The Board, 1947.

Woollatt, Lorne H. *The Cost-Quality Relationship on the Growing Edge.* New York: Teachers College, Columbia University, 1949.

[9] Retail sales indexes are published monthly (annual summaries in July) in: U.S. Department of Commerce, *Survey of Current Business.*

7

TAXATION AND PUBLIC SCHOOL FINANCE

THE MATTER of deciding how much to spend on public education has been identified as an important task that has widespread effects and challenges the best of vision, information, and leadership among the citizenry and its school boards and legislatures. The counterpart of the task is the question of where the money should be obtained. Answering this latter question is equally as challenging and involves the whole matter of taxation and fiscal policy for all of the interrelated services and demands made upon the state and the localities.

In any school system the determination of how the schools are to be financed must, of course, depend on the character of the state's tax system. The types of taxes from which the schools receive support may be an important factor in public attitude toward education and may even be reflected in the educational quality of the schools concerned. Acknowledgment of these ideas makes the matter of taxation one of critical importance for educational leadership.

The urgent and practical problem of taxation is in politics, and in the contention and bids for funds the schools must be well represented.

Since education is a state function, it should have a first claim on the state's resources. It is thus the obligation of the state to provide the structural features of a plan for financing its schools. In such a plan the agencies delegated with carrying out the state's educational function should be enabled to utilize whatever revenue sources are conveniently available to them, and these sources must generally be supplemented by revenue that is accessible most readily on the state level.

Besides striving for a sound system of taxation in its school finance

113

plan, public policy must also seek to achieve a sensitive balance between citizen sacrifice and the direct overburdening of the revenue sources available to the agencies delegated with carrying out the state's educational function.

In designing the school finance plan as well as in attempting to achieve the balance of effort in taxation within this plan, the informed educator must give guidance and help to the legislature. It is, therefore, critically important that educators understand the interrelationships that exist in any tax system. Educators must also be conversant with the basic principles and concepts of taxation and their implications for the effectiveness of the public schools.

I. INTERGOVERNMENTAL FISCAL RELATIONSHIPS

Public education is a unique form of government in America that has special provisions to insure it as a nonpartisan, nonsectarian, classless service. It can perhaps best be viewed in its legal framework as extending from the locality up to the state level, and yet as a form of government it is separate and parallel with other types of government. Even though education enjoys this unique position structurally and functionally in terms of all other American government, it must be financed from the taxes that support other public services. In this sense it must be viewed as an integral part of the total state and local government.

The public schools derive their financial support from all levels of government—federal, state, and local. They may, therefore, be affected by tax problems arising at any of these three levels. They may also be affected by shifts in the responsibility for the support of various governmental functions.

This interrelatedness of support highlights the need for a coordination of revenue sources. Newcomer,[1] in pointing out the proliferation of unplanned, uncoordinated taxes, cited New York City as an example of having over 150 separate federal, state, and local taxes, 10 of which accounted for more than 95 per cent of the total yield. This desperate need for coordination—perhaps a good deal of integration—of taxes brings into focus one of the fundamental conceptions of taxation. This concept is that no level of government (federal, state, or local) can ignore other levels or kinds of government in considering the nature of its tax structure. This concept has become increasingly important with the phenomenal rise in public expenditures which has been accompanied by increased tax burdens and much more overlapping of taxes.

[1] Mabel Newcomer, *Taxation and Fiscal Policy* (New York: Columbia University Press, 1940), p. 17.

The total problem of fiscal relationships is complicated by a multiplicity of various governmental units, subunits, tax authorities, commissions, boards, districts, etc. The most crucial problems in public finance arise because of an unrealistic relationship between the fiscal capacity and the administrative responsibility of some of these governmental units. This is particularly true in the case of school districts. Recognition of this unrealistic relationship between capacity and responsibility must be met by either dedicating (earmarking) specific taxes, sharing taxes among the various echelons of government, providing grants-in-aid from one level of government to another, or altering the function of a particular governmental unit to fit its fiscal capacity.[2] The solution to these problems lies in devising improvements that are in harmony with some of the widely accepted basic concepts of taxation.

2. ESSENTIAL OBJECTIVES OF TAXATION

It is inevitable that political institutions and historical conditions will be reflected in the tax system of a nation or state. Because of America's democratic social order, a number of "objectives" of taxation have evolved. Other goals of taxation have emerged as a result of broad experience in the administration of tax laws across America or because of various economic analyses and theories concerning taxation. Some of the more important objectives of taxation, discussed in the following paragraphs, are (1) balanced taxation, (2) growth and vigor of the economy, (3) effective tax administration, and (4) tax justice.

Balanced taxation

One of the essential concepts of taxation is that any individual tax must be viewed in its relationship to all other taxes in operation in the given tax system. According to some persons, all taxes are bad, particularly the ones they must personally pay. Actually, some taxes are more objectionable than others. The important meaning of balanced taxation is that each proposed addition or modification in the tax system needs to be in harmony with an over-all tax design. It follows, therefore, that no tax can be evaluated except in the context of the total tax structure.

Any change in a state's tax system is generally a serious matter and should be preceded by a very careful study by competent, tax-trained personnel. This is an important principle to follow, but in many

[2] National Conference of Professors of Educational Administration, *Problems and Issues in Public School Finance* (New York: Bureau of Publications, Teachers College, Columbia University, 1952), pp. 113–37.

cases the political climate and timing may not make such a study feasible. In such a situation the only alternative is to make the best possible decisions concerning tax changes in the light of a cursory examination of the existing tax structure. It is important to remember that taxation is a very urgent and complex problem and that it is immersed in politics. There are political considerations to be made in contemplating tax changes as well as sound principles of taxation.

As an illustration of the application of this principle, let us suppose that under serious pressure for additional tax revenues some school people suggest a raise in the state sales tax as a means of obtaining additional and critically needed school funds. Before seriously advocating such a change, these people should seriously consider the balanced tax principle involved.

In this case, the proposed tax itself has a certain pattern of impact. The sales tax is the kind known as a regressive tax. This means that it is a tax whose burden is distributed inversely as compared to income. The citizen with a $1,000 income thus pays a larger percentage of this in sales taxes than does the citizen with a $5,000 income.

This recognition that the sales tax places the major burden on the lower income groups demands an examination of the total tax system. If this examination reveals that the lower income groups are already carrying a heavy share of the total tax burden, then it would seem grossly unjust to advocate an increase in the sales tax. If, however, there appears to be a fairly equitable sharing of the present tax burden, then any increase in the sales tax which is regressive should be offset by a tax that is progressive, such as a tax on income. (A progressive tax is one that places the major burden on the higher income groups.) Thus, in a currently balanced tax structure any regressive type of tax should be offset by a progressive type of tax in order to equitably distribute the tax burden over all taxpaying groups. This is an expression of the principle of balanced taxation.

Growth and vigor of the economy

World wars and the Great Depression have drastically changed the historical viewpoint toward taxation in America. In the past, taxation was viewed primarily as an instrument for raising revenue to pay the expenses of government. Today it is firmly recognized that taxation serves more than this function of raising funds. It may serve as a stimulus or control and must be positively related to the functioning of the American economy. This means that taxation must be designed and coordinated with the problems of the total economy. Careful considerations must be made so that harmful effects of taxation are avoided or minimized. Detrimental elements of our economy can be curtailed and positive aspects can be encouraged through taxation. Taxation can and should exert beneficial influences and stability for the economic and social well-being of our nation.

The role of taxation through its controls and stimuli must be to promote and maintain prosperity without inflation. Two significant aspects of our peacetime economic system are involved here—consumption and investment. The success of our free enterprise system demands the maintenance and encouragement of adequate markets for the tremendous amount of consumers' goods produced by our nation under efficient full-employment. Another essential is that the incentives for investments and work be maintained so that further efficiency and higher standards of living are progressively achieved. A well-planned and administered tax system can be instrumental in establishing and maintaining these essentials.

Effective tax administration

Administering taxes is almost as important as the policy imposing them. Effective administration as a tax objective calls for minimized costs and difficulties in collecting taxes. In addition, the aim is to obtain reasonably complete and accurate payments of all taxes legally due. If poorly administered, an otherwise equitable tax may become quite unjust. A tax becomes unfair if either avoidance or evasion is possible for large numbers of persons or businesses.

Effective tax administration is a function of the nature and form of the tax imposed as well as the integrity and vigor of the administrators. While some taxes are easily enforced, others provide "constant temptation to marginal individuals whose honesty is directly proportional to the effectiveness of the machinery for enforcement." Detection of tax evaders is usually an expensive service and is considered uneconomical unless it brings in more money than it costs.

Effective tax administration is only possible in a situation that is relatively free from political controls. In addition, adequate funds must be available for the employment of an adequate number of competent, professional personnel with the authority to administer the tax system as well as conduct research for its continuous improvement.

Tax justice

In terms of good tax theory, there are some generally accepted principles of taxation. A very concise statement of these is as follows:

1. Rich or poor, every citizen should pay his equitable share of taxes.
2. Taxes should be direct rather than indirect. It is difficult to determine just where the final impact of a tax really is. It is sometimes possible for one tax-paying group to shift a tax to an entirely different group. This is particularly true of business taxes.
3. Taxes may be levied for social control as well as for revenue. There are many taxes whose primary purpose is not revenue. Tariffs, chain-store taxes, taxes on narcotics, and taxes on margarine are obviously of this type.
4. Taxes primarily for revenue should be levied either in proportion to benefit or in proportion to ability. Motor vehicle taxes, for example, are benefit taxes to the extent that they are earmarked for highway costs. The progressive personal income tax, where some allowance is made for personal needs through exemptions, is a good example of a tax on ability.[3]

The principal difficulty with effecting an equitable tax system, however, lies not in the lack of recognition of sound tax principles. The difficulty lies in the human element involved, and this also includes the various legislatures that determine policy on tax matters. How one interprets "justice" generally depends upon what kinds of taxes affect him personally. As far as the individual is concerned, the best tax is of course the one that shifts the burden to someone else. Thus, it is impossible to achieve a tax system that is ideal for everyone. There are too many conflicting interests involved.

In order to bypass the block suggested by the subjective interpretation of justice, it is helpful to conceive of three facets of tax justice. These various facets are related to the tax objectives already presented and are listed in a kind of priority of consideration.

A first concept of tax justice is one that demands the effective administration of tax laws already in effect. This implies: (a) curbing dishonesty, (b) removing technicalities that provide for loopholes and unwarranted exemptions, (c) revamping poorly-structured or obsolete laws that hinder effective local government, and (d) eliminating extremely objectionable taxes from the tax system.

A second concept of tax justice calls for the extension of the tax system to cover tax bases not currently covered. Such extensions are necessary to achieve more equity in order that all individuals and groups pay their fair share and only their fair share of the total tax burden. The fair share is generally determined by levying taxes in proportion to ability-to-pay or in proportion to benefits received. This may call for new kinds of taxes or a broader coverage for taxes already in effect.

[3] Adapted in part from Mabel Newcomber, *op. cit.*, pp. 32–33.

A third concept of tax justice is an expression of the goal of balanced taxation in the over-all tax structure. As mentioned before, this means that some taxes may need to be reduced in order to offset the tax burden currently imposed upon certain segments of the population. A general sales tax or a property tax, for example, may be highly regressive, but may be counterbalanced by progressive income and inheritance taxes so that the tax system may be proportional or even progressive.

Of course, the shades of meaning of justice must still be hammered-out in public policy, but these various concepts of justice need their advocates.

3. LOCAL TAX STRUCTURES

The use of local taxes by the school districts of America varies widely. In the theory and practice of public school finance the ability to tax locally is essential. It is this power that gives the districts "local lee-way" to experiment, to exceed the minimum program prescribed by the state, and to adapt its school program to effectively serve the needs of the locality. It is the local tax structure that can reflect and encourage local initiative—that element considered so vital to educational quality in the American school systems. Local tax structures can probably best be discussed by treating the property tax separately from all other kinds of local taxes.

The property tax

The property tax is of vital importance to the schools. The extent of reliance on this tax in a school district may appreciably influence local attitudes and have a direct bearing on citizen interest and therefore educational quality. The property tax, however, is also the mainstay of all local government. In almost all states it provides the largest single source of tax money.[4]

Because of the dominant position of the property tax, it is the key to many tax problems. This tax has failed in recent years to supply adequate revenue. It is largely because of this that state assistance to school districts and other local units of government has been magnified.

There are a number of major factors that account for this general failure of the property tax. These include: (a) the failure of assessed valuations to rise proportionately with rising price levels; (b) the decline in the base of legally taxable resources because of exemptions;

[4] Among the various states, the property tax provided in 1953 an average of 38.4 per cent of state and local general revenues.

(c) the imposed limitations on tax rates; (d) the natural inequality in the distribution of taxable property; and (e), in some areas, an increase in population because of national defense activities without an accompanying increase in taxable property to support the additional services required for the larger population.[5]

Beginning with the depression years, nonproperty taxes have replaced property taxes in the form of shared taxes or grants-in-aid. This movement to find revenue to supplement the property tax at the local level of government has greatly intensified the need for coordination of taxes among all levels of government. Some observers also maintain that the pendulum has swung too far with the result that the property tax has been neglected and does not now bear its fair share of the total tax burden.

Property tax burden

In any state one frequently hears or reads of the relatively excessive share of the total tax bill that is carried by property. Along with this, of course, goes the plea that this, the property tax, be reduced. Since this sort of plea strikes directly at the heart of the school program, it is important that the educator be equipped to at least get at the real facts of the case.

One of the ways frequently used to get at the facts about the burden on property is to make comparisons with other districts or with other selected states or with the average burden on property in all states. Information of this nature can be obtained from publications of the U.S. Bureau of the Census and the U.S. Department of Commerce. This approach may be fruitful, but it must be recognized from the outset that fundamentally the idea of tax burden is a subjective concept. Even comparative low rankings do not completely refute the charge that property taxes are too high. They simply indicate the relative use made of the property tax.

Another means of getting at the real facts of taxation is to make a comparison with all other taxpayers of the type of taxpayer affected most. In a rural district, for example, this would mean citing some of the following relevant tax facts about farmers:

1. Rising farm income and typically lagging assessments of property during and following World War II have substantially diminished the proportionate amount of property taxes paid by the farmer in relationship to his income.
2. The federal government's policies of farm produce price supports

[5] Jewell J. Rasmussen, *An Economic Appraisal of State and Local Taxation in Utah* (Salt Lake City: Utah Education Association, 1954), p. 3.

takes much of the risk out of farming at the expense of other tax-paying groups.

3. Other elements in the tax structure also favor the farmers. A sizeable portion of the real income of farmers escapes income taxation for several reasons: farmers generally own their own homes or can count rental as a business expense; they produce more than other groups for their own consumption; and surveys conducted by the U.S. Bureau of Agricultural Economics and the U.S. Bureau of the Census have revealed biases toward underreporting of income by farmers.[6]

In contrast, the income of the urban worker is reported accurately through the withholding system. And, because the city worker does not produce any of his own food, he pays more income and sales taxes than does the farmer. A similar case would need to be made for the specific group of taxpayers involved.

There is one other approach to the problem of property tax over-burden. This is a rule-of-thumb measure suggested by Mort and Reusser. They suggest that for all school purposes a figure of $8 per thousand of current sales value be taken as a point of reference as to when property begins to be overburdened.[7] This figure represents the average tax rate for schools in the state of New York prior to the inflation of prices (1939–40). It is supposed to represent only the lower edge of overburden on property. In their definition of this $8 per thousand reference figure, Mort and Reusser point out that many states do not have a single school district that can be classified as having an overburdened property tax for school purposes.

Property tax administration

The administration of the property tax is an important function. Effective property tax administration not only demands complete honesty on the part of the personnel involved but also calls for adequate provisions for competent, impartial help and essential facilities as well as some degree of political and statutory freedom. It is widely recognized that a good property tax law can be wrecked by poor administration. A mediocre tax law can often be made to work reasonably well by good administration.

In many states there is a strong tendency toward the withdrawal from state use of the property tax. Thirty-three states levied taxes on general property in 1933. By 1953 this number had been reduced to

[6] See Edward L. Henry, "The Farmer's Tax Burden," *National Tax Journal*, IV (December, 1951), 341–50.

[7] Paul R. Mort and Walter C. Reusser, *Public School Finance* (2d ed.; New York: McGraw-Hill Book Co., Inc., 1951), pp. 87–88.

25, and only eight of these used this state property tax for school purposes.[8]   The general feeling is that the property tax "belongs" to the local communities and should be levied, assessed, and collected locally.   It is also recognized, however, that there is a definite state responsibility involved.   Thus, the property tax should be developed as a "tax locally levied, assessed, and collected, but centrally supervised and equalized."   It is imperative that there be strong, active state administration in the assessment process.   This is particularly true when the state provides for an adequate equalization program for school or other purposes.   Anything less than state-wide uniformity in assessment will penalize certain districts and thus promote tax inequities.

In addition to the basic equalization and supervision function of the state department of taxation, this agency also has a research responsibility for continuously making objective studies of the economic and administrative aspects of state and local taxes.

There are many reasons why the property tax should be continued as the major source of local revenue.   As important as the property tax is, it is widely recognized that this tax has been "weakened by continued inequalities in assessments, growing exemptions, and rigid rate-limitations."   A rather detailed examination of each of these three crippling devices will now be made.

Assessment practices

Without doubt, the almost "chaotic confusion" which characterizes the property assessment field continues to be the weakest point of the property tax.   Although assessment methods have improved in recent years, gross inequalities continue to be a major cause of dissatisfaction with this tax.   Some states, of course, are better than others.   It appears that in some states there might be "open rebellion" about the tax assessment situation if individual property owners would take the time to find out how the valuation of their own property compared with that of similar types in other neighborhoods and other counties.

The assessment of buildings and improvements has caused the most difficulty throughout the nation.   This is primarily because of the marked changes in building costs and the shrinking value of the dollar since the beginning of World War II.   This has generally resulted in a widening difference between assessed and fair market value of older buildings.   Assessors have generally been reluctant to increase the assessed value of older buildings since they have believed that changes in the price levels were temporary, or that it was unfair

[8] National Education Association, Research Division, "State Legislation Affecting School Revenues, 1949–1953," *Research Bulletin*, XXXII (October, 1954), 145–47.

to add to valuations when it was apparent that the present owner could not realize the difference on such increased values. However, this practice of maintaining property assessments at prewar levels is no longer defensible.

Another important objection to prevailing methods of assessment of buildings and improvements is the amount of property that may escape taxation. The common practice is for local assessors to use building permits and personal observations to detect and locate new buildings and improvements on old buildings. In many areas, however, building permits are not required. Even where permits are essential, much improvement work is done without permits and since reappraisals are usually slow to be made, much improvement work remains undetected and therefore untaxed. Only complete and frequent reappraisals will satisfy this shortcoming.

Land assessments may also be criticized for overlooking some properties. It is essential that a tax map be maintained in the local assessor's office as an assurance that all taxable property is covered on the tax rolls. Some suggest that high school students might gain some worthwhile educational experience and also render a contribution by undertaking a project of producing a comprehensive tax map of their community or school district.

In land and building assessment it is common practice to hire local people in order to get a more valid appraisal of property. This practice has the advantage of providing persons familiar with the yields of land or fair values of buildings involved. It also has the serious disadvantage, however, of letting a man classify the property of his neighbors, friends, and relatives. Local assessments are further complicated by frequent turnover of staff, lack of skill and training in appraisals, the influence of political and personal considerations in discretionary decisions, low salary scales, and limited funds and personnel for thorough and up-to-date assessments.

The level of assessment or the ratio maintained between the true or fair cash value and the assessed value of property is also in need of attention in many states. Most tax authorities agree that this difference should be small since low levels of assessment give a false appearance of inadequate local tax resources and distort the effect of any imposed tax rate limitations.

Property tax exemptions

A large number of exemptions represent a serious limitation to the effective use of the property tax in some states. There are, of course, certain exemptions that can be justified on social, economic, administrative, or other grounds. In some states, however, there are abuses of even the deserving forms of exemption. Some examples that warrant careful scrutiny are the exemptions of income-yielding business properties held by religious, charitable, and educational institutions, the possible pyramiding of exemptions within families, or the under-assessments which are concessions over and above the legal exemptions to war veterans.

More serious than the abuses of deserving exemptions, however, are the nondeserving exemptions so prevalent in some states. Careful reconsideration should be given to any exemptions of tangible personal property, certain able-bodied veteran exemptions, incentive exemptions for industrial real estate, federal-owned real estate exemptions, and low-rent housing and homestead exemptions.

A word of caution may be appropriate. As in the case of considering any tax, proper appraisal of any exemption demands the consideration of the specific, total tax system. For example, few tax students would defend the trend toward confining the property tax to real estate only. A tax on other tangible property may not, however, seem completely warranted in view of an existing tax structure. To this issue, Sly and Miller point out that:

> As a matter of general tax policy, there may be a question whether a state . . . which already has corporate and individual income taxes and a consumer sales tax, should properly tax inventories of merchandise, raw materials, and semi-finished goods, and livestock of farmers, either at the same rates as real estate or as part of the general property tax at all. Such inventories are a current asset, have value solely for the purposes of re-sale, and are taxed as economic goods by the other three taxes.[9]

Tax rate limitations

The third crippling device that weakens the property tax is rigid tax rate limitations. The Great Depression gave rise to the adoption of property tax limitations.

The total effect of tax rate limitations has been very unfavorable. Although contrived as a means of limiting the burden of taxation, they have in reality only deprived local boards of their discretion in sensible budget-making. In addition, they have represented a needless complication in the levying of taxes. These rate limitations have in a real sense tended to shift the decision-making from the local districts where it belongs to the legislature where it is diffused, insensitive, and certainly not in the best interests of education.

[9] John F. Sly and William Miller, *Tax Policies in Utah* (Salt Lake City: Utah Legislative Council, 1954), p. 68.

In operation, the rate limitations on the property tax actually serve as a guide and ceiling for school expenditures. It is perfectly clear that the use of an allowable millage levy alone cannot be a satisfactory guide to the real burden on local taxpayers. Even more ridiculous, however, is the implicit assumption that an allowable millage can be a defensible means of determining the quality of the educational program.

General over-all tax rate limitations are unwholesome and can be discarded with the assurance that local tax rates will be effectively limited by the willingness of the local citizenry to tax themselves. Even more critical, however, is the practice of imposing a number of specific limitations. There is absolutely no justification for depriving locally elected representatives of a choice of expenditure programs best suited to the needs of their own communities. This is essentially the hampering effect of rigid tax rate limitations which are geared to specific purposes of expenditure. The effect of these restrictions is to take the control of the schools away from the local school boards. The result is that "local control over educational destinies is as dead as if it had been transferred to a state agency."[10]

Besides these devastating effects of tax limits, there are other reasons why they should be completely abandoned. An examination of the basic purpose of property tax limits reveals that they really do not limit taxes. On this point, Sly and Miller reveal some important information by stating:

As the result of some 20 years of experience with a wide variety of property tax rate limitations, competent observers are generally agreed that such limitations may sometimes succeed in restraining the taxation of property, but generally fail to restrict the total tax burden; and even tend to increase it by compelling the adoption of new and additional forms of taxation at the state level. This conclusion is based upon a considerable variety of tax limitations, and their operation in the depression period 1932–1941—a time during which a number of property tax limitations were adopted together with state sales or income taxes.

The notion that property tax limits actually limit the burden of taxation is dispelled by an examination of the experience of states with and without limits between 1942 and 1953 . . .

Tax limits are no longer operating as they did in depression times—when they held local property taxes down and forced state replacement taxes upward. States with property tax limits did not experience any less increase than states without such limits in per capita local property tax between 1942 and 1953; the average local increase in tax limitation states was even greater than that among other states over this period.[11]

[10] Mort and Reusser, *op. cit.*, p. 101.
[11] Sly and Miller, *op. cit.*, pp. 71–72.

Nonproperty taxes

Having the locality make substantial contribution for the support of local services is generally considered wholesome. This is particularly true as far as education is concerned. The principle is well established that strong local interest is essential for good schools and that this interest is promoted by an awareness among the taxpayers that local funds provide for the local school program.

This principle of substantial support is valid, of course, only if sufficient revenue is available to the local boards so that they might exceed the minimum requirements prescribed by the state. In an era when the local property tax is persistently plagued with inefficient administration, restrictive rate limitations, poor assessments, and growing exemptions, the acceptance of the principle of substantial local support poses the problem of how this can be accomplished.

Despite the rapid increase in the amount of state aid, at mid-century the local and county governmental units supplied almost 60 per cent of public school revenues. More state aid and more efficient use of local resources is one way to solve this problem. Another way appears to be through broadening the tax base of local governmental units.

In addition to the property tax, which has traditionally been the mainstay of local government, many localities and school districts have long had the authority to collect some minor nonproperty taxes such as licenses and poll taxes. These older nonproperty revenue sources, however, have had little fiscal importance.

Under the pressures of needed funds, the localities, and especially the cities, have sought new sources of tax revenues. Consequently, almost every tax source that has been used by states has now been utilized by some municipalities and counties. The types of nonproperty taxes reported as being used by city school systems in a poll conducted in 1950 include the following in order of their frequency of mention:[12]

1. Sales and gross receipts
2. Income and payroll
3. Admissions and amusements
4. Cigarettes and tobacco
5. Business and occupations
6. Parking meters
7. Motor fuel

[12] National Education Association, Committee on Tax Education and School Finance, *New Sources of Local Revenues for Public Schools* (Washington, D.C.: The Association, 1950), p. 19.

8. Poll
9. Utilities
10. Liquor
11. Severance
12. Municipally owned services
13. Property transfer
14. Hotel rooms
15. Gambling devices
16. Motor vehicles
17. Race tracks
18. Employee privilege
19. Fire insurance
20. License fees
21. Fines
22. Advertising
23. Soft drinks
24. Parking lots

The state legislature must, however, give the localities the specific authority to levy certain types of nonproperty taxes. Nevertheless, in some instances, such as Pennsylvania, the law permits local bodies to levy a tax on any item taxable by the state that is not being taxed at the time. Under such permissive legislation a great number of new taxes came into use. In Pennsylvania after the first year of the permissive act of 1947, local subdivisions, including school districts, "had levied 505 new taxes with amusement (120) and severance (120) heading the list."[13]

During the past two decades nonproperty taxes have become increasingly important in some of the larger municipalities. While nonproperty taxes contributed only 8 per cent of the total tax revenues of cities of 100,000 or more population in 1930, this proportion had risen to 23 per cent by 1948.[14]

Although nonproperty taxes may appear to some to be a new source of revenue for schools, their many limitations should also be recognized. Cornell[15] found a high correlation between the amount of the property tax base and that of the nonproperty tax base. This means that nonproperty taxes fail to relieve the burden on property in sparsely settled areas where the need for relief sometimes appears to be greatest. Another limitation of the nonproperty taxes is that the ones most frequently authorized are consumption taxes which bear hardest on those persons who are least able to pay. In addition,

[13] *Ibid.*, p. 16.
[14] *Ibid.*, p. 13.
[15] Francis G. Cornell, *A Measure of Taxpaying Ability of Local School Administrative Units* (New York: Teachers College, Columbia University, 1936).

many of these taxes are indirect and since they are administered in a local area they are relatively easy to evade and may frequently be the cause of intercommunity competition and conflict. The use of non-property, local taxes has the further disadvantage of causing an uncoordinated proliferation of taxes that tends to keep administrative costs high as well as to complicate an already complex tax structure.

In order to save money and simplify the administration of local, nonproperty taxes by eliminating the duplication of tax collection agencies, some states have served as the collecting agency and have distributed the tax monies according to the original amounts collected in the localities. The chief disadvantages of this practice are (1) that it favors those local units that are economic centers and obtain a portion of their taxable resources from neighboring communities, and (2) that it "leaves differences in fiscal abilities as they are and merely increases inequalities in services."[16]

4. STATE TAX STRUCTURES

Since education is a state function, the responsibility of a state in providing for schools cannot be shrugged off by granting increased taxing powers to local school units. Although innovations, experimentation, and improved services can probably be financed best from local tax sources, the state has the responsibility for furnishing an adequate foundation program and providing sufficient local tax leeway to exceed the minimum program required by the state. The state must, therefore, have a sound tax system to meet its obligations.

The importance of the state as a major taxing unit has only been recognized within the past quarter of a century. Since the 1920's there has been a shifting of more and more of the revenue needs to the state level of government. In 1932, when a total of $6.3 billion represented all state and local taxes, the state taxes accounted for only $1.9 billion of this amount.[17] By 1942 all state and local taxes amounted to $9.6 billion, of which more than half, or $5 billion, was paid in state taxes.[18] In 1952 all state and local taxes amounted to approximately $19.1 billion, $11 billion of which was paid in state taxes.[19] Clearly the trend is toward the increasing importance of state taxes.

[16] Arvid J. Burke, *Financing Public Education in the United States* (New York: Harper & Bros., 1951), p. 171.

[17] U.S. Bureau of the Census, *Historical Review of State and Local Government Finances, Special Studies* No. 25, June, 1948, Tables 21 and 22.

[18] *Loc. cit.*

[19] Rasmussen, *op. cit.*, p. 129.

The state's role as a major taxing unit became apparent as the states began to use various taxes other than property. For the most part, this development has taken place since the 1920's. Figure 6 portrays the use made by the various states of some of the nonproperty taxes since 1928. The increasing use of nonproperty taxes by the states as shown in Figure 6 has been accompanied by a decreasing reliance on the state property tax. Whereas 33 states levied taxes on general property in 1933, only 25 states used this tax in 1953.[20]

Elements of a defensible state tax system

There are three major criticisms made against state tax systems in general. These are that the state tax structures are (1) too complicated in their taxation of business, (2) too regressive in their general nature, thereby placing an unduly heavy burden on the low-income segment of the population, and (3) too irresponsive and uncoordinated with the federal fiscal policy so that some state tax programs may actually counteract federal actions.

Keeping these three objections in mind, it is appropriate to examine the nature of some of the specific taxes that can be defensibly used in a state's tax system. The source from which taxes are collected is probably more important than the amount raised when one takes into consideration the effect on the economy and the equity of the tax system to all the people of the state.

Outlining a "model" state tax system is fraught with difficulties such as established traditions and constitutional provisions, degree of urbanization, and differences in the amount and nature of the basic resources among the various states. In order to avoid these difficulties, only those elements of a tax system that have widespread support in current tax theory will be discussed.

Consumption taxes

The family of taxes that exacts a levy on commodities and transactions and whose ultimate incidence is generally the price the consumer pays for goods and services is known as consumption taxes. This group of taxes is frequently classified into three groups:

1. The sales tax, which in two decades has assumed the leading role in state taxation, is a regressive tax levied upon retail sales of tangible personal property or upon sales of services such as public utilities or amusements.

[20] National Education Association, Research Division, "State Legislation Affecting School Revenues, 1949–1953," pp. 145–46.

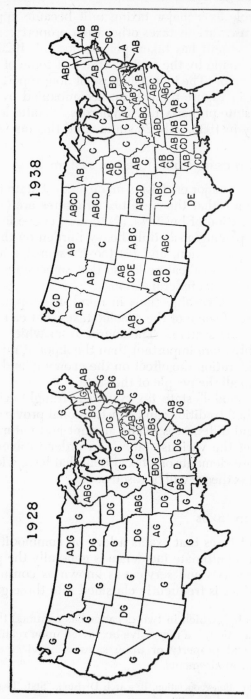

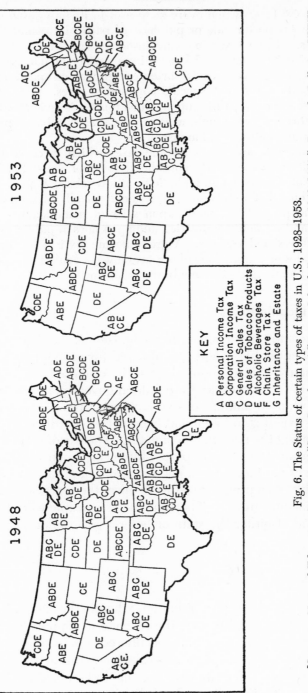

KEY

A Personal Income Tax
B Corporation Income Tax
C General Sales Tax
D Sales of Tobacco Products
E Alcoholic Beverages Tax
F Chain Store Tax
G Inheritance and Estate

1953

1948

Fig. 6. The Status of certain types of taxes in U.S., 1928–1953.

[Sources. National Education Association, "State Legislation Affecting School Revenues, 1949–1953," *Research Bulletin*, XXXII (October, 1954); "State Tax Legislation Affecting School Revenues, 1939–1943," *Research Bulletin*, XXII (October, 1944); and U.S. Department of Commerce, *State Tax Collections* in 1953.]

2. The excise taxes which every state uses in its imposition of some form of tax on the sale or purchase of particular commodities or services. These taxes in many instances are firmly established, regressive in nature, and known by a variety of names, such as selective sales taxes, excise taxes, sumptuary or spending taxes, commodity taxes, and specific commodity taxes. The principal services and commodities upon which this tax is levied in the various states are motor fuels, alcoholic beverages, tobacco products, pari-mutuel betting, and amusements.

3. Gross receipts and gross income taxes which, because of their similarity, are frequently considered together, have the leading virtues of simplicity and high yields at low rates. A gross receipts tax is one that exacts some revenue from all sales of tangible personal property at retail, upon sales of manufactures, wholesalers, and extractive industries, and upon sales of public, personal, and professional services. A gross income tax is a levy upon all these sales or transactions plus a tax on wages, salaries, rent, interest, dividends, and other nonbusiness income.

Personal income taxes

The net income tax is commonly recognized as the most rational, scientific, and equitable means ever devised for raising revenue in a modern economy. Since about three-fifths of the states, the local governments in four states, and the federal government use this tax, there is a substantial amount of overlapping in the use of this progressive tax. Much is to be gained from better coordination among the agencies using the personal income tax. The use of this tax by all levels of government can be supported by the arguments that this tax effectively taxes net income as a good measure of ability to pay, and it has the ability, as a progressive tax, to offset the regressive tax load on the lower income groups. There are but few people who advocate the withdrawal of either the state or federal governments from this tax source.

Property taxes

With the exception of those situations wherein the state levies and collects the property tax but uses the revenue to support locally administered services, it is almost universally recognized today that the property tax should play a very minor role, if any role at all, in financing state government. Its extensive use should be exercised by local governmental units, including school districts.

Corporation net income taxes

Any system of business taxation should not only help provide the necessary revenues of government but should also exert a wholesome influence on economic growth and the stability of the economy. It is widely recognized that corporation net income taxes can do this, and, as a result, this tax is firmly established in the tax structures of two-thirds of the states. This tax was introduced because the property tax proved unsatisfactory in reaching all business assets and also because of the difficulty of assessing corporate property.

Severance taxes

Severance taxes are of the nature of privileges, licenses, or occupation taxes levied on persons engaged in the business of mining, cutting, or in other ways severing for commercial purposes the natural resources from the soil or water.

Excepting a few states, severance taxes provide only a minor source of revenue. In a small number of states like Texas, Louisiana, Minnesota, and Oklahoma, however, this tax is significant and yields from one-third to one-seventh of all state revenue. The issue concerning this tax is whether or not it should assume a larger role in many other states that have large amounts of natural resources. Those persons advocating that this tax should figure more prominently in the state tax structures point out that since mineral deposits are rarely spread out through all local taxing units, a state severance tax enables the entire state to benefit. Furthermore, they contend that since minerals especially are the state's heritage, and once extracted, cannot be restored, the severance tax is justified, particularly if it can be made effective in curbing waste and promoting the optimum use of natural resources. Certainly the severance tax warrants careful consideration and study in every state having a considerable amount of mineral deposits.

Death and gift taxes

Although more than three-fourths of the states impose death and gift taxes, such taxes constitute only a minor source of state revenue. These taxes are not levies on ownership of property, but on the act of transferring this ownership. There are four types of such taxes now in use by the states: the inheritance tax, an estate tax that is independent of the federal levy, an estate tax based on the federal levy, and a "differential estate tax designed to absorb the difference between state duties otherwise imposed and the maximum credit allowed under the 1926 federal act."

Since the receipt of a gift or bequest increases the economic resources of an individual, under the "ability to pay" principle there should be taxation of such transfers. It is generally recognized that because of certain inherent difficulties this should be a tax treated separately from an income tax, and although the Federal Government currently uses this same tax, the states do not impair this source of revenue by their using it. What is needed is a coordination between the two levels or taxing agencies.

Taxes on banks, insurance companies, public utilities, and other businesses

One of the criticisms of state tax systems is their taxation of businesses. On this point state tax structures are accused of arbitrariness, complexity, and a lack of integration or coordination of taxes with the possibility of providing a repressive influence on business. The trend in the literature on taxation in recent years has been to deemphasize this form of taxation.[21] In any event, the separate taxation of each type of business warrants careful investigation in each state.

5. POTENTIAL SOURCES OF REVENUE FOR SCHOOL SUPPORT

There are a number of untapped financial sources for school support. The extensive use of nonproperty taxes on the local level has been advocated by some as the major avenue open for additional revenue for schools. Others have looked at some entirely new source, such as tideland oils, or have eyed expanded federal aid as a generous source of funds to take care of the critical educational financial needs of America. Still others have advocated the more efficient use and administration of present tax sources as the best answer to the problem of securing additional revenue for schools.

The authors believe, of course, that no source of potential school revenues should be overlooked; however, their emphasis is on the more effective and efficient use of present tax sources.

It is acknowledged that nonproperty taxes may be a rich source of local school revenue for the larger units such as sizeable municipalities and counties. However, this source is fraught with the difficulties of tax overlapping, duplication of collecting agencies, and adverse effects such as intercommunity competition and conflict.

[21] Rasmussen, *op. cit.*, p. 36.

Because of these complications, it appears to be a logical and more economical solution to leave most of these taxes to be administered on a state basis and have their proceeds equitably distributed to all localities.

Recognition is also made of the very promising prospects for expanded and increased federal support of education. Although such appropriate congressional action would provide a tremendous boost to the solution of some of the problems of school finance, it cannot be hoped to be a panacea. America will still face the problems of state responsibility, local interest and initiative, and structural and operational effectiveness of local school units.

Regardless of the action taken on the use of additional nonproperty sources of local revenue or the expansion of federal aid to education, there still remains the obligation to improve state and local tax structures in the interest of tax justice as well as in the best interests of our over-all economy. Conscientious study and effort to improve existing state and local tax structures can frequently reveal tremendous new potentials for school support. In achieving a balanced, equitable state and local tax system that will effectively meet the public service needs of a given state, loopholes, evasions, and more effective administrative methods are apt to be discovered that can in large measure meet the needs identified. What is most needed is a program of research and tax improvement that is coordinated on all levels of government—local, state, and federal.

TOPICS FOR STUDY AND DISCUSSION

1. Can the money needed for the future school program be provided from present tax revenue sources in your state? In your district?
2. In the interest of tax justice and adequacy, should new sources of revenue be made available to finance schools in your state? In your district?
3. What is the property tax rate limitation in your state? Is it an impediment in the provision of a better educational program in your district?
4. At what rate is property assessed in your state? Are assessments equalized on a state-wide basis? Enumerate any changes in assessment practices that you would recommend for your state.
5. List the taxes used in your state for the support of schools and indicate the proportion of the total revenue that is received from each source.
6. When was the last comprehensive study of taxation made in your state? What are some of the evidences one might look for in order to determine whether or not a tax study is needed?
7. Does the assessor for your district have a tax map? What are the advantages of such a map?

SELECTED REFERENCES

BURKE, ARVID J. *Financing Public Schools in the United States.* New York: Harper & Bros., 1951, chaps. V–IX.

MORT, PAUL R. and WALTER C. REUSSER. *Public School Finance,* 2d ed., New York: McGraw-Hill Book Co., Inc., 1951, chap. XXVIII.

National Conference of Professors of Educational Administration, *Problems and Issues in Public School Finance.* New York: Bureau of Publications, Teachers College, Columbia University, 1952, chap. IV.

National Education Association, Committee on Tax Education and School Finance, "New Sources of Local Revenues for Public Schools," Washington, D.C.: The Association, 1950.

National Education Association, Research Division, "State Legislation Affecting School Revenues, 1949–1953," *Research Bulletin,* XXXII, October, 1954.

RASMUSSEN, JEWELL J. *An Economic Appraisal of State and Local Taxation in Utah.* Salt Lake City: Utah Education Association, 1954.

SLY, JOHN F. and WILLIAM MILLER. *Tax Policies in Utah.* Salt Lake City: Utah Legislative Council, 1954.

8

STATE LEADERSHIP IN FINANCING PUBLIC EDUCATION

TRACING THE historical development of state departments of education in the United States can give some keen insights into the functions and potential of this important office in American education. Since the middle part of the nineteenth century when state school offices were quite firmly established, the whole character of American public education has changed. With these changes in education has come the necessity of changing the status and role of the state departments of education. Many of the functions formerly entrusted to the local school units have been shifted to the state level and other functions have simply been added. Some of the permissive aspects of education have become obligatory. Increased demands on local school units and the growing complexity of state operations are reflected in bulky school codes and sizeable state school office staffs. The duties of the chief state school officer have changed greatly from simple clerical, statistical, and exhortatory tasks to those that demand expert judgment and considerable professional knowledge and skill.

It is appropriate that the top level leadership in our states be competent, well-trained, professional persons. Public education in our democratic form of government demands the finest kind of constructive statesmanship for the important positions in the state department of education. This becomes completely apparent in the realm of school finance where subtle, inadvertent, and insidious shifts of control can be effected unless those persons in key positions are alert and sensitive to such shifts.

137

I. THE STRATEGIC POSITION AND ROLE OF
THE STATE EDUCATION DEPARTMENT

When American education is viewed broadly, it becomes apparent that the various state departments of education have a very important role. If for no other reason than the recognition of the official legal status of these departments, their importance and potential can be seen to be great. These agencies are singularly situated for working with local school units. In addition, they are in an unmatched position for coordinating educational activities throughout their respective states and in working with other branches and agencies of state government and volunteer organizations as well as with federal education activities. As far as educational finance is concerned, the state department of education is in a strategic position for carrying out certain functions that are critically important within each state and serve the state as a whole.

Principal functions

The principal functions of the central state agencies are broadly classified as operational, judicial, regulatory, and leadership. A state department of education includes the state board of education, the chief state school officer, and the staff of the department. Forty-two states have state boards of education but the specific responsibilities given to state departments of education may vary greatly from state to state. In addition to the control and supervision of elementary and secondary education, which is a responsibility generally vested in a state department of education, this agency may also have jurisdiction over other educational agencies. For example, in many states the state department of education has control over teachers' colleges and normal schools, trade schools, adult education, junior colleges, schools for the deaf and blind, and other educational programs.

It thus becomes a function of some state departments of education to operate institutions or activities in much the same way as a local administrative unit must be operated. Functions of this type performed by state departments of education are commonly classified as *operational.*

In recognition of the distinction between educational and strictly legal matters, the state departments of education have commonly been given the responsibility for rendering judgments on controversial issues arising in school districts.[1] Thus the central educational

---

[1] See Robert R. Hamilton and Paul R. Mort, *The Law and Public Education* (Chicago: The Foundation Press, Inc., 1941), chap. 3.

agency, through the state superintendent, functions as an arbiter by dispensing justice and rendering judicial decisions. This is referred to as the *judicial* function.

As far as the control and supervision of elementary and secondary education is concerned, the state department of education has the obligation to carry out its assignments made by legislative or constitutional action. As a state agency it must provide the prudential checks or devices necessary to insure that educational activities within the local units are carried out in a way that safeguards the interests of all the people of the state. Thus, the state department of education has the task of assuring the observance of minimal educational standards or regulations throughout the state. This is called the *regulatory* function and is an expression of prudence in the establishment and enforcement of basic standards or procedures which safeguard funds and matériel. This function has become increasingly important because of the notable and somewhat alarming trend of having an increasing amount of control reside with the state departments of education. This trend is unquestionably a reflection of the consolidation of local units and the increasing proportion of state funds that have become available for educational support. Quite naturally, therefore, this regulatory function has been primarily designed to control budgetary procedures and methods of accounting, auditing, and reporting to the public. However, this regulatory function also extends to buildings, teacher certification, curriculum, and other educational matters.

The state department of education, however, must exercise a role that reaches beyond the mere prudential functions of formulating and enforcing standards. It must also be viewed as a possible contributor to the educational enterprise that is carried on in each locality. This calls for a positive service from state departments of education that attempts to improve the educational program, strengthen local vigor and initiative, and encourage pilot schools and experimentation. These activities are broadly classified as *leadership* functions and are considered as constituting "the major responsibility of state departments of education."[2] In the area of school finance these leadership functions would call for the continuous improvement of the state's fiscal policy in educational matters. It would also mean attempts by the central agency to provide for better budgetary, auditing, and accounting procedures that would not only continue to meet the demands made of these activities as prudential safeguards but would encourage vigorous local support and initiative with a maxi-

---

[2] National Council of Chief State School Officers, *The State Department of Education* (Washington, D.C.: The Council, 1952), p. 21.

mum exercise of local control. The state leadership function also implies the providing of expert, resourceful persons who can help local units to solve their own educational problems. In this capacity, representatives of the state department of education gain recognition from the quality of their suggestions and performance instead of undue deference to their positions and status.

Organization and operation

The effectiveness and efficiency of a state department of education, like that of a local administrative unit, depends in large measure upon its organizational structure.

The state education agency in many states is so obviously inadequate and cluttered with functions that are not primarily educational that its efficiency is seriously impaired. Tracing the development of the state department of education in almost any given state reveals some rather obsolete arrangements that have remained through the years and serve to hamper operations. Unfortunately, some states have tended to preserve these obsolete organizational arrangements by specifying them in the laws.

The wide diversity in organization and practice among the state education departments may be viewed as an extensive experiment. However, modernization and continuous evaluation of functions within these state administrative units should progressively eliminate some of these antiquated or poorly placed activities and responsibilities. Only in this way can state education machinery be improved to the point where it can effectively meet current needs.

2. THE ROLE OF STATE EDUCATIONAL LEADERSHIP AS RELATED TO THE VARIOUS BRANCHES OF GOVERNMENT

The development of education has witnessed an increasing complexity of fiscal arrangements and a situation wherein many agencies participate in the operation of schools. One of the leadership responsibilities of the state department of education is to work with federal and local, as well as other state agencies in order to coordinate the educational programs throughout the state. By performing this task effectively, the state education agency can greatly reduce unnecessary overlapping and duplication of services and improve the efficiency of educational endeavors.

Relationships with the executive branch

One of the notable trends in state government in recent years has been the increased centralization of responsibility in the governor. The power of the executive branch of state government has thus increased. Much of this increase has come about through the creation of a number of staff agencies which deal with various phases of government common to several state functions. Examples of such agencies are those given control over purchasing, state planning, and budgeting. All of these have some influence on education.

In some states the governor may appoint state boards of education. In others, he may serve as an ex-officio member of the state board of education. Through his appointive power, his veto power, or through his approval of the educational budget before it is presented to the legislature, the governor may play a key role in influencing educational administration and educational policies.

In view of this important and influential relationship which the executive branch of state government has with education, it seems logical that considerable effort be made to establish and maintain a wholesome, positive working relationship between the executive department and the state education agency. An annual hearing or conference might be provided by law wherein the governor and some members of the legislature review educational plans, problems, and budgets.[3] Such conferences should serve to stimulate interest and provide for a sharing of ideas.

Relationships with the state legislature

One of the original reasons for the creation of state departments of education was to provide information, advice, and leadership to the state legislature.

It is through the legislature that the people of the state express their will and desires concerning the organization and operation of education. And it is the state legislature that should be the sole agency for determining general legal policy and providing finance for public schools. Obviously, one of the most important responsibilities of the state department of education, then, is to keep the legislature completely informed of the needs, problems, and general conditions of public education within the state.

The state department of education plays a strategic role in the development and improvement of educational policies and school

[3] See Paul R. Mort, *Principles of School Administration* (New York: McGraw-Hill Book Co., Inc., 1946), pp. 133–34.

support.   It must continuously study and service the state's fiscal policy as it relates to education, and it must discern those elements which facilitate and those that hamper the operations of the various local administrative units.   Advice to the legislature must be given in such a way that a sensitive balance is maintained by providing, on the one hand, an adequate amount of state aid to local units and, on the other hand, requiring sufficient local sacrifice to maintain vigorous local interest in the schools.   It is through such provisions, and the tax leeway given to local units, that each community can furnish itself with more than the minimum of educational opportunity and thus provide the state with a dynamic force for continuously making school improvements.

An obligation also rests with the state department of education for carrying out legislative mandates and regulations as well as presenting the needs of education.   These activities must be carried out in such a way as to develop confidence of the legislators in the ability and integrity of those who administer the state's programs of public education.

It is the additional responsibility of the state education agency to take a leading part in the drafting and initiation of sound legislation concerning the schools.   By advising against ill-considered, hastily-drawn school legislation, the state department of education can do much to preserve the autonomy and effectiveness of local units, and thus maintain a strong state-system of education.

Relationships to federal education activities

There are many federally supported, educational activities that directly or indirectly affect the various state systems of education. Although the extent, cost, and nature of federal educational activities are discussed in Chapter 9, there are a significant number of these programs that involve the various state departments of education and thus warrant some mention here.

Some valid criticisms have been leveled at the Federal Government for its lack of a unified educational policy, and for the numerous uncoordinated and overlapping educational activities it sponsors that are diffused through its many agencies.[4]   The general pattern, however, is for those educational activities that are administered through the U.S. Office of Education to be channeled generally through the several state departments of education.   It is the observance of this pattern that will help strengthen the traditional state responsibility

[4] Hollis P. Allen, *The Federal Government and Education* (New York: McGraw-Hill Book Co., Inc., 1950), pp. 15–59.

for education and will assuredly mean the most efficient utilization of the various federally sponsored programs.

Regardless of the initiating federal agency, the channeling of all federal activities in education through the states' central educational agencies will give the state some needed control of these programs. It also assures a coordination and lack of duplication of services and can be useful in the over-all, long-range planning done at the state level. The need for such a pattern of relationships between the state and federal governments has become accentuated in recent years because of the increasing complexity and number of federal programs and because of the complaints registered by local superintendents of the numerous federal agencies and authorities with whom they have had to work directly.[5]

3. OPPORTUNITIES AND OBLIGATIONS IN WORKING WITH LAY CITIZENS

One of the major purposes of a state department of education has been to provide leadership and information to the public at large. It has only been in recent years, however, that this process of information-giving between the state school office and the public has been recognized as being most wholesome when it operates in both directions. This means that deliberate efforts must be made to provide a free flow of ideas and information not only from the state education department to the people of the state but also from the public back into the state school office.

The people of this nation have always been the great source of strength for education. The relatively recent trend of having large numbers of citizens participate in an official advisory capacity or in the actual formulation of policy is significant for American education.

Perhaps the grandest illustration of this wholesale involvement of citizens in the development of educational policies and guides for action occurred in the process of the 1955 White House Conference on Education. Across America, the citizens in nearly every locality were invited to meet together and discuss the problems of their schools, and the problems of school finance were given prominent recognition. Representatives of these community conferences met in statewide conferences that provided some valuable ideas and resolutions for use at the state level. And, of course, representatives from the state conferences met in Washington where, through small group meetings and a "filtering" process, the "grass roots" ideas were incor-

[5] American Association of School Administrators, *The American School Superintendency* (Washington, D.C.: The National Education Association, 1952), p. 343.

porated into some significant resolutions and recommendations for public education in America.

The officers of the various state departments of education must continually strive to broaden the extent of participation in educational affairs and share decision-making with the lay public. New York State recently completed a study that involved 75,000 persons. Another of the promising practices for accomplishing this objective of wide participation has been used in Connecticut where some regional councils have been organized to consider educational problems. Another recommended practice has been for the state education department to provide for periodic budget hearings or conferences on its programs and operations.[6] It is in these conferences that the representative lay citizens and local school board members can be helpful in giving advice and suggestions for the continued improvement of the operations of the state school office.

4. THE RELATIONSHIP BETWEEN THE STATE DEPARTMENT OF EDUCATION AND THE LOCAL ADMINISTRATIVE UNITS

Tradition and the deep conviction of the people of the United States seem to hold that the local school district should be endowed with administrative and financial powers in order to serve as the basic operating unit in American education. It is also recognized, however, that in order for the local units to function effectively, state leadership and state financial support must be available.

The central problem involved in the relationship that is thus established between state departments and local units is that of providing the needed funds and services while still preserving the autonomy and integrity of the local unit. State departments of education, in attempting to serve in this general framework, have undergone a process of functional evolution. At the present time it appears that less and less emphasis is being placed on the regulatory function and more and more emphasis is given to advisory and consultative services. The emerging role of the state departments appears to be that of a liaison agency between the local district and the state that gives particular emphasis to the leadership functions of the office.

This newer viewpoint on state-level services holds that adequate and dynamic leadership practically eliminates the necessity for invoking compliance procedures. Thus the role of the state department becomes one of making expert professional and technical services available with the aim of strengthening local school programs and helping local units to more effectively help themselves.

[6] Mort, *op. cit.*, p. 133.

SOME SPECIFIC STATE DEPARTMENT SERVICES IN SCHOOL FINANCE

As an illustration of some of the kinds of services related to school finance that may be provided to local units by the state school office, the following should be suggestive:

Regulatory:

1. Formulate guides for local school accounting, budgeting, bonding, etc.
2. Conduct audits.
3. Provide mandated services such as budget reviewing, checking capital outlay plans, etc.
4. Collect information necessary for approvals for financial reimbursements or appropriations.

Leadership:

1. Prepare handbooks for local administrators to facilitate procedures related to school finance problems.
2. Sponsor inservice conferences, institutes, and workshops for local school board members, administrators, and school business officials.
3. Operate a clearing house for sharing up-to-date information on new developments in school finance and business management.
4. Advise local school officials on organization and administration and problems of school finance.
5. Cooperate with training institutions for the improvement of administrator education programs.
6. Conduct research studies as a basis for evaluating school finance policies and practices.
7. Develop basic school finance policies for suggested use on the state and local levels.
8. Stimulate experimentation and leadership within the local administration.
9. Provide consultant field services to assist local units.

The leadership in the state department of education must be constantly on the alert in rendering these services to see that local control is maintained and local initiative fostered. It is relatively simple to abuse some services such as audits or budget reviews. If the reviewing or auditing bodies are empowered to challenge the policy-making authority of the local school board, then these functions are "out-of-bounds" and represent a threat to the "home rule" and integrity of the entire education system.

Stimulating lighthouse programs, experimentation, and the diffusion of good educational practice

It is the duty of the state department of education to encourage and vigorously promote the operation of schools that pioneer with educational innovations and experiment with new educational practice. These are commonly referred to as "lighthouse" schools.

The stimulation of these "pilot" or leader schools requires that these schools be well supported financially and that a very permissive climate prevail in the school and community as far as tryout of new ideas is concerned.

State department personnel are in an advantageous position to recognize good educational practice and to share this information with the various local units throughout the state. A research project in Pennsylvania, however, revealed that the state agency exerted only moderate influences in the diffusion of certain adaptations studied and that an active state interest was not found in the early stages of diffusion.[7]

Some appropriate guides for action on the state level that would be helpful in the stimulation and diffusion of good educational practice are as follows: (1) encourage local units to identify their needs and meet these with creative imagination and state services whenever appropriate; (2) be continually on the lookout for new ideas and new practices and encourage and help nurture these wherever they are found; (3) provide adequate state services as they are needed in the local units; (4) conduct basic research studies on how good practices are most efficiently diffused; (5) assemble, evaluate, and distribute to local units those research findings, descriptions of good practices, and other helpful bits of information that can be utilized for the improvement of schools.

5. OTHER PROFESSIONAL ACTIVITIES AND OBLIGATIONS OF THE STATE DEPARTMENT OF EDUCATION

In addition to the school finance responsibilities of the state department of education that have already been discussed, there are others that deserve special mention.

---

[7] Paul R. Mort and Francis G. Cornell, *Abstracts from American Schools in Transition* (New York: Bureau of Publications, Teachers College, Columbia University, 1946), p. 105.

Cooperating with educational associations and institutions

One of the important obligations of the state department of education is to cooperate with voluntary educational associations and with private schools and higher institutions in planning and carrying out educational improvements for the state. The state school office must take the initiative in such a program since it is in the most favorable position to coordinate the efforts of all such agencies.

Publications

Bulletins, handbooks, and other printed materials related to school finance that are designed to promote better schools are produced and distributed by state departments of education. Such media have become one of the important services rendered by these central agencies.

Although some state departments issue publications that are excellent, others reflect through their bulletins an obsolete organization and philosophy. This is particularly true in some of the traditional annual or biennial bulletins that are issued. In many cases these contain only repetitive, uninteresting, and almost irrelevant information and statistics that are of little use to anyone and reflect only that amount of design that reveals it to be a replica of previous similar reports.

It is essential that state departments of education periodically make a critical review of their publications in order to make them more informative and useful.

Research activities

Although the state department of education should be in a strategic position to conduct educational research, the unfortunate truth is that many of the state school offices are ineffective and unproductive in this critically needed service.

Despite the tremendous leadership potential of the state school offices, research activities are organized in less than half of them. In many of these, the organized research done is almost wholly devoted to preparing the annual report and has little significance as far as research for improvement of practice is concerned. Actually, it is the state department of education that should take the initiative to sponsor and coordinate all education research activities throughout the state.

Our need in education for continuous and basic research is acute.

This is especially true in the area of school finance. Competent personnel, adequate facilities and funds, and freedom from political controls are all necessities for a strong and useful research program in a state school office.

Without a research program, the schools become stagnant and lethargic as far as their adaptability is concerned. With a vigorous and systematic research program, intelligent educational progress is a possibility that desperately needs to be promoted at the state as well as at the local level.

TOPICS FOR STUDY AND DISCUSSION

1. Give a report on the historical development of the state department of education in your state.
2. Enumerate some of the specific activities of the state department of education in your state as they are related to the operational, judicial, regulatory, and leadership functions.
3. Give a report on the general organization of your state department of education with particular reference to the school finance services.
4. Evaluate the relationships that exist between your state department of education and (a) the governor, (b) the legislature, (c) the lay citizenry of the state, (d) local school districts within the state, and (e) the state education association and other groups or agencies interested in education.
5. Make a constructively critical evaluation of the annual or biennial report of your state department of education.
6. List the organizations in your state that carry on a systematic program of research in the problems of school finance. Evaluate the effectiveness of this program.

SELECTED REFERENCES

American Association of School Administrators. *The American School Superintendency.* Washington, D.C.: The National Education Association, 1952.
ALLEN, HOLLIS P. *The Federal Government and Education.* New York: McGraw-Hill Book Co., Inc., 1950.
HAMILTON, ROBERT R. and PAUL R. MORT. *The Law and Public Education.* Chicago: The Foundation Press, Inc., 1941.
MORT, PAUL R. *Principles of School Administration.* New York: McGraw-Hill Book Co., Inc., 1946.
MORT, PAUL R. and FRANCIS G. CORNELL. *Abstracts from American Schools in Transition.* New York: Bureau of Publications, Teachers College, Columbia University, 1946.
National Council of Chief State School Officers. *The State Department of Education.* Washington, D.C.: The Council, 1952.

9

FEDERAL PARTICIPATION IN THE SUPPORT
OF EDUCATION

WHAT SHOULD be the role of the Federal Government in the financing of education in America? This question has been a burning issue and still remains unsolved.

Some people believe that an extensive program of federal monies for the elementary and secondary schools would be contrary to the American tradition, a violation of the long-accepted legal principle that education is a state function, and a further step toward the deterioration of America's unique system of public education which is nourished through local sacrifice, interest, and participation.

Others contend that substantial federal support for education in the various states is critically essential to the welfare of the nation. These people amass statistics and marshal arguments to show the wide differences in educational need, ability, and opportunity among the states. These arguments are buttressed by pointing out that the population of the United States is mobile and migratory, that some kind of responsibility exists for the welfare and enlightenment of all Americans, and that our nation, embroiled in a world-wide crisis and exercising a position of international leadership, must exert more effort to improve the education of its people if it would meet existing and future challenges to our democratic, free society.

Public opinion in America has been divided on this issue. Most of the evidence available, however, indicates that the majority of the people in the United States favor a more substantial program of federal aid to the public schools. This is borne out by a number of

149

polls[1] and by the White House Conference on education which was held late in 1955. In the White House Conference about two-thirds of the 2,000 delegates favored a substantial federal support program for schoolhouse construction. On the question of federal aid for general operation and maintenance of America's public schools, only about half the delegates favored such a program of support. The delegates to this Conference were presumably representative of the American people since they had, for the most part, been selected through their participation in a series of "grass roots" education conferences held in the various states.

Congressional attempts to implement substantial federal aid programs for public schools have been repeatedly stymied because of political, racial, or religious issues.

The various issues involved in the question of federal aid to the elementary and secondary schools of America can best be understood by (1) getting a historical perspective on the problem, (2) examining the current status of educational activities supported by the Federal Government, (3) analyzing the methods of distributing federal funds for education, (4) reviewing some of the arguments on the federal aid problem, and (5) considering some of the basic principles to be recognized in any program of federal support to the public schools.

I. HISTORICAL PERSPECTIVE ON FEDERAL AID TO EDUCATION

The history of federal support of education can be conveniently separated into two divisions: the first is a policy of federal grants for the general support of schools; and the second is a policy of conditional grants for the promotion of specific aspects of education.

Grants for the general support of education

The basic motive of early federal support for education is eloquently expressed in the famous Northwest Ordinance of 1787 which declared that "Religion, morality, and knowledge being necessary to good government and the happiness of mankind, schools and the means of education shall forever be encouraged."

Although Vermont, Kentucky, and Tennessee were admitted after the passage of this early ordinance, the first state to receive any direct benefits was Ohio in 1802. Section 16 of every township in Ohio was

---

[1] Typical of such polls is the one conducted by Roper and reported in *Life*, XXVIII (October 16, 1950), 46–47; and by Gallup's American Institute of Public Opinion reported in most American newspapers on March 22, 1956.

dedicated for school purposes. This same designation of school lands continued for all but three new states admitted to the Union after the beginning of the nineteenth century. The three states not receiving these benefits were Maine, whose land was part of Massachusetts and not the national domain; Texas, which was annexed as a sovereign state; and West Virginia, which seceded from Virginia during the Civil War.

With the admission of Oregon in 1848, all subsequently admitted states received two sections of every township for school purposes (16, 36), and since the admission of Utah in 1896, all new states have received four sections of land for schools (2, 16, 32, 36).[2]

Taken together, all of these school lands given by the Federal Government to the various states would amount to more than 73 million acres, or an area as large as the states of Ohio, Indiana, and Illinois combined.[3]

In addition to the regular sectional land grants, the Federal Government made other grants to the states for school purposes. One of these was a series of gifts of saline land, or an equivalent acreage, to the states. This practice began with Ohio, became the equivalent of two full townships with Indiana, and, with the exception of Utah in 1896, this procedure was terminated after the admission of Colorado in 1876.[4]

Another special grant, which also began with the admission of Ohio, was the practice of giving for internal improvements within the new state 5 per cent of the proceeds from the sale of public lands therein. During the first fifty years this policy was in effect, some states diverted this money into their permanent school funds, and, by Congressional act, such procedure became mandatory for all states admitted after 1860.[5]

Other special grants, of which only a part has gone for the benefit of schools, included the Federal Government's giving to the new states a title to all swamp lands, and allowing all states 25 per cent of the revenue derived from federal forests and nonmetallic deposits and 37½ per cent of all revenues received from federal leases and royalties.[6]

[2] This is with the exception of Oklahoma which received two sections and $5 million in gold to compensate for land in Indian Territory.
[3] Ellwood P. Cubberley, *State School Administration* (New York: Houghton Mifflin Co., 1927), p. 26.
[4] *Ibid.*, p. 31.
[5] *Ibid.*, p. 32.
[6] Arthur B. Moehlman, *School Administration* (2d ed.; New York: Houghton Mifflin Co., 1951), p. 461.

Conditional grants for the promotion of specific aspects of education

The Federal Government's early policy was that of providing schools with grants which were unspecified as to their particular use. This policy was radically changed in 1862 with the passage of the Morrill Act, which provided for the establishment of the land-grant colleges. This was followed by the Second Morrill Act, the Hatch Act, the Smith-Lever Act, and others which were concerned with experiment stations, agriculture, and home economics extension work, and did not directly affect the elementary and secondary schools of America.

In 1917, however, the passage of the Smith-Hughes Act provided for vocational education in the secondary schools. Under this law a Federal Board of Vocational Education was created and state boards for vocational education were to be organized within the various participating states. Although this program was to be offered only to students who were at least fourteen years old, the statute provided for federal cooperation in a number of other related facets including the preparation of vocational teachers and supervisors, paying teachers' salaries and other necessary expenditures, and conducting studies as to needs and course offerings in agriculture, home economics, trades, industries, and commerce.

A number of laws passed by Congress since 1917 have been aimed at either supplementing or extending the Smith-Hughes program. These included the George-Reed Act of 1929, the George-Ellzey Act of 1934, the George-Deen Act of 1937, and the George-Barden Act of 1946. All four of these laws provided for additional supplemental appropriations for the Smith-Hughes program, and the third-mentioned law provided for extending the program to include distributive education and vocational guidance.

Federal aid to America's elementary and secondary schools, however, has not been limited to vocational education. As a result of the Great Depression of the 1930's, a number of federal activities were begun that had some effect on the schools either because of direct aid or because of the establishment of some supplementary, parallel, or competitive educational function.

These emergency activities, which included the alphabetically designated programs of C.C.C., N.Y.A., W.P.A., and P.W.A., were terminated with the advent of World War II in the early 1940's. While the Civilian Conservation Corps established its own educational program and the National Youth Administration simply provided aid for needy students, the Federal Emergency Administration of Public Works and the Works Progress Administration provided for the refurbishing, extending, and constructing of public school buildings.

The national defense efforts associated with World War II gave rise to some new federal activities associated with education. As early as 1940, under the control of the U.S. Office of Education, a series of intensive, short-term training courses at the secondary level were given to workers whose jobs were linked with the national defense efforts. In 1941 the Lanham Act was passed by Congress and, among other provisions, this act authorized the construction of many public school buildings in temporary federal housing projects.

Two other significant federal programs began in the 1940's. One of these was the school lunch program which was administered through the Department of Agriculture and was initiated as a means of disposing of food surpluses that accumulated after the great wartime demand had diminished. The other was the Servicemen's Readjustment Act of 1944 together with Public Law 16 for the rehabilitation of World War II veterans. These laws provided for educational opportunities for all servicemen whose education had been interrupted or who had sustained injuries requiring re-education as a result of World War II.

During the early 1950's, other important school legislation was enacted by Congress. A modification of the "G.I. Bill of Rights" was provided for veterans of the Korean War, and two laws were enacted to provide funds for school operation and maintenance (P.L. 874) and school building construction (P.L. 815) in areas where federal activities resulted in overburdened school systems.

2. THE CURRENT SCOPE OF FEDERAL ACTIVITIES IN EDUCATION

It should be carefully noted that the preceding discussion of federal aid to education has been confined solely to those activities having a direct effect on the state systems of elementary and secondary public schools. Such activities, however, give only a very limited description of the extent of federal activities in education. A comprehensive analysis of all federal participation in education reveals an enormous amount of interest and activity. A complete listing of annual federal expenditures for education is staggering. The Hoover Commission, for example, in its Task Force report on public welfare showed that federal funds obligated for educational programs during the school year 1948–49 amounted to about $3.7 billion.[7]   Another study by the Legislative Reference Service of the Library of Congress revealed that in 1949–50 approximately 300 separate and distinct programs of education were operating in the various federal departments at an annual cost of more than $3.6 billion for 255 of these programs.[8]   A large proportion (81 per cent) of this money was devoted to veteran education and training.

For comparative purposes it is interesting to note that the total amount expended by all the public school systems in the United States was only $2.9 billion in 1945–46, $4.3 billion in 1947–48, and $5.8 billion in 1949–50.[9]

The numerous educational programs that are federally supported are associated not only with the public schools but with private schools, universities, vocational rehabilitation, farming, business, government, military service, office management, health, currency, thrift, research, civil defense, law enforcement, handicaps, veterans' education, citizenship, penal institutions, surveys, social security, occupied areas, conservation, national parks, libraries, apprenticeship, and others.[10]   A more complete analysis of all of these federally sponsored educational activities reveals (1) no over-all federal policy on education seems to exist; (2) the responsibility for education is scattered throughout the governmental structure and ranges from functions of the Department of State to the Smithsonian Institute, and from the District of Columbia to the various islands and outposts under the jurisdiction of the United States, and from the education of Indians to R.O.T.C. programs and military academies; and (3) the result is some rather serious overlapping, competition, and duplication.

It is of interest to notice that the great emphasis in federal activities in education is concerned with post high-school or higher education levels.   Fewer than 15 per cent of the federal activities in education are concerned with the population of the elementary and secondary schools in the form of school lunches, school buildings, vocational education, etc.[11]

The extent of the many uncoordinated and overlapping educa-

[7] The Brookings Institution, *Functions of the National Government in the Field of Welfare* (Washington, D.C.: U.S. Government Printing Office, 1949), p. 590.

[8] Charles A. Quattlebaum, *Federal Educational Activities and Educational Issues Before Congress* (Washington, D.C.: U.S. Government Printing Office, 1951), p. 567.

[9] See Chapter 1.

[10] Clayton D. Hutchins, Albert R. Munse, and Edna D. Booker, *Federal Funds for Education*, U.S. Office of Education Bulletin No. 14 (Washington, D.C.: U.S. Government Printing Office, 1954), pp. 3–12.

[11] *Ibid.*, p. 3.

tional activities sponsored by the Federal Government serves to focus attention on one of the central issues involved in expanding federal aid to the elementary and secondary schools of America. Some people are concerned with the fact that the Federal Government spends heavily for education through many agencies and for many diffused purposes while some of our states, because of a lack of money, operate their elementary and secondary schools in obsolete buildings, with poorly prepared teachers and with excessive class sizes. The question is raised as to whether it might not be sounder public policy to shift the financial emphasis of federal support of education so that more funds would be available for capital improvements and operation of the elementary and secondary schools. It is contended by some that such a shift in emphasis would, in time, reduce the pressing necessity for many of the educational programs for adults.

3. METHODS OF DISTRIBUTING FEDERAL FUNDS FOR EDUCATION

In considering the topic of federal aid to education, it is important to review the most significant patterns of support used by the Federal Government in sponsoring various phases of education. The specific methods of distributing federal funds vary with each program because of the kind of aid provided and the purpose for which Congress authorized the funds.

In describing some 56 different programs of federal support to education, Hutchins, Munse, and Booker suggest the following general classification of methods used in distributing federal funds for education.[12]

Land area

The early land-grant assistance was essentially a policy of giving federal support for education in proportion to the amount of land area held by each state. Of the states that received for school purposes the one or more sections of land in every township, it is apparent that the larger the state was geographically, the more benefits it received.

This method of distributing federal support was for general educational purposes and had no federal controls. The state receiving the land was considered competent to establish its own policies. This practice resulted in gross mismanagement and squandering of most

[12] *Ibid.*, pp. 14–18.

of these grants in the older states, but a more prudential administration of them in the states admitted after 1850.[13]

In advocating expanded programs of federal funds for the elementary and secondary schools of America, some people have cited this pattern of support to illustrate that federal aid programs are possible without any federal control.

Population

The first instance of allocating federal support for education in proportion to population was through the Morrill Act of 1862. This act established the land-grant colleges and was the beginning of a federal policy of "stimulation of special activity" in education.

In this law, each state received 30,000 acres of federal lands for each senator and each representative in Congress. This meant that the amount of the federal grant to each state was roughly proportional to its total population.

Population has also served as a basis for distributing federal funds for agricultural extension services and experiment stations as well as for vocational education. School lunch funds and federal monies for the recent school facilities survey have been apportioned on the basis of the school-age population. Funds for federally impacted areas have been allotted on the basis of average daily attendance data.

Some authorities have advocated that proposed federal aid programs to the elementary and secondary schools should use the number of school-age children as the basis of distribution.[14] It is argued that allocating to the states a given amount of money per school-age child, instead of on the basis of some calculated formula, would reduce the possibility of federal control, result in some measure of equalization, and probably enhance the chances of Congressional enactment of a program of federal aid.

Matching funds

Beginning with the Smith-Lever Act of 1914 and followed by the Smith-Hughes Act of 1917 and several subsequent laws, the Federal Government established a policy of requiring states to match federal appropriations in the support of certain educational activities. The aim of such federally supported programs was to stimulate a specific

[13] Cubberley, op. cit., pp. 26–27.
[14] Edward M. Tuttle, "A New and Different Approach to Federal Aid for Education," American School Board Journal, CXXX (February, 1955), 74.

phase of education. The matching provision was used as a device to assure that state and local funds for the particular activity might not be reduced as federal monies were received.

In proposing new legislation for federal aid to elementary and secondary education, this matching feature has very few advocates. Part of the reason for such a lack of enthusiasm for any kind of matching plan is the recognition that under such a program in vocational education, federal control increased greatly over curriculum, class size, equipment, personnel employed, and even methods of instruction.[15] Other reasons for objecting to the matching pattern of federal support are that such a program tends to favor the wealthier states, puts a strain on state and local tax resources, and unduly favors certain activities.

Equalization programs

In order that educational effort in the several states will be equivalent, the equalization concept holds that in any federal aid program requiring state contributions, these contributions must be proportional to the income or wealth of the people of the states. This concept also holds that in the distribution of federal funds the less wealthy states will receive proportionately greater amounts of money.

The equalization method has been used to a limited extent by the Federal Government in the distribution of school lunch funds. Proportionately larger amounts of money are allocated to the states with relatively low per capita income by requiring lower state and local matching rates.

In recent years several of the federal aid to education bills considered by Congress have contained provisions for equalization. This has been most frequently provided for by authorizing the distribution of funds to the several states in an inverse proportion to their income per capita. Such provisions have been found in proposals for aid in school operation and maintenance as well as those seeking funds for schoolhouse construction.

The interest in equalization features of any proposals for federal aid to education is only a relatively recent phenomenon. Mort and Reusser point out that as it applied to federal support, the equalization concept was slow in being accepted.[16] It was not until the mid-1940's that explicit recognition was given to the foundation program idea as developed by Strayer and Haig in the early 1920's. Because

[15] Moehlman, *op. cit.*, p. 466.
[16] Paul R. Mort and Walter C. Reusser, *Public School Finance* (2d ed.; New York: McGraw-Hill Book Co., Inc., 1951), p. 558.

TABLE 7. Variations among the states in ability and effort to finance education

State	School-aged children per 1000 wage-earning adults 1950	Per cent of school-aged children in school 1951-52[b]	Income payments per capita 1952[a]	Income payments per pupil in A.D.A. 1950-51[a]	Relative financial effort made to support public schools (per cent of income spent for schools) 1950-51	Average value of public school property per pupil 1949-50[a]
UNITED STATES	403	84.7	$1,639	$10,662	2.27	$454
NORTHEAST						
Connecticut	324	82.7	2,080	15,922	1.89	579
Maine	457	88.6	1,361	7,828	2.22	323
Massachusetts	342	76.8	1,745	14,833	1.80	610
New Hampshire	390	72.4	1,530	11,909	2.16	432
New Jersey	312	82.5	1,959	15,834	2.12	595
New York	305	79.9	2,038	17,340	2.00	790
Pennsylvania	372	77.0	1,710	12,388	2.13	556
Rhode Island	334	71.6	1,655	15,667	1.75	649
Vermont	458	79.0	1,336	8,439	2.79	367
NORTH CENTRAL						
Illinois	334	76.2	1,983	15,942	1.92	687
Indiana	404	91.5	1,685	11,314	2.36	348
Iowa	423	91.3	1,545	9,340	2.79	428
Kansas	407	94.4	1,698	9,198	2.66	592
Michigan	400	84.2	1,815	11,707	2.31	591
Minnesota	419	81.1	1,491	9,780	2.76	499
Missouri	381	86.7	1,583	10,945	1.86	396
Nebraska	409	85.7	1,566	9,807	2.37	494
North Dakota	529	80.1	1,223	7,867	3.04	493
Ohio	369	83.7	1,881	11,993	1.90	509
South Dakota	472	84.6	1,258	8,926	3.00	440
Wisconsin	408	72.8	1,649	12,364	2.24	616

WEST					
Arizona	514	89.1	1,498	8,945	3.39	445
California	327	92.8	2,032	12,983	2.36	427
Colorado	420	89.7	1,618	10,642	2.37	495
Idaho	521	90.3	1,438	7,769	2.83	381
Montana	440	85.2	1,697	10,646	2.72	477
Nevada	345	115.2c	2,250	14,120	1.97	643
New Mexico	595	86.4	1,331	7,213	3.70	388
Oregon	381	91.3	1,733	10,996	2.80	596
Utah	568	94.9	1,450	6,885	2.94	422
Washington	374	98.7	1,810	11,428	2.37	642
Wyoming	445	95.4	1,607	10,200	3.12	477
SOUTH					
Alabama	578	86.1	1,012	4,981	2.69	142
Arkansas	563	86.9	951	4,869	2.44	242
Delaware	368	78.1	2,260	17,119	1.92	543
Florida	383	93.4	1,319	8,651	2.38	323
Georgia	536	88.8	1,137	6,118	2.31	220
Kentucky	537	81.4	1,135	6,536	2.16	233
Louisiana	514	78.5	1,206	7,230	3.30	289
Maryland	378	79.8	1,761	13,129	1.87	439
Mississippi	622	92.4	818	3,539	2.66	137
North Carolina	570	87.7	1,049	5,257	3.02	261
Oklahoma	482	99.0	1,285	6,582	3.34	433
South Carolina	642	88.9	1,099	5,043	2.83	184
Tennessee	503	87.1	1,126	5,943	2.30	152
Texas	456	82.9	1,452	9,224	2.58	363
Virginia	464	85.4	1,322	7,922	2.21	342
West Virginia	552	88.6	1,232	5,850	2.84	330

SOURCES: a. Research Division of the N.E.A., *Educational Differences Among the States* (Washington, D. C.: National Education Association, 1954).
b. U. S. Office of Education, *Statistics of State School Systems, 1951-52* (Washington, D. C.: U. S. Government Printing Office, 1955), p. 48.
c. This figure is accounted for by the relatively large transient population of Nevada.

of implicit control features, some objection is held toward attempts to apply the foundation program idea to a plan of federal aid for education.

Other methods of distribution

Some use has been made of several other methods and combinations of methods of distributing federal funds for education.

Flat-grants—equal allocations for all—have been used to a limited extent in the Federal Government's appropriations to the land-grant colleges, experiment stations, and agricultural extension services.

In a few instances, the Federal Government has completely financed some educational services. Illustrations of this practice are found in veterans' education, schools for Indians, the service academies, and research activities.

The nontaxable status of federally owned property gives rise to payments by the Federal Government to local school districts. These payments are made in lieu of taxes which would be available for schools if there were no loss in tax revenue because of property ownership by the Federal Government. In those instances where such ownership causes an increase in the educational load, additional federal funds are made available to the school district.

4. CHILDREN, WEALTH, AND EDUCATION

The overwhelming majority of the American people believe that public education in the United States should continue to be controlled primarily by the states and local communities. When it comes to the question of financing the schools, however, there are some honest differences of opinion about where this responsibility should reside. Some persons contend that the several states and localities can and should finance their public elementary and secondary schools without assistance from the Federal Government. Others maintain that not only are currently available federal funds desirable but that substantial increases in federal aid must be promptly forthcoming if public education in America is to serve its noble and needed functions.

Regardless of the position one takes on the federal aid issues, there are some pertinent facts about children, wealth, and education within the various states that warrant some careful consideration. These facts are given in Tables 7 and 8 and, taken together, they present a rather forceful argument for some kind of abrupt change in the present patterns of school support.

The various states differ markedly in their ability and effort to finance education. Table 7 reveals that one of these differences lies in the proportionate number of children to be educated. On a state-wide basis it can be seen that some states like Mississippi and South Carolina have twice as many school-age children per 1,000 wage-earning adults as do states like New York and New Jersey.

Even if the per capita income payments in all states were equal, it becomes apparent that the wide variation in the ratio of children to adults would still leave a great disparity among the states in their ability to support education. The differences in ability due to the proportionate numbers of children are actually greater than they may at first appear. In the public financing of education, it seems that the ability to support schools decreases more than in a direct ratio to the proportionate number of children to be educated. Clark[17] suggested that in comparing states and communities, those with only half as many children per 1,000 wage earners in reality have not twice the ability, but four times as much ability to support schools as do those states and communities with twice as many children per 1,000 wage earners.

Instead of being nearly the same, however, the per capita income varies widely among the several states. A more extensive analysis would also reveal that over a 20-year period, the Middle Atlantic, Pacific, and New England regions have been consistently the wealthiest and that the Southern regions have been the poorest.[18] This leads to the unfortunate conclusion that, in general, the states with the largest number of school-age children per 1,000 wage earners are also the ones with the smallest per capita income. Furthermore, these states are generally the ones with the smaller percentages of school-age children in school and, therefore, if comparisons are made on the basis of income payments per pupil in average daily attendance, even more marked differences are seen in the ability of the states to support education. This tends to reinforce the conclusion that, by-and-large, where the educational load or need is greatest, the ability is lowest.

In some states the people are putting forth nearly twice as much effort to finance public schools as are the people in other states (see Table 7). In addition, it can be seen that the amount of effort exerted does not appear to be closely related to a state's ability. It is evident, however, that many of the states with the least ability are making greater-than-average effort.

[17] Harold F. Clark, *The Effect of Population Upon the Ability to Support Education* (Bloomington, Indiana: Bulletin of the School of Education, Indiana University, 1925), vol. II, No. 1, p. 20.
[18] Ralph C. Geigle, "Relative Efforts of the States to Support Public Education," *Elementary School Journal*, LII (December, 1951), 221–28.

TABLE 8. Educational differences among the states

State	Median years schooling of population over age 24 1950[a]	Per cent of population over age 24 with less than 5 years schooling 1950[a]	Current expenditure per pupil in A.D.A. from state and local public sources 1950-51[a]	Military rejections due to educational deficiencies 1940-1944[b]	Per cent of rejections for failing the A.F.Q. test 1950-51[a]	Per cent of voting age population that voted in presidential elections 1952[a]
UNITED STATES	9.1	11.0	$217	12.3	16.4	65.3
NORTHEAST						
Connecticut	9.8	8.9	265	5.6	9.1	75.9
Maine	10.2	6.7	161	5.3	14.6	64.5
Massachusetts	10.9	7.9	245	4.0	3.7	74.0
New Hampshire	9.8	6.3	228	5.4	4.8	77.8
New Jersey	9.3	9.2	289	5.1	10.6	69.6
New York	9.6	9.5	324	2.8	10.8	68.9
Pennsylvania	9.0	9.4	243	3.9	7.0	65.0
Rhode Island	9.3	9.7	254	4.8	5.1	77.8
Vermont	10.0	5.5	215	3.8	12.9	66.5
NORTH CENTRAL						
Illinois	9.3	7.8	278	2.3	5.2	75.1
Indiana	9.6	6.6	231	3.5	7.0	74.5
Iowa	9.8	3.9	244	4.5	4.8	75.2
Kansas	10.2	5.0	223	5.2	5.2	70.2
Michigan	9.9	7.5	243	4.2	9.8	65.6
Minnesota	9.0	5.8	245	1.8	1.3	72.6
Missouri	8.8	8.4	185	5.5	14.5	71.2
Nebraska	10.1	4.9	225	2.7	7.6	69.1
North Dakota	8.7	8.8	228	3.7	10.7	77.2
Ohio	9.9	6.9	198	3.0	11.8	69.2
South Dakota	8.9	5.8	232	1.7	6.4	73.9
Wisconsin	8.9	7.2	244	3.7	4.2	71.4

WEST						
Arizona	10.0	14.2	247	20.9	15.2	52.4
California	11.6	6.8	269	4.8	7.1	70.1
Colorado	10.9	7.1	217	5.3	8.1	71.6
Idaho	10.6	4.5	202	1.9	3.3	78.5
Montana	10.1	6.3	263	2.5	5.2	73.2
Nevada	11.5	6.8	239	4.7	9.2	71.5
New Mexico	9.3	18.0	225	15.4	25.7	63.5
Oregon	10.9	4.3	275	1.4	2.2	67.2
Utah	12.0	4.3	175	2.3	1.9	79.6
Washington	11.2	4.7	248	1.4	3.8	71.5
Wyoming	11.1	5.7	274	4.4	4.7	73.7
SOUTH						
Alabama	7.9	22.6	118	28.9	39.2	24.9
Arkansas	8.3	19.8	107	25.5	39.2	37.8
Delaware	9.8	9.7	288	9.2	14.6	79.1
Florida	9.6	13.8	184	18.7	28.3	50.0
Georgia	7.8	24.2	123	29.4	30.2	30.0
Kentucky	8.4	16.8	122	16.6	22.2	60.0
Louisiana	7.6	28.7	217	29.7	38.7	40.4
Maryland	8.9	10.9	216	14.6	13.9	57.5
Mississippi	8.1	25.2	85	29.2	40.4	24.3
North Carolina	7.9	21.1	143	22.9	34.6	52.1
Oklahoma	9.1	10.9	197	9.4	17.2	69.2
South Carolina	7.6	27.4	118	33.3	56.0	30.7
Tennessee	8.4	18.3	124	21.1	36.4	46.2
Texas	9.3	15.8	209	22.8	21.1	42.9
Virginia	8.5	17.5	152	24.8	28.9	31.3
West Virginia	8.5	13.7	150	12.0	21.8	77.4

SOURCES: a. Research Division of the N.E.A., *Educational Differences Among the States* (Washington, D. C.: National Education Association, 1954).
b. Research Division of the N.E.A., *The Facts On Federal Aid for Schools* (Washington, D. C.: The Association, 1949).

The average value of public school property per pupil is also given in Table 7. This may be taken as a general index of ability and effort of the several states.

The wide educational differences among the states is presented in Table 8. In general, the states cited as having low per capita income and a high proportion of children to educate are the same states that provide a relatively low level of expenditure per pupil for their schools. Similarly, it is generally these same states that have a relatively low educational level among their adult populations. This same tendency prevails when one examines some of the apparent effects of education. By-and-large, the states that seem to be low in ability and educational status are the ones with low voting records and with high rates of military rejections due to educational deficiencies.

Despite the complications presented by racial differences, parochial school enrollments, and urban and rural factors, the information presented in Tables 7 and 8 poses some very real problems to the American people. This is particularly true if their general norm holds to the concept of equality of educational opportunity as being the "inalienable right" of every citizen. In an age that demands the development of our country's precious human resources for national security and world leadership, it is obvious that some significant improvements must be made in our systems of public education. It requires little imagination to see that the continued existence of poor schools is a threat to our free, democratic way of life as well as to our nation's social, political, and economic well-being.

5. THE ISSUES INVOLVED IN THE QUESTION OF FEDERAL AID FOR ELEMENTARY AND SECONDARY SCHOOLS

For a third of a century a concerted effort has been made by the National Education Association and other groups to encourage Congress to enact a law providing for an expanded program of federal aid for the elementary and secondary schools of America. Some of the proposed bills have provided for general grants to the various states. Others have omitted provisions for school buildings and transportation. And still others have been restricted to aid for school construction. The one thing all of these bills have had in common has been their failure to be enacted into law.

The nonpassage of these numerous bills has been due to several fundamental issues involved in the problem of federal aid to education. The major issues center around (1) equalization, (2) states' rights, (3) federal control, (4) support of nonpublic schools, and (5) racial segregation.

Equalization

The preceding discussion and the conclusions drawn by the authors in connection with Tables 7 and 8 represent some of the arguments used by persons favoring an equalization program of federal aid to education. A summary of the case for equalization is expressed in the following paragraph.

The states differ widely on their ability to finance education as well as the extent to which they provide educational opportunities for their children and youth. In general, it appears that the states with the most children per capita have the least resources and provide the least amount of money per child for school purposes. Consequently, the educational opportunities for many American children in several states are grossly inadequate, and the entire country is penalized by the resultant waste of undeveloped human resources. This waste is revealed by such measures as educational deficiencies of draftees for military service and estimates of the number of illiterates in our population. In view of such conditions, and the fact that America's population is highly mobile in crossing state boundaries and in moving from one region of the United States to another, some people maintain that the nation's general welfare demands that the Federal Government take the logical and educationally-sound next step of applying nationally the principle of state equalization. Such a program would recognize that an adequate educational opportunity is an individual right and a democratic necessity, regardless of where a child lives. The additional money required to effect such an essential scheme would represent a sound investment in the social and economic well-being of the nation.

Those Americans who oppose any such program of equalization reject the foregoing arguments. Their contentions are summarized in the following points. First, it is held that the need is greatly exaggerated by the lobbyists who are trying to get the federal aid bills passed. Second, the bills presented to Congress are primarily general aid measures and not equalization provisions, otherwise they would provide aid to only a few states instead of giving funds to all states. Third, the amount of money spent is not a true measure of the amount of equalized educational opportunity because of the differences in state school systems and the varying degrees of efficiency of district organization within the states. Fourth, there is no accurate formula for measuring the true ability of the states to support education. And, fifth, the concepts of equality of educational opportunity and compulsory attendance, as presented by professional educators, are open to question and must be examined very carefully because of the tremendous size of the present national debt and the great expense involved in the Federal Government's becoming committed to any such program of federal aid to education.

States' rights

In the course of more than 150 years the people of the United States have evolved a program of universal education which is legally a function of the various states but has beeen largely community-centered and community-administered. Few people are in favor of changing this general pattern of state responsibility with local concern and operation.

The proponents of expanded federal aid to education contend that such a program should in no way jeopardize America's traditional system of responsibility and control of education. On the contrary, they maintain that a federal aid bill can and must be so written that it preserves states' rights and strengthens local systems and boards of education throughout America. These advocates point out that the United States has had a program of federal aid to education for more than a century-and-a-half. Because of this long history of federal interest in education, it may be safely assumed that the Federal Government may continue to make grants to public education in such a way that the rights of the states will not be seriously diminished in their exercise of the education function.

The opponents of expanded federal aid to education see this issue of states' rights in an entirely different light. To these persons, further federal aid is unquestionably an infringement since education is a state and not a federal function. Furthermore, they contend that such aid can only serve to weaken the local district, which is the very element in our systems of public education that needs strengthening most. This whole idea of going to Washington for "federal handouts," as these people call such aid, is symptomatic of a weakening of the integrity of the American people. The people in the states and local communities can and must solve their own educational problems. It is the local sacrifice and interest that has given America's schools their strength and made education the most unfettered public enterprise in the United States. It is a poor pattern of support for the states to send tax money to Washington where the federal bureaucracy uses part of it to sustain itself and sends the remainder back to

the states for schools.   A much better pattern, argue those opposed
to federal aid to education, would be to restore to the states some of
the taxing power usurped by the Federal Government.   With this
increased taxing power, the states could adequately take care of their
own educational problems.

Federal control

The issue of federal control of education is one with many facets
and many different interpretations.   For example, some individuals
and groups repeat the slogan of "federal aid without federal control,"
while others sincerely believe that such an arrangement is completely
impossible to achieve.   Some people subscribe to limited federal control of education.   Others use this as the principal argument against
any kind of extension of federal aid to education.

Those who favor some federal control of education believe that it
should be very limited.   They believe that it is quite improbable that
the Federal Government will ever again make educational grants over
which it has no control, and that it is simply not good administration
to make blanket appropriations without specific accounting.   These
people concur in the belief that federal aid should strengthen state
and local control, initiative, and efficiency in education.   All of this
can best be achieved, however, by setting up some well-established,
precisely defined standards that will improve education.   Because of
the obsolete and extravagant organizational structure, the low level
of professional preparation required of teachers, and other serious
shortcomings within many states, some persons have advocated a few
qualifying standards related to the minimum size of a school district,
the minimum amount of teacher preparation, and the maximum size
of classes.[19]   By such standards it is believed that federal aid can be
effectively used as a kind of lever to raise educational standards
throughout America rather than to perpetuate some of the inefficient
units and educational practices that currently exist.   One of the principal disadvantages of specifying such standards in a federal aid bill,
however, is that it seems to make its enactment much more difficult.

The people who advocate federal aid with no federal control believe that any centralized control may encourage educational progress during the initial stages of the program, but that such control
eventually means uniformity and stagnation.   They point out that
public education has already drifted toward some federal control and
that such a trend is dangerous and must be reversed.   They contend

[19] Willard B. Spalding, "Without National Standards Federal Aid Would Be
Wasted Effort," *Nation's Schools,* XLVI (July, 1950), 29–31.

that federal aid without federal control is possible because the Federal Government can make general purpose funds available to the various state departments of education. Such funds should be furnished with a very minimum of compliance features. A full reporting of the use of such funds should be made to the Federal Government as a matter of general public information as well as an adequate safeguard against state expenditures of such federal funds for anything outside the broad educational purposes for which they were made available. Such audits could also be useful to Congress in shaping its future policies.

Throughout the implementation and extension of any expanded federal aid to education program, extreme care must be exercised to see that the control of the public schools is not unintentionally shifted toward the Federal Government.

Support of nonpublic schools

Since about 90 per cent of nonpublic elementary and secondary school enrollments in America are under the jurisdiction of some church organization, this issue is really one of granting public funds to sectarian schools. To some people, such a practice represents a fundamental breach in the wall between church and state that was erected by the First Amendment to our Federal Constitution. Others take a completely different view of the problem. Each group can find support for its position in the seemingly contradictory court decisions of the various states and even in the decisions of the United States Supreme Court.

Those persons favoring federal aid for nonpublic schools justify their position by the "child-benefit theory." This theory holds that many of the services of the public schools, such as health inspections, welfare services, transportation, child accounting, recreation, guidance, etc., are really general community services. Because a child attends a nonpublic school is no legitimate reason why he should be deprived of these essential community services which, it is argued, are of a completely nonsectarian nature. In view of the fact that the nonpublic schools in the United States educate approximately one eighth of the American school children, and taking the stand that whatever public money is given for education in nonpublic schools is given for strictly nonsectarian services and supplies to the children and not to the school, it is thus argued that such federal aid provisions will in no way violate America's policy of separation of church and state.

Those who oppose any kind of federal aid for nonpublic schools believe that if the child benefit theory is carried to its logical conclusion, it will simply divert funds from public to nonpublic schools. Furthermore, since the fundamental purpose of the parochial school is to promote and strengthen the sponsoring church organization, to some people the giving of tax money to a church school is indistinguishable from giving tax money to the church itself and is therefore a violation of the Federal Constitution.

Since 1930, the strong and continuous pressure from the leadership of the nonpublic schools for federal support has been met with vigorous opposition by the National Education Association and other groups. The result has been that this thorny issue has constituted one of the principal blocks in the passage of an expanded federal aid to education bill.

Racial segregation

Another block to the passage of expanded federal aid to education bills has been the amendments made to require the states to provide school facilities open to all children, regardless of their racial characteristics. Such a provision is, of course, in conformity with the requirement of the most recent United States Supreme Court decisions which have ruled that segregated schools were unconstitutional.

The difficulty of such an amendment is that even though it may be professionally sound, it is not politically expedient since it aligns the southern states against the passage of a federal aid bill.

TOPICS FOR STUDY AND DISCUSSION

1. What are some of the benefits that might accrue if the Federal Government should adopt a foundation or minimum program for all of the United States? What might be some of the disadvantages?
2. If you were to advocate that federal aid should be given only to those districts that could meet certain minimum qualifications, what would be the nature of the specific standards you would recommend?
3. In what ways does the principle of support and control (see Chapter 3) have a bearing on the problem of federal aid?
4. Evaluate the Smith-Hughes program in your state. Give consideration to the main purpose of the law, its effect on other aspects of the school program, and its impact on the least wealthy districts.
5. Defend the contention that communities with only half as many children per 1,000 wage earners have not twice, but four times the ability as those states with twice as many children per 1,000 wage earners. Be specific in your arguments.
6. Per capita retail sales is sometimes cited as one of the manifestations

of the differences in education among the various states.[20] Which states or region do you think would stand out as being low on this measure? Can you defend such a measure? Explain.

SELECTED REFERENCES

CUBBERLEY, ELLWOOD P. *State School Administration.* New York: Houghton Mifflin Co., 1927.

GEIGLE, RALPH C. "Relative Efforts of the States to Support Public Education," *Elementary School Journal,* LII (December, 1951), 221–28.

HUTCHINS, CLAYTON D., ALBERT R. MUNSE, and EDNA D. BOOKER. *Federal Funds for Education* (U.S. Office of Education Bulletin No. 14), Washington, D.C.: Government Printing Office, 1954.

MOEHLMAN, ARTHUR B. *School Administration.* 2d ed. New York: Houghton Mifflin Co., 1951.

MORT, PAUL R. and WALTER C. REUSSER, *Public School Finance.* 2d ed. New York: McGraw-Hill Book Co., Inc., 1951.

National Education Association, Research Division, *Educational Differences Among the States.* Washington, D.C.: The Association, 1954.

National Education Association, Research Division, *The Facts on Federal Aid for Schools.* Washington, D.C.: The Association, 1949.

QUATTLEBAUM, CHARLES A. *Federal Education Activities and Educational Issues Before Congress.* Washington, D.C.: Government Printing Office, 1951.

U.S. Office of Education, *Statistics of State School Systems,* 1951–52. Washington, D.C.: Government Printing Office, 1955.

[20] National Education Association, *Educational Differences Among the States,* p. 28.

PART III

MANAGEMENT OF SCHOOL FUNDS

10

BUDGETARY PROCEDURES

THE NEED for a sound budgetary procedure for the public schools is no longer a debatable question. In the early history of the public schools, the salary paid the teacher was about the only money outlay required. The modern school, however, is different. There are numerous services and activities which must be financed and each merits its just portion of the dollar.

The school is a social institution and its financial support rests with the people. The purposes for which this money is spent and the controls exercised over the spending are affected by the wishes of the society. The more a society demands of its institution, the greater is the need for sound budgetary procedures.

I. DEVELOPMENT OF THE BUDGET

The word "budget" was derived from the old French word *bougette,* meaning bag, wallet, or pouch. In England the word "budget" was first applied to a wallet or box in which the Chancellor of the Exchequer kept his papers. By 1760 the word "budget" was commonly applied to the financial statement made by the Exchequer. The budget system has been used for a great number of years by the governments of England and Canada. The United States government, however, did not make use of the budget system until 1921, when Congress passed the law requiring a budget for the Federal Government. Charles G. Dawes, later a Vice-President, was appointed the first Director of the Budget by President Harding. Although the Federal Government did not make use of the budget until 1921, business and industrial concerns had used budgetary procedures for a number of years.

Development in the public schools

In 1922, Twente[1] made a comprehensive study of school budgetary procedures practiced in 363 cities. This study showed that the practices in these school systems were undeveloped and nonstandardized. In these cities the charters frequently provided for combining the city and school money into one single budget. This study also showed that there was little agreement among the several state laws concerning school budgetary procedures.

The first functional approach to scientific management of the school monies was made by Moehlman in 1925.[2] He set forth in detail the procedures to be followed in making a school budget for a large school system. Engelhardt and Engelhardt[3] outlined the various steps to be used in preparation and use of the budget.

DeYoung, in 1932, repeated the study made by Twente and sampled 813 cities scattered throughout the United States. He found that there had been some progress made during the ten years. There was more uniformity in state requirements and in practices followed by many of the cities.[4]

In 1949, Chase and Morphet[5] reported that in thirty-one states the school officials had the responsibility for the preparation and approval of school budgets except in certain types of districts in a few of the states. In eleven states the school budgets had to be submitted to some other local political body for approval of all items and the total amount. In five other states the local political body approved only the total amount of the budget; this meant that in sixteen states all the schools were fiscally dependent. In those places where the budget commission or the local budget approving agency had complete authority to change any item in the budget, there was likely to be conflict and confusion. In reality the budget approving agency would control the details of the school policy.

Although budgeting in the public schools is approximately thirty-five years old, the procedures have not become well established and

[1] John W. Twente, *Budgetary Procedures for a Local School System* (Montpelier, Vt.: Capital City Press, 1932).

[2] Arthur B. Moehlman, *Public School Finance* (Chicago: Rand McNally & Co., 1927).

[3] N. L. Engelhardt and Fred Engelhardt, *Public School Business Administration* (New York: Bureau of Publications, Teachers College, Columbia University, 1927), chap. 22.

[4] Chris A. DeYoung, *Budgetary Practices in Public School Administration* (Evanston, Ill.: Northwestern University Press, 1932).

[5] Frances S. Chase and Edgar Morphet, *The Forty-Eight State School Systems* (Chicago: Council of State Governments, 1949), pp. 154–56, 238.

are not considered essential by many administrators. Too many administrators are satisfied by filling out forms required by the state which show sources of income and items of expenditures. The functional approach—the budget being an expression in dollars and cents of the educational program—is a responsibility of the chief administrator and the board of education, and it should not be neglected.

2. THE BUDGET AS AN EDUCATIONAL INSTRUMENT

The budget defined

One of the early definitions of the budget was given in 1921 by Arthur E. Buck of the Bureau of Municipal Research. He stated: "The budget, in the strict sense of that term, is a complete financial plan for a definite period, which is based upon careful estimates both of the expenditure needs and the probable income of government."[6] Mr. Buck, in his book *Public Budgeting*, stressed the fact that the budget is "a plan of action for the future."[7] He pointed out that budgeting was more than filling in the forms and estimating receipts and expenditures. It involves policies, decisions, programs, and performance.

The present-day concept of the school budget is far more than a group of figures, graphs, tables, and charts which give the anticipated income and expenditures for a definite period of time. It is a complete story which tells of the cooperative effort in a community for providing an educational program which will improve community learning for all people. Such a story tells of the community's educational development over the years and projects the planning into the future. It points out those areas where improvement must be made to meet the ever changing social and economic conditions. The budget may be described as an over-all picture of the school as it is and what is desired by the people through cooperative planning.

Budgeting as a continuous process

Budget building is not a periodic activity. It is a continuous process from year to year. It is a process through which the school receives the greatest possible benefits as a result of educational planning over a long period of time. The laws governing the school systems in the several states require periodic budgets which are usually for one year. The periodic or annual budgets, however, are merely

6 Arthur E. Buck, *Budget Making* (New York: D. Appleton Co., 1921), p. 2.
7 Arthur E. Buck, *Public Budgeting* (New York: Harper & Bros., 1929), p. 4.

applications of the over-all continuous planning of the governmental body. The annual budget represents an actual legally expendable financial allowance over a fiscal year. The fiscal year is usually from July 1 through June 30. In some schools, however, the fiscal year corresponds to the calendar year. In general it may be said that the annual budget carries the educational program forward one year toward the long-range goal.

Functions of the budget

Although the budget itself is only an administrative instrument for controlling the financial outlay of the school district for a period of time, the process through which it is developed is an important function. It is a basis for democratic action on school problems pertaining to the whole community. Lay groups and professional workers have an opportunity to work together in planning and deciding upon the problems which must be solved. These groups can concentrate on broad policies and leave the details to the specialists. It is through these democratic procedures that the people gain an understanding of the requirements of the schools and a willingness to furnish the necessary financial support.

The budget projects the school program into the future. Only through this means can assurance be given that the schools will meet the ever changing needs of the whole community. Year-by-year steps may be taken to meet the projected programs.

The budget gives an overview of the total educational program. It is a means of giving the board of education, the administration, and the local citizens a view of the system as a whole. Each part of the educational program and its relationship to the total program may be seen. It is through this means that each part of the program will receive a just proportion of the finances. No one part of the school program should be sacrificed for another part. There may be times, however, when some phases of a total program cannot be carried forward as fast as may be desired because of limited finances. In such cases the citizens should have a voice in determining which should have priority.

Another important function of the budget is to improve the administration of the school system. The budget is based upon an accepted educational program and charts a course of action to be followed. Such procedure enables the forces to work as a unit with assurance of full cooperation from all concerned. The budget requires the administrator to have work plans for each department of the school, to foresee expenditures, to estimate receipts, to set up budgetary controls, to purchase economically, and to analyze and evaluate each part of the school program.

A well planned and administered budget not only improves the administration of the school system but also stimulates confidence among the taxpayers of the community. They can see that good business practices are being followed. A detailed expenditure forecast is a means of convincing the taxpayers that the board of education and the administrator are following good, accepted business practices.

The budget calendar

It has been pointed out that budgeting is a continuous process. The calendar of events is a means of setting up a guide for planning the year-round activities in connection with making the budget. The calendar should not be considered as an inflexible instrument but rather as a guide for planning, and it cannot be the same for all schools. It should show what things are to be done, who is to do them, and when they are to be done.

Figure 7 is an illustration which may be followed in making out a budgetary calendar. Such a plan should be worked out by the administrator in cooperation with the board of education and the administrator's co-workers.

Date to be done	Activity	To be performed by
September 20	Appointment of committee to consider curricular changes and new textbooks	Superintendent and administrative council
September 25	Report to Citizens Committee	Superintendent and member of the board
January 10	Requisitions from teachers	Principals
March 1	Report from the committees	Chairmen of committees
March 15	Presentation of tentative budget to citizens committee	Superintendent and selected board members
April 1	Annual meeting to approve budget by board	Superintendent
July 1	Beginning of new accounts	Business office

Fig. 7. Budgetary calendar. This is an illustration, not a complete calendar.

Cycle of operations

Because taxes are levied and governmental expenditures are usually approved each year, the budget document is made annually. This annual document must fit into the general pattern of continuous planning of the total educational program, just as nine months of school work fit into the total educational program of a child. Each year there are certain operations which must be completed for the development of the budget document. They are (1) preparation, (2) presentation and adoption, (3) administration, and (4) appraisal. These steps are known as the cycle of operations, and all are essential for the administration of a sound educational program.

3. PREPARATION OF THE BUDGET

Budget-making involves both legislative and executive functions. Certain policies must be adopted by the legislative body before the final budget document may be prepared by the executive officer. These policies should be the outgrowth of the thinking of lay citizens of the community and should include such factors as (1) tax rates to be levied, (2) major changes to be made in educational programs, and (3) the capital outlay program to be carried out.

The actual preparation of the budget, the executive function, should be executed in light of the policies and decisions made by the legislative body. There are threee major steps in the actual preparation of the budget: (1) developing an educational program to meet the demands and needs of the community, (2) translating the educational program into costs or expenditure estimates, and (3) recommending the means of financing the expenditures in light of the major financial policies set up by the citizens and the board of education. The parts of the budget may be compared to an equilateral triangle.

ACTION OR EDUCATIONAL
PROGRAM

Fig. 8. Parts of a school budget.

All three sides or parts must be equal or the triangle will fall apart. The same may be said of the budget. Figure 8 illustrates the parts of the budget.

The educational program, the base of the triangle, should be determined as the first step in making the budget. The second step is to determine the amount of money needed to carry out the educational program. The third step is to raise a sufficient amount of money to meet the expenditure needs. In actual practice, however, the income or revenue of a district is often set by the state constitution, laws, or other political bodies over which the school officials have no control. In this case the available money becomes the base line and the educational and expenditure programs must be cut to equal the finances. Too often (for the good of public education) this practice must be followed by school administrators.

The educational or action program

The educational program of the annual budget presents the action plan of work for the ensuing year and should not duplicate the work of other governmental or nongovernmental agencies of the community. This part of the budget is probably the most significant aspect since it charts the educational course of action for the ensuing twelve months, and it should fit into the long-range educational plans of the community.

The kind and extent of education to be provided is determined by answering such questions as:

1. What should be the purpose of education?
2. What are the special community needs to be met during the year?
3. What is the best type of school organization for the particular community?
4. What should be the upper and lower limits of free education in the community?
5. What should be the supervisory program?
6. What should be the inservice training program for teachers and other employees?
7. What should be the qualifications of the teachers?
8. What should be the salary schedule?
9. What should be the policy pertaining to financing co-curricular activities?
10. What should be the policy on furnishing books, supplies, and materials free to pupils?
11. What should be the teacher-pupil ratio?
12. What should be the kind of school plants constructed?

These and numerous other similar questions and problems should be answered by the parents, patrons, teachers, pupils, school board members, and administrators as the basis upon which the educational program is built. It must be said, however, that in planning the educational program the leadership should not get so involved in the details that the fundamental elements of curricula, services, personnel, and housing are neglected.

The fundamental issues concerning the educational program having been agreed upon, the next problem is to translate this program into costs or expenditures for the next fiscal year.

The expenditure plan

Translating the educational program into an expenditure plan is an important and difficult task. The extent to which the educational plans are realized depends upon the accuracy of estimating the actual costs for operating the total program for the ensuing fiscal year. The estimated expenditures must balance with the estimated income. There are so many factors which involve judgment in estimating future costs that every possible aid should be used by the administrator.

There are certain legal provisions which may affect the expenditures of a school district. These provisions may come from the city charters in cases of a city school, or from statutes, state constitutions, or federal regulations. The city charters contain statements relative to the control of the financing of the schools. It is not uncommon for the state statutes to set up certain standards such as minimum salaries, classifications or divisions of funds or how a certain fund may be used. The state constitution may limit the amount of tax rate that may be voted by the citizens of the district. For example, the constitution of North Carolina limits the amount of taxes that may be voted by the people for current expenses to an amount not to exceed fifty cents on the one hundred dollars valuation. There are certain regulations which control the amount of money a school district may receive through vocational aid. Therefore, the administrator must study carefully all regulations, state and local, which may affect the expenditures and amount of money available.

There are two methods used widely by administrators in translating educational specifications into expenditures—the detailed analysis method and the lump-sum method. The former is used by those administrators who actually try to make the budget a sound educational instrument. The latter is used by those administrators who have not considered the importance of the budget in the operation of a school program.

Accurate estimation of expenditures is accomplished through a detailed analysis of past costs and present needs of the school. An important guide for the analysis of costs is found in the records or accounts for the past several years. A good accounting system will reveal the cost of services, materials, and equipment by function, character, and location. These data will reveal trends and enable one to project fairly accurate costs for the future. The lump-sum method of estimating expenditures fails to reconcile educational needs with expenditures. In other words, it is a method of guessing at the future costs and may or may not be accurate. Morrison brings out the point that such a method places the responsibility for the results upon the administrator.[8]

Where there is a wide latitude in the amount of possible revenue which may be secured by a vote of the people or by the legislative body, administrators have found it desirable to present minimum and desirable needs. Each staff member makes requests on two levels, the *minimum* and the *desirable*. The minimum is interpreted to mean the actual needs for maintaining the department, and the desirable includes everything which would be needed for improvement beyond the minimum. These minimum and desirable requirements are translated into minimum and desirable expenditures in the preliminary budget. This method would require two columns for estimated expenditures, one for the minimum and one for the desirable. It is thought that such a method will encourage the legislative body to make added improvements in the total educational program. It at least gives the members of the legislative body a chance to make choices for an extended educational program beyond the bare minimum.

Collecting data for expenditure estimates. Administrators have found it valuable to have a budget file, consisting of a few manila folders, in which they place information pertaining to the budget gathered during the year.[9] This file may contain information on costs, budget changes, insurance premiums due, requests made by individuals, and any other information which may be needed in the actual process of estimating expenditures. Such a method helps to insure a more complete budget and also helps to make more accurate estimates.

The use of a standard list of supplies and equipment is also an aid

[8] H. C. Morrison, *The Management of School Money* (Chicago: University of Chicago Press, 1932), p. 509.
[9] DeYoung, *op. cit.,* p. 61

in estimating expenditures.[10]   This standard list should not be static nor so standardized that new materials and equipment cannot be secured.   Such a list will be of great value in determining unit costs and may be used for a request form from individual teachers, departments, and schools.

An accurate record of purchases by items is an aid not only for making a standard list of supplies and equipment but also for estimating future expenditures.   Figure 9 shows such a record, which may be kept in a visible index file.   This record may be keyed to the purchase order file, which would show the departments or schools using the item.

Date	Purchase Order	Quantity	Purchased from	Unit Price	Total

Description of item_____

Name of item _____ No._____

Fig. 9. Item purchase card.

Classifying the Expenditures.   There is a definite need of classifying all expenditures according to the accounting forms used by the school system.   The character classifications of expenditures for schools have been fairly well standardized throughout the country.[11]   They are as follows:

1. Administration (general control)
2. Instruction
3. Auxiliary Services
4. Operation of Plant
5. Maintenance of Plant

[10] See Chapter 20 for a sample of a supply list.

[11] See *Financial Accounting for Public Schools*, Circular 204, rev. August, 1948 (Washington, D.C.: Office of Education, Federal Security Administration, 1948), pp. 16–34.

6. Fixed Charges
7. Capital Outlay
8. Debt Service

Each of these may be subdivided into several different divisions as will be shown in this chapter under the format of the budget. The divisions under the character headings depend largely on the legal requirements of the state, the use of the accounts, and the size of the school system.

Some administrators also divide the expenditure side of the budget into classifications based upon the school organization—elementary, junior high, and senior high school. Others may divide the expenditures according to buildings. This latter division is especially valuable for estimating cost of operation and maintenance. The division of expenditures will depend to a great extent upon the size of the school system. In general, however, the character classifications are the major divisions of the expenditures.

Work Procedure for Organizing Material. The administrator will save time in preparing the budget if he plans some organization for recording the estimated expenditures as he collects his data. This form may differ somewhat from the final budget. It has been found very satisfactory to make large work sheets such as the one shown in Figure 10 for recording the historical data pertaining to the budget.

Character Classification	Actual Expenditures			Current Budget	Requests	
	1950–51	1951–52	1952–53		Minimum	Desirable
1. Administration						
a. Board of Education Secretary's Office						
b. School Census						
c. Etc.						
Total						

Fig. 10. Sample work sheet for collecting budget data.

This form, when completed in all of the character classifications, will be a rough draft of the expenditures. No doubt the administrator will need numerous other supplementary forms for assembling these data. The historical data of expenditures for the past three years enable the administrator to make comparisons. Wherever great variations in the historical data, the current budget, and requests for the next year are noted, detailed explanations should be made.

A well-proportioned expenditure plan. The expenditures should be well proportioned—that is, each part of the school system should receive its just share of the money according to its needs. Although there cannot be any standard percentage for each part of the budget, it is a good practice to make some comparisons. The United States Office of Education publishes every two years a bulletin entitled *Statistics of State School Systems,* which gives percentages of money spent in each character classification by the size of the city. Some school officials use the Research Division of the National Education Association for securing such data. In any event, a comparison of the local school with similar schools will give an indication whether the amount of money spent in each character classification is in line with what is spent in other schools.

The following table shows how such a comparison may be made.

TABLE 9.   A comparison of the local school expenditures with expenditures of twenty cities similar in size

Character Classification	Per Cent of Money Budgeted in	
	Other Cities	Local School System
Current Expense	88.3	86.6
1. Administration	3.1	4.6
2. Instruction	72.2	70.4
3. Auxiliary Service	4.2	7.1
4. Operation of Plant	12.3	13.2
5. Maintenance of Plant	5.1	3.4
6. Fixed Charges	3.1	1.3
Total Current Expense	100.0	100.0
Debt Service	8.3	9.3
Capital Outlay	3.4	4.1
Total Costs	100.0	100.0

It is also well to make comparisons with previous years. If there are marked differences of percentages between years in certain character classifications, an explanation should be made. For example, the percentage for maintenance cost may be unusually high one year because of extensive repairs, or the percentage for capital outlay may be high because of a new building that is to be constructed. In making a comparison with other schools or for past years, consideration must be given to the local situation at the present time. That the percentage is higher in one character classification and lower in another is no indication that the local budget is not well proportioned. It does, however, give a point of departure for studying the whole problem. If the percentages compare favorably with those of other schools, it is an indication that the amount of money being spent in each character classification is fairly well proportioned.

Allowance for Contingencies. Setting up contingent allowances in the school budget is a much debated question. Some people feel that contingencies lead to extravagance and others feel that contingencies are necessary. In reality, a large contingent allowance is out of harmony with the philosophy of budgetary procedure. If expenditure estimates are carefully planned, contingencies are not so essential. It may be well to set aside a small amount of money and label it an "emergency fund" and use this fund only upon the approval of the board of education. This procedure will eliminate extravagance and at the same time provide money for the unforeseen.

Some school officials operate in the belief that certain items of the budget should be padded. There are two apparent reasons for such practice—first, that the person or persons who finally approve the budget will always cut it a certain amount and second, that a padded budget is more easily administered because a balance for contingencies will be assured. Such a practice not only defeats the purpose of the budget but also is dishonest. If an administrator follows the practice of padding the budget, he may expect the approving agent and the lay citizens to find it out within due time and lose respect for the school officials. The administrator should make an honest attempt to prepare an accurate estimate of expenditures and let it be known that services will be curtailed if the budget is cut. Honesty will win out in the long run.

Transfer of unexpended balances from one character classification to another, if permitted by law, should be made only by the board of education. In some states the laws do not permit transfers, especially debt service. The executive officer should be given authority to transfer small unexpended balances within the same character classification of expenditure. Good budgetary procedures, however, will eliminate the necessity for most transfers.

The financial plan

The third part of the budget is the financial plan. In some places this part of the budget must be considered first because too often the income for a school district is a set amount. It is a better technique, however, for the budget maker to develop the educational program and then to determine the amount of money needed to carry out the program. If it is then found that the needed revenue cannot be secured, a decision can be made on which services can best be delayed or curtailed.

Sources of revenue for the support of public education vary greatly from state to state. In general, however, the school receipts are derived from federal, state, county, and local sources. In most schools the amount of money coming from the Federal Government is relatively small. The method and amount of appropriations of state money will vary from state to state. In some few states over 75 per cent of the money needed to operate the local school will come from the state; in others, less than 20 per cent will come from this source. In general it may be said that a very small percentage, less than 7 per cent, of money for the support of public education comes from the county government. It is only in those states which operate some form of a county unit that the county plays an important role in financing public education. The county funds are greater than the local funds in only seven states. In a vast majority of the states over 40 per cent of the money for financing public education comes from the local unit of administration. This local money is derived to a great extent from the general property tax.

In most cases the amount of money received from the Federal Government and the state can be estimated fairly accurately each fiscal year. The money derived from local sources cannot be estimated so easily. No "rule-of-thumb" can be adopted in estimating receipts. The procedures are somewhat like those for preparing estimates of expenditures.

A study of previous receipts by years and sources is essential for the budget maker if he is to make an accurate estimate for the future. Figure 11 is designed to show the percentages of receipts by sources for the past several years. Such information will give some trends which will be helpful in estimating future receipts.

Since a high percentage of school receipts is derived from property taxes, a careful study should be made of the assessed valuation of property, tax rates, and collections. Figures 12, 13, and 14 give information concerning valuation of property, tax rates, and collections. These are suggestions for the budget maker. He should design those forms which will tell the best story of the tax structure and which will give the most help in predicting future income of the school district. Too much emphasis cannot be placed upon estimating future receipts. If actual receipts do not coincide fairly closely with the estimated receipts, there will be a tendency for board members and citizens to feel that the budget maker's techniques are not sound, and consequently they are apt to lose faith in the administration.

Fig. 11. Amount and per cent of receipts by source for the past five years.

Date _____

Year	Total Receipts	Sources									
		Federal		State		County		Local			
								Taxes		Other	
		Amt.	Per cent	Amt.	Per cent	Amt.	Per cent	Amt.	Per cent	Amt.	Per cent
195_											
195_											
195_											
195_											
195_											
Estimate For 195_											

Year	Assessed Valuation			Total Enrollment*	Amount of Valuation Back of Each Pupil
	Personal	Real	Total		
195_					
195_					
195_					
195_					
195_					
Estimated for 195_**					

* Either enrollment, membership or average daily attendance may be used.

** These may have to be estimated if the tax record books are not complete at the time the budget is made. In that case it may be well to carry the historical data for 10 to 15 years.

Fig. 12. Total assessed valuation of property and amount of valuation back of each pupil.

The information given in Figure 12 may be shown effectively by the graph in Figure 13.

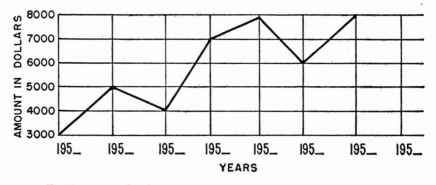

Fig. 13. Assessed valuation of property back of each child, by years.

Figure 14 gives a method of showing the relationship of tax rates used for schools and other purposes by years.

Years	Total	Rate in mills or cents				Per cent for Schools
		State	County	City	Schools	
195						
195						
195						
195						

Fig. 14. Property tax rates for all governmental agencies.

Figure 15 is designed to show the percentage of taxes collected each year for school purposes. It may be well to make a more detailed analysis of back taxes collected than is given in this form. A careful

Year	Total Assessed Valuation	Rate	Total Amount Assessed*	Amount Collected			
				Current	%	Back Taxes	%
195_							
195_							
195_							
195_							
Estimated For 195_							

*Total amount assessed equals Rate times Assessed Valuation.

Fig. 15. Assessed valuation of property and taxes collected.

study of taxes collected is essential in projecting local receipts, since this source is such a large per cent of the school funds. The economic conditions of the country have great effect on payment of taxes.

After having compiled the necessary historical data relative to income, the administrator should show the over-all picture of the income such as is illustrated in Figure 16. This form will enable members of the board of education and the local citizens to make certain comparisons before the budget is adopted. It is to be noted that the items under each source will vary according to state laws and local conditions. For example, if the school does not operate a lunch program under Federal Government auspices, this item of receipts would not be included. It is thought that at least three years of estimated and actual receipts should be given in order to show the trends. Probably five years would be much better than three.

Classification of Receipts. To link the budget with the accounting system used by the school system, the receipts should be classified as to source and destination.[12] The source classification refers to the political subdivision which distributed the money, namely, federal, state, county, or local. Fund classification refers to the legal divisions of the school accounts. The names of these funds will vary from state to state. It is essential not only to show the sources of the money but also to show the amount to be appropriated for each fund.

Balancing the Budget. One of the purposes of a budget is to see that no more money is spent than is available. It is almost impossible to balance exactly the expenditure and the revenue plans because judgment, prediction, and certain other variables, such as changing prices, continue to be present after the budget has been adopted.[13] There does need to be effort made, however, to keep the expenditures slightly less than the anticipated income. The fiscal year for many schools ends June 30, and often money for the new year does not come to the treasurer for some months. In many cases local taxes are not collected and turned over to the schools until toward the end of the calendar year. Therefore, a cash balance is almost necessary at the end of each fiscal year. If there appears to be a decrease in income, expenditures must be reduced. If the school follows the practice of carrying over a cash balance at the end of each fiscal year, a slight deficit may be absorbed by reducing the cash balance. In general, however, schools must operate upon the theory and practice of a balanced budget.

4. THE BUDGET FORMAT

The format of the budget depends to a great extent upon the group to whom it is to be presented and also upon the size of the administrative unit. If only a small group of people are to review the budget, it may be typed. If a great number of people are to review the

---

[12] See Chapter 11 for a detailed explanation of accounting for receipts.
[13] Arvid J. Burke, *Financing Public Schools in the United States* (New York: Harper & Bros., 1951), p. 438.

Fig. 16. Estimated and actual tax receipts by source.

Sources	Amount Received by Years						
	195- & 195-		195- & 195-		195- & 195-		195- & 195-
	Estimated	Actual	Estimated	Actual	Estimated	Actual	Estimated
1. Federal							
a. Voc Aid							
b. Lunch Program							
c.							
Total							
2. State							
a.							
b.							
c.							
Total							
3. County							
a.							
b.							
Total							
4. Local							
a. Current Taxes							
b. Back Taxes							
c.							
d.							
Total							
Grand Total							

budget, then it should be mimeographed or printed. Smaller school systems will likely have to rely upon mimeographing because of the cost involved in printing.

The general make-up of the budget should be attractive and neat. It should be written in simple language. The use of technical or professional terms should be avoided. A good quality paper, good workmanship, and ample illustrations will add to the appearance of the document. If the budget is printed, selected pictures of the school system will be very beneficial for a more complete understanding by the lay people. The same form, pictures, and illustrations should not be used year after year. In other words, the budget should be something new each year and should be so attractive that people will be eager to study it.

Approximately three-fourths of the states provide by law certain prescribed forms to be used for reporting the anticipated receipts and expenditures to approving bodies. These forms should be used for reporting to the proper authorities. However, they are not ample for presenting the budget to the board of education and the citizens of the community. A more complete budget is necessary.

Outline of contents

No two budgets will be alike. Therefore, it cannot be said that any one budget is right. The outline of a budget is presented and perhaps it will give some notion of the specific contents.

I. Table of Contents
II. Letter of Transmittal
III. The Educational Program
    A. Functions or purposes
    B. The organization of the school system
    C. The supervisory program
    D. The teaching staff
        1. Qualifications
        2. Experience and tenure
        3. Salary schedule
    E. The curricula, including changes proposed
    F. The nonteaching employees
    G. The pupils—enrollment, drop-outs, etc.
    H. Teacher-pupil ratio
    I. Supplies and equipment, including libraries, shops, etc.
    J. Activities
    K. Others

IV. Estimating Expenditures
    A. Detailed estimate of each character classification of the budget
    B. Supporting data for detailed estimates
    C. Summary of estimates
V. Estimating Income
    A. Analysis of all income
       1. Federal
       2. State
       3. County
       4. Local
          a. Valuation of property
          b. Per cent of taxes collected
          c. Assessed valuation back of each child
          d. Comparative study on tax rates
    B. Summary of receipts
VI. Comparison of Estimated Expenditures and Receipts
VII. The Long-range Educational Program for the Schools
VIII. Conclusions

5. PRESENTATION AND ADOPTION

The budget must be adopted by the proper approving agents. In some schools the board of education is the approving agent. In other schools there may be two or three approving agents such as the city council, board of education, and state board of education; and in still other schools there may be public hearings before the final adoption of the budget. In most cases the approving authorities are stipulated in the state laws. However, in some cases the approving authorities are named in the charters of the cities.

Time for presentation and adoption

The budget should be presented and adopted well in advance of the beginning of the new fiscal school year. The legislative body should be kept well informed on major problems while the budget is being prepared; then there will not be great changes at the adoption time. Advance notice should be given the board when the budget is to be adopted, and each member of the board should be supplied with the complete budget well in advance of the date so that he may have time for study. At the time for the adoption the administrator or designated officer should make an oral presentation of the whole budget. If the budget has been well prepared and clearly presented, its chances for adoption will be greatly enhanced. If the budget has to be presented to other bodies than the school board, a definite calendar should be prepared and the presentations made at the required time.

The resolution by which the budget is adopted should be carefully stated and recorded in the minutes of the approving authority. It is a good plan to make the adopted budget a part of the minutes. The tax levying authority should be notified of the levy to be made on all property. All other persons concerned with the budget should be notified of the board's final approval.

Publicizing the budget

Ample publicity should be given the budget. This may be done through the newspapers, public hearings, addresses, and special publications. This publicity should precede the formal adoption of the budget, and after it has been adopted the citizens should be told of the outcome. Publicity for the budget is necessary because the schools belong to the people, and it is the people who provide the money. A well-informed public will tend to reduce criticism of the school system. Although the amount of money being spent on public education is small in comparison to other governmental costs, there are many people who question the efficiency of the schools.

6. ADMINISTRATION OF THE BUDGET

After the budget has been adopted the next step is its administration. Unless the budget is followed as closely as possible, there is little reason for making it. The budget is a financial plan to guide the administrator or a member of his staff in the spending of money for the fiscal year.

Transferring budget to accounting forms

The budget should be transferred from the minutes of the board of education to the accounting records. These accounting records will be different in the schools of the several states. Basically there are two types of bookkeeping forms; one type utilizes the columnar distribution of receipts and expenditures, and the other consists of regular standard bookkeeping forms.[14] The columnar system is usually a uniform system required or suggested by the state and follows the pattern set up by the National Advisory Committee on School Records and Reports.[15] There are also an increasing number of

[14] See Chapter 11 for a description of the columnar system.
[15] United States Office of Education, *Financial Accounting for Public Schools,* Circular 204, rev. August, 1948 (Washington, D.C.: Federal Security Agency, 1948).

schools which are using machine accounting. Whatever form of accounting system is used, provisions should be made to call the administrator's attention to the original authorization and to the unencumbered balance in each account.

There are a number of reasons why the budget should be transferred to the accounting system. Among the reasons are[16] (1) making the historical record complete, (2) authorizing the expenditures, (3) controlling the expenditures, (4) encumbering the funds, (5) facilitating ready references, (6) preparing the periodic reports, and (7) aiding in auditing the accounts.

Accounting records and working methods are valuable to budgetary control, but they are secondary to good management. The administrator must be ever alert to see that the intent of the budget is followed. The budget is a *thing* and is no better than the administration. It takes good administration to make plans and then put those plans into operation. Judgment is necessary at all times, and the administrator must use it in the administration of the budget.

7. APPRAISAL OF THE BUDGET

The appraisal of the budget is the last step in the cycle of operation. It is one of those important steps which is often overlooked. It is through the appraisal that the board of education and administrator are able to know if the budget is really functioning in the administration of the school system. It is only through an honest appraisal that improvements will be made in the budgetary system.

How appraisals are made

There are a number of devices which may be used to appraise the effectiveness of the budget system. Operational and postaudits described in Chapter 14 can do much to bring about improvements in the budget. Regular reports to the board of education showing actual receipts and expenditures in comparison with estimated receipts and expenditures will enable the controlling body to pass judgment upon the degree of accuracy of the budget. These reports will also serve as a good medium for keeping the board informed on the administration of the budget.[17]

Appraisal forms[18] are often used by administrators for evaluating the effectiveness of the budget. These forms, however, are rather

---

[16] DeYoung, *op. cit.*, pp. 324–25.
[17] See Chapter 12 for suggestions for such reports.
[18] See DeYoung, *op. cit.*, chap. XIV.

difficult to use because of the great variation in the form and content of the school budget in different communities. A form designed for a particular school would have *some* value, especially if it is used over a period of years.

Probably the best method to use in the appraisal of the budget is to study it day by day throughout the entire school year. Through accurate accounting and reporting, one may see some of the weaknesses and make the necessary changes the next year. The budget will improve and will aid the educational program in proportion to the degree that the administration plans, administers, and evaluates the current document. No budget can be better than the administrator chooses to make it. Whether it is a servant to the educational program depends upon the administrator. The budget is an instrument to aid the educational program and should be considered as such at all times. At no time should the budget be an end product; but it should be a means to an end, that is, a better educational program for the whole community.

TOPICS FOR STUDY AND DISCUSSION

1. Why did budgetary procedures progress more rapidly in business than in governmental groups?
2. Why are school administrators slow in following good budgetary practices?
3. Work out a budget calendar for your school.
4. Who should help develop the budget? Take an actual situation and list persons or groups who should assist in developing the budget.
5. Make an outline showing what you would include in the educational program of a budget. Why is this part of the budget often neglected?
6. What are the laws of your state relative to budgetary procedures for schools?
7. How would you determine whether your budget is well proportioned?
8. What are some of the limiting factors in regard to financing schools in your district?
9. What are the sources of revenue for your school?
10. Select several budgets and compare the tables of contents. What conclusions can you draw?
11. Examine several budgets and make a list of topics which would make suitable newspaper stories.
12. What are the purposes of budget hearings? Would you advise such a hearing if it is not required by law? Why?

SELECTED REFERENCES

American Association of School Administrators. *School Boards in Action,* Twenty-fourth Yearbook. Washington, D.C.: National Education Association, 1946, pp. 153–55.

BOLMEIER, EDWARD C. "Variations in Control over City School Budgets," *American School Board Journal,* CXIII (September, 1946), 23–25.

BUCK, A. E. *Public Budgeting.* New York: Harper & Bros., 1929.

BURKE, ARVID J. *Financing Public Schools in United States.* New York: Harper & Bros., 1951, chap. XVI.

DEYOUNG, CHRIS A. *Budgeting in Public Schools.* New York: Odyssey Press, Inc., 1936.

GROSE, C. HERMAN. "The Educational Plan of the School Budget," *American School Board Journal,* CVIII (February, 1944), 23–24.

MORT, PAUL R., and WALTER C. REUSSER. *Public School Finance.* 2d ed. New York: McGraw-Hill Book Co., Inc., 1951, chap. XIX.

National Education Association. "Fiscal Authority of City Schoolboards," *Research Bulletin,* XXVIII (April, 1950), 56–59.

PITTENGER, BENJAMIN FLOYD. *Local Public School Administration.* New York: McGraw-Hill Book Co., Inc., 1951, chap. XXV.

11

FINANCIAL ACCOUNTING

IT CANNOT be said that a school system is good because it has acceptable business practices, but it may be said it is not the best without them. A school is not operated as a business enterprise to show a financial profit, but it is operated to show an educational profit. This profit of the school is measured in terms of effective educational services rendered to the children and adults of the community. Without sound general accounting, accurate cost accounting, auditing, budgeting, and financial reporting, the school cannot operate in an effective and efficient manner and it will not render the best possible services.

I. FUNCTIONS OF ACCOUNTING IN A SCHOOL SYSTEM

The general function of financial accounting in a school system is to help carry out the purposes of the school. To be specific, the functions are (1) helping to develop the educational program, (2) meeting the legal requirement as to expenditures of funds, (3) giving data for cost studies, and (4) furnishing the necessary information for budget building and reporting. All of these functions are essential for a superintendent to administer a sound educational program.

Developing the educational program

In a commercial enterprise the purpose of accounting is to furnish the management with those financial facts essential to efficient and intelligent administration. Likewise, in a public school system the administration must be supplied financial facts because educational problems have their financial implications. Whether it is the type of

198

school organization, curricula, qualifications of teachers, or any other educational plans, the problem of costs will be a determining factor. Only a very limited number of school systems are able to design an educational program of any kind without considering the element of cost. Whether it is a school for a small district or a school system for a city of more than a million people, accounting of school money is essential for developing an educational program and a financial plan for its implementation.

Legal requirements

The board of education and the administrator operate a school system under the law of the state. *Fund* accounting is usually required by the state laws. Certain revenues are restricted as to use, and the accounting system must show that all provisions of the laws have been complied with. For example, the authors are acquainted with one state that has a special fund known as the *Free Textbook Fund.* The state derives the money for this fund from taxes on foreign (out of state) insurance companies which write insurance in the state. This money is appropriated to the several districts, and each district is required to spend this money according to the state law. Therefore a separate account—receipts and expenditures—must be kept for this fund. Some states will have as many as five or six different *funds;* others will have only two.

Some city schools have certain restrictions imposed upon them by local municipal authorities which are as stringent as the state laws. The administrator must be acquainted with the state laws and local regulations and keep accounting records which will fulfill these requirements.

Cost studies

If an administrator is to act intelligently in developing new policies or in modifying old ones, he must know costs within his own systems; and he must also be able to compare costs in similar schools.[1] Cost accounting is a means of stating the expenditures in terms of work done or services rendered. Although it cannot be worked out as objectively in education as in the industrial world, it can be used to a considerable advantage in measuring the educational performance of any school system. In the computation of costs identical units must be used. The accounting system used must give accurate data for working out cost studies.

[1] Harry P. Smith, *Business Administration of Public Schools* (Yonkers-on-Hudson, N.Y.: World Book Co., 1929), p. 144.

Budgeting and reporting

Probably no other function of general accounting is more important than that of furnishing information for budgeting and reporting. The data used for building a budget estimate for the ensuing year must be based upon the experience of the past year. This experience will be shown through the accounting records. The success of the school system is largely the result of sound budgetary practices. Securing the finances for a proposed budget depends to a great extent upon the reports of the school system to the board of education and to the citizens of the community. Budgeting and reporting are so closely tied to each other that it is hard to separate the two. Each depends upon the other and both are essential for the development of an educational program which will give maximum service. A complete discussion of the budget is given in Chapter 10 and of reporting in Chapter 13.

2. CHARACTERISTICS OF A GOOD ACCOUNTING SYSTEM

Record keeping is a problem that deserves careful consideration whether it is for the individual, for private enterprise, or for a public institution. In a public institution such as a school system there are laws and rules and regulations of state and local boards which must be considered in setting up a system of financial accounting. The characteristics of a good financial accounting system are similar to those of any system of records.

Adequacy

Financial records must be complete in every respect. They should serve all the ordinary business purposes that are obtained from bookkeeping. The records should be so designed that the responsible person will be protected from carelessness. The accounting system should make possible a comparison of receipts, expenditures, and costs of the local school system with other schools. The necessary information for making reports to the local board, the state department, and the United States Office of Education should be easily obtained from the accounting records.

Availability

All information desired from the financial records should be easily securable for the efficient administration of the school system. Information which cannot be secured when desired is of little value.

The records must provide for proper distribution, posting, balances, and cumulative summaries.

Simplicity

Financial records should be simple and easily kept up-to-date but complete enough to tell the whole financial story. A minimum number of separate forms should be used, and provisions should be made for collecting only those data which are usable. The forms used in the financial accounting should be easily obtained and simple enough for the average office clerks to use with a minimum amount of assistance from the business manager.

Uniformity

The accounting system should be uniform throughout the state, and the state system should be similar to that recommended by the U.S. Office of Education. The classifications, nomenclature, and definitions should follow those practices accepted in the field of school accounting. The same classification should be used year after year to facilitate cost studies.

Permanency

An accounting system should be designed so that the records may be kept over a period of years. Most state laws require financial records to be on file for two to five years. If the records are bulky, they will be hard to store in a fireproof vault. Every possible effort should be taken to preserve records for the historical values.

3. THE ACCOUNTING SYSTEM

The financial accounting system should provide for an accurate record of all receipts and expenditures. There is no one system used by all schools throughout the country. Each state should have a system designed to meet the particular needs of the state and at the same time be uniform in certain aspects with the systems used throughout the country. Figure 17 shows in a chart form the records which are needed to meet the legal requirements of a state and also meet the uniformity requirements of all systems.

Coding accounts

Classification of receipts or expenditures is a relative matter and may be divided into any number of divisions. The main purpose of a classification is to facilitate accounting practices. In making a classi-

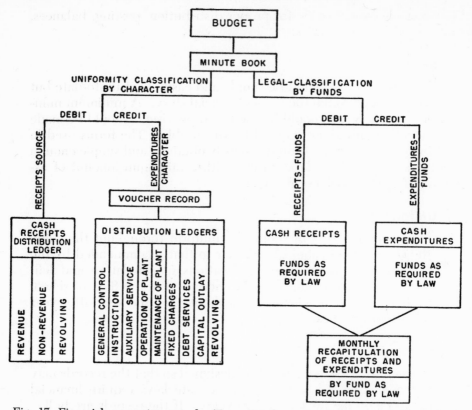

Fig. 17. Financial accounting records. (From Grieder and Rosenstengel, *Public School Administration* [New York: The Ronald Press Co., 1954], p. 456.)

fication division of either receipts or expenditures, the classifier must take care not to divide them into parts which will have little significance. When the classifications are once made, the divisions should be followed over a period of years. The use of codes will aid accounting procedures and cost accounting. Each state usually has its own code system. Some of the codes suggested are alphabetic, others numerical, and still others a combination of both. There is a code system which was worked out by a committee of the National Education Association and the National Association of School Business Officials which is used in a number of states. There are, however, many variations in the several states. The extent to which a code system is used will depend largely upon the size of the school system and the degree of breakdown desired by the administration. It may be said that the system of codes adopted or used in the state accounting system should be used by the local system.

As an example, the Iowa State Department of Education[3] designed a system for coding receipts and expenditures to meet the needs of the state. Although the system of coding is not much different from those used in other states, it does meet the needs of fund accounting set by law in the state. The codes for receipts are:

GENERAL FUND

1000–1399   Revenue receipts
1400–1479   Nonrevenue receipts

SPECIAL COURSES FUND

1480–1499   Revenue receipts

SCHOOLHOUSE FUND

1500–1599   Revenue receipts
1600–1699   Nonrevenue receipts

Ample opportunity is given for additional numbers to be used for the several sources of money in each fund.[4] For example, district taxes would be a revenue receipt for the general fund and would be coded 1010, and premium on original bonds would be a nonrevenue receipt for the schoolhouse fund and would be coded 1605.

The coding of expenditures is similar.[5] The following gives the main *character* classification of expenditures with some of the subdivisions and the codes:

CODE   CHARACTER CLASSIFICATION

100–199   GENERAL CONTROL ADMINISTRATION (Paid from general fund)

100–124	Administration salaries
100	Salary of superintendent
105	Salaries of superintendent's assistants
125–149	Administration office supplies
125	General office expenses
135	Census
150–159	Legal and consultation services
150	Auditing
155	Legal advice
160–179	Travel expense
160	Board of education
165	Secretary
170	Superintendent
180–199	Other costs

[3] *Uniform Financial Accounting for Iowa School Districts*, Research Bulletin No. 15, April, 1954 (Des Moines, Iowa: Department of Public Instruction, 1954).

[4] See section 4 which follows for the sources of money classified as revenue and nonrevenue receipts.

[5] See section 5 of this chapter for the divisions of character classifications.

200–299 INSTRUCTION (Paid from general fund)
    200–219 Salaries of high school personnel
        200   Salaries of principals
        210   Salaries of teachers[6]
    220–244 Clerical and professional services
        220   Salaries of clerical help
        240   Professional library
    245–259 Instructional supplies
        245   Art
        246   Audio-visual aids
    260–264 Textbooks and supplementary readers
    265–269 Library books and supplies
    270–289 Supplementary instructional activities
    290–299 Other costs

300–399 AUXILIARY SERVICES (Paid from general fund)
    300–329 Transportation
        300   Salaries
        305   Supplies
    330–349 School lunch
        330   Salaries
        335   Food
    350–359 Health services
        350   Salaries
        355   Supplies
    360–369 Community services
        360   Salaries for adult education
        362   Other expenses of adult education
        363   Public library
        365   Playground
    370–379 Revolving account
    380–399 Other costs

400–499 OPERATION OF PLANT (Paid from general fund)
    400–409 Salaries
        405   Custodians
    410–439 Supplies
    440–459 Utilities
    460–499 Other services

500–599 MAINTENANCE OF PLANT (Paid from general fund)
    500–519 Buildings and grounds
        500   Labor
        505   Materials
    520–569 Service plants
        520   Labor for repair to heating plant

[6] If the expenditure is for junior high school personnel, J follows the number and if the expenditure is for elementary school personnel, E follows the number.

525   Material for repair to heating plant
570–589 Furniture and equipment
  570   Labor
  575   Material
590–599 Miscellaneous costs

600–699 FIXED CHARGES (Paid from general fund)

 600–604 Insurance premiums
 605–629 Rent
 630–659 Assessments
 660–699 Other costs

700–799 CAPITAL OUTLAY (Paid from general fund)

 700–719 Additions
  700   Equipment
  705   Furniture
 720–769 Alterations
  720   Labor
  725   Materials
 770–799 Other costs

800–839 DEBT SERVICE (Paid from general fund)

  800   Interest short time loans
  805   Judgment bonds
  810   Others
 840–899 Transfers to schoolhouse fund

900–959 CAPITAL OUTLAY (Paid from schoolhouse fund)

 900–909 Sites
 910–914 Buildings
 915–944 New service systems
 949–959 Alterations

960–999 DEBT SERVICE (Paid from schoolhouse fund)

 960–969 Payment on bonds
 970–979 Interest on bonds
 980–989 Other debt service
 990–999 Transfer to general fund

The codes and classifications are about the same as will be found in many other state systems except that the provisions for payment of short term debts which have not been voted by the people and the payment of certain capital outlay accounts are paid from the general funds.

4. CLASSIFICATION OF RECEIPTS

School receipts come from many sources, such as local property taxes, state appropriations, federal grants, bonds, sale of property, tuition, etc. Receipts are classified as to funds and source.

Fund accounting

The state law will determine the fund classification. Fund classification means that certain receipts are restricted in use and must be accounted for as stipulated by law. For example, some states provide for a *General Fund* and a *Building Fund*. All money received by the local district for operating the school system for the current year is placed in the general fund, and all money received for plant maintenance and construction will be placed in the building fund. In North Carolina the law provides for three funds, *Current Expense, Debt Service*, and *Capital Outlay*. These three funds coincide in name with the three major classifications of expenditures. Some states have as many as six funds. The Missouri law stipulates that certain money must be placed in either *Teachers, Incidentals, Free Textbooks, Interest, Sinking*, or *Current Building* fund. It seems unnecessary to have over two or three funds. Certainly six different funds are entirely too many. The greater the number of funds, the more complicated is the accounting system.

In those states which have fund accounting the laws require that both receipts and expenditures be allocated by funds, and transfers usually cannot be made except as stipulated by law. The states which use fund accounting require state reports which must be made out in light of the different funds. Figure 18 shows a cash register, receipts and expenditures, which may be used for fund accounting. It is to be noted that Columns 7 and 8 on the receipt side of the ledger and Columns 6 and 7 on the disbursement side are for the different funds. There must be as many different columns as there are funds. The form presented in Figure 18 and the other forms presented for accounting of receipts and expenditures are suggested by the National Advisory Committee on School Records of the United States Office of Education, Circular 204, revised August, 1948.

In those districts which use the treasurer system this cash register may be kept by the treasurer. In any event the receipts should be recorded regularly as received by the school system. The recording of disbursements may be done at regular intervals. Some schools have followed the practice of using a different colored check for each fund. For example, if there are three funds, there would be three different colored checks. This procedure will facilitate recording. The cash register should be balanced monthly.

Source classification of receipts

To secure uniformity in reporting through the county and state to the U.S. Office of Education, the receipts should be classified as to

Receipt Register—Year Ending June 30, 19—

Date	FROM WHOM	FOR	Their Number	Receipt Number	Total Amount	FUNDS	
						Name Fund 7	Name Fund 8
1	2	3	4	5	6	7	8
		Amount Brought Forward					

Disbursements Register—Year Ending June 30, 19—

Date Paid	Warrant or Check No.	Date of Warrant or Check	TO WHOM ISSUED	BANK WHERE PAID	AMOUNT PAID—FUNDS		
					Name Fund 6	Name Fund 7	8
1	2	3	4	5	6	7	8
				Amount Brought Forward			

Fig. 18. Cash book for fund accounting.

source.   Classification as to source has become fairly well standardized throughout the country.   Grouping receipts in such manner
facilitates an analysis of amounts each year and provides a convenient
basis for comparison over a period of years and with those of other
school systems.

The classifications of cash receipts as to source are (1) *revenue,* (2)
nonrevenue, and (3) *revolving fund.*

Revenue receipts are those which do not result in increasing the
school indebtedness or in decreasing the school property, and the
sources are the following:

1. Appropriations and subventions from federal and state government for special or general aid
2. Money raised from local (county, township, district, or city) taxation for current expense, capital outlay, or debt service
3. Income from permanent school funds
4. Interest on deposits or short loans
5. Tuition
6. Gifts
7. Fines and penalties
8. Rents
9. Fees
10. Net receipts from revolving funds

Nonrevenue receipts are those which result in an obligation of the
district for future payment and may or may not decrease the assets.
The sources are as follows:

1. Receipts from sale of bonds
2. Premiums on bonds
3. Temporary loans
4. Sale of property (not material which has been purchased for resale)
5. Insurance adjustments
6. Refunds

Revolving fund receipts are gross receipts which the board of education receives when it acts as an agent.   If the board of education
spends money for cafeteria supplies and then serves lunch, the gross
proceeds are known as revolving fund receipts.   The revolving fund
receipts also include money received from the sale of all types of supplies, books, etc.   It is to be noted that the gross amount from the
sale of an article is a revolving fund receipt.   The net profit from
the sale is entered in the account book as a revenue receipt.   Figure
19 shows a cash receipt ledger.   This ledger has provisions for two
different funds.   If there are more than two or three fund accounts

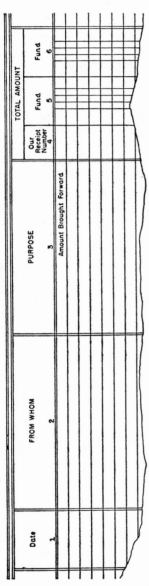

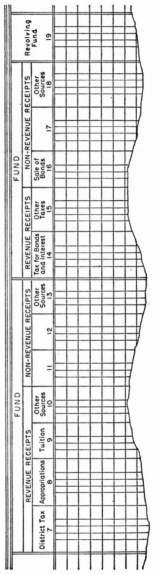

Fig. 19. Cash receipts ledger as to source.

required by law, it will be impossible to combine the *fund* accounts and *source* accounts into one cash ledger. In that event both cash receipt ledgers as shown in Figures 18 and 19 should be used. The number of divisions under revenue (Columns 7, 8, 9, and 10) and under nonrevenue (Columns 11, 12, and 13) may be increased. This will depend upon the local or state form.

5. CLASSIFICATION OF EXPENDITURES

It is necessary to make a proper classification of all items of expenditure if a true and accurate financial record is to be of significant value to the administrator. Where fund accounting is required by law, all expenditures must be classified as to fund and recorded in the disbursement register of the cash receipts register as shown in Figure 19.

There are several methods of classifying expenditures. The most widely used is the functional or character classification. Some schools will also use the object and location classifications. The size of school and the use of the records will determine the different classifications. The basic classification, however, is *function* or *character*. This classification is recognized by the U.S. Office of Education, and all its reports are based on this breakdown of expenditures. The general plan for *character, object,* and *location* classifications is as follows:

Character Classification
    I. Current Expense
        A. General Control (Administration)
        B. Instruction
        C. Auxiliary Services
           1. School Services
           2. Transportation
           3. Community Services
        D. Operation of Plant
        E. Maintenance of Plant
        F. Fixed Charges
   II. Capital Outlay
  III. Debt Service

Object Classification
        1. Audits
        2. Board of Education
        3. Clerical Work
        4. Drayage
        5. Heating
        6. Legal
        7. Repairs

8. Supplies
9. Telephone
10. Textbooks

This list may be as broad as a school system may desire. An agreement should be reached as to the breakdown which is desired, and some code system should be used to designate the objects.

Location Classification. The location classification is usually broken down as to individual schools within the system. A code system is assigned each school. If the administration desires a breakdown different from that of individual schools, the classification may be by divisions, such as elementary, secondary, vocational, kindergarten, night school, or any other convenient division.

Encumbrance of funds

Good budgetary procedure demands that all funds be encumbered at the time purchases or contracts for services are made. The encumbrance record is designed to assist the administrator in controlling commitments so that the several accounts will not be overdrawn. Unless such a record is kept, it is conceivable that there might not be sufficient money to operate the schools for the whole year. For each item of the budget there should be an encumbrance record sheet such as that in Figure 20.

As contracts are signed or purchase orders are made, the amount is recorded on the encumbrance record under the column "amount encumbered" and added to the previous "balance outstanding." When payments are made, the amount is recorded under the column "amount paid" and is subtracted from the "balance outstanding." The balance outstanding is in effect the amount which must be reserved to pay bills due. The sum of all balances outstanding at any one time will be the amount the school system owes.

Voucher or warrant register

The voucher register is the book of original entry in the accounting of expenditures. After invoices are approved for payment and the voucher-check, check, or warrant has been prepared with the different classifications coded, the items are then entered in the voucher register. This register is arranged so that the character classifications can be easily entered. The current expenses are separated from debt services, capital outlay, and revolving funds. Figure 21 shows a voucher or warrant register.

ENCUMBRANCE RECORD

Year_____   School _____   Fund_____

Account Title_____   Code Number_____

	Date	Refer- ence	Explanation	Amount		Balance Out- standing
				Encum- bered	Paid	
	1955					
1	July 1	P.O. 9	Book Supply Co.	60|00		60|00
2	July 6	P.O. 11	Ronald Press Co.	100|00		160|00
3	July 10	v. 1	Book Supply Co.		60|00	100|00
4	July 15	v. 2	Ronald Press Co.		100|00	0|

Fig. 20. The encumbrance record.

Distribution ledgers

The distribution ledgers are directly related to the voucher register. Each distribution ledger is a breakdown of a major character classification. Although the subdivisions of each major character classification vary among the several states, there is a tendency to make them more uniform. The distribution ledgers presented herein are those which have been recommended by the U.S. Office of Education in the publication *Financial Accounting,* Circular 204, revised August, 1948.

General Control (Administration). Those expenditures entered under general control in the voucher register are recorded in a general control distribution ledger. The subdivision for this distribution ledger should include at least the following:

> Board of education and secretary's office
> > Salaries
> > Supplies
> > Other expenses (This may be subdivided by use of codes.)
> General and educational administration
> > Salaries
> > > Administrative
> > > Clerical

Voucher Register

Date Entered	In Favor of	Voucher No.	Fund	Code	WHEN AND HOW PAID		Grand Total	DISTRIBUTION OF CURRENT EXPENSE							Debt Service	Capital Outlay	Revolving
					Date	Ck.-W. No.		Total Current Expense	General Control	Instruction	Auxiliary Services	Operation	Maintenance	Fixed Charges			
July 1	BUDGET ESTIMATE																
																	1
																	2
																	3
																	4

Fig. 21. Voucher or warrant register.

213

Supplies
Other expenses
Business administration
Salaries
    Administrative
    Clerical
Supplies
Other expenses

Figure 22 shows the distribution ledger used for general control.

Instruction. The distribution ledger designed for instruction deals primarily with expenses incurred relative to the actual classroom teaching. The items which are recorded under instruction in the voucher register are recorded in this distribution ledger and should include at least the following subdivisions:

Salaries
    Supervisors
    Principals
    Teachers
    Other instructional staff such as counselors
    Clerical
Textbooks
Teaching supplies used by staff and pupils
    Agriculture
    English
    Home-making
    Industrial arts
    Science
    etc.
Other expenses of instruction

Figure 23 shows the distribution ledger for instruction.

Auxiliary Services. The distribution ledger (recommended for use) for auxiliary services includes those subdivisions which formerly were divided into two different registers, auxiliary agencies and co-ordinate activities. This one ledger, auxiliary services, has three main divisions as shown in the following outline:

A. School services
    Medical (salaries, supplies, and contractual services)
    Dental (salaries, supplies, and contractual services)
    Nurse (salaries, supplies, and contractual services)
    Welfare work (salaries and supplies)
    Extracurricular activities
    Lunchroom deficits

DISTRIBUTION LEDGER

General Control (Administration)

Date	To Whom, For What, or Voucher Number	Code	Total	Board of Education and Secretary's Office				General and Educational Administration				Business Administration			
				Salaries		Supplies	Other Expense	Salaries		Supplies	Other Expense	Salaries		Supplies	Other Expenses
				Administrative	Clerical			Administrative	Clerical			Administrative	Clerical		
	Code Number														
	Budget Appropriation														

Fig. 22. General control distribution ledger.

Instruction

Date	To Whom, For What, or Voucher Number	Code	Total	Salaries					Textbooks	Teaching	Other Expenses of Instruction
				Supervisors	Principals	Instructional Staff		Clerical Assistants			
						Teachers	Other Instructional Staff				
	Code Number										
	Budget Appropriation										

Fig. 23. Instruction distribution ledger.

B. Transportation
  Publicly owned and/or contracted
    Administration (salaries and supplies)
    Operation (salaries and supplies)
    Maintenance (salaries, supplies, and contractual services)
  Contractual services
  Payment to parents in lieu of transportation
  Insurance on equipment and employees
C. Community services
  Public libraries (salaries and supplies)
  Public recreation (salaries and supplies)
  Community center (salaries and supplies)
  Services to private or parochial schools
  Custodial costs in residential schools

Figure 24 shows the distribution ledger for auxiliary services.

Operation of Plant. All items of expenditures necessary for keeping the physical plant open and ready for use are charged to this character classification. Care must be taken to exclude from this classification those items belonging to maintenance and capital outlay. The items included in this ledger are as follows:

Salaries and wages of engineers and custodians
Supplies for engineers and custodians
Fuel
Power and light
Water
Telephone
Freight, drayage, and express
Laundry
Care of grounds, walks, trees, shrubs, flowers, etc.

Figure 25 shows the distribution ledger for the operation of plant.

Maintenance of Plant. Expenditures for the upkeep or restoration of any part of the physical plant, either through repairs or replacements, are charged to the maintenance of plant. Care must be taken to exclude those items belonging to operation of plant or capital outlay. Costs of maintenance of plants include grounds, building, and equipment.

Grounds
  Salaries
  Supplies
  Contractual services
Buildings and mechanical services
  Salaries

AUXILIARY SERVICES

A – School Services

B – Transportation

C – Community Services

Fig. 24. Auxiliary services distribution ledger.

217

Operation of Plant

Date	To Whom, For What, or Voucher Number	Code	Total	Salaries and Wages	Engineers' and Janitors' Supplies	Fuel	Light and Power	Water	Other Expenses of Operation
	Code Number								
	Budget Appropriation								

Fig. 25. Operation of plant distribution ledger.

Repairs and Replacements (Maintenance) of Plant

Date	To Whom, For What, or Voucher Number	Code	Total	Grounds		Buildings and Mechanical Equipment			Educational Equipment and Furniture			Other
				Salaries	Supplies and Expenses	Contractual Services	Salaries	Supplies and Expenses	Contractual Services	Salaries	Supplies and Expenses	Contractual Services	
	Code Number											
	Budget Appropriation											

Fig. 26. Maintenance of plant distribution ledger.

218

Supplies
Contractual services
Educational equipment, including furniture
  Salaries
  Supplies
  Contractual services

Figure 26 shows the distribution ledger for the maintenance of plant.

Fixed Charges. Those items of expenditure which are rather stable and recurrent, such as insurance, sickness allowance, retirement, and rent, are charged to fixed charges. If an insurance premium is evenly divided each year, the whole amount is charged to this account. However, if it is paid only once every three or five years, one year's cost is charged to fixed charges and the remainder to capital outlay as a prepaid charge. The amount deducted from a teacher's salary for retirement and then paid to the retirement system is charged to instruction and not to this account. The amount which the board pays to match the teacher's contribution is charged to fixed charges. The following gives the major subdivisions of fixed charges:

Insurance
Judgments
Sickness allowance or excess payment to substitute teacher
Retirement
Rent
Payment to other school systems, such as tuition
Refunds

Figure 27 shows the distribution ledger for fixed charges.

Capital Outlay. Capital outlay expenditures include anything except supplies, which results in an increase of the assets of the school. This expenditure must result in an increased asset and not a replacement. Purchase of items of equipment for resale to students is not charged to capital outlay. The major charges to this account are the following:

Sites and improvement of sites
New buildings
Additions to buildings
Alterations to buildings
Equipment
  Library books
  Furniture
  Laboratory equipment

Fixed Charges

Date	To Whom, For What, or Voucher Number	Code	Total	May Be Allocated to Pupil Costs						Should Not Be Allocated to Pupil Costs		
				Insurance Premiums	Judgments (or Payment in Lieu of court decision)	Sickness Allowances (or Excess Payments to Substitute Teachers)	Payments to Teacher or Civil Service Retirement Funds	Rent	Other	Transfers to Other School Systems for Tuition, etc.	Refunds	Other
	Code Number											
	Budget Appropriation											

Fig. 27. Fixed charges distribution ledger.

Capital Outlays

Date	To Whom, For What, or Voucher Number	Code	Total	Sites and Improvement of Sites	New Buildings	Additions to Buildings	Alterations to Buildings	School Library Books	Equipment	
									Furniture, Laboratory Equipment and Fixtures	Busses and Other Transportation Equipment
	Code Number									
	Budget Appropriation									

Fig. 28. Capital outlay distribution ledger.

220

Typewriters
Buses and other transportation equipment

Figure 28 shows the distribution ledger for capital outlay.

Debt Services. All payments to reduce outstanding indebtedness are charged to this account. The major subdivisions are the following:

Retirement of
    Short-term loans
    Warrants or bills of previous year
    Bonds
Payment of interest on
    Short-term loans
    Warrants
    Bonds
Payment to sinking fund for bond retirement, if such plan is used

Figure 29 shows the debt service distribution ledger.

Prorating items of expenditures

Certain items of expenditure will cut across several character and/ or location classifications. For example, the general administrative offices of a small city school system are located in a building housing elementary children and the custodians may take care of the whole building. It would not be correct to charge the total cost of custodial services to the elementary school. Such expenses may be prorated on the basis of per cent of floor space used by each division. A similar problem relative to heat may be involved, and the cost may be prorated on the basis of per cent of cubic feet of space in each division. Such problems should be anticipated, and the method used for prorating costs should be agreed upon by the administration and followed so that accurate cost accounting may be made. The use of codes will be valuable in prorating expenditures.

6. MONTHLY RECAPITULATION OF RECEIPTS AND EXPENDITURES

The accounting system should provide for an accurate and simple monthly statement of each fund which is required by the state law. Such a record is known as the recapitulation of receipts and expenditures. Figure 30 shows such a form. This form may be designed to

Debt Service From Current Funds

Date	To Whom, For What, or Voucher Number	Code	Total	Retirement of:			Interest Payment in:			Payments to Sinking Funds For Bond Retirement
				Short-Term Loans	Warrants or Bills of Previous Year	Bonds	Short-Term Loans	Warrants	Bonds	
	Code Number									
	Budget Appropriation									

Fig. 29. Debt service distribution ledger.

FUND

Year and Month 1	Balance in treasury at beginning of month 2	Received during month 3	Total receipts and balance for month 4	Expended during month 5	Balance in treasury at close of month
JULY	$250.00	$152.89	$402.89	$200.50	$202.39
AUGUST	202.39				
SEPTEMBER					
OCTOBER					
NOVEMBER					
DECEMBER					
JANUARY					
FEBRUARY					
MARCH					
APRIL					
MAY					
JUNE					

RECONCILEMENT OF BALANCES
BALANCE OF THIS RECORD WITH TREASURER
JUNE 30, 19__

1. Balance as shown by this book.......... $ _____
2. Outstanding checks or drafts unpaid...... $ _____
3.   Total of lines 1 and 2.............. $ _____
4. Treasurer's balance per bank certificate.. $ _____

Sign _____
Note: Person reconciling account should sign above.

FUND

Year and Month 1	Balance in treasury at beginning of month 2	Received during month 3	Total receipts and balance for month 4	Expended during month 5	Balance in treasury at close of month 6
JULY	$3,150.00	$453.11	$3,603.11	$200.00	$3,403.11
AUGUST	3,403.11				
SEPTEMBER					
OCTOBER					
NOVEMBER					
DECEMBER					
JANUARY					
FEBRUARY					
MARCH					
APRIL					
MAY					
JUNE					

RECONCILEMENT OF BALANCES
BALANCE OF THIS RECORD WITH TREASURER
JUNE 30, 19__

1. Balance as shown by this book.......... $ _____
2. Outstanding checks or drafts unpaid...... $ _____
3.   Total of lines 1 and 2.............. $ _____
4. Treasurer's balance per bank certificate.. $ _____

Sign _____
Note: Person reconciling account should sign above.

Fig. 30. Monthly recapitulation of receipts and expenditures.

MANAGEMENT OF SCHOOL FUNDS

fit into the regular accounting book. Provisions may be made for any number of funds. It is to be noted that provisions are made for reconciliation of balances at the close of the year.

7. THE GENERAL LEDGER

The use of the cash books, voucher register, and distribution ledgers is most desirable for budgetary control. There is, however, a need to have a general summary account, especially when large sums of money are involved, to give the administration a quick overview of the financial status of certain major accounts. This may be accomplished through the use of the general ledger account. The number of general ledger accounts will depend altogether upon the local needs. They may be kept according to the different funds or to any other division of the accounting system. The following shows an illustration of a general ledger account set up for current expense used as a general fund.

General Ledger Account-General Fund

Date	Item	Folio	Debit		Credit	
July 1	Estimated receipts	J.V.1	$600,000	00		
July 20	Received from state	C.B.1			$200,000	00
July 31	To balance		400,000	00		
Aug. 1	New estimate of receipts		$400,000	00		

Fig. 31. General ledger account for a particular account or general fund.

It is to be noted that the illustration shows how this account is closed and a new balance is obtained. This account shows a summary and can be used for comparison over a period of time.

8. MACHINE ACCOUNTING

The traditional equipment for school accounting has consisted of books and forms. These books and forms have been hand posted. Today, some accounting machines are very desirable, even in the small schools if the quality of the business services are to rise to the level of instructional services. In the larger schools a number of different machines are used. One of the least expensive machines that can be used advantageously in schools with fifty or more teachers is the pegboard type which permits written forms and carbons to be superimposed and locked in perfect register. This device is adapted to the preparation of two, three, or more forms simultaneously. It is especially useful in payroll and account payable procedures (see Figure 39, Chapter 12).

An example of a more expensive type of equipment is the National's new "142" payroll and distribution machine which prints five records in one operation. This machine has a tax computer which automatically indicates withholding taxes, social security, state taxes, or other variable deductions based on a percentage of gross earnings. The pay check, pay statement, employee's earning record, payroll journal, and check register are all created in a single operation. Gross and net pay are automatically computed, and up-to-date balances for earnings and withholdings are figured and printed on each employee's record. The depression of a single key causes instant, simultaneous printing on five records, all of which appear in original print.

Companies such as the Burrough Adding Machine Company, National Cash Register Company, or Remington Rand, Inc. will design forms and machines to meet the needs of a school system. The forms can be designed to furnish the same information that has been given in this chapter. There are, however, certain general considerations that should help determine whether a school should acquire accounting equipment beyond the typewriter, adding machine, and the calculator. They are:

1. The size of the administrative unit
2. The original cost of the machines
3. The number of automatic features of the machine
4. The number of the existing operations that can be performed by the machine
5. Number of records now used and number desired for future use should be carefully studied and reduced to the minimum
6. Simplicity of the machine or the ease of training personnel to use the machine
7. Service facilities of the vendor for the machine
8. Service facilities of the vendor in preparation of forms
9. Saving of time of the office personnel
10. Reduction of time needed to perform basic operations such as paying employees

The cost of the equipment is determined by the number of automatic features; therefore, those operations which have infrequent use or which can be eliminated should be considered. The total situation should be analyzed before purchasing the machines and forms designed to do the essential operations. Except in the largest school systems, the purchase of individual machines for specific jobs may lead to the waste of funds. Only by multiple use of machines can maximum economy be assured.

TOPICS FOR STUDY AND DISCUSSION

1. Why should a school system maintain an accounting system, since it does not operate for profit?
2. How can an accounting system help develop the educational program?
3. Should the characteristics of an accounting system be similar to those of any good record system? Why?
4. What are the different funds required by law in your state?
5. What are the sources of income for your school system?
6. What codes are used for the different character classification in your state?
7. Secure a copy of the accounting system used in your state and compare the cash books with those given in this book. What difference do you find? Why?
8. Make a list of schools in your district, and then make a code for each to be used in coding expenditures as to location.
9. Indicate in the space preceding each of the following items in Column A the number indicating the proper classification as shown in Column B.

Column A	Code	Column B
—— 1. Premium for fire insurance	100	General Control
—— 2. Load of coal	200	Instruction
—— 3. Beakers for science	300	Auxiliary Services
—— 4. Expense for Board of Education	400	Operation of Plant
—— 5. New handsaw	500	Maintenance of Plant
—— 6. Principal's salary	600	Fixed Charges
—— 7. Interest on bonds	700	Capital Outlay
—— 8. Salary for mowing lawn	800	Debt Service
—— 9. Grass seed		
—— 10. New grate for furnace		
—— 11. New school bus		
—— 12. Rent		
—— 13. Refund to student for tuition		
—— 14. Library books		
—— 15. New desk for superintendent		

10. What general ledger accounts should the bookkeeper for your school keep?

SELECTED REFERENCES

American Association of School Administrators. *School Boards in Action.* Twenty-fourth Yearbook. Washington, D.C.: The Association, 1946, chap. VI.

ENGELHARDT, FRED and FRED VON BORGERSRODE. *Accounting Procedures for School Systems.* New York: Bureau of Publications, Teachers College, Columbia University, 1927, chaps. III–IV.

FOSTER, EMERY M. (ed.). *Financial Accounting for Public Schools.* U.S. Office of Education, Federal Security Agency, Circular 204, rev. 1948. Washington, D.C.: Government Printing Office, 1948.

GRIEDER, CALVIN and WILLIAM E. ROSENSTENGEL. *Public School Administration.* New York: The Ronald Press Company, 1954, chap. XX.

MORT, PAUL R. and WALTER C. REUSSER. *Public School Finance,* 2d ed. New York: McGraw-Hill Book Co., Inc., 1951, chap. XII.

12

PAYROLL ACCOUNTING

ORDINARILY ONE might think that the office practice in regard to payroll accounting in the public schools would be a simple, "cut-and-dried" process since most salaries are contracted in advance. This is not the case, however, since the procedure used in the average school system is the product of custom rather than the result of scientific study. It is the purpose of this chapter to point out certain procedures and recommended practices which should be of value in developing a sound system of payroll accounting.

I. FUNCTIONS OF PAYROLL ACCOUNTING

Payroll accounting like all other phases of business administration of public schools does not have an end in itself. It is a means to the end. It is one of those activities of the business department which is essential for carrying out the best possible educational program for the children of the community. Developing and maintaining good morale among the professional and nonprofessional employees is essential for a good school system. If the morale among the employed personnel is to be the best, the employees must receive their pay on time and have a feeling that their personal records are adequate, accurate, and up to date. To meet these conditions the payroll division[1] has a definite function to perform.

Another function of the payroll division is prudent management of all funds to be used for the payment of employees. The division is responsible through the administration to the board of education

---

[1] A payroll division is a person or a group of persons responsible for the work done in connection with paying employees. In a small school system the division may have only one secretary while in a large system there may be ten, twenty, or more persons.

228

and indirectly to the citizens of the community for the proper accounting of all funds. There must be not only honesty but also accuracy in handling of funds.

A third function of the payroll division is to serve as a tax collecting agency. The withholding federal tax law makes it mandatory for the school system to deduct a certain per cent of each employee's pay. Proper accounting of such taxes must be made. The federal law also requires the administrator to report at the close of the calendar year the amount paid to and taxes withheld from each employee. Those states which have retirement systems also require the local boards to deduct certain amounts each month and transmit these deductions to the proper officials. Other deductions such as group insurance, and hospitalization are often made at the request of employees. Prudent care and management of the deductions place additional responsibility upon the payroll division.

2. PRINCIPLES OF PAYROLL ACCOUNTING

Payroll accounting in a school system is the one single business aspect of school administration which deals with the greatest per cent of the school's revenue. Approximately 80 per cent of the current expense dollar goes for payment of salaries. Even in a small administrative unit there are a number of employees of the board of education who must be paid regularly, and a system of payment cannot be neglected. In the larger school systems there will be hundreds of employees who must be paid monthly or semimonthly and a definite plan or procedure must be followed to insure prompt and accurate payments. Regardless of the size of the school unit, there are some fundamental principles of payroll accounting which should be followed.

Principles or policies adopted by the board of education

There are some over-all principles of payroll accounting which should be recognized by the board of education and made a part of the rules and regulations. Among these are:

1. The adoption of a salary schedule which clearly states the classification of the employee, the date regular salary increments are granted, and the absences allowed with and without pay. The board of education may have a need for making changes in the salary schedule from time to time. However, these changes should be made known to all employees and made a part of the rules and regulations.
2. The adoption of a plan for handling substitutes, with pay scheduled for each class of worker.

3. The adoption of a plan for granting vacations, especially to those persons who are employed for twelve months.

4. The establishment of pay dates for all classes of employees. Paying different groups of employees on different dates makes it easier for the payroll division to get out the pay since the work is scattered throughout the month. If the pay date should fall on a holiday, the checks should be delivered to the employees the preceding day. In some administrative units teachers are paid on very irregular dates. The laws of the state will often stipulate that teachers will be paid at the end of each school month which is twenty teaching days. The authors have known many teachers who have gone as many as six to eight weeks without receiving pay checks. Often the fourth month of school will begin sometime during the first week of December, and the schools will be dismissed for Christmas vacation before twenty days have been taught, and the teachers will not be paid until sometime in January. If for some reason the school should fail to open immediately following the holidays, the teachers will not receive pay until late in the month of January. There does not seem to be any justification for such laws and practices. However, many systems pay the teachers on the first of each month and some pay twice a month. The nonteaching personnel are usually paid at the first of each month, but sometimes they are paid twice a month. Boards of education and administrators should establish regular pay dates and pay on those regular dates. Employees will then know how to plan their personal affairs.

5. The adoption of a plan of employing teachers and nonteaching personnel to be paid on a nine-month, ten-month, twelve-month, or some other basis. Whatever the plan may be, the employees should be informed of it. Many schools follow the practice of employing nonteaching personnel for twelve months' work and pay, and teachers for nine months' work and pay. It is becoming more common today to employ teachers for nine months' work and spread the pay over twelve months. Again the state laws must be taken into consideration before a definite plan is established. It would seem that teachers would have better morale if they received pay twelve months each year. Certainly record keeping and payroll practices would be simplified if all employees were paid on the calendar twelve months' plan.

6. The authorization of a proper person to notify the payroll division of all additions, transfers, preparations, or other changes pertaining to the employees. Responsibility must be placed in some one person because this is the basis of all legal payroll payments. In a small system this person may be the superintendent of schools and in a large system it may be the superintendent or an assistant superintendent in charge of personnel.

7. The adoption of a plan for making deductions from individuals' pay other than those deductions required by state or federal laws.

In many cases, today, teachers and other groups wish to take advantage of hospitalization, insurance, or other payroll deduction plans. Therefore a definite plan should be formulated and approved or adopted by the board of education so that the payroll division will be able to make the necessary deductions and to pay the proper person or company. Even though deductions require extra work for the payroll division, the convenience of the employees should be considered.

Principles set by the payroll division

There are some fundamental principles of payroll accounting that should be recognized by the payroll division. Whatever payroll system is planned, it must satisfy the school system for which it is designed. There are certain local conditions which will have a direct bearing upon the payroll system. The size of the administrative unit and the availability of equipment are two controlling factors. A small administrative unit, which has few employees, will probably not need nor be able to provide the machines which will be necessary in the large schools.

The system should be flexible so that changes may be made with the least possible effort. A few years ago very few deductions besides those for absences were necessary. Today, however, there will be some three, four, or more deductions made from an employee's pay check, and the number of deductions will not always be the same for all employees.

The system should be simple both from the standpoint of understanding and operation. Secretarial assistants change rather rapidly in these days when positions are easily secured. Therefore, the system must be such that one with a minimum experience will be able to do the work. Care must be taken so that adequacy is not sacrificed for simplicity.

The system must provide adequate information for the administration. Certain reports are required of each school system, and the information collected by the payroll division must be adequate to furnish the necessary information. Since salaries are by far the largest single item of expenditures, it is most desirable to give a true functional distribution which will aid the administrator for budgetary purposes.

The system must meet certain standards of uniformity. Today the necessity for keeping records for a long period of time requires certain uniformity for filing purposes. The system should be such that a clear and complete picture of all financial transactions pertaining to each employee, and all employees or a group, will be understood many years hence by persons who may be interested in certain information.

The system must meet the legal requirement. Each state has specific legal requirements pertaining to records, reports, and so forth. The payroll division has the responsibility for designing a system that will meet these requirements.

The system should be centralized. The work of payroll making should be done as much as possible in the central office. Principals and other administrative officers should be relieved of such work with the exception of reporting personnel absences and substitute services. These reports should be simple but complete.

3. PAYROLL PROCEDURES

The main objective of the payroll division is to execute the contractual agreement relative to pay, made by the board of education with each individual employee. This objective implies that accurate payments on the date agreed upon will be made and it also implies that there will be funds available when needed. Such an objective requires careful planning. It means that there are certain operations that must be executed on time and that definite procedures must be followed by all concerned.

Payroll regulations

In light of the general policies adopted by the board of education and those set by the payroll division, a set of regulations governing payroll procedures should be developed. These regulations or procedures should be mimeographed and a copy placed in the hands of each administrative officer who has been delegated a payroll responsibility.

Authorization of persons on payrolls

It was pointed out in section 2 that the board of education should adopt a policy which would designate one person to authorize the additions, transfers, and separations of employees. When a change is made in the payroll the authorized person should notify in writing the payroll department and the administrative officer responsible for keeping the record of attendance. This notification should be

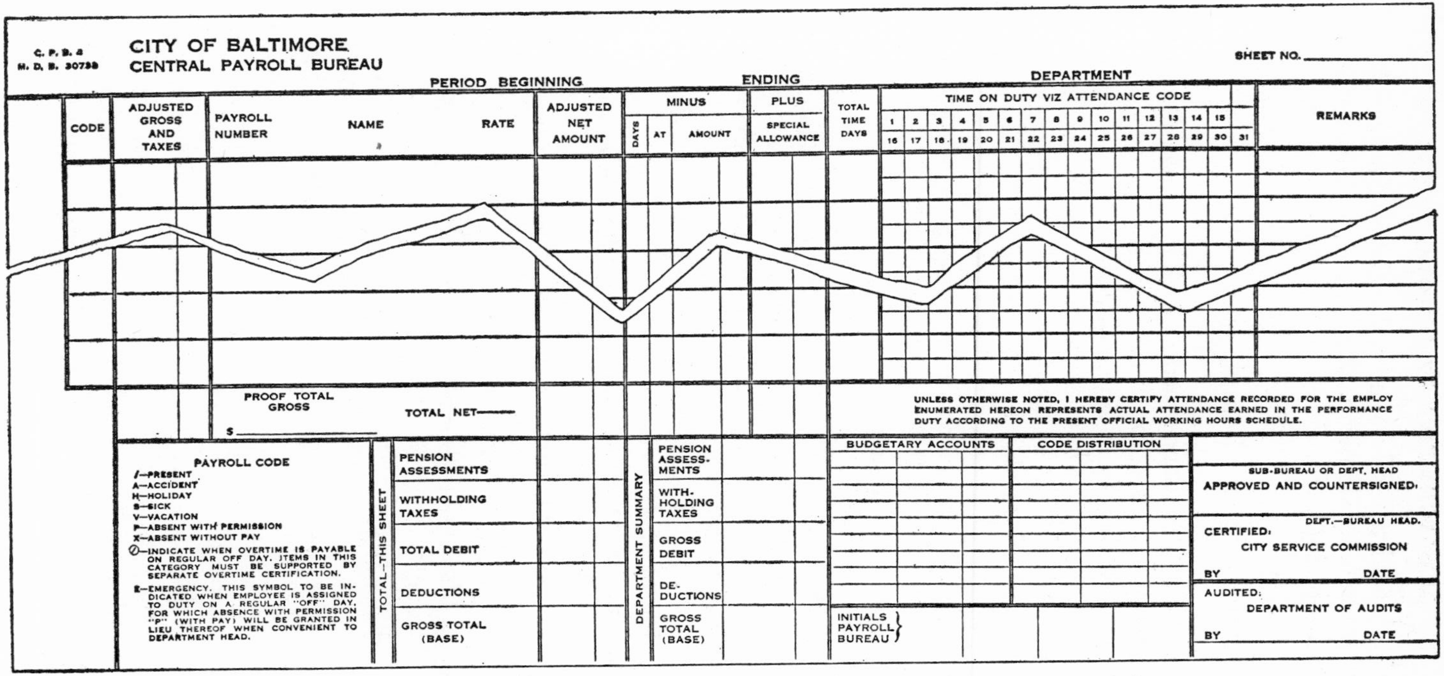

C. P. B. 4
M. D. B. 30738

CITY OF BALTIMORE
CENTRAL PAYROLL BUREAU

SHEET NO. ____

PERIOD BEGINNING ENDING DEPARTMENT

CODE	ADJUSTED GROSS AND TAXES	PAYROLL NUMBER	NAME	RATE	ADJUSTED NET AMOUNT	MINUS DAYS	MINUS AT	MINUS AMOUNT	PLUS SPECIAL ALLOWANCE	TOTAL TIME DAYS	TIME ON DUTY VIZ ATTENDANCE CODE	REMARKS
											1 2 3 4 5 6 7 8 9 10 11 12 13 14 15 / 16 17 18 19 20 21 22 23 24 25 26 27 28 29 30 31	

PROOF TOTAL GROSS $____ TOTAL NET——

UNLESS OTHERWISE NOTED, I HEREBY CERTIFY ATTENDANCE RECORDED FOR THE EMPLOY ENUMERATED HEREON REPRESENTS ACTUAL ATTENDANCE EARNED IN THE PERFORMANCE DUTY ACCORDING TO THE PRESENT OFFICIAL WORKING HOURS SCHEDULE.

PAYROLL CODE
/—PRESENT
A—ACCIDENT
H—HOLIDAY
S—SICK
V—VACATION
P—ABSENT WITH PERMISSION
X—ABSENT WITHOUT PAY
⊘—INDICATE WHEN OVERTIME IS PAYABLE ON REGULAR OFF DAY. ITEMS IN THIS CATEGORY MUST BE SUPPORTED BY SEPARATE OVERTIME CERTIFICATION.
E—EMERGENCY. THIS SYMBOL TO BE INDICATED WHEN EMPLOYEE IS ASSIGNED TO DUTY ON A REGULAR "OFF" DAY, FOR WHICH ABSENCE WITH PERMISSION "P" (WITH PAY) WILL BE GRANTED IN LIEU THEREOF WHEN CONVENIENT TO DEPARTMENT HEAD.

TOTAL—THIS SHEET: PENSION ASSESSMENTS; WITHHOLDING TAXES; TOTAL DEBIT; DEDUCTIONS; GROSS TOTAL (BASE)

DEPARTMENT SUMMARY: PENSION ASSESSMENTS; WITHHOLDING TAXES; GROSS DEBIT; DEDUCTIONS; GROSS TOTAL (BASE)

BUDGETARY ACCOUNTS CODE DISTRIBUTION

INITIALS PAYROLL BUREAU

SUB-BUREAU OR DEPT. HEAD
APPROVED AND COUNTERSIGNED:
DEPT.—BUREAU HEAD.
CERTIFIED:
CITY SERVICE COMMISSION
BY DATE
AUDITED:
DEPARTMENT OF AUDITS
BY DATE

Fig. 32. Report of employee's attendance by principal to payroll department—large school. (Courtesy Baltimore Superintendent of Schools.)

the basis of all legal payroll payments made by the board of education. This step seems a simple matter, but it is essential if an accurate payroll is to be maintained.

Reporting attendance of employees

Some kind of an attendance record of all employees is the basis of an adequate payroll system, for through such a record overpayments and underpayments may be avoided, thus reducing work for the payroll department. The attendance record of each employee of the administrative unit should be kept each day on a form (such as is shown in Figures 32 or 33) by the principal of the building to which the employee is assigned. Those employees not assigned to a particular building should report at some central point each day and the attendance should be kept and reported by some designated person. The report of attendance should give the day-by-day record of each employee and also give reasons for absences. The attendance report should be simple and require the minimum amount of time and effort on the part of the responsible persons who must make up the report. The main work and all calculations should be done by the central payroll division. In some schools the payroll division types the names on the attendance record before it is sent to the principal at the beginning of each reporting period. Such a plan will assure that the names are correct and written in proper order.

Those persons who are absent and expect pay for the days absent should be required to furnish a report to the payroll division indicating date of absence and reason. Some school systems require a report from a physician certifying that the employee was ill and not able to perform his regular duty. Most school systems, however, do not require the doctor's certificate. A statement made by the teacher on a form as shown in Figure 34 is usually the only requirement. The form could be on a 3″ x 5″ card for convenience in filing and it should be sent to the payroll department with the employee's attendance reports. The approval or denial of the absence report should be made before the payroll division makes any calculations. The payroll division should have the attendance reports on a certain day before each pay day. If the school pays on the first day of each month and if the payroll division needs ten days to complete the work, the attendance record should be sent to the payroll division on the twentieth of the month. Such a plan would require that the attendance be from the 20th day the preceding month through the 19th day of the current month.

PRINCIPAL'S REPORT OF ABSENCES
OF TEACHERS FOR MONTHLY PERIOD ENDING

_____ 19____

_____ School

Roll of Teachers Other employees	Cause (See code below)	No. days Ab.	Date of absence	Name of substit.	No. days sub.	Supt's remarks

Code

    I. - Personal Illness
    F. - Illness or death in family
    A. - Attendance at professional meeting
    V. - Visiting classes or other schools
    D. - All other causes
       ATTACH STANDARD FORM F-SL-1

WHERE NO ABSENCE IS RECORDED THE TEACHER WAS PRESENT EVERY DAY.

THIS REPORT IS DUE FIVE SCHOOL DAYS BEFORE THE END OF EACH MONTH.

    I certify that the above report of absence of teachers for the period indicated is correct.

_____ Principal

_____ Date

Fig. 33. Report of employees' attendance by principal to payroll department—small school.

```
┌─────────────────────────────────────────────────────────────┐
│                      _____ School                            │
│                                                               │
│                  Certification of Absences                    │
│                                                               │
│   In all cases of absence from duty on the part of all        │
│   employees of the Board of Education, and if compensation    │
│   is expected for such absence, the absentee shall fill in    │
│   the following report:                                       │
│                                                               │
│   Absence began _____   │
│                          (Give hour and date)                 │
│                                                               │
│   Returned to duty _____   │
│                          (Give hour and date)                 │
│                                                               │
│   Give cause of absence_____   │
│                                                               │
│   _____   │
│                                                               │
│                                                               │
│   I certify that the above facts are true.                    │
│                                                               │
│                          _____  _____  │
│                          (Employee's Signature)     (Date)    │
│                                                               │
│   The absence is approved or denied.                          │
│                                                               │
│                          _____  _____  │
│                          (Signature of Authority)   (Date)    │
└─────────────────────────────────────────────────────────────┘
```

Fig. 34. Employee's excuse for absence.

Reporting substitute services

At the time the attendance report of employees is forwarded to the payroll division, a report of substitute services should be made by the principal. Figure 35 shows a form which is used for reporting substitute services.

Some schools follow the practice of requiring each person who does supply work to turn in a report of services rendered. This gives a check on the accuracy of the principal's report. Figure 36 shows a form which may be used by substitute teachers. If this form is required it should be sent to the payroll division on the same date that employees' absences are reported.

```
_____
|                                                        |
|              _____School                            |
|                                                        |
|   Principal's Report of Substitute Teachers for Payroll.|
|                                                        |
|   _____School.  For period beginning_____and ending |
|                                     (Date)             |
|               _____                                   |
|               (Date)                                   |
|_____|
```

Signature of Supply Teacher	Date of Beginning Work	Substituted For	Total Number of Days

(Signature of Principal)

Fig. 35. Principal's report of substitutes.

The payroll

Upon receipt of the attendance records and reports of substitutes, the payroll clerk should prepare the payroll. A careful check should be made of the names of regular and substitute employees on the payroll and the attendance record. The names on the payroll and attendance record may be typed in one operation before the beginning of the pay period. The payroll clerk will then extend all calculations which may include extra pay earned and deductions such as absence, federal tax, contributions to retirement system, hospital care, and others which have been approved. In some schools the attendance record and payroll are on the same form so that when the computations are entered on the attendance record it becomes the payroll (see Figure 32). If the equipment used for writing these records is manually operated, such a combination may save time. Figures 37 and 38 give different forms of payrolls which may be used. When

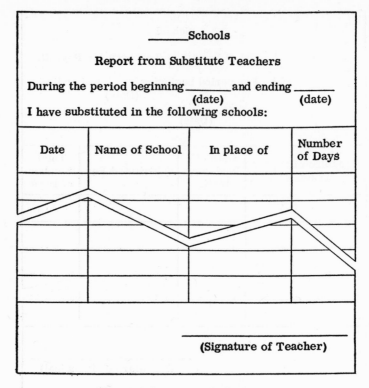

_____Schools

Report from Substitute Teachers

During the period beginning_____and ending_____
        (date)   (date)

I have substituted in the following schools:

Date	Name of School	In place of	Number of Days

_____
(Signature of Teacher)

Fig. 36. Substitute teacher's report.

the payroll has been completed it should be checked and, if possible, by a second party. If there are two clerks in the office, one may work out the payroll and the second person do the checking. In large city systems there will be a number of employees in the payroll division and the work will be divided. After the payroll is checked it should be sent to the controller (if there is one), or to the person designated by the board, to be approved. In many schools the business manager or the superintendent will be the authorized person to approve the payroll.

Writing checks and posting accounts

After the payroll is approved the payroll division writes the checks and makes entries on the individual employee's record, the voucher register, and the distribution ledgers. In small schools this work will be done by hand. In larger schools there should be a machine which

_____ Schools

PAYROLL

Sheet No. _____

Pay Period Ending _____

Names	Classification	Annual Salary	Monthly Salary	Add Extra	Absence Deductions	Net Pay Earned	Earned Deductions				Others	Net Payment	Warrant or Check No.
							Fed. Tax	Retirement	Hosp. Ins.	Others			

Fig. 37. Payroll of employees. This payroll must be remade each month.

Name	Position	Annual Salary	Monthly Salary	First Begins .... Month Ends				Twelfth Begins .... Month Ends				Total for the Year			
				Deductions		Absences	Amount Paid	Deductions		Absences	Amount Paid	Deductions		Absences	Total Amount Paid
				Fed. Tax	Retirement			Fed. Tax	Retirement			Fed. Tax	Retirement		
1															
2															
3															

Fig. 38. Payroll record. This payroll provides for writing names once and extending amounts each month.

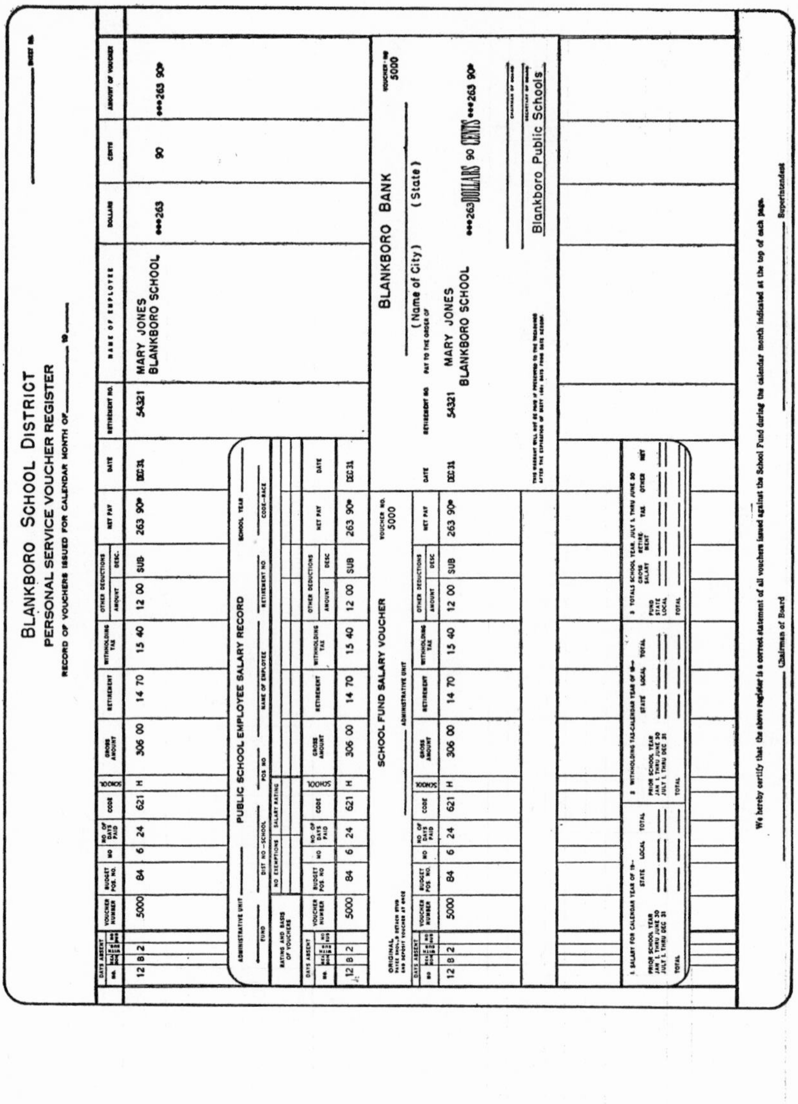

Fig. 39. Pegboard system for writing checks and recording information on employee's record and voucher register.

will record information on individual employee's record and the voucher register, and write the check in one operation. Figure 39 shows a pegboard system so arranged that the writing lines are perfectly aligned. The same information appearing on all three forms is written in one operation. This is not only a time-saving device but also a means of eliminating errors. It is to be noted that the three forms which are presented in Figure 39 may be designed for any school system.[2]

The individual employee's record

Today it is essential that a complete record be kept for each employee. This record should contain at least the following information: (1) name of employee, (2) local address, (3) retirement, and Social Security Number if the school system is under the federal law, (4) position, (5) salary and position on schedule, (6) number of exemptions[3] (7) space for recording absences, (8) spaces for all deductions, (9) gross salary, and (10) provisions for working out total salary and all deductions for the calendar years. It is to be noted that the employee's salary record card given in Figure 39 has spaces provided to calculate all deductions over the calendar year, although the employees are paid on the regular fiscal school year, that is, July 1 through June 30. These employee records should be filed in the same relative position as the name appears on the payroll. Should the employee discontinue his service with the administrative unit, the record should be filed for future references. It will be much easier to refer to this record than those in the accounting book. If the school system is so small that it cannot afford a machine for writing these records, a clerk should be assigned the task of keeping similar records.

The payroll or voucher register

It is to be noted in Figure 39 that the information is copied on the personal service voucher register at the time the check and the employee's record are made out. The same information is required but the voucher register is used for the persons in a particular school. If the information which is given on the voucher register is recorded in the distribution ledgers and to fund accounts, a space should be left after the last name, with the same code number, for the purpose

[2] There are at least three firms that manufacture the necessary equipment and the representative will be glad to help design the forms to meet local needs.
[3] The school system should use the regular federal forms and require the employee to notify the payroll officer when there is a change in his status.

of making totals. Only the totals will need to be posted on the distribution ledgers and fund accounts.

The check or warrant

In Figure 39 a form of a check is presented. It is to be noted that the voucher part of the check contains the same information that is recorded on the individual's record and the payroll or voucher register. The individual has a right to see the several deductions which have been made. This will enable him to keep his own accounts and make comparisons. The authors believe that the most desirable method of payment for services is by check.

If the warrant system is used, the warrant will be treated as a check by the treasurer who will then write one check each pay period to the bank for payment of all warrants. This system is likely to be used when the treasurer is a lay person. Another system which is used by some schools is for the treasurer of the board of education to draw a check on the school fund for the total amount of salaries for the month and to deposit it to the credit of a designated person, the paymaster, who draws checks against this account, on his own signature, for the payment of the employees. Under all conditions checks made of safety paper should be used and if an error is made on a check, the check should be marked *VOID* and another one used. Most school systems make provisions for two persons to sign all checks. Often the second signature is made by the use of a rubber stamp. In North Carolina, the superintendent, who is also the secretary of the board of education, signs the checks as one of the two persons required by law.

Delivery of checks to employees

The laws of some of the states require the disbursing officer of the school system to either deliver in person or mail the checks or warrants to the employees. This practice is not followed in many school systems. A common practice is to deliver the checks to the school and the principal places each employee's check in his school mail box. It is not a good practice for the principal to go into the classroom and hand the check to the teacher. A sound practice is to assign a person, who has taken no part in preparing the payroll, to deliver the check.[4] Although the records of the board of education are public property and may be inspected by any citizen, the pay check of an employee should be placed in an envelope and sealed before it is delivered.

[4] Frank B. Howell, "Efficient Payroll Accounting," *School Executive*, LXIII (August, 1944), 33–35.

Payment of deductions withheld from individuals

It was pointed out in section 2 of this chapter that deductions beyond those required by law should be approved by the board of education. Deductions mean more work for the payroll division; however, the board of education should be willing to render this service if it is more satisfactory and convenient for the employees.

The usual practice of paying the Federal Government is to draw one check monthly for the total amount which has been deducted from all employees and deposit it in a local bank to the credit of the government. At the end of the calendar year the payroll division must certify to the District Director of Internal Revenue and each employee the total amount of wages paid and the total amount which has been withheld for taxes. The Internal Revenue Service will furnish the form to use. It is Form W-2 and is in triplicate. The original or copy A is sent to the District Director of Internal Revenue and duplicates (copies B and C) are sent to the employee on or before January 31 following the calendar year. In some of the states a copy of the withholding tax statement must be sent to the state revenue department.[5]

The deductions made for retirement and the contributions made by the board of education must be sent to the retirement division of the state. The retirement system usually supplies the forms to be used by the payroll division for regular payments. Some states require this money to be transmitted monthly and others quarterly.

Deductions made for insurance, hospitalization, and so forth are usually paid monthly. The companies usually furnish the schools with a regular form to use, and often the names and the amount due are typed on the form by the company. This reduces the work of the payroll division.

Cancelled pay checks

All returned cancelled checks should be compared with the payroll they cover, by some person who has taken no part in preparing the payroll. After cancelled checks have been compared they should be filed in the same order as the names appear on the monthly payroll and voucher register. Such procedure will aid the auditing of the records. Too much care cannot be taken in handling payroll records

---

[5] In such cases it will be more economical for the administrator to purchase Form W-2 made up for typing five copies at one time. The Amsterdam Printing and Lithographing Co., Amsterdam, New York, will provide these at reasonable cost.

and procedures. This is not a reflection on the honesty of individual workers but merely good business management.

4. AN EVALUATION OF PAYROLL ACCOUNTING

A careful study should be made from time to time of the payroll procedures used in a school system. The several different jobs should be analyzed and studied with a view to making the needed improvements. It may be well to call in representatives from companies for suggestions and also persons from industry who have been successful in this work. There are a few general questions one would need to answer positively before he could say the payroll procedures are satisfactory. Among these:

1. Are employees paid on time?
2. Are time schedules checked by more than one person?
3. Are pay checks accurately written?
4. Are substitutes' time reported accurately?
5. Are the individuals' records adequate to meet the present needs?
6. Are forms used that will require the minimum of time?
7. Are the employees satisfied with the present methods used in delivering checks?
8. Are all possible safety precautions essential for protecting school funds being used?
9. Are accounting machines used which provide the necessary information for the administration?
10. Are records filed so that auditing will be facilitated?

TOPICS FOR STUDY AND DISCUSSION

1. What principles or policies has your board of education adopted relative to payroll accounting?
2. What procedures should be followed by a group of employees who want to take out group insurance and use the payroll deduction plan?
3. When are the teaching and nonteaching personnel in your school system paid? Are the dates for paying employees set by the board of education or by the state laws?
4. How is teachers' attendance reported to the payroll division in your school system?
5. Enumerate the reasons why each school system should keep a complete individual employee's record.
6. Evaluate the method used in the delivery of your pay check.
7. Evaluate the payroll procedures used in your school system.
8. Should the payroll division be directly responsible to the business manager or to the superintendent of schools?

SELECTED REFERENCES

BRAINARD, A. D. "School Pay-Roll Procedures," *American School Board Journal*, CIX (August, 1944), 32–34.

BURKE, ARVID J. *Financing Public Schools in United States*. New York: Harper & Bros., 1951, pp. 502–5.

CALBORN, E. JANE. "Installing a School Payroll System," *American School Board Journal*, CXXVII (August, 1953), 45.

CARMICHAEL, FORREST V. "We Switched to Machine Accounting and are Money Ahead," *Nation's Schools*, LIII (March, 1954), 108–12.

LINN, HENRY H. *School Business Administration*. New York: The Ronald Press Co., 1956, chap. VIII.

MORT, PAUL, and WALTER C. REUSSER. *Public School Finance*. 2d ed. New York: McGraw-Hill Book Co., Inc., 1951, pp. 233–34.

TAYLOR, BARBARA. "Machine Accounting in Small Schools," *American School Board Journal*, CXXVIII (March, 1954), 47–48.

13

FINANCIAL STATEMENTS, REPORTS, AND COSTS

PUBLIC EXPENDITURES of funds have mounted to an all-time high during the past decade. The governmental activities, especially on the national level, demand a greater proportion of the dollar than has ever been known in the history of the country. Although public education costs have also mounted to an all-time high, the increase has not been so great when the value of the dollar and the increased enrollment and services are considered. Nevertheless, the cost of public education is sufficiently high to attract the attention of the taxpayers. There are tendencies to hold the line or even to reduce local tax burdens when federal taxes are high. Since support of public education is primarily through local and state taxes, the administrator must do everything possible to show the lay citizens that continued support is essential for maintaining a modern, up-to-date educational program. Financial statements, reports, and cost studies are means of informing the board of education and citizens of the community about the conditions of the schools.

I. FINANCIAL STATEMENTS

The members of the board of education are representatives of the people and are responsible to them. The superintendent is the chief executive officer of the board and is directly responsible to the board. One of the functions of the chief executive officer is to familiarize the members of the board with the conditions of the schools. When the budget is adopted the board should have a complete understanding

246

of the financial conditions of the school.   Each month the administrator should report to the board on the income and expenditures of the school district.

Basic principles for making financial statements

The board of education is responsible for adopting policies, appraising results, and interpreting the school to the people.   It is only through a clear understanding of the financial conditions of the school that the board is able to carry out its functions.   The superintendent, who is responsible for executing the program, must know the financial facts and present them to the board members in the most significant manner.   If financial statements are to be of the most value to the administration and the members of the board of education, the following principles are suggested as guides:

1. Statements must be developed in accordance with accepted business practices.
2. Data must be accurate.
3. Statements must be consistent with the budget and accounting forms.
4. Statements must be easily understood.
5. Each statement must serve a purpose.
6. Statements must be arranged for easy interpretation.
7. Statements must be easily prepared.
8. Statements must be presented at regular intervals.

While the basic principles for the preparation of financial statements are generally recognized, there is much to be desired in reporting to the boards of education.   Careful consideration is needed on the part of the administration if the board of education and citizens are to understand the financial conditions of the school.

Kinds of financial statements

The number and kinds of financial statements will vary with the school systems.   The statements should give a true picture of the current financial condition in relation to the school budget.   The budget is the controlling instrument for all financial transactions, and the administration should report monthly on its effectiveness.   Statements should be made to show the status of each fund.   Fund accounts are legal accounts and must be shown separately.   Figure 40 is a form which may be used monthly to show the status of cash receipts in relation to the budget estimates of receipts.

The above form not only provides a means of keeping an accurate

Source of Receipts (1)	Total Receipts for Past Year (2)	Budgeted or Estimated Receipts for Current Year (3)	Receipts for Current Month (4)	Total Receipts to Date (5)	Receipts Anticipated for Remainder of Year (6)
1. State appropriations 2. Special state money 3. Local taxes 4. Etc. (List all major sources of income as shown in budget)					
Totals					

Fig. 40. Cash receipts report.

account of income from all sources but also provides a means of comparing the income with the anticipated yearly income and the income for the past year. The list "sources of receipts" should give the same breakdown that is used in the budget. Such a statement will enable the administration to keep a close check on all receipts, and it will show the trends of a particular source.

It has been pointed out in Chapter 10 that the state laws determine the number of different fund accounts that must be kept. Many of the state laws do not permit transfer of money from one fund to another. Therefore, an accurate monthly statement showing the balance in each fund is essential. Figure 41 is a form which may be used for showing the balances in each fund.

Funds	Total Receipts and Balances from July 1 to Date	Disbursements Including Present Month's Bills	Balances After Paying Current Bills	Balances One Year Ago
List by name different funds required by law				
Totals				

Fig. 41. Balances in each fund.

The board of education approves the budget, which gives the administration authority to make the expenditures of money for the execution of the budget. The administration should report to the board

Code	Budget Items	Budget Appropriations	Last Balance	This Month's Bills	New Balances
	List of items should be the same as shown in budget				
Total					

Fig. 42. Disbursements and balances by budget items.

Source of income:	Anticipated for Year	Received					
		July	August	September		June	Total
Federal							
1. Vocational							
2. Other							
State							
1. Permanent							
2. Equalization							
3. Tuition							
4. Other							
Local							
1. Current taxes							
2. Back taxes							
3. etc.							
Totals							

Fig. 43. Monthly statement of receipts.

monthly the status of the budget.   Figure 42 shows a monthly financial statement of expenditures and balances in each item of the budget.

In addition to the administrator's regular monthly statements for the board of education information, there are other statements which are valuable to the administration.   For example, one of the most valuable statements for analyzing income is the monthly receipt statement, which is presented in Figure 43.

Financial statements will differ in different types of school systems. Those school systems which are fiscally independent will require a different statement from those which are fiscally dependent.   The differences, however, in financial responsibility do not alter the need for financial statements.   The control of income and expenditures of a local school system requires regular statements of financial conditions in order to check forecasts when the budget was made with the realities existing each month.

2. REPORTS

Financial reports of superintendents are of long standing.   Some of the early reports were first made in the school systems of Cleveland in 1834, New York City in 1843, Chicago in 1853, and St. Louis in 1854.   Although financial data did not occupy a prominent place in the early reports, consideration was given to the major classifications of receipts and expenditures, teachers' salaries, and certain cost studies.[1]   There is a broader concept of the financial report today than there was in the earlier reports.   In the earlier reports the data were presented without interpretation, while today administrators find it necessary to employ many of the techniques used in commercial advertising in presenting the financial facts to the citizens of the community.   Financial reports may be classified into the following groups: (1) reports for the local general public, (2) reports to county or other intermediate units, to the state, and to the U.S. Office of Education.

Reports to the public

It is reasonable for the citizens of a community to expect that the superintendent of schools will report from time to time on the financial conditions of the school district and the needs of the schools.   There is no one method which can be used in all communities.   Each com-

---

[1] Paul R. Mort and Walter C. Reusser, *Public School Finance* (2d ed.; New York: McGraw-Hill Book Co., Inc., 1951), p. 274.

munity must be studied in order to find the most effective means. Some administrators make use of many media, while others rely primarily upon the budget[2] and the annual report.

There has been a considerable change in the annual report in recent years. Formerly the annual report was a statistical report without illustrations. Today, reports are made more attractive and readable through the use of pictures, charts, and graphs. An attempt has been made to present an annual report that is attractive and interesting to the average lay person. The format of the report will determine its effectiveness. It should have an attractive cover, an appealing title, a good table of contents, good paper and readable type. The contents should be planned with a definite purpose, and only those materials which will carry out the purpose should be used.

Some school administrators are questioning the value of the annual report because of the limited circulation and the cost, and are developing a number of special reports throughout the year. Each special report will consider only one phase of the school program and will be very short and easily understood. These special reports are given wide circulation throughout the school district. By the use of charts, pictures, and a limited amount of statistical material, a short, attractive report can be of much value in reporting the financial conditions of the school district to the citizens.

A short newsletter published at regular intervals has proved an excellent means of keeping the public informed, especially in the smaller communities. Each letter will deal with a particular aspect of the school system. This letter must be well written and attractive. Wide circulation at a minimum cost can be given to this type of report.

Reports to state

State laws require some type of report from each school system. These reports are statistical and financial. The state department of education designs the report which is to be made by the local administration. These administrative reports should be integrated into a system whereby information may be taken from the accounting system. There has been a tendency in some states to require a number of different reports from each administrative unit, thereby causing undue time and work. State reports should be simple and call for only those data which are essential for securing a true picture of the entire state and at the same time meeting the requirements of the state laws. The present cooperative program of the chief state school offi-

[2] See Chapter 13 for discussion on the budget.

cers and the U.S. Office of Education may bring about more uniformity in the reports which will be made and also provide that the data secured will be of more value. It is imperative that all state reports be compiled with extreme care if the data are to be of value in state studies. A good system of state reports integrated with the U.S. Office of Education reports is valuable for securing information on education over the country as a whole and for research purposes.

3. COSTS

Cost accounting has always had an important place in the management of a business. It is essential for the manager of a factory to know how much labor and materials cost for producing any particular item. Business spends much money making time and motion studies. Only through studies can production costs be reduced. Although schools are not operated on the same principles as business, the administration can improve in management by using some practices which have proved beneficial to business.

Importance of cost studies

The greatest values derived from an analysis of the educational program of a school system through costs are in managing the finances, in determining school policies, and in gaining lay support of the program.

Educational costs provide facts and information for the management of the business affairs of the school system. Although it may be difficult to allocate all costs associated with a given service or product used in the schools, much improvement is being made through the use of better accounting and more adequate records. For example, the administration may wish to know what type of fuel would be the most economical to use in a new building which is being planned for the community. It is possible through cost studies to calculate the cost of heating a cubic foot of space with coal, oil, or gas and to come to a reasonably scientific decision. Likewise, it may be necessary for the administration to know the cost of labor on a certain project in order to determine whether the district can afford to duplicate the same at another school. It is only through cost studies that it is possible to make such decisions. If the administration is to manage the schools most economically, cost studies are essential.

The board of education is always confronted with making policies for a school system. The basis for final decisions upon many policies involves cost studies. For example, what will be the policy of the board of education on charging for the use of certain building facili-

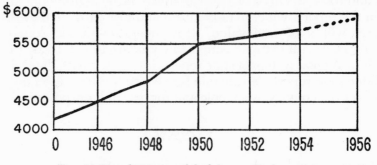

Fig. 44. Trends in cost of fuel for a school system.

ties, such as the gymnasium? No final decision can be reached until basic costs have been determined for heat, water, light, and janitorial services. The knowledge that some phase of vocational work will cost the district a given amount of money is a factor in determining the extent to which such courses will be given. The fact that a certain course costs twice as much as another course may be helpful in deciding whether to continue it. In no case, however, should the cost factor be the sole determinant in making such decisions, for there are other factors involved. Cost is only one factor in making a decision pertaining to school problems.

Accurate cost studies are essential in presenting financial information to lay citizens. The average person better understands and appreciates the problems involved in financing public education if he is able to see what it costs to operate certain phases of the school program. It is far more significant to a parent to know that it costs $295.50 to educate a child for a year than to know that it costs over four million dollars to educate the children of the city. Table 10 illustrates how certain cost studies were presented to the lay citizens of Albuquerque, New Mexico. This information appeared in the *Public School Journal,* which was published by the public school system.

Over 40 per cent of the money for the support of public education in the United States comes from property taxes. Costs for schools are high or low depending upon the taxpayer's general attitude toward education and his tax bill. It is only through a conscious effort to provide adequate, accurate, and honest cost facts that the lay citizens can be expected to formulate a favorable opinion toward the school system, since they are paying high taxes. These cost studies must be presented in such a manner that they can be easily understood. The use of charts and diagrams will aid in presenting facts.

TABLE 10. Cost per pupil and average daily attendance—Albuquerque Public Schools

Average Daily Attendance......	Elementary Schools 16,901		Junior High Schools 4,817		High Schools 3,404		Total All Schools 25,128		
	Pupil Cost	Expenditure	Pupil Cost	Expenditure	Pupil Cost	Expenditure	Pupil Cost	Expenditure	Percentages
Instruction......	$142.49	$2,409,131.03	$145.75	$702,153.76	$187.04	$636,693.51	$149.16	$3,747,978.30	83.3
Operation of School Plant	11.00	185,964.22	12.78	61,554.61	17.48	59,489.12	12.22	307,007.95	6.8
Maintenance of School Plant...	5.69	96,175.98	4.98	23,968.86	6.25	21,259.65	5.63	141,404.49	3.2
Auxiliary Services......	4.28	72,394.66	7.88	37,934.47	6.41	21,819.01	5.26	132,148.14	3.0
Administration......	4.02	68,020.29	4.02	19,380.92	4.02	13,699.09	4.02	101,100.30	2.3
Fixed Charges......	2.76	46,746.39	2.04	9,802.93	2.37	8,062.58	2.57	64,611.90	1.4
Total Current Expenses......	$170.24	$2,878,432.57	$177.45	$854,795.55	$223.57	$761,022.96	$178.86	$4,494,251.08	100.
Debt Services......	14.26	241,149.87	14.16	68,707.95	14.27	48,565.08	14.26	358,413.90	
TOTAL......	$184.50	$3,119,573.44	$191.71	$923,503.50	$237.84	$809,588.04	$193.12	$4,852,664.98	

ADMINISTRATION: Office Salaries; Office Supplies; Postage; Telephone; Telegraph; Other Administration Expenses.

INSTRUCTION: Salaries of Principals, Supervisors, Clerks; Teachers' Salaries; Supplies used in Instruction; Library Supplies; Textbooks; Other Instructional Expenses.

OPERATION OF PLANT: Janitors' Wages; Janitors' Supplies; Fuel; Light and Power; Water; Other Expenses of Operation.

MAINTENANCE OF PLANT: Repair of Buildings; Repair and Replacement of Equipment; Upkeep of Grounds; Workman's Compensation.

AUXILIARY SERVICES: Health Service; Bus Transportation.

FIXED CHARGES: Property Insurance; Rents; Group Insurance.

DEBT SERVICE: Interest on Bonded Debt; Sinking Fund.

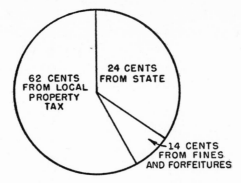

Fig. 45. Source of the school dollar.

Figure 44 illustrates how trends of school costs may be presented. One may look at the chart and see at a glance that it is costing the school district more money for heating the school system.   It might be of much value if a similar chart were presented to show the increase or decrease in cost of fuel per ton. Likewise, a chart may be used to show the number of tons of fuel used each year or to show certain unit costs.

Where does the school get its money? Many people may have the idea that all the money comes from local taxes or from the state. A simple chart explaining the source of all school money may favorably alter the attitude of many people toward the school.   One can see at a glance that 62 cents comes from local property taxes, 14 cents from fines and forfeitures, and 24 cents from the state. A similar chart showing how the school dollar is spent is easily presented.   These and all other types of charts are valuable for presenting information on school costs to the citizens who support the public schools.

Comparative costs

Most people feel that taxes and death are two sure things.   There is not much discussion concerning death but there is always much discussion concerning taxes. Whether it is in a period of high prices or low prices, taxes are always hard to pay.   Since a large proportion of school costs is borne by property taxes, complaint is often heard concerning high educational costs.   The administrator should make comparative cost studies of the services rendered by the schools and other governmental agencies of the community or state.   How much of the tax dollar goes for lighting the streets of the city?   How much is spent on streets?   What does it cost per day to keep a person in jail? What does it cost per day to keep a person in a mental institution? These and numerous other comparative studies may be made and presented to the citizens of the community to help build a more favorable attitude toward supporting public education.

Comparative cost studies with other school systems often aid in getting a better understanding of public education. The U.S. Office of Education publishes each two years a report which gives the expenditures per pupil in city school systems by sizes of cities. The administrator can secure these studies and present cost studies of his school system in comparison with cities of similar size throughout the United States. Likewise, the state department of education publishes cost studies for the state. Oftentimes groups of superintendents within a state organize and work out worthwhile studies for their systems. Comparative cost studies are essential for gaining local support for public education.

Units of measurements for cost studies

The unit of measurement that is chosen for use in making cost studies is of prime importance. Unless the same unit of measurement is used, comparative cost studies are of little value. The units of measurement selected should be readily defined and of common use. There are certain units which have been widely used for a number of years. Some of these are the following:

Item of Cost	Unit of Measurement
Total educational cost	Average daily attendance
Current expense cost	Average daily attendance
Building costs	Cubic or square foot
Instructional cost	Average daily attendance or per pupil clock hour
Supervision cost	Teacher supervised
Instructional supplies cost	Per pupil
Janitorial supply cost	Square foot floor space
Cleaning cost	Square foot floor space
Subject cost	Pupil hour
Maintenance cost	Square foot floor space
Heat cost	Cubic foot
Water cost	Average daily attendance
Administrative cost	Average daily attendance
Ability to support cost	Per capita income
Effort to support cost	Average daily attendance
Food or lunchroom cost	Meals served

It is not always an easy matter to determine the unit of measurement to use. If comparative costs are to be made, the unit chosen should be the same. If comparative studies are not to be made, the administrator may select the unit which will be the easiest to understand. However, a unit which has more or less been accepted as a standard of measurement may be more signficant in the future. Cost studies are valuable if used correctly. However, a word of caution must be given in that costs do not tell the whole story. They are only one factor in the total situation.

TOPICS FOR STUDY AND DISCUSSION

1. What values have financial statements?
2. Draw up forms you would use in making a monthly financial statement to a board of education.
3. What is the relationship between financial statements and the accounting system?
4. Make a skeleton outline of the financial report you would include in the superintendent's annual report.
5. What kind of financial report would you give to the local newspaper for publication?
6. How would you prorate administrative expense if you were making a cost study of instructional supplies?
7. Show trends of current expense costs in your school for the past twenty-five years.
8. Compute the cost in your school for elementary education.
9. Make a study of transportation costs in your school system. What unit of measurement is the most satisfactory to use?

SELECTED REFERENCES

BURKE, ARVID J. *Defensible Spending for Public Schools.* New York: Columbia University Press, 1943, chaps. VI, IX, and X.
DAVENPORT, K. S., and H. H. REMMERS. "Educational Achievement as Compared with Money Spent on Schools," *School and Society,* LXI (May, 1945), 333–35.
HATTON, OTIS C. "Gearing Good Will Along with School Funds," *Nation's Schools,* XLII (September, 1948), 23–25.
MORT, PAUL R., and WALTER C. REUSSER. *Public School Finance.* 2d ed. New York: McGraw-Hill Book Co., Inc., 1951, chaps. VIII and XIV.
REDDING, C. D. "Annual Report for the Small School," *Nation's Schools,* XXX (December, 1942), 8–19.
SOPER, WAYNE W. "Educational Costs and Their Analysis," *Review of Educational Research,* XVII (April, 1947), 155–62.

14

FINANCIAL SAFEGUARDS

ALL SCHOOL MONEY collected for a district is a public trust for which the board of education is held responsible. The superintendent of schools as the executive officer of the board must set up sound financial safeguards against individual dishonesty, carelessness, or mismanagement. The necessary precautions for safeguarding school funds are (1) a sound system of custodianship of the money, (2) bonds for school officials, (3) safeguards for deposits, (4) sound administrative procedures, and (5) audits.

I. CUSTODIANSHIP OF SCHOOL MONEY

The state laws determine, to a great extent, the form and manner of providing for the custodianship of school money. The laws, in a number of cases, are not complete or adequate and the administrator has the responsibility of setting up a sound system.

Different custodial systems

A study of the state laws and present practices shows that there are many officials charged with the custody of school funds. At least four district school custodial systems are used at the present time. They are:

1. The school board treasurer system. The board of education appoints a person, who may or may not be a member of the board, to serve as the district treasurer. This person receives a small stipend for his services and often acts as the financial advisor to the board of education.

2. The clerk or secretary-treasurer system. In some of the states the laws provide that the board of education appoint a clerk or secretary who

will serve as the treasurer. This person is usually a full-time employee of the school system and may or may not be the superintendent of schools. If he is not the superintendent of schools, he is likely to be designated as the business manager of the school system.

3. The governmental treasurer system. The state laws which provide for this type of system designate the treasurer of the governmental unit, such as the town or city, township or county, as the treasurer of the school system. Usually he does not receive any extra stipend for the work and is not an employee of the board.

4. The depository system. The board of education selects a bank to be the custodian of the school funds, and an official of the bank acts as treasurer. All money due the district is sent directly to the bank. The school district uses a voucher or warrant system for payment of bills. The vouchers or warrants are issued by the administration and serve as orders for the bank to pay. The official of the bank will cash the vouchers and then issue a check on the school account for one or more vouchers. A monthly statement of receipts and expenditures is made to the board of education. Beach[1] points out that the depository acting as the treasurer has much merit because of the safety features and competent personnel for handling of funds.

Responsibilities of the custodian of school money

In most states the duties of the custodian of school money or the treasurer of the board of education are defined by the state laws. The laws, however, are very meager in a number of cases. Therefore the board of education, through its rules and regulations, should state definitely the responsibilities of the treasurer. The following should be included:

1. He shall deposit all money in the depositories as designated by the board of education.
2. He shall keep an accurate account of all money according to funds (legal accounts).
3. He shall pay all accounts when properly approved.
4. He shall be bonded.
5. He shall make all reports required by law and the board of education.
6. He shall advise with the administration relative to financial problems of the district.

2. BONDING SCHOOL OFFICIALS

Although state laws generally provide for bonding school officials, many of the laws are very general; and some boards of education are

[1] Frederick F. Beach, *The Custody of School Funds* (New York: Bureau of Publications, Teachers College, Columbia University, 1933), p. 12.

very lax in their procedures. Many school employees who handle school money are not bonded even when required by law, and oftentimes the nature of the bonds offer little or no protection.

Who should be bonded?

All school employees who are responsible for or who are associated with the handling of school money should be bonded. Linn and Joyner state:

as a general rule, that all individuals directly responsible for the collection, custody, disbursement, and general management of school funds and supplies, and by whom an act of wrongdoing or negligence may result in monetary loss to the school district, should be bonded.[2]

The practice of requiring all persons to be bonded does not imply that all persons are dishonest. Rather, it is a precautionary measure to protect the schools from carelessness, inefficiency, robbery, or any other form of mismanagement.

As a general rule, board members do not actually handle school money; therefore, they need not be bonded. Other officials, however, such as the treasurer, secretary, and/or superintendent, should be bonded. Tax collectors should be bonded; however, they are not usually under the control of the board of education but are under the supervision of the state. Not only the officials of the board of education but also certain employees should be bonded. Among the employees who should be bonded are (1) bookkeepers, (2) auditors, (3) certain clerks, (4) storeroom managers, (5) cafeteria managers and cashiers, and (6) activity treasurers for individual schools.

Some persons are opposed to bonding school officials and employees on the premise that they are honest and that bonding adds additional expense which seems unnecessary. Sometimes an argument is also presented that good supervision and sound management make bonding unnecessary. Bonding those people who handle money is a part of good management. School money is a public trust of the board of education, and every precaution possible should be observed so that it will be used for the education of the youth of the community.

What amount of bonds should be carried?

The question is often asked "for what amount should an individual be bonded?" Although this is a hard question to answer because of

[2] Henry H. Linn and Schuyler C. Joyner, *Insurance Practices in School Administration* (New York: The Ronald Press Co., 1952), p. 327.

the great number of factors involved, it may be stated that the amount of the bond should equal the largest amount of money the individual has under his control at any one time. There are many factors, however, that the board of education should consider before deciding upon the amount of the bond for a particular individual. Linn and Joyner suggest an answer to the following questions before deciding upon the amount of bond for any particular individual or position:

1. What is the total amount of funds for which he may be responsible during the year, or during his term of office?
2. What is the total amount of money for which he may be responsible at any one time?
3. What kind of accounting system is used?
4. How frequently are audits made of his accounts?
5. What is the nature of these audits?
6. Who makes the audit: local officials, superior officers, local citizens, surety company auditors, state auditors, or private auditors (certified public accountants)?
7. Does the individual sign checks and warrants alone or must they be countersigned by others?
8. Is he liable for funds on deposit in banks?
9. How frequently are his accounts checked and balanced by other individuals (not audited)?
10. To what extent do deputies and assistants handle the funds for which he is responsible?
11. If his term of office is for several years, is there a cumulative liability on his bond?
12. Is he responsible for the handling of several different funds and accounts so that shortages may be covered up by transfers?
13. What are the local state laws or court decisions pertaining to liability on surety bonds?
14. What special safety devices are used to protect the funds, such as check-writing equipment, "safety" check paper, seals, safes, vaults, and so on?
15. Are the responsibilities and duties of his office so divided that collusion will be made more difficult?
16. How frequently must he turn over any monies coming into his hands to officers or depositories?
17. Does he keep public accounts in banks in his own personal account or are they deposited in a public account?
18. Has he had sufficient training and experience, either in business or in other public work, so that he is capable of filling the position successfully?
19. Does he have a good character and reputation?
20. Does he have any financial standing so that in the event of loss

beyond the penalty of his bond, recourse may be had to his personal estate?[3]

In light of the answers to the above questions, the board of education may be more able to determine the amount of protection necessary. Although the questions may be answered correctly and show a high degree of security, there still remains the problem of protecting the funds in case of loss. From the standpoint of recovery of a loss, the amount of the bond should be large enough to guarantee full protection.

Classes of bonds

Personal and corporate surety bonds are in use today. A personal surety bond is that type which requires one or more persons to guarantee the fidelity of the individual who is responsible for handling money or to cover the faithful performance of the duties of the office. This type of bond was one of the earliest methods used for bonding officials in this country and is still used today in many school districts. In many cases the state laws require a surety bond but fail to state the kind of bond. There are some advantages of the personal bond in that it is obtained rather easily and quickly, does not cause embarrassment through answering questions required by bonding companies, and costs, if anything, very little. The disadvantages, however, outweigh the advantages. Some of the disadvantages are as follows:

1. A person signing the bond seldom realizes the full extent of his liability in case of losses due to negligence on the part of the official or losses beyond the control of the official. The signer usually considers he is guaranteeing the fidelity of the official.
2. Sometimes the laws favor the person who signs the bond.
3. The official may feel obligated to the person signing the bond and go beyond the law to render favors.
4. The person signing the bond may die or become insolvent before the expiration of the bond and no other security will be secured, thereby leaving the funds unprotected.
5. The person signing the bond is not always willing to pay if there should be a loss. If the case is taken to court and judgment rendered against the individual, it may be difficult to find resources from which the loss may be collected.
6. Personal securities are frequently worth much less than the amount of the bond.

[3] *Ibid.*, pp. 330–31.

7. The credit of the surety may be impaired by his signing the bond.
8. The personal surety may be ruined financially if he is required to pay a large loss.
9. Immediate payment of losses may be hard to collect although the personal surety is financially able to meet the obligations.

The corporate surety bond is a bond purchased from a company organized for the purpose of guaranteeing a loss or losses. This type of bond is being used more extensively each year. The use of the corporate surety bond has some distinctive advantages over the use of personal bonds. Some of these advantages are:

1. The corporate surety companies afford greater protection than personal sureties. Surety companies operate under certain governmental controls which tend to assure their ability to meet their obligations.
2. The principal is not under an obligation to the surety.
3. Corporate surety companies pay claims promptly.
4. Through a process of investigation, an applicant who is not a good risk is often kept from being given a responsible office.
5. Applicants can secure surety without embarrassment.
6. Surety companies put forth effort to cause individuals who have defaulted to make restitution or suffer legal penalties.
7. Surety companies will help supervise business methods of schools in order to prevent losses.

The use of the corporate surety bond is receiving more consideration each year by school officials. Although it is being recognized as one of the best means to insure the safety of money, there are some alleged disadvantages. They are:[4]

1. Corporate surety bonds are expensive.
2. Sometimes settlements are delayed because the company tries to avoid payment on some technicalities.
3. Some people are embarrassed by the personal questions which the company asks on the application.
4. The red tape involved for securing a bond is a nuisance.
5. The period of time necessary to secure a corporate bond is often much longer than that required for a personal bond.
6. The company stipulates the terms and conditions under which the bond is furnished.

These alleged disadvantages are not serious and should not discourage any school board from requiring its officials and employees to be bonded. The most serious disadvantage is the cost of the bond. Boards of education should feel that the cost of bonds is a good insurance investment for the district.

[4] Adapted from *ibid.*, pp. 305-7.

Types of corporate surety bonds

There are four different types of surety bonds that are used by school districts. They are (1) individual, (2) position schedule, (3) name schedule, and (4) blanket.

The individual corporate surety bond is, as the name implies, a bond for any given amount on a particular person. This was one of the first types of corporate bonds used by schools but is becoming less popular today. This bond would protect the school from any losses as a result of the action of the individual in any position he might be assigned.

The name schedule bond is somewhat similar to the individual bond. The bond would cover a number of individuals. The amount of liability on each individual is shown opposite his name. It is a means of bonding several individuals in one bond. Addition and deletion of names are necessary as changes are made.

The position schedule bond is similar to the name schedule. In place of the names appearing on the bond, the several different positions will appear on the bond. This type of bond eliminates additions and deletions of names and is of considerable advantage if the turnover of employees is great.

The blanket type of corporate surety bond is gaining in use over the other types mentioned. This type of bond gives the school district protection from any losses which might result from any employee's actions. The North Carolina State Board of Education purchases such a bond covering all money in all the schools of the state. Automatic additions and deletions of names are made without notice to the company and without adjusted premiums during the year. It is a bond which offers the maximum of security with the least amount of effort in keeping it up to date. Applications have been simplified, and the rates are rather low in comparison with other types.

3. SAFEGUARDING DEPOSITS

Selection of depositories

The selection of depositories for school funds should be based upon two fundamental considerations—security of funds and service to the administrative unit. In the past, the accepted procedure was to seek bids from banks in terms of interest paid on the daily balance. This procedure is not practicable today. Too often banks are selected for personal or political reasons without any consideration of security. Such procedures should be discouraged.

In general it may be said that the board of education should select for a depository only those banks which have a paid-up capital stock and surplus equal to at least $200,000. The amount of the funds to be placed in any one bank should not exceed 50 per cent of capital and surplus. Consideration should also be given to the nature of the clientele of the bank. In a bank which depends upon a single industry for business or secures a large per cent of its deposits from public funds the chances for failure are greater than in one which has a diverse clientele and a small per cent of the deposits from public funds. The competence of management is also an important factor in selecting a bank to serve as a depository.

Security of deposits

The Federal Deposit Insurance Law insures deposits up to $10,000. The amount of deposits of a school fund in excess of $10,000 should be secured by corporate surety bond or collateral. Some state laws permit the use of personal bonds for security of deposits. It is felt, however, that personal bonds do not afford the security necessary for public school money. Since most banks have such large deposits and the income from deposits is so small, some banks object to purchasing corporate surety bonds to protect public funds. If the bank will furnish a corporate surety bond, it is one of the best means of safeguarding the deposits, for the bonding company will not issue the necessary bond without a thorough investigation of the bank. Many boards of education, however, follow the practice of requiring the bank to furnish collateral in the nature of state or federal government bonds. Such procedure does not require the bank to pay out a sum of money to furnish security for the deposits. At the same time, however, the school funds are fully protected.

4. SOUND ADMINISTRATIVE PROCEDURES

A sound system of business administration is one of the best means of safeguarding public school funds. No school administrator should feel that the public school money is fully protected unless the best possible business practices are put into operation in the handling of the financial affairs of the school district. State laws are very meager on specific practices to be carried out by the administrator. The rules and regulations of the board of education should be rather definite on certain administrative practices, but at the same time the administrator should have the authority to go beyond the prescriptions set up by the board and establish the best practices possible.

Specific safeguards

Some of the administrative safeguards which should receive consideration are the following:

1. Using an adequate accounting system
2. Using sound budgetary procedures
3. Requiring complete and regular reports by the accounting officer and treasurer to the board of education and the public
4. Requiring an annual audit by a certified public accountant
5. Having all checks or warrants countersigned by a second party, who does not handle the funds
6. Requiring two individuals to take part in the act of disbursing money
7. Making all payments by checks or warrants and not by cash
8. Requiring the individual who receives the money (cash or check) to make a deposit in the bank
9. Using special safety devices, such as check-writing equipment, "safety" check paper, and the like
10. Requiring all accounts to be checked and balanced periodically by others than the regular bookkeeper
11. Placing responsibility for certain work upon an individual
12. Maintaining a good system of financial publicity
13. Requiring signed, serially numbered receipts when money passes from one person to another
14. Depositing all money in the approved bank the day it is received
15. Requiring proper authorization before disbursements are made
16. Reducing the number of separate funds to the minimum required by law

There will be wide differences in practices prevailing in the school systems throughout the country. The smaller school systems are handicapped to some extent in not having adequate personnel for executing sound administrative safeguards. Nevertheless, the administrator has the responsibility of organizing the administrative personnel so that there will not be any chance for the loss of funds through neglect, carelessness, or mismanagement.

5. THE AUDIT

Auditing of financial records has long been recognized as an essential in business. Business concerns are operated for a financial profit; and all interested parties demand that they be protected from fraud, losses, mismanagement, and improper expenditures for funds. Since schools are not profit-making institutions, the demands for auditing the financial accounts have not been so great.

Present practices in school auditing

The provisions for school audits as set forth in the state laws will vary from state to state. Some of the states do not have any legal requirement for an audit, others require all districts to have an audit once each year, and others require an audit of certain school systems. In a recent study, McGrew[5] reported that thirty-two states require the school districts to have their financial accounts audited. Twenty-six of these states require the audit to be made annually, although in five cases the laws did not include all the districts of the states. There are four states which require all districts to have audits, but the laws do not specify an annual audit.

There are a number of states which leave the problem of audits in the hands of the boards of education. In some states the audits are made by committees of citizens appointed by the local board of education. This practice is particularly true in smaller districts.

About half of the states have some plan for state auditing.[6] The two state agencies used for auditing local district funds are the state department of education and the state auditing department. A great number of the states, however, require the local boards of education to employ private auditors.

Although there has been a marked increase in the number of schools which require an annual postaudit during the past twenty-five years, there remain many school systems which never have a true audit made of the financial records. In some districts the post examination of the financial records is so superficial that it hardly deserves to be described as a postaudit. One is inclined to say that sound business practices, especially audits, in the public school systems of the country are woefully inadequate and that school administrators should not be satisfied with the present conditions. A goal for school administrators should be, *all school accounts must be audited by competent authorities at least once each year.* Nothing less than this insures proper safeguards for the funds which have been intrusted to them for the education of the boys and girls of the country.

Types of audit

Auditing may be divided into two major types—internal or continuous, and external. The internal or continuous audit includes what

[5] James W. McGrew, *Safeguarding Local School Funds, A Plan of Auditing the Accounts of New Jersey School Districts* (Trenton: N.J., New Jersey State Chamber of Commerce, November, 1950).
[6] Council of State Governments, *The Forty-Eight State School Systems* (Chicago: The Council, 1949), p. 157.

is often classified by the public administrator as the preaudit, current audit, and operational audit and is performed by the regularly employed personnel of the board of education. The external audit is usually called the postaudit by the public administrator and is performed by an accounting firm employed for that particular purpose.

Internal or continuous auditing is an important part of fiscal control. It involves budgetary procedure including the legal adoption as is reflected by the minutes of the board of education, budgetary control, and appraisal of the work done in the school system. This form of auditing is carried on each day, and at the end of each month a summary of the past month's operation should be reported to the board of education. The business department, under the direction of the superintendent of schools, should execute the internal or continuous audit.

The external or postaudit is often referred to as a public audit. There are three different kinds of public audits which may be made of the school financial records. They are (1) the balance sheet audit, (2) the examination audit, and (3) the detailed audit.

The balance sheet audit involves the verification of the financial conditions of the school district as of a given date and does not contemplate the verification of all transactions over a given period of time. The auditor does not concern himself with details of certifications of income and expenditures but does concern himself with the verification of the assets and liabilities at a given date. This type of audit is not so valuable to schools as it is to business concerns. It may be used, however, at the time a school district is interested in selling bonds.

The examination method of auditing is becoming more popular with business and no doubt will prove very satisfactory for schools. This form of audit relies upon the sampling or test check method and does not verify each item of expenditures and receipts. All transactions are classified according to months, and the auditor makes some definite plan of checking a certain number of items in each month. He might test check the third, fifth, or any other set number of items. This type of audit considers the consistency of the accounting methods and does sufficient test checking to verify accuracy. Such an audit does not require the time needed for the detailed audit and is much less expensive.

The detailed audit is similar to the examination audit. It differs, however, in that each transaction is verified. The auditor starts at a certain time, known as the "cutting off point," and covers the verification of all transactions up to another "cutting off point." The period may vary as to the length of time. Normally, the period of time should cover the fiscal school year. This is the type of external audit which is usually used by boards of education. It is much more expensive to make than the examination type. Many boards of education which are not required by law to have an audit hesitate to employ an auditor because of the expense. In such cases, consideration should be given to the examination type of audit.

The external or postaudit should be made annually immediately following the close of the fiscal year. Although the business office does not make this audit, it can facilitate the work by using good business procedures and maintaining good internal or continuous audits.

Reasons for auditing

When one speaks of making an audit, many people have a notion that it is a process of detecting something wrong with the accounts. Although this may be one reason for making an audit, there are others which are probably of as much or more value. The reasons for making an audit are as follows:[7]

1. To give assurance of the correctness of all financial reports made at the close of the fiscal year
2. To prevent fraud by the personnel's knowing that all accounts will be audited
3. To detect any fraud which might have taken place during the past fiscal year
4. To check on the consistency and accuracy of record-keeping
5. To protect the employed personnel concerned with the business administration of the school
6. To assure the general public that the personnel of the business department are honest
7. To give the general public a feeling of security concerning the public school money
8. To furnish unbiased financial information concerning the schools
9. To assist the administration in installing newer business practices
10. To secure expert professional services for improving the accounting system

Functions of the audit

The functions of the external or postaudit are closely related to the reasons for making it. The functions, however, should be considered in the light of the values derived from the audit. If the postaudit is to be of the most value possible, the auditor should have some knowl-

---

[7] W. E. Rosenstengel, "The Annual Financial Audit," *American School Board Journal*, CII (May, 1941), 42.

edge of all phases of school administration, especially budgetary procedures, cost studies, and school records.

Although matters of fiscal policies governing the schools are the functions of the board of education, the audit should develop many financial facts into a form which will make them useful to the administration and the board in making decisions to adopt, to retain, or to reject certain procedures or programs. Budgetary procedures should be improved as a result of a good school audit. The audit report should show in columnar array the actual expenditures along with budget appropriations and likewise actual receipts along with anticipated receipts.

"One of the main purposes of the audit is to furnish financial facts for publicity purposes. The citizens are investing their money and entrusting it to the administration and are entitled to know whether or not their money is going to the cause of education. The best way to give the citizens the necessary confidence in the business administration of the schools is to have public auditors make an annual audit of *all* financial records."[8]

The public will accept the information presented in the audit as true and accurate. Certain parts of the audit should be lifted out of the report and published for special emphasis. Therefore, the auditor should aim to present this material in a manner that the average person can understand. Some of the material, however, will have to be interpreted to the newspapers so that it will appear interesting and understandable to the lay citizens.

A good audit will offer suggestions for the improvement of the accounting procedures. Auditors have opportunity to come in contact with the newer and more efficient practices used in private and other public business and can offer many suggestions which may be applied to business management of a school system. Oftentimes these suggestions, if used, will save the school district more than the cost of the audit.

A vast majority of school administrators, school business managers, and other employed personnel are honest. There are times, however, when some people of a community will question the integrity of some or all of them, and the school audit provides a means of assuring the citizens that the school funds are being spent according to the plans of the board of education. The audit is a means of checking all accounts against possible fraud.

The audit serves as a basis for helping to evaluate the entire school program. It gives an opportunity to make such studies as unit costs,

---

[8] Calvin Grieder and William E. Rosenstengel, *Public School Administration* (New York: The Ronald Press Co., 1954), p. 436.

complete analysis of the indebtedness and the insurance programs and plant depreciation. Last but not necessarily least, the audit provides an excellent means for organizing financial information concerning the school system for archival purposes.

Steps followed in making an external audit

The external or postaudit should not be limited to checking the accuracy of the accounting records but should show a true statement of the fiscal affairs of the school district. If the business administrator knows something of the work of the auditor, he can facilitate the work by having all records in order. The following gives a summary of the steps followed in making the external audit:

1. The balance in each fund for the beginning of the period is verified by reconciling the bank statement, the treasurer's report, the account books, and outstanding checks or warrants.
2. The receipts are verified by checking treasurer's account and accounting books and comparing these with statements from tax collectors, certificates of appropriations from state and any other governmental agency which appropriates funds to the school, and duplicate receipts of any miscellaneous receipts. Auditors will take samplings and make direct verifications of the receipts from the several sources.
3. A comparison will be made of anticipated receipts as given in the budget by sources and those actually received.
4. An examination will be made of all items of expenditures recorded in accounting books in comparison with the minutes book of the board of education, purchase orders, rendered bills from vendor, cancelled checks or warrants, and check stubs. If the purchase order, bill from vendor, and cancelled check or warrant are attached to the voucher jacket and placed in order as recorded in the accounting books, auditing will be facilitated. Monthly payrolls should also be in order as recorded in accounting books. The auditor will likely make a sample verification of accounts paid.
5. A verification of outstanding bills will be made.
6. The balance at the close of the auditing period is verified by reconciling the bank statement, the treasurer's books, the account books, and outstanding checks or warrants.
7. A comparison will be made of the budget allotment and the actual expenditures of each character classification shown in the budget.
8. A study of the insurance program should be made by verification of the insurance policies and the insurance record.
9. A verification of outstanding indebtedness as shown by the bond register and amount of payment will be made.
10. A study will be made of the accounting books as to accuracy and completeness.

Any discrepancies discovered by the auditor should be explained if possible. Improvements in the accounting procedures or business practices should be recommended by the auditor where necessary.

Contents of the audit

Although the contents of the audit will vary with the legal requirements of the state and the auditor, the following lists the minimum essentials of a complete report:

1. Letter of transmittal
2. Comments and supporting data which includes statement of bonded indebtedness and report on insurance in relation to value of property
3. Balance sheet
4. Statement of receipts and disbursements as to source and destination. (Where fund accounting is required by law, a statement of each fund must be made.)
5. Exhibit of receipts, showing a comparison with anticipated budget amounts
6. Exhibit of expenditures, showing a comparison with budget estimates
7. Statement of the disposition of cash. (Divided according to funds, if provided by state law.)
8. Statement of each miscellaneous account

State laws are not specific in stating the contents of the audit. The auditor usually sets the pattern to be followed. If the administrator knows enough about auditing, he may be able to advise with the auditor in developing a report which will be more meaningful to the board of education and the citizens of the community. A good audit made by a competent public accountant is an asset to the administration of the business affairs of the school system.

TOPICS FOR STUDY AND DISCUSSION

1. What form of custodianship of funds is provided by law in your state?
2. What are the requirements in your state for a school depository?
3. What rules and regulations does your district have concerning the custodianship of the school money?
4. What provisions do your state laws make relative to bonding persons who handle school funds?
5. What school officials in your district are bonded? How much is the bond?
6. What kind of bonds are used in your school for bonding officials?
7. What are the disadvantages of a personal bond?

8. How are the school deposits of your district secured?
9. Evaluate the administrative procedures used in your school relative to safeguarding school funds.
10. Are the financial records in your district audited? By whom?
11. Write out a set of criteria for evaluating a school audit.
12. What are the laws of your state relative to auditing school records?
13. Does the business manager of your school system make internal audits? If so, make a study of them and write out your recommendations of their effectiveness.
14. What are the functions of an audit?
15. Make a study of your financial accounts. Are they in order so that auditing may be facilitated?

SELECTED REFERENCES

American Association of School Administrators. *The American School Superintendency.* Thirtieth Yearbook, Washington, D.C.: National Education Association, 1952, chap. VII.

Burke, Arvid D. *Financing Public Schools in the United States.* New York: Harper & Bros., 1951, chap. XX.

Grieder, Calvin, and William E. Rosenstengel. *Public School Administration.* New York: The Ronald Press Co., 1954, chap. XIX.

Linn, Henry H., and Schuyler C. Joyner. *Insurance Practices in School Administration.* New York: The Ronald Press Co., 1952, chap. IX.

Linn, Henry H. *School Business Administration.* New York: The Ronald Press Co., 1956, chap. VII.

Mort, Paul R., and Walter C. Reusser. *Public School Finance.* 2d ed. New York: McGraw-Hill Book Co., Inc., 1951, chap. XI.

Remmlein, Madaline K. *School Law.* New York: McGraw-Hill Book Co., Inc., 1950, chaps. VIII, X.

15

CAPITAL FUNDS AND DEBT SERVICE

ADMINISTRATORS OF school systems throughout the United States will be concerned with financing school improvement programs for a great number of years. Billions of dollars will be spent to construct new plants, to modernize old buildings, and to provide new equipment of all types for the oncoming school population. Since there is a lag in construction programs in comparison with the present-day needs and since all predictions indicate a much larger pupil enrollment for the future, school authorities must give serious consideration to the problem of providing adequate funds to meet the capital outlay needs. All too often the school authorities on the local level are not able to solve the problem because of the many limitations placed upon them by traditions and state laws. Therefore, they are forced to look to another local governmental agency, the state, or even the Federal Government for assistance.

The management of capital funds and debt service activities are closely interrelated and in many instances the management of either one involves the other. For the purpose of this discussion, the capital fund has to do with the money which has not been used to actually pay for a particular physical asset such as land, building, or equipment. On the other hand, debt service has to do with money obtained to make payments for funds advanced to secure physical assets or services.

The major problems and procedures involved in the management of capital funds and debt service activities will be discussed in this chapter. It is realized that there is no one best method of managing these activities for all school districts. Therefore, several different methods, practices, and procedures will be presented.

I. REASONS FOR CAPITAL FUNDS OR INDEBTEDNESS

Traditional method of financing school plant construction

The provision for capital funds has been regarded, since colonial days, as a responsibility of the local school district. As late as 1939, Thurston[1] reported that no state was furnishing as much as a million dollars per year for school plant construction. Since 1945 there has been an awakening concerning state responsibility for financing capital outlay costs for school plants.[2] Although the state is entering the area of financing capital outlay, the local units are still forced to finance large construction programs which cannot be paid out of current money. Therefore, borrowing seems to be the only practical solution for raising sufficient funds to finance the needed school plants. Going into debt permits a school district to acquire new and needed facilities in a current fiscal period and allows the cost to be spread over a reasonable number of years.

Emergencies

A second reason for creating a capital fund or going into debt is to meet an emergency which cannot be paid out of current expenses. If a school plant is partially destroyed by a wind storm or fire, it usually becomes necessary for the district to seek capital funds immediately. Although most districts will have insurance to offset the loss, the cost of rebuilding will likely require additional funds. Emergencies cannot be anticipated to such a degree that they may be financed out of current expense. Therefore a capital fund obtained by borrowing seems to be the common way of meeting emergencies.

Refunding

Boards of education, like individuals, sometimes have found it necessary to reorganize debt payment plans. There are various reasons for such a condition. It may be due to the lack of accurate planning to meet outstanding debts, to the decline in revenue for numerous reasons, or to the securing of lower interest rates on callable bonds which had been issued when interest rates were high. Under these

---

[1] Lee M. Thurston, "State Aid for Construction," *The Nation's Schools*, XXIII (May, 1939), 29–30.

[2] The most detailed report on state programs is Erick L. Lindman *et al.*, *State Provisions for Financing Public-School Capital Outlay Programs*, U.S. Office of Education, Bulletin 1951, No. 6 (Washington, D.C.: Government Printing Office, 1951).

or other circumstances it is occasionally necessary for the board of education to reorganize its present debt payment plan and pay the outstanding debts with money received from a new bond issue. Such bonds are known as refunding bonds.

Most of the states have strict laws relative to the issuance of refunding bonds. The finance officer of the school districts should make a careful study of the state laws and be sure that all legal requirements are satisfied. The authors believe that careful planning of the financial program will eliminate, in most cases, the necessity for issuing refunding bonds. There are times, however, when refunding is a necessary, sound, and feasible financial procedure.

2. METHODS OF FINANCING CAPITAL OUTLAY

In most school districts the financing of capital outlay and current expenses is different. Capital expenditures may require greater amounts during periods of construction programs than can be met from annual tax resources, while current expenses may be paid by fairly uniform tax rates from one year to another. At the present time, when building needs are so great, even larger districts are unable to finance the necessary capital outlay programs without going into debt. Because the construction of buildings makes relatively large expenditure demands on the local units, a number of different plans have been adopted for financing outlay programs. Also, newer methods for financing capital outlay are being given careful consideration by a number of states and the Federal Government.

Pay-as-you-go-plan

If possible, it is highly desirable to finance capital outlay programs out of current income. However, the taxing power in a vast majority of school districts is too limited to permit the use of this plan. This is true, especially today, when the capital fund needs have increased so much in comparison with the increased taxable wealth, and when the concept exists that total capital funds must be locally financed. The objectives of the pay-as-you-go plan are to save interest charges on borrowed money and to place the cost of the improvements on the citizens who authorize them. One of the main reasons more school systems have not adopted the pay-as-you-go plan has been the burden of past indebtedness. Unless the several states and the Federal Government share in the construction cost of the present building needs, there will be fewer districts in the future using this plan than there have been in the past. A district must have a high valuation of taxable property, a low tax rate, moderate building needs, and a small indebtedness before it can consider the pay-as-you-go plan for financing capital outlay programs.

Reserve funds

A capital reserve fund is similar to a depreciation reserve fund. Both presume that funds will be set aside annually and allowed to earn interest. The capital reserve fund will be used to finance a project when needed while the depreciation reserve fund will be used to replace the item being depreciated when it is worn out. The reserve fund method is a fairly economical way to finance building, especially in periods of high prices, high interest rates, or both. There are, however, only a very few school districts that can postpone the building program until a reserve fund has been established. If school districts, during World War II, had looked ahead and set up reserve funds, many of our current building problems would have been easier to finance. Many districts, however, had heavy indebtedness and did not feel it profitable to build capital reserves and pay off bonds at the same time. Whenever a district is free of debt and is not in the need of a new plant immediately, the reserve fund method should receive careful consideration. The investment of reserve funds should receive careful management under the supervision of adequate state laws so that school boards will not lose money which the citizens have paid for future use.

Bonds

As a method of financing capital outlay, issuing bonds has been accepted more than any other plan. Although the payment of the bond and the interest results in a greater total cost, the plan is more feasible and it has the advantage of spreading the cost over a period of years. Even in large cities where the pay-as-you-go or reserve fund plans may be feasible, school administrators are often faced with the necessity of making capital improvements to such an extent that bonding seems to be the only practical solution.

A bond is an obligation issued by a corporation or government to pay a principal sum of money on a certain date, with interest. In the case of a school district, it would be an obligation made by the board of education to pay the amount of the bond and interest on a certain date. Chatters and Tenner[3] have classified bonds in several ways.

[3] Karl H. Chatters and Irving Tenner, *Municipal and Governmental Accounting* (Englewood Cliffs, N.J.: Prentice-Hall, Inc., 1946), p. 418.

One of the classifications which is of particular value to the school administrator is the method of retirement.

Serial Bond. The serial bonds are so named because they are paid off, as a rule, in a given order. So many are paid at the end of the first year, so many at the end of the second year, and so on, until the whole issue has been paid. There are three commonly used methods for retirement of serial bonds.

If the population of the community is fairly stable and if the building needs have been met, the method of paying equal annual payments on the principal is sound. The total payment, principal and interest, will be much less toward the final payments. An illustration of such a schedule for the retirement of a $1,000,000 bond issue for a ten-year period at 3 per cent is shown in Table 11.

TABLE 11. Example of a ten-year serial equal payment on principal bond issue, $1,000,000 at 3 per cent

Principal	Bonds Retired	Interest Payment	Total Annual Payments
$1,000,000	$ 100,000	$ 30,000	$ 130,000
900,000	100,000	27,000	127,000
800,000	100,000	24,000	124,000
700,000	100,000	21,000	121,000
600,000	100,000	18,000	118,000
500,000	100,000	15,000	115,000
400,000	100,000	12,000	112,000
300,000	100,000	9,000	109,000
200,000	100,000	6,000	106,000
100,000	100,000	3,000	103,000
Totals	$1,000,000	$165,000	$1,165,000

An annual payment of $100,000 on the principal, plus the interest of $30,000 would make the total payment for the first year $130,000. The total interest charge for the ten years would be $165,000. The total cost over the ten years would be $1,165,000.

There are times when a new bond issue should be fitted into the existing indebtedness of the district. In such cases, unequal annual payments are suggested. For example, a school district floats a bond issue of $500,000 for a period of ten years at 3 per cent interest and the present indebtedness will not be paid for at least five years. However, the board feels that the total payments should not exceed $80,000 because of the excessive tax burdens. Table 12 illustrates how

TABLE 12. Example of a ten-year serial bond tied to old bond issue, $500,000 at 3 per cent

Payment on Old-Issue Interest and Principal	Bonds Retired on New Issue	Interest Paid on New Issue	Total Annual Payments
$ 45,000	$ 10,000	$ 15,000	$ 70,000
35,000	20,000	14,700	69,700
25,000	30,000	14,100	69,100
15,000	40,000	13,200	68,200
5,000	55,000	12,000	72,000
	65,000	10,350	75,350
	70,000	8,400	78,400
	70,000	6,300	76,300
	70,000	4,200	74,200
	70,000	2,100	72,100
$125,000	$500,000	$100,350	$725,350

the payments of the principal on the new issue may be varied from year to year to meet the financial conditions of the school district.

The total amount of interest will be greater in such an arrangement because of the small initial payment made on the principal. Such a plan of payment is often necessary because of outstanding indebtedness.

A third plan of payment of serial bonds is known as the annuity plan, which provides for the total payment, principal and interest, to be approximately equal each year. The payments on the principal would be relatively smaller in the early years and larger in the later

TABLE 13. Example of a ten-year serial annuity bond issue, $500,000 at 3 per cent

Principal	Bonds Retired	Interest	Total Payments
$500,000	$ 44,000	$15,000	$ 59,000
456,000	45,000	13,680	58,680
411,000	46,000	12,330	58,330
365,000	48,000	10,950	58,950
317,000	49,000	9,510	58,510
268,000	50,000	8,040	58,040
218,000	52,000	6,540	58,540
166,000	54,000	4,980	58,980
112,000	55,000	3,360	58,360
57,000	57,000	1,710	58,710
Totals	$500,000	$86,100	$586,100

years. Table 13 gives an illustration of payments for a $500,000 bond issue for a period of ten years at 3 per cent interest.

The extent to which the total annual payments may be equal depends upon the denomination of the bonds. The example as given in Table 13 used $1,000. The total annual payments did not vary as much as $1,000.

Various provisions may be used in working out payment schedules. There are a number of factors which must be taken into consideration before the schedule of payments is to be made, such as stability of assessed valuation of property, old indebtedness to be paid, possibility of new indebtedness before present issue has been retired, and the tax rate to be levied.

Term Bonds. The whole amount of a term bond (sometimes known as "straight bond") issue is paid off at one time and the length of the term is usually a relatively long period. They are called either *sinking fund* or *nonsinking fund* bonds. Sinking fund bonds provide that money for the redemption be accrued annually over the life of the bonds. By this means the district will have a sufficient amount of money to pay off the bonds at maturity. The term bond is an expensive way to finance capital improvement. Although term bonds were used by schools extensively in the 1920's, they are seldom used today. Many of the states have laws prohibiting the issuing of term bonds by school districts.

Serial-redemption Sinking-fund Bond. This type of bond is a combination of the sinking fund and serial bond. It is a term bond in that all the issues are scheduled to mature on the same future date and it is callable. The district is required to vote continuing tax levy for the life of the bond and the annual collection from the levy is pledged to the sinking fund. The sinking fund must be used each year to call as many bonds as the amount will redeem. The bonds are numbered serially and are called in order. This type of bond has all the good qualities of a serial bond but none of the disadvantages of the sinking fund bond. The district is protected against unfavorable fluctuations in depression years and accelerates the payment on the principal in inflation periods. If school districts would have had such bonds during the 1940's, many more schools would have paid more on the indebtedness. Such bonds should have careful consideration by administrators.

Length of bond issues

A satisfactory upper limit on the period of a school bond issue has never been established. Most commonly, bonds have been issued for twenty-year terms.   There are, however, great numbers issued for thirty years. If a bond issue can be paid off in ten to fifteen years, it is highly desirable.   Certainly, the period should be as short as possible so that the debt will not hamper the current operation of the school system.

Legal aspects of bonding

The school district is created by the state and its power to issue bonds is regulated by the constitution and the statutes.   Some form of supervision by the state or county agency of local bond issues is required and state approval is becoming more common each year.   All the states have legal provisions covering the issuance of bonds for capital outlay.   All but three states require elections to be held on the proposed bond issues.   In most of the states a regularly qualified voter may participate in the election.   However, a few states restrict the voting to taxpayers or property owners.   In about two-thirds of the states a simple majority vote is sufficient to decide the outcome, while about one-third require a majority of 60 to 67 per cent for approval of the issue.[4]

Debt limitations usually pertain to all outstanding indebtedness. In most cases the limit of indebtedness is stated in terms of a percentage of the total valuation of taxable property, ranging from 2 to 40 per cent.   There are, however, some cases where the limitation is based upon maximum debt that may be incurred in any one year.   A school board which plans to vote bonds should employ an attorney, preferably a bonding attorney, to guide and direct the procedure of the board's actions through the bond issue.   The employment of an attorney does not, however, lessen the administrator's responsibility of having a thorough knowledge of the state laws relative to bond issues.

State support of capital funds

It was pointed out in the beginning of this chapter that there has been an awakening to the fact that the state has a responsibility for financing capital outlay for school plants.   Florida was the first state, in 1945, to introduce a plan for making capital outlay a part of the state foundation program.   Other states are taking more and more responsibility for providing capital funds.   Some are making grants, others are using some type of an equalization plan, and still some few are not giving any support for capital funds.

[4] Calvin Grieder and William E. Rosenstengel, *Public School Administration* (New York: The Ronald Press Co., 1954), p. 529.

Lindman *et al.*[5] state some fundamental characteristics which can be used in developing a satisfactory state program for financing capital outlay. They are:

1. Each state should make provision for state assistance in the financing of capital outlay programs.
2. The state program for financing school buildings should be scientifically developed.
3. State plans for financing capital outlay should be developed as an integral part of the foundation program of education.
4. Any acceptable program should provide adequately and equitably for all essential school plant needs.
5. Provisions should be made in the program for some state grants rather than for loans alone.
6. The state plan should provide for both emergency and long-range needs.
7. The program should be financed through an equitable combination of state and local revenues.
8. The funds should be derived chiefly from current state and local revenue.
9. The program should be administered by the state department of education.
10. An objective formula for apportioning funds should be incorporated in law.
11. The program should provide for equitable tax effort.
12. Each local school system should have a reasonable margin of local tax leeway or bonding capacity.
13. The program should place maximum emphasis on local responsibility and state leadership.
14. Comprehensive local school plant studies should be required.
15. Each local school system should develop and adopt a long-range program.
16. The state program should assure all necessary facilities in all permanent school centers.

Today, when a vast majority of school districts are so far behind in school plant needs, there should be some emergency provisions by the state for providing capital funds. The funds could be provided by the state on a loan and grant basis. Local districts should not be required to issue bonds or levy taxes which would be an excessive effort. The formula used for the apportionment for such aid "might well provide that the districts will pay back to the state in accordance with their ability over a period of years."[6] If a district could not af-

[5] Erick L. Lindman *et al.*, *State Provisions for Financing Public-School Capital Outlay Programs*, U.S. Office of Education, Bulletin 1951, No. 6 (Washington, D.C.: Government Printing Office, 1951), pp. 154–57.
[6] *Ibid.*, p. 159.

ford to repay the whole amount needed in a certain number of years, the excessive amount might be considered a grant. The state should take the leadership of such a program so that the local units will be able to provide the necessary facilities which are so badly needed in so many places.

School building authorities or holding companies

Since World War II, new innovations for financing school construction have come into use. The "holding companies" and "building authorities" are legalized in some states.[7] The companies furnish the money to finance the building projects and rent the facilities to the districts until the debt is paid, at which time the district is given the title of the property. Lindman *et al.* state:

For such a plan to be effective, however, it must be carefully integrated with a long-range financing program so that capital outlay funds provided currently by the state [if any is given] can be used toward retiring those bonds [loans]. If that is not done the least wealthy districts will not be in position to provide the facilities needed because they will not be able to make the necessary payments.[8]

This method of financing capital outlay is a means of getting around the constitutional limitation of debt which is a problem of many districts. Some school authorities do not believe this method of financing capital funds is the solution to the crisis in schoolhouse construction. It does, however, enable some districts to provide the facilities which could not otherwise be obtained.

Federal aid for capital funds

The need for federal aid to education has been discussed for years. These discussions have usually been centered toward support for the total education program. Not until the year 1955 had there been so much discussion relative to the Federal Government's giving aid for capital funds. Preceding the first White House Conference ever to concentrate entirely on education, which was held in Washington in late November, 1955, over 3,600 local meetings throughout the nation were held to discuss educational problems. At these local meetings there were nearly one-half million people in attendance. One of the problems discussed with some of the local groups was "How Can We Finance Our Schools—Build and Operate Them?" The need for more money for capital funds to provide adequate hous-

---

[7] Some of the states which have such programs are Kentucky, Indiana, and Pennsylvania. South Carolina has a form of state aid which might be classified as State Building Authority.
[8] *Ibid.*, p. 159.

ing for the children was foremost in the thinking of thousands of individuals.

The President, speaking on film to the 2,000 participants at the White House Conference, said that federal aid "was in the heart of the problem." He went on to say "that . . . if the Federal Government doesn't step in with leadership and with providing credit and money where necessary, there will be a lack of schools in certain important areas. And this cannot be allowed." A majority of the participants at the conference agreed that federal funds must be provided for school plant needs. The federal funds, however, "should never be permitted to become a deterrent to state and local initiative."

The President in his January, 1956, State of the Union message asked Congress to provide "an effective program of federal assistance to help erase the existing deficit of school classrooms." In a budget request made January 12, 1956, the President asked Congress for $1.25 billion or $250 million a year, in direct grants. He said that "such a program should be limited to a five-year period, [and] must operate to increase, rather than decrease local and state support of schools." There was a bill presented to Congress which provided for the features suggested by the President but it was defeated.

3. SHORT-TERM SCHOOL INDEBTEDNESS

Short-term indebtedness is usually limited to borrowing money for some reason to pay current expenses. As a general rule school districts cannot borrow money to pay current expenses unless there is statutory authority to create such indebtedness. Short-term borrowing is usually the result of some emergency such as the failure to collect the anticipated revenue. In such cases anticipated warrants or notes are issued pending the receipt of taxes or some other anticipated income. However, the amount of warrants or notes issued may not exceed the anticipated revenue. The state laws will describe how such warrants or notes must be issued, and it is generally considered a condition of borrowing that as the anticipated receipts are collected the income must be used to retire the anticipated warrants or notes. It is not uncommon for the law to stipulate the amount of the notes or warrants in relation to the total anticipated income. The common amount is about 80 per cent. In most cases, the tax anticipation warrants or notes bear interest with the maximum rate set by law. If warrants or notes are issued in anticipation of tax levies for a certain year, they do not augment the existing indebtedness. The payment of the warrants or notes must be paid out of the income for that particular year, regardless of when the income is received by the school district.

In some states it is permissible for school districts to create short-term indebtedness through what is known as *Bond Anticipation* notes. Such notes are issued against authorized bonds which for some reason have not been sold. When the bonds are sold the notes are paid out of the bond proceeds. This is a practice used to give the school district immediate working capital so that the project will not be delayed. It is also used in some school districts to delay the issuance of the bonds until the greater amount of the authorized issue is needed. The amount of interest paid out on the bond anticipation notes will usually be much less than the interest on the total bond issue. This is often a real economy to the school district.

4. ADMINISTRATION OF SCHOOL BONDING PRACTICE

The school administrator should be thoroughly acquainted with the principles and practices of school bondings, since the need of obtaining capital funds through voting and issuing school bonds will continue for many years. Whenever bonds are voted by the people, it is imperative that the proceeds be used only for the purposes stipulated within the authorization. If the voters authorize a definite number of bonds to be issued, the board of education does not have to issue the total amount at once. The board has a continuing power and may issue new bonds at any time, provided that the total does not exceed the amount voted by the people.

Several suggestions are presented in this section for the administrator when he is faced with the problem of providing capital outlay funds by a bond issue. In presenting these suggestions it is assumed that a careful study of needs has been made.

Relationship of new debt to total expenses

It is not an uncommon practice for a school district to vote bonds for payment of a new school plant without the administration determining in advance the effect of the new indebtedness upon the total cost of the school. A new school plant will likely require additional custodial services and supplies, more heat and electricity, increased insurance premiums because of increased cost of construction, and added instructional costs. All of these increased costs must be paid from current expenses. In addition to these current expenses there will be interest and bond payments to be made—all of which will likely result in an increased tax rate for the school district. These additional costs should be anticipated in the advance of building new plants.

There are school districts today which have built additional plants and are trying to operate them on the same current expense budget as was in use before the new building was constructed. In these cases one will likely find poor housekeeping standards and buildings which are deteriorating rapidly. It is false economy to construct expensive buildings and not provide the necessary current expenses which will assure adequate upkeep.

Many school districts have not been out of debt for a great number of years and will likely not be for years to come. There is a tendency to postpone maturity payments of new bonds until older issues are paid so that tax rates will not be increased. This practice is questionable. It results in large interest payments and it may hinder progress in the future. It is a good practice to begin retiring bonds as soon as possible after they are sold even though tax rates are increased.

Creating good credit rating

A good credit rating is as essential for a school district as it is for an individual. The market for school bonds will depend to a great extent upon the credit rating of the district.[9] The interest rates are often determined in light of the credit rating. The rating which a school district receives is based not only upon the financial condition and management but also upon economic and sociological factors of the district. Credit agencies[10] are interested in knowing certain facts about the amount and nature of the debt, such as reason for creating the debt, the character of all outstanding debts, whether the debt has increased or decreased, method of payment of debt, and whether or not the bonds are tax-exempt.

The economic and social factors which have bearing on the credit rating are: character of the population, resources of the community, density of population, employment situation, stability of the income of the community, and general progress of the total community.

The financial conditions and management of the school district are important considerations in establishing a good credit rating. Some of the financial conditions considered are: (1) trends in valuation of taxable property, (2) relation of assessed valuation to true valuation of property, (3) trends in tax rates, (4) trends in tax collections, (5)

[9] Among the best known credit agencies are: Dun and Bradstreet, Inc., Moody's Investors Service, and Poor's Publishing Co., all of New York City.

[10] Karl H. Chatters and A. M. Hillhouse, *Local Government Debt Administration* (Englewood Cliffs, N.J.: Prentice-Hall, Inc., 1939), pp. 282–87.

trends in local income other than tax sources, (6) tax limitations set by law, and (7) state aid for indebtedness.

The efficiency of the school administration is not overlooked by rating agencies. If the management of the financial affairs shows that good business practices are being followed, the credit rating will be more favorable. If sound budgetary procedures are followed, if financial safeguards are evident, if the school seems to be meeting the approval of the citizens and business men in the community, the investment houses will tend to be more interested in purchasing the bonds. Careful cooperation with bond dealers, prompt preparation of credit reports, and courtesy to representatives of investors will build goodwill in the investment circles and will aid in the selling of the bonds.

The bonding attorney

Some boards of education retain legal advisors at all times, while others secure such services when needed. In some situations the district or county attorney serves the boards of education in the area. Whatever the situation may be, if the board of education is holding an election with a view to issuing bonds, a bonding attorney should be employed. Most local attorneys are not approved as bonding attorneys. This lack of approval is not a reflection on the competence of the local lawyer; it is merely that investors will require the approving opinion of a legal bonding specialist. It will save both time and money for the board of education to employ the bonding attorney at the very beginning of the procedures which take place leading to the issuing of bonds. The fees paid to a bonding attorney will vary with localities but usually they are a small fraction of 1 per cent of the bonds.[11]

There are a number of documents which must be certified as to their authenticity. The *Twenty-Seventh Yearbook* of the American Association of School Administrators lists the following:

1. Statement of assessed valuation
2. Sworn statement of debt
3. Minutes of board meeting at which resolution to borrow was passed
4. Citation of legal authority to borrow
5. Resolution authorizing school election to approve the bond issue
6. Notice of election
7. Certificate of publication of election notice
8. Form of ballot

[11] Lists of nationally known bond attorneys may be secured from local banks, bond dealers, and *The Bond Buyer,* New York, N.Y.

9. Proceedings canvassing election returns
10. Certificate of public official showing that election returns are certified public record
11. Advertisement of sale
12. Certificate of publication of sale notice
13. Certificate of sale and award
14. Resolution confirming sale
15. Certificate of signature on bonds
16. Copy of bond form
17. Nonlitigation certificates
18. Treasurer's receipt for payment for bonds[12]

Selling bonds

Bonds must be sold. The most common method of bond disposal by the school district is the sale of the total issue to a broker or a syndicate of bidders. These bidders or buyers act as "wholesalers" of the bonds and are willing to pay a better price if the bonds can be resold readily. Brokers have found through experience that individual investors expect certain rather simple but still very important standards of bonds. They are:[13]

1. Bonds should be attractively printed or engraved on good, high-grade paper with adequate protection against forgeries or counterfeiting.
2. Bonds should be of one thousand dollars' denomination.
3. Bonds should be nonregistered, with provision for optional registration.
4. Bonds should be in coupon form.
5. Bonds and interest should be payable in a large financial center.
6. Bond maturity schedules should be arranged so that purchases may be made in blocks of five or ten thousand dollars.
7. Bond prospectus should be prepared giving complete information on the bonds and financial condition of district.[14]

Getting bids on bonds

In most of the states the local boards of education have the responsibility for selling the bonds. In a few states, a central state

[12] American Association of School Administrators, *American School Buildings,* Twenty-Seventh Yearbook (Washington, D.C.: The Association, 1949), pp. 303–4.

[13] For detailed suggestions on "Planning a Bond Issue to Meet Investor's Wishes," see Henry H. Linn (ed.), *School Business Administration* (New York: The Ronald Press Co., 1956), pp. 359–62.

[14] For suggestions on contents of bond prospectus see Henry H. Linn, *Practical School Economics* (New York: Bureau of Publications, Teachers College, Columbia University, 1934), p. 366.

agency handles the marketing of all bonds issued by local political subdivisions. In those districts which have the responsibility of selling the bonds, attention should be given to obtaining a number of good bidders. The school officials should try to find a time when the market is not "flooded" with similar issues. The bonds should be sold on the basis of sealed bids. The time, place, and manner of receiving bids should be advertised in financial journals[15] and in newspapers of wide general circulation. The bid calls should be made far enough in advance of the sale so that bidders will have sufficient time to examine the prospectus and analyze the information about the bonds and district.

The business official of the school district should answer inquiries from bond dealers promptly. A delay in answering any correspondence relative to the bond sales may reduce the number of bidders and thus cause a very poor sale of the total issue. The board of education should adhere to time as stated in the call for bids—when the bids will be accepted and when all bids will be opened. Promptness in these matters will be appreciated by the bidders.

Choosing best bid

Choosing the best bid out of several different bids of a total bond issue is not always an easy task. Bonds are generally sold by sealed bid or auction sale and if split rates, premiums, or discounts have been offered by the bidders it becomes quite a task to calculate the best bid. Assistance from the financial experts who may be present will often help the board of education determine the most satisfactory bid. As a general rule the bidders will have formal calculation sheets and interest tables with them and will be able to calculate the best bid very quickly.

School bond records

It is not only essential to keep an accurate record of the minutes leading up to the issuance of a school bond, but it is also essential to keep a complete and accurate record of all bonds sold and interest paid. The record should provide the following:

1. Purpose of issue
2. Date of sale
3. Amount of bonds sold
4. Rate of interest
5. Name and address of purchaser
6. Name and address of ultimate owner, if possible

[15] *The Daily Bond Buyer* is a good example.

7. Denomination of bonds by serial numbers
8. Dates of payments of interest and principal
9. Amount of payments of interest and principal
10. Paying agent
11. Amount of debt service charges
12. Record of canceled coupons and bonds paid

All bond payments and interest due should be paid on time. State laws usually make it mandatory that the money collected from taxes for payment of principal and interest on bonds must retain its specific identity. The mixing of funds is usually prohibited and must be used for the specific authorized purpose of payment of bonds and interest.

5. PUBLICITY FOR SCHOOL BOND ELECTIONS

Interpreting needs to the public

Today when taxes and the cost of living are high, school officials cannot take for granted that a school bond issue will be voted by the citizens. Much time and strenuous effort are needed to win the approval of any major financial program. School administrators must realize that the citizens are not always aware of the critical needs of the school and that the school must compete with other community activities for financial support. The voting public must be informed of the existing facilities, new facilities needed, the financial condition of the district, the amount of money necessary for the new facilities, and the effect the bond issue will have upon individuals' taxes. After all is said and done, the extent that taxes will be increased will determine in large measure the way an individual votes when he goes to cast his ballot.

Although school officials try to carry out a continuous public relations program, it becomes necessary to conduct a systematic campaign to put over a bond issue. The media for such a campaign are many; however, a few suggestions which have been successful are outlined below:

1. Organize a citizens' committee representing all phases of community life—business, labor, professions, housewives, industry, the press, and so on. Be sure that this group of citizens understands the proposition and has all the necessary information about the needs of the school district, the costs, population trends, etc.
2. Get the members of the citizens' committee to visit the schools and get firsthand information on the needs of the school district.
3. Furnish the individuals of the committee with all information which may be desired.

4. Hold open meetings of the board of education and invite citizens to attend.
5. Furnish newspapers with usable materials for news stories and feature articles. Make use of photographs for publication.
6. Make a set or two of slides and script for use in presenting facts to the public.
7. Conduct neighborhood meetings.
8. Organize a speakers' bureau and furnish speakers with the necessary information.
9. Procure television and radio coverage.
10. Obtain endorsements of the proposed bond issue from organizations and individuals.
11. Send to each home the directions for voting. This will include place for voting, copy of ballot correctly marked, and the time that the polls will be open.
12. Organize "get-out-the-vote" committee for election day.
13. Get committees of Parent-Teacher Association to organize "car pools" for transportation to polls and also furnish "baby sitters" where needed.
14. Deliver "dodgers" giving important facts on the bond issue to each home the night before election.
15. Repeat—repeat, and repeat the facts about the needs of the schools. Do not rely upon any one media, use many.

Reporting to the public on use of bond proceeds

Too often school officials do not report to the citizens on the use of the bond proceeds. A systematic plan should be used to tell the citizens how their bond money was used. It is well worth the expenditure of funds to print a report on the expenditure of the bond money and send it to each home. The report should show pictures of new plants, classrooms, and other facilities. A good story should be included describing the facilities and what the facilities mean to the educational program of the children. Cost studies should also be worked out so that the layman can understand how his money was spent. School administrators should feel that they owe the lay people an accurate and complete account of all funds voted. This will make the next bond issue more easily carried, especially if the citizens feel that they are getting value received for the taxes being paid.

6. MANAGEMENT OF BOND MONEY

When invest funds?

When bonds are delivered to the purchaser, the board of education will have the responsibility of management of the money received.   If for some reason the construction of a school plant is not started immediately, the major portion of the bond money should be safely invested until it is needed.   However, in about ten states the boards of education are not authorized to invest any type of school funds.   The investment of idle funds is a business proposition and will save the school district the much needed money.

Kinds of investments

The investment of school funds should be so planned that any amount of the account can be liquidated when needed without cashing the entire investment.   The investment of the school fund should be such that there would be no question of its safety.   Probably the most satisfactory investment would be placed in United States Government securities, such as Treasury bills, certificates, notes, or bonds. There are times when a board of education may wish to purchase state or local government bonds.   Often these securities are not as readily marketable as those of the U.S. Government.

Safeguarding the funds[16]

In order to be sure that capital funds are on hand when needed, the administrator must safeguard all deposits in a bank in excess of the $10,000 protected by the Federal Deposit Insurance Corporation.   This safeguarding may be made through effecting a depository agreement with the bank.   The bank should deposit with the nearest Federal Reserve Bank government bonds equal to the deposit of the school district and to be held in escrow for the protection of the deposit.   No administrator can afford to take any chances with the safety of the school funds.

TOPICS FOR STUDY AND DISCUSSION

1. Why has the financing of capital funds been considered for so long a responsibility of the local school district?
2. What are some of the problems that confront the local unit in financing capital outlay?
3. What are the advantages and disadvantages of using the pay-as-you-go method of financing capital outlays?
4. What type of bonds may be issued in your state?
5. Why are serial bonds more desirable than straight or sinking fund bonds?
6. When should a school district use refunding bonds?

[16] See Chapter 14 for a more complete discussion on this subject.

7. What do the school laws of your state say concerning the issuance of refunding bonds?
8. How are capital funds obtained in your state?
9. Work out payment schedule for a twenty-year annuity schedule of a $2,000,000 bond issue at 2½ per cent interest. Bonds will be issued in $1,000 denomination.
10. What is the maximum length of a bond issue in your state?
11. What are pro and con arguments relative to school building authorities or holding companies?
12. Can you justify federal support for school plant construction programs? Why?
13. If your state furnishes capital funds, evaluate the method used.
14. Should state funds for capital funds be used to pay bonded indebtedness? When?
15. What is the maximum amount of bonds that your school district may issue by a vote of the people?
16. Why is a campaign necessary for voting a bond issue?
17. When should a board of education invest school funds?
18. Do the objections to general federal aid for education apply with equal force to school construction aid? Why?

SELECTED REFERENCES

American Association of School Administrators. *American School Buildings.* Twenty-Seventh Yearbook. Washington, D.C.: The Association, 1949, pp. 288–308.

ARNOLD, WILLIAM E., and WILLIAM B. CASTETTER. "Problems of Business Administration," *Review of Educational Research,* Vol. XX, No. 2, April, 1950.

BURKE, ARVID J. *Financing Public Schools in the United States.* New York: Harper & Bros., 1951, pp. 318–22 and 446–73.

GRIEDER, CALVIN, and WILLIAM E. ROSENSTENGEL. *Public School Administration.* New York: The Ronald Press Co., 1954, chap. XXIII.

HUTCHINS, CLAYTON D., and ALBERT R. MUNSE. *Public School Finance Programs of the United States.* (U.S. Office of Education, Misc. No. 22.) Washington, D.C.: Government Printing Office, 1955.

LINDMAN, ERICK, et al. *State Provisions for Financing Public-School Capital Outlay Programs.* (U.S. Office of Education, Bulletin 1951, No. 6.) Washington, D.C.: Government Printing Office, 1950.

LINN, HENRY H. *School Business Administration.* New York: The Ronald Press Co., 1956, chap. XII.

National Conference of Professors of Educational Administration. *Problems and Issues in Public School Finance.* New York: Bureau of Publications, Teachers College, Columbia University, 1952, chap. XXII.

REMMLEIN, MADALINE K. *The Law of Local Public School Administration.* New York: McGraw-Hill Book Co., Inc., 1953, chap. II.

16

INTERNAL ACCOUNTING[1]

IN THE PRESENT-DAY public school system, especially the high school division, the management of business affairs has become big business. One often hears and sees statements relative to "Our system of free public education," but if one investigates or has had or has a child in school he immediately begins to question whether education is free to all youth. It is not an uncommon practice to charge fees to students for the privilege of pursuing certain courses. Some of the courses for which fees are often charged are music, typing, sciences, and industrial or vocational courses. In some schools a fee is charged for each course a student may wish to pursue, while other schools do not charge any fees.

One of the large sources of money which must be managed in the average school is student extra-class activity money. This money is derived from the extra-class fees, athletic contests, plays, concerts, special programs of all kinds, sales, and numerous other ways. As a matter of fact, the cost to the student who participates in the so-called extra-class activities is almost unbelievable.[2]

In addition to the fees from extra-class activities, there is the fund relative to the management of the cafeteria. In some schools the management of this fund is a responsibility of the principal while

[1] For the purpose of this chapter, "Internal Accounting" means the mangement of all the money handled by a school which may be obtained from all sources other than those funds appropriated by the board of education. This money from the several sources of the school will be called the "Activity fund." The management of the activity fund is usually under the immediate supervision of the principal.

[2] See Harold C. Hand, *Principal Findings of the 1947–48 Basic Studies of the Illinois Secondary School Curriculum,* Bulletin No. 2 (Springfield, Ill., 1949), pp. 54–64 for a good example of costs for pupils who participate in extra-class activities.

in others the management of the cafeteria money is a responsibility of the central business office of the school district.[3]

From the several sources of income found in a school one will see that a large sum of money must be managed. Even in a small school there may be two or three thousand dollars handled each year. In some of the large schools the amount may be more than $50,000 a year. The management of such large sums of money is an administrative responsibility which should receive careful consideration.

The purpose of this chapter is not to present the pros and cons on extra costs to students nor to discuss extra-class activities but to present a sound and practical plan for managing those finances of a school which will be called the *activity fund.*

I. THE ROLE OF THE BOARD OF EDUCATION IN THE MANAGEMENT OF THE ACTIVITY FUND

School administrators will agree that it is not the function of the board of education to do the administrative work in connection with the management of the activity fund. They will also agree that the board of education has a function of making some general policies pertaining to the management of this fund. The methods used in raising funds, what accounts will be handled by the school, what fees if any will be charged students, and the general business practices to be followed are some of the problems which should receive attention in the rules and regulations of the board of education. Authorities in the field of school administration will agree that the board of education should accept, if not provided by law, the same responsibility over the activity funds as is accepted over the regular public school money.

How will activities be financed?

It is the responsibility of the board of education to determine whether activities will be financed through appropriations from public money or through admissions, dues, and other money-making plans. Today, one will find many different plans for financing the activities of the schools. In some schools the boards of education appropriate funds for the support of some of the activities, while in other schools the boards do not aid any of the activities from the regular school funds. In the latter cases, raising of funds to support the activities presents many problems.

---

[3] See section 4 of this chapter for a more detailed discussion on management of cafeteria funds.

In a recent study[4] of some 125 junior and senior high schools in Maryland, it was found that about 38 per cent of the schools charged activity fees which ranged from 50 cents to ten dollars and that about one half of the schools charged class dues ranging from one dollar per year in the seventh grade to six dollars per year in the twelfth grade. This study also showed that approximately 65 per cent of the schools charged students admission to attend athletic games.   The prices of admission ranged from five cents to one dollar depending upon the type of contest.   In addition to the above-mentioned expenses, sometimes students were charged for (1) attending plays and other programs, (2) receiving the school paper and year book, (3) attending movies in the schools, (4) attending dances and other social events, (5) going on class trips, (6) graduating expenses, and (7) participating in all other types of activities found in the schools.

Similar studies have been made in other states[5] with about the same findings.   These studies point out that the principals of the schools are forced to raise money through many means in order to finance the activities of the school.   These costs to students are sometimes called "hidden tuition," because activities are essential in the modern educational program.   It is very doubtful if one can find many administrators who will not agree that most school activities are valuable in the educational program.   If an activity does not have an educational value it should not be incorporated into the school program.   Many of the so-called activities are as valuable to some students as some of the regular class offerings.   If the activities have educational value, why should they not be financed in the same manner as other parts of the educational program?   The board of education of a school system should establish a policy on how school activities will be financed.   Such a policy should state which activities will be financed from public funds and which ones will be financed by the pupils.   Also such a policy should give some consideration to the maximum amount students should be expected to pay to participate in activities.

Shall fees be charged students who pursue certain courses?

In many of the public school systems charging of fees has become part of the regular financing programs.   All types of fees are charged both elementary and secondary school pupils.   Some of the more common fees being charged by the schools are library, supplementary

---

[4] Willard L. Hawkins, "Can Parents Afford to Send Their Children to High School?" *Nation's Schools*, LII (July, 1953), 51–54.

[5] See Harold C. Hand, *op. cit.*

readers, science, music, art, industrial arts, commerce, home economics, and numerous others. The number and amount of the fees will depend to a great extent upon the degree the schools are being supported by public funds. Many administrators feel that the amount of money available from public sources is not sufficient to operate the schools, and they establish the practice of charging fees for purchasing the necessary instructional materials. Such a practice is nothing short of charging tuition. If public schools are to be free to all boys and girls who live within the administrative unit, there does not seem to be any justification for charging fees. It is very questionable whether the charging of fees by boards of education is legal. Many students are unable to pursue certain courses in some schools because of the fees. If public schools are to be financed by the public through a system of taxation, all children should have the same opportunity to pursue courses without regard to their ability to pay. The board of education should express its feelings on the practices to be followed relative to charging fees in the schools of the administrative unit and let them be known to all concerned.

Which accounts shall be the responsibility of the school?

The different accounts which a principal is responsible for managing will vary in the different administrative units. In some districts the principals will manage all funds collected within the school. In others, the business offices of the boards of education will manage the funds received from fees and cafeterias and leave only the activity money as the responsibility of the principals. It is doubtful if any one person can say which is the better practice. Much depends upon the general administrative setup of the district and the beliefs held by the members of the board of education. It is essential, however, for the board of education with the advice of the superintendent to take definite action on this problem and state in the policies or rules and regulations of the board who will be responsible for the supervision of the several different funds. After such a policy has been stated, the chief administrator has the responsibility to see that the different funds are managed according to the mandates of the board. Such a procedure is good business management because responsibility to manage funds can be placed on certain employees.

Shall money be collected by teachers for outside agencies?

Although funds collected through the schools for outside agencies such as the United Forces, the Red Cross, the March of Dimes, and so forth are not usually handled in the same manner as internal school accounts, the boards of education have certain responsibilities relative to this problem. Some boards of education have regulations preventing the collection of money from students for outside agencies, while others do not have any regulations concerning such funds. These outside agencies usually have worthy causes for money, but whether or not the administrators and teachers should be expected to serve as collecting agencies for these organizations is debatable. Some people feel that the schools which are collecting these funds place undue pressure on those students who are not able to give. Others feel that the students get good training in citizenship through such drives. If funds are to be collected, they should be handled in a business-like way so that everyone concerned will be protected from the consequences of carelessness, waste, or misappropriation. The board of education should adopt policies preventing or regulating the collection of all funds for outside agencies.

Shall rules and regulations be adopted by the board of education for the management of internal accounts?

It is not an unusual thing to hear of some principal permitting unsound management of funds collected in his school. He may even be accused of dishonesty or misappropriation of funds. Often such cases are the results of unfounded rumors. But whatever the facts of the cases may be, damages to the individuals and the schools have been done. In far too many schools no definite internal accounting system has been developed and approved by the board of education. One of the early authorities in the field of extracurricular activities emphasized the importance of a sound business plan for the control of funds handled in a school system. He said, "the school that provides a favorable situation for loose practices in handling money is little short of criminal. The crime is not so much that some pupils, teachers, or board members have an easy chance to be dishonest. It is rather that, as a result of the school's muddling along, pupils come to think that public business should be handled that way."[6] The board of education should adopt rules and regulations which will insure safe business management of all internal accounts.

What business management procedures should there be in the rules and regulations of the board?

Although the board of education should not carry out the administrative procedures of the school system, it should set up broad policies

[6] Elbert K. Fretwell, *Extra-Curricular Activities in Secondary Schools* (New York: Houghton Mifflin Co., 1931), p. 446.

or rules and regulations by which the schools should be administered. The board of education is responsible through the administrators for all funds handled in all schools and should insist that sound business practices are followed.   As an example of rules and regulations which would guarantee sound business procedures, the following is presented:

1. A simple uniform accounting system should be used by all the schools in the system.[7]
2. All funds of a school should be handled by a central treasurer who should be appointed by the board of education upon the recommendation of the principal of the school and/or the superintendent of schools.
3. The central treasurer should be bonded by a corporate surety bond. The amount of the bond should equal the largest amount of money entrusted to the treasurer at any one time.
4. All money received by the central treasurer should be deposited in an approved bank, or banks, in one account known as ——School Activity Fund.
5. A receipt should be given when money is passed from one person to another.
6. In general, all accounts should be paid by checks. It may be necessary, however, for the central treasurer to handle a petty cash fund not to exceed (state amount).
7. A definite system for purchasing should be carried out.
8. Budgetary procedures should be followed. The final approval of all budgets and charges should be a responsibility of the principal.
9. A monthly summary statement should be made in quadruplicate— one copy for students, one for the principal, one for the superintendent, and one filed by the central treasurer.
10. The accounts of the central treasurer should be audited annually by a certified public accountant.
11. All funds should be deposited in the bank or banks daily, if possible.
12. A definite plan for selling all tickets should be followed.
13. The central treasurer should make an annual report.
14. A system of training all student treasurers of the several activities should be followed.
15. A simple statement of procedures used in the internal accounting system should be worked out and distributed to all students and interested citizens.

The inclusiveness of the procedures approved by the board of education will depend upon the school system. The beliefs held by the

[7] If a suggested uniform system has been worked out for all schools of the state by the state department, a principals' organization, or any other organization, such form should be used.

principals and superintendent concerning the management of internal accounts should have some influence upon the policies adopted by the board. For example, if the administrator of a small school system did not believe in the central treasurer system, he would not want the board of education to adopt some of the principles set forth in this section. The administrators should be interested in having the board adopt some general fundamental policies to be followed in handling internal accounting.

2. ORGANIZATIONAL PLANS

The plan of organization for internal accounting used by a school system will depend largely on the sizes of schools, personnel, methods of financing activities, collection of fees, management of cafeteria, and the general policies of the board of education.

The central treasurer plan

Most school authorities today will agree that there should be one person appointed by the board upon recommendation of the principal to serve as the treasurer of the school. Although the principal of the school is the responsible person, he should not actually keep the records. If the school is not large enough for the employment of a full-time controller, and most schools are not, a member of the teaching staff should be appointed as the bookkeeper or central treasurer.[8]

All money which is the responsibility of a particular school, regardless of source or destination, should be received and disbursed through the central treasurer. If it is only a matter of transmitting to the board of education certain money collected as fees by the teachers, the transaction should be completely executed through the central treasurer.

Bonding central treasurers

The central treasurers of all the schools of the system should be bonded.[9] The blanket type of corporate surety bond is probably the most satisfactory for large administrative units with a number of schools. Automatic additions and deletions of names may be made without notice to the company and also without adjusted premiums. In a small school with only one person serving as a central treasurer the name or position schedule would be satisfactory. The payment

---

[8] The words Controller and Central Treasurer will be used to mean the person appointed by the board of education to handle all funds of the school.

[9] See Chapter 14, section 2 for a complete discussion on bonding school officials.

for such bond should be made by the board of education. If the board does not see fit to pay the cost of the bond, probably the most satisfactory method would be to charge a prorated per cent to each account. The total amount of the bond should be at least equal to the greatest amount of money handled by the treasurer at any one time.

The budget system

All funds raised and spent for the several activities of a school should be operated on the budget plan. Those funds which are collected by the school, the principal, teachers, or students, and are transmitted directly through the central treasurer to the board of education or to an outside agency should not be included in the budget of the school. The students of the school secure excellent training in handling finances through the budget procedures. The participation in developing the activity budget is a sound business practice which the pupil may carry over in handling his personal finances. Probably no other activity offers a better opportunity for pupils to gain experience in solving financial problems cooperatively—which is so often needed by adults in working with community projects.

The budget of each activity should have three parts which are: (1) the program or work which the club or any other activity wishes to undertake, (2) the cost for carrying out the program or work, and (3) the means or methods of raising the necessary funds needed to meet the costs.

There are schools which permit each activity to work out its budget and present it to the student council for approval. After the council has approved the budget it is presented to the principal for final approval, and then he transmits it to the central treasurer as the operating budget of the activity. If the activity ticket is used, the officers of each club or group know what per cent of the total receipts from the sale of such tickets goes to the several different activities. The individual activity budget plan is used more in those schools where each activity has the responsibility of raising its own money through dues and other means. The individual budgets could be in the form as presented in Figure 46.

If an activity wishes to change its program of work and the financial outlay, the officers would have to make a request for supplementary budget approval through the council and principal. The central treasurer would recognize any changes made in the budget. The central treasurer would not permit expenditures to exceed the actual income nor would he recognize expenditures greater than those antici-

_____SCHOOL					
BUDGET FOR _____ _____					
Name of activity				Date	
Anticipated Receipts			**Anticipated Expenditures**		
Sources	Amount		Projects	Amount	
1. Balance	$15	00	1. Thanksgiving Program	$10	00
2. Dues	16	00	2. (List others)		
3. (List all sources)			3.		
4.			4. Anticipated Balance		
Totals			Totals		
Explanations					
Program or Work of Club: (Sufficient pages should be used to tell the complete story of the program proposed by the activity)					
Detailed plans on how money is to be raised:					

Fig. 46. Budget for an activity.

pated plus any additions approved. Such a budget plan will necessitate a careful check on actual income compared to anticipated income by the central treasurer and the activity treasurer.

The budget plan which is gaining favor in a number of schools is one which is made by the student council. The council appoints a budget committee.[10] This committee secures the work program and financial needs from each activity and then it makes a tentative budget according to the anticipated resources of the school. This budget is presented to the council for consideration. After the council has approved the budget it is then presented to the several different activities and to the principal for consideration. If the members of an

[10] Faculty members and students are usually on the budget committee; however, the membership will vary from school to school.

TOWNSBORO SCHOOL BUDGET
FOR SCHOOL YEAR OF

_____

	Income			Expenditures	
Sources	Receipts Past Year	Antici- pated Receipts	Account Titles	Expend- itures Last Year	Antici- pated Expend- itures
Balance	172.18	189.42			
Activity Tickets	2000.00	2200.00	Assembly	180.00	200.00
Basket Ball	600.00	550.00	Choir	80.00	78.00
			Band	500.00	600.00
Band Concert	125.00	200.00	Etc.		
Debates	175.00	160.00			
Football	1800.00	1950.00			
Etc.			To Balance	189.42	200.00
Totals			Totals		

Approved.

Officers of Council

_____

Principal _____

_____

(See supporting data attached)

Fig. 47. School budget by student council.

activity object to its budget, a delegation may appear before the student council budget committee for a hearing. If in the judgment of the principal the budget is not satisfactory, he should report his findings to the budget committee with a complete explanation. After the budget is finally adopted by the council, it should be approved by the principal. In some schools the superintendent and board of education must also approve the budget in its final form. The approved budget is transmitted to the controller as the working budget of the school. The final form of the budget as approved may be presented as shown in Figure 47.

Training treasurers

Provisions should be made yearly to instruct the treasurers of the several different activities in their duties. The central treasurer should do this work. All forms and records used by each activity and those of the central treasurer should be thoroughly explained. Every treasurer should be supplied with the forms such as requisitions, deposit slips, receipt books, and the activity account book. The treasurer should be taught how to make the entries in the account books, how to strike a balance, and how to compare the balance with the balance given on the monthly report of the central treasurer. At the close of the year the account books of the several treasurers should be audited by a committee from the activity and turned over to the central treasurer. The account book used by each activity treasurer should be a simple ledger type of book which shows receipts and expenditures.

Sale of tickets

In too many schools the sale of tickets to athletic events and other school activities is carried out in a haphazard manner. All tickets should be purchased in rolls and numbered. Different colors may be used for different events and different classes of purchasers. If the school has a full-time controller or central treasurer, he is the most likely person for the job of giving tickets to students to sell. At the time the student is given his tickets for sale he signs a form in duplicate showing the number and kind of tickets he has received. The duplicate copy is held by the controller and the original is given to the student receiving the tickets. Such forms may be made up in a receipt type of book. Figure 48 shows a simple form which may be used.

At the time designated, all money for tickets sold and the unsold tickets should be turned in to the controller and a receipt such as shown in Figure 49 should be issued in duplicate. The original copy of Report of Tickets Sold should be given to the student and the duplicate matched with the duplicate of Tickets for Sale. These duplicates should be filed as part of the central treasurer's records. If the school does not have a central treasurer to do this work, sponsors of the home room may follow the same plan.

At the time of the event the persons selling tickets should be

TICKETS FOR SALE

This is to certify that I have received the following tickets:

    Number_____to_____inclusive for adults @ (price)

    Number_____to_____inclusive for children @ (price)

Event_____

Date_____

                                    _____
                                   (Signature of Student)

Fig. 48. Receipt of tickets for sale.

charged with a roll or rolls of tickets beginning with certain numbers, and after the event the amount of cash should be checked with the number of tickets sold. The records of these sales should also be filed. Such a plan as presented may seem like an undue amount of work and

REPORT OF TICKET SALES

Received from_____
                            (Name of student)

_____Adult tickets sold @ _____ total _____
   (Number)

_____Adult tickets returned
   (Number)

_____Children tickets sold @_____total
   (Number)

_____Children tickets returned
   (Number)

                         Total money received $_____

Event _____   _____
                             Signature of Controller

Fig. 49. Report of ticket sales.

precaution, but it is good business procedure and a protection to all concerned.

Manual of accounting

A complete manual of the accounting procedures used in a school should be prepared and distributed to the pupils, members of the board of education, and interested citizens. This manual should cover methods of handling all accounts, purchasing, payments of bills, budget system, sale of tickets, the work of the treasurers of the several activities, and all forms used in connection with the work. It should be given wide circulation among students and citizens of the community. The manual must be written in clear, simple style so that it may be understood by those who do not have technical knowledge on the subject.

Auditing[11]

The organizational plan of internal accounting should provide for an annual audit of the accounts by a certified public accountant. Most school systems have found it advisable to employ the same auditor to audit the activity accounts of the several schools and the funds of the board of education. The activity accounts should be audited after the close of the school term or the fiscal year. The report of the auditor should be made in triplicate, one copy for the board of education, one for the principal, and one for the central treasurer. Publicity should be given to the auditor's report.

Other safeguards

Provisions must be made for the controller or central treasurer to have adequate time to do his work and to see the students and faculty members. An office convenient to all personnel of the school should be provided. The necessary equipment and supplies should be furnished.

Provisions must be made for the central treasurer to make the necessary bank deposits including cash received from the sale of tickets to an entertainment or contest held at night. School officials should not follow the practice of leaving a large sum of money in the building during the night.

The board of education should approve the bank or banks in which all activity money will be deposited. If the amount of money on hand at any one time is greater than the amount guaranteed by the federal

[11] See Chapter 14 for discussion on audits.

insurance plan, the board should require some form of security from the officials of the bank.[12] The administrators and the board of education should take all possible precautions to see that the activity fund is protected.

3. THE ACCOUNTING PROCEDURES

Although the accounting system used in a school system should be simple, it should be adequate to meet the need of the school and to insure good business practices. The size of the school will to a certain extent determine the types of account books or records which should be used. There are, however, certain records and forms that should be used in any school system if a sound financial system is to be operated. This section will be devoted to the forms and records which may be used by a school.

Receipts

The receipt is an important record whenever money is passed from one person to another. All treasurers of the several organizations and all faculty members who may collect money from students for any reason should issue a receipt. The receipt should be signed in duplicate, with the original given to the person from whom the money was received and the duplicate left in the book.

In issuing a receipt the following information should be filled in:

```
TOWNSBORO SCHOOLS
     RECEIPTS

Number _____              Date _____

   Received from_____ Amount_____

   _____dollars.

   For:  Account name_____


                          _____
                          Signature of person receiving money
```

Fig. 50. The receipt.

12 See Chapter 14.

```
┌─────────────────────────────────────────────────┐
│              TOWNSBORO SCHOOLS                    │
│              CENTRAL TREASURER                    │
│               DEPOSIT TICKET                      │
│                                                   │
│   Deposit No._____        Date _____      │
│   This deposit covers all money received by (name of person) │
│   for general receipts no.____through no.____. The money │
│   is to be deposited to the following accounts:   │
│                                                   │
│       Name of Accounts            Amount          │
│                                  $_____          │
│        (The several accounts                      │
│         may be listed or left    _____           │
│         vacant to be filled in.) _____           │
│              Total               $_____          │
│                                                   │
│   Receipts and ticket checked by                  │
│                                _____    │
│                                (Signature of Controller) │
└─────────────────────────────────────────────────┘
```

Fig. 51. Deposit ticket used by organizations.

(1) receipt number,[13] (2) date, (3) name of person from whom the money was received, (4) fund or account to which the money should be deposited, (5) the amount of money, and (6) signature of the person receiving the money. Receipt books with duplicate receipts consecutively numbered may be purchased from office supply dealers. Some schools may prefer to have their own receipt books printed and numbered. Figure 50 shows one form of a receipt.

Depositing money with controller

All persons, organization treasurers and others, who receive money from different individuals should have the responsibility of depositing the funds with the controller or central school treasurer. A form of a bank deposit ticket should be used. Figure 51 shows such a form. The controller will be able to verify the amount of money on the deposit ticket by comparing it with the receipts. This deposit ticket should be made out in duplicate. The original is for the controller and the duplicate for the individual making the deposit. This dupli-

[13] It is a better plan to have all receipts numbered consecutively.

cate should be filed with the receipts. The controller uses the original for posting his accounts.

Depositing money in bank by controller

The controller should use regular bank deposit slips made out in duplicate for depositing all money into the bank. The sum of his bank deposit slip should equal the sum of all the central treasurer's deposit tickets covered by the deposit. The duplicate bank deposit slip should be fastened to the several deposit tickets and filed according to the date of the bank deposit. Receipts handled in this manner may be easily checked by the auditor.

Petty cash

It is usually necessary for the controller to keep a small petty cash fund. The size of the fund will depend upon the policies of the school system. A check should be drawn on the bank for petty cash money, and the central treasurer as controller should keep an accurate account of all cash paid out and charge the payments to the proper accounts. It is a good practice to require a receipt when cash is paid and place the receipt in petty cash drawer. When the cash runs low the total of the receipts should equal the amount to be drawn by check to make the cash equal the total amount on hand at any one time. The petty cash fund should be closed out at the end of the year.

Purchase system

An organizational plan for internal accounting should provide for a uniform system of purchasing all materials needed by the school. Such a plan is a sound business procedure and is necessary for budgetary control. There are several different purchasing methods used. A method which has been found to be satisfactory is known as the central purchasing plan. In this plan the central treasurer is the one person given the authority to sign purchase orders. All requests for material or services are made by the organizations on requisitions. When the organization wishes to purchase anything, the organization treasurer makes out a requisition in duplicate, Figure 52, with the necessary information filled in. The requisition is signed in duplicate by the sponsor and any other officers of the organization as agreed upon by the student council, and then the original requisition is delivered to the central treasurer who issues a purchase order, Figure 53. The central treasurer should check the account as to available funds before writing the purchase order. The organization treasurer

TOWNSBORO SCHOOL
REQUISITION

Date_____

Name of organization_____ Req. No. _____

The following material is requested from

_____ or a check_____
(Name of firm)   Address

Unit	Quantity	Description	Unit Price	Total

Sponsor   Treasurer

Other   Other

Fig. 52. Requisition blank from an organization.

should also record in his ledger the number and amount of the purchase. If the exact amount is not known, an estimate should be made and recorded in pencil and corrected when the bill is returned. The central treasurer should write the purchase order in duplicate. The original is for the vendor and the duplicate is clipped to the requisition and placed in the file of unpaid bills. When the vendor sends a bill for the material, the bill is fastened to the requisition and duplicate purchase order and then the account is ready for payment. If the organization desires money instead of a purchase order, a check may be written and notation made on the requisition. In such case the organization should secure a statement or receipt of purchases and file it with the central treasurer. Although this system may seem complicated, it will assure control of purchases by the school and it will also give the students experience in good business practices as well as assuring them that their money is being protected.

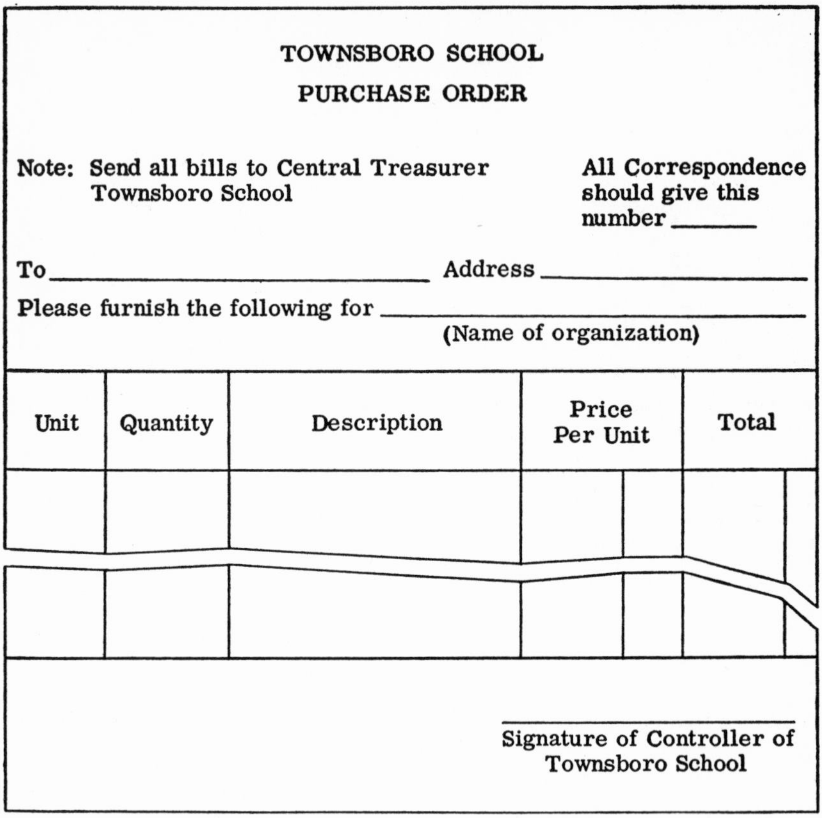

TOWNSBORO SCHOOL

PURCHASE ORDER

Note: Send all bills to Central Treasurer   All Correspondence
       Townsboro School   should give this
                                               number _____

To _____ Address _____

Please furnish the following for _____
                                 (Name of organization)

Unit	Quantity	Description	Price Per Unit	Total

_____
Signature of Controller of
Townsboro School

Fig. 53. Purchase order for activity fund.

Payment of bills

All accounts should be paid by check. A large checkbook containing two or three checks to a page may be secured from any bank, and for a small fee the bank will provide checks with the name of the school printed upon each. No check should be issued in payment of any item for which an invoice has not been furnished to support the issuance of the check. The checkbook stub should be filled out at the time the check is written. After a check is issued in payment of an invoice or bill, the invoice should be marked paid, with the date and check number entered on the invoice. The invoice should then be filed in consecutive order according to the number of the check by which it was paid.

It is quite possible that an invoice submitted for payment may cover several purchases that are to be paid from two or more accounts.

```
┌─────────────────────────────────────────────────────┐
│                 TOWNSBORO  SCHOOL                     │
│                 VOUCHER  JACKET                       │
│                                                       │
│   Pay to_____ Amount___            │
│   Covering purchase orders numbered_____        │
│   Paid by check number_____ Date _____        │
│                                                       │
│        Accounts Charged              Amount           │
│        _____                _____          │
│        _____                _____          │
│                                                       │
│                    Total      $   _____           │
│                                                       │
└─────────────────────────────────────────────────────┘
```

Fig. 54. Voucher jacket for activity fund.

In such a case one check is written for the total amount of the invoice, but the check stub should show the amount that is to be charged to each account. All the purchase orders covered by the invoice should be fastened to the invoice and marked as indicated in the preceding paragraph.

The voucher jacket

Some school systems use the voucher jacket system. The voucher jacket may be an envelope in which to place duplicate requisitions, duplicate purchase orders, and the invoice for filing. The cancelled check covering the payment of the invoice is also placed in the jacket. This makes it possible to file easily all transactions pertaining to a purchase. Figure 54 shows a voucher jacket that may be used.

The accounting record

There are many different systems of accounting used throughout the country. The states have been slow in adopting a uniform method of accounting for the activity funds. If there is not a uniform plan used throughout the state, each school district should adopt a uniform system for all schools of the administrative unit. If the schools are rather small and there are only a few different accounts in each school, the columnar system will be very satisfactory. However, if there are as many as fifteen different accounts or if there is one account with

Date	Description	Ref. No.	Bank Account		Athletics		Z Club	
			Pd. In	Pd. Out	Pd. In	Pd. Out	Pd. In	Pd. Out
1.								
2.								
3.								
Etc.								

TOWNSBORO SCHOOLS

CASH ACCOUNT

YEAR 19—

Fig. 55. Columnar cash account.

TOWNSBORO SCHOOL CASH BOOK										
Date	Description	Ref. No.	Code	Paid In		Paid Out		Balance	
9/1/56	Any Activity	4	6	200	15			200	15
9/2/56	Any Firm	2	4			85	15	115	00
9/3/56	Another Activity	3	5	20	00			135	00
Etc.									

Fig. 56. Cash book.

many transactions, the columnar system will not be as satisfactory as the separate cash and ledger accounts.   Figure 55 shows a columnar cash account.

The purpose of the cash account (Figure 55) is for recording in a consecutive manner according to date and number all deposits made in the bank and all checks issued.   The total cash balance in the bank and the balance of each individual account may be found at any time. It is to be noted that all receipts or deposits are entered in the cash account as *Paid In* to the bank account and to the individual account, and all expenditures or checks issued are entered as *Paid Out* to the bank account and to the individual accounts.

The cash account may be balanced at any time.   The total of each column should be entered in small pencil figures under the last entry in the book.   The book is in balance if the sum of the *Paid In* columns for the individual accounts equals the *Paid In* column under the bank account and the sum of the *Paid Out* columns for the individual accounts equals the *Paid Out* column under the bank account.   The difference between the *Paid In* and *Paid Out* columns under the bank account represents the cash balance.   Likewise the difference between the *Paid In* and the *Paid Out* in the individual account will give a cash balance of the account.   If the *Paid Out* is greater than the *Paid In,* then the account is overdrawn.

If there are many different accounts, the controller will find it more satisfactory to use a cash book and a ledger sheet for each individual account.   Figure 56 shows a form of a cash book which is easy to keep and it provides for a balance at all times.

It is to be noted that the cash book makes provision for using a code number for each account.   The school should assign each account a

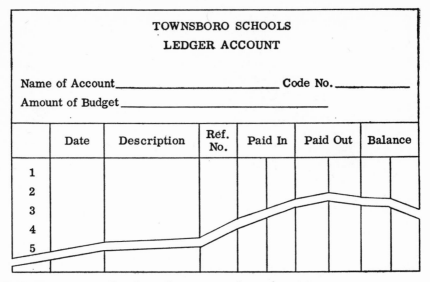

Fig. 57. Ledger account for each activity.

code number. Such a code should be simple and made known to all organizations. The following illustrates a simple code which may be used:

Name of Activity or Account	Code
Athletics	1.
Baseball	1.1
Basketball	1.2
Football	1.3
Debating	2.
Y. Club	15.
Boys	15.1
Girls	15.2
Z. Club	20.

The code number should always appear on communications pertaining to an individual account.

The ledger for each individual account is shown in Figure 57.

The posting of the receipts to this ledger sheet would be made from the cash book and the deposit ticket. The posting of the expenditures should be from the cash book and the check stub or voucher jacket. A balance may be obtained after each transaction.

Reconciliation of bank account

At the end of each month, the bank will render a statement to the school and return the checks which have been paid and charged to the account. The balance shown by the bank statement will rarely

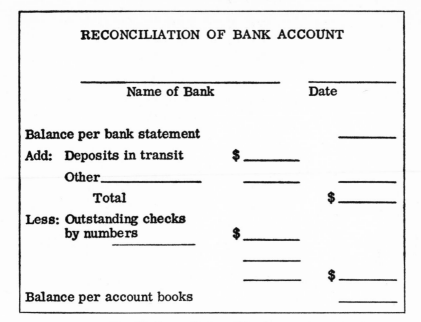

Fig. 58. Reconciliation of bank account.

agree with the controller's cash account balance. The procedure for reconciling the bank statement is as follows:

1. Arrange in numerical order the returned cancelled checks.
2. Refer to the preceding reconciliation statement and note the outstanding checks to see if they appear in the present statement.
3. Check the deposits as shown in cash book and duplicate slips with deposits shown on the bank statement. If these agree, this part of the statement is correct. If the two do not agree, trace the error and make correction.
4. Compare the cancelled checks with the entries in the cash book. Place a check ($\sqrt{}$) mark in the cash account book beside the entry for each cancelled check. Make a list by number of outstanding checks from the preceding month, if any, and those outstanding for the current month.
5. Prepare the reconciliation statement as shown in Figure 58. The deposits in transit added to the bank balance minus outstanding checks should equal the balance given in the cash book. If the books do not balance, recheck through same procedure until error is found.

Report of controller

The controller should prepare a monthly report showing receipts and expenditures of the several different funds. One copy should be

TOWNSBORO SCHOOL

REPORT OF CONTROLLER

For the period beginning_____and ending_____

Account	Cash Balance 1st of Period	Receipts for Period	Total	Disburse- ments for Period	Cash Balance End of Period
1_____	$_____	$_____	$_____	$_____	$_____
2					
3					
Totals	$_____	$_____	$_____	$_____	$_____

Fig. 59. Report of accounts, made by controller.

filed with the principal, one with the superintendent, one posted for student information, and one filed in the controller's records. The form shown in Figure 59 may be used.

The treasurers of the several organizations should be encouraged to check their records with the report made monthly by the controller. Should there be a difference in any one of the accounts, the treasurer of the organization should report to the controller and the two check the records until the error is located. Such a practice will encourage the treasurers of the several organizations to keep accurate records and it will also help develop good morale among the students relative to the safety of the activity funds.

In addition to the monthly reports, the controller should also prepare an annual report at the close of the school year. This same form used for the monthly reports may be used for the annual report. Effort should be made to pay all bills and get all checks cashed before closing the books. The annual audit should be made after the annual report has been made. There should be a policy by the school officials indicating what will be done with the balances in the several accounts of any organizations which will not function the following year. Some schools follow the policy of transferring such funds to the student council's account.

4. MANAGEMENT OF CAFETERIA FUNDS

The management of cafeterias is not the same in all the school systems of a state and often it will be different in the several schools of an administrative unit or district. Likewise the financial accounting will be different. In general, it may be said that the management and financial accounting will be carried out by the officials of each school or the whole school system.

Individual school control

If the control and management of the cafeteria is the responsibility of the principal of the school, it is likely that the financial accounting will also be the responsibility of the principal. There are some principals who have this responsibility but delegate the financial accounting to the central treasurers; others delegate the accounting to cafeteria managers, and still others actually do the accounting. The authors question the advisability of the principal doing the actual accounting work. Although the principal is responsible, he should delegate this work to the central treasurer or controller.

If there are several schools within a school system operating under the individual school plan, the superintendent, principals, central treasurers, and cafeteria managers should work out a business management plan which could be used in all the schools. After such a plan has been worked out it should be presented to the board of education for approval.

In a great number of schools the cafeteria account is kept separately by the central treasurer and the money is deposited in an approved bank as a special account. The accounting records could be similar to the ones described in section 3 of this chapter. If there is a need for a detailed breakdown of receipts and expenditures, a columnar ledger may be used as shown in Figure 60. Although the divisions made in the receipts and expenditures as shown in Figure 60 are the ones generally used, others may be added or substituted according to the needs of the school system.

Definite policies should be established relative to purchasing procedures, receiving and checking supplies and materials purchased, and certifying accounts to be paid. The manager of the cafeteria usually has this responsibility. Some supplies such as staple groceries including canned food should be purchased in quantities large enough to justify bids. Payment of all accounts including labor should be made by check.

TOWNSBORO SCHOOLS
CAFETERIA LEDGER ACCOUNT
Year 19____ - 19____

Date	Descrip-tion	Ref. No.	Total Distributed		Lunch Room Receipts					Lunch Room Expenditures				
			Receipts	Expenses	Student Fees	Adult Fees	F.D.A. Payments	Other Receipts	Total Receipts	Food	Labor	Equipment	Other Expenses	Total Expenses
1948 9|6		1		88 20										
9|7		2		50 00									50 00	50 00
9|8		1	.75 00		72 60	2 40			75 00					
9|8		3	84 95											
9|8		1	66 00											

The routine for handling cash should be planned. Some of the problems in this connection are (1) who will get the necessary change needed each day? (2) how will this change be secured? (3) who will check the cashier? (4) what will be done with the daily receipts? and (5) who will make the deposits in the bank? Although these problems seem simple, they are very important and must be executed daily. In many schools the central treasurers will handle all of this work with the exception of serving as the cashier.

School system control

Some school systems have the financial control of all cafeterias centered in the business managers' offices. In such a system there is often a manager in charge of all the cafeterias who has the responsibility of purchasing, checking purchased materials, certifying bills and payrolls to be paid. The manager will need to delegate much of this work, but he will be responsible for it. The accounting records are usually kept by a bookkeeper in the business office.

The problems connected with handling cash receipts under this system are about the same as those mentioned under the individual school control system. The cashiers should be checked by someone designated by the cafeteria manager, the cash sent to the central business office, and the money then deposited in the bank.

The central business office ordinarily deposits all cafeteria funds in one account but keeps records as to receipts and expenditures for each cafeteria. This will enable the management to know whether or not each cafeteria is making the necessary profits. Most cafeterias are operated on a very narrow margin.

The national school lunch program

The National School Lunch Act, which was passed in June, 1946 by the 79th Congress, authorizes the distribution of funds and allocation of surplus commodities to the public schools of the several states. The purpose of the act was "to safeguard the health and well-being of the nation's children and to encourage the domestic consumption of nutritious and agricultural commodities and other foods, by assisting the states, through grant-in-aid and other means, in providing an adequate supply of food and other facilities for the establishment, maintenance, operation, and expansion of nonprofit school lunch programs."[14] The state educational agency of each state must disburse the funds to all the public schools.

[14] *State Provisions for School Lunch Programs*, U.S. Office of Education, Federal Security Agency, Bulletin 1952, No. 4 (Washington, D.C.: Government Printing Office, 1952), p. 3.

Legislative authorization for the establishment of school lunch programs will be found in all the forty-eight states.[15] The state formulates its rules and regulations concerning the (1) physical plant and facilities, (2) personnel, (3) finances, and (4) food care and management. Many of the states have developed a very comprehensive set of records and reports which must be kept up by the principal of the school. Many principals find that the reports required to operate a cafeteria under the federal lunch program are very time consuming. Each state should try to hold the number of reports to the minimum. The number and kinds of reports required in many of the states cause some people to question the advisability of the whole program, although these same people realize the values that the children are receiving.

Personnel for the cafeteria

The personnel needed for an efficient cafeteria will depend upon the size of the school and upon the plan for administering the several cafeterias in the school district. In a large administrative district there should be at least one person to supervise all the cafeterias. This person should have special training in institutional management. In addition to the supervisor, there should be a manager of each cafeteria. The manager should be trained for the work, be able to keep the records, and handle all the phases of the lunchroom operation. The number of cooks, dishwashers, and other helpers for each cafeteria will depend upon the number of pupils being served, the number of service lines, and the equipment being used. In general, a cafeteria well-equipped with power machines including a dishwashing machine and serving 450 to 500 pupils will need one manager and at least four cooks and helpers. All workers should be required to have health certificates. The laws of the state usually set up standards of health for persons working in cafeterias. Pay schedules and work hours are often decided upon by the local administration. Certainly all lunchroom personnel should receive the same consideration as other employees of the school system.

TOPICS FOR STUDY AND DISCUSSION

1. Does the board of education have a legal responsibility in the management of the activity funds?
2. How are the activities in your school financed?
   What improvements would you suggest?
3. Does your school charge fees? Why?

[15] See *ibid.*, p. 9, for the types of authorization provided by each state.

4. What are the arguments pro and con concerning collection of money by the school for outside agencies?
5. What rules and regulations does your board of education have concerning the management of activity funds?
6. Explain the plan used in your school for activity fund accounting. What suggestions would you make for the improvement of the system?
7. What persons in your school are bonded? Why? When should a teacher be bonded?
8. Evaluate the practices used for auditing the accounts in your school.
9. Evaluate the method used for selling tickets in your school.
10. Do you need treasurers of the different organizations if you have a controller? Why?
11. Work out a plan for purchasing you would like to see in operation in your school.
12. How are the cafeteria funds in your school managed?

SELECTED REFERENCES

AKERLEY, HAROLD E. "The Budget Procedure—Step by Step," *School Executive,* LXVII (November, 1947), 46–47.

DOUGLASS, HARL R. *Modern Administration of Secondary Schools.* Boston: Ginn & Co., 1954, chap. XIX.

FRENCH, WILL, J. DAN HULL, and B. L. DODDS. *American High School Administration.* New York: Rinehart & Co., Inc., 1951, chap. XXIV.

HALLEY, ROBERT R. "A Student-Body Budget in a Small Rural High School," *American School Board Journal,* CXIX (July, 1949), 28.

HAWKINS, WILLARD L. "Can Parents Afford to Send Their Children to High School?" *Nation's Schools,* LII (July, 1953), 54–56.

JACOBSON, PAUL B., WILLIAM C. REAVIS, and JAMES D. LOGSDON. *Duties of School Principals.* Englewood Cliffs, N. J.: Prentice-Hall, Inc., 1950, chap. XX.

JOHNSON, EDGAR G., and ROLAND C. FAUNCE. *Student Activities in Secondary Schools.* New York: The Ronald Press Co., 1952, chap. XIV.

STOUT, MENARD W., and G. BAKER THOMPSON. "What Is Effective Administration of Pupil Activity Finances?" *Bulletin of the N.A.S.S.P,* XXXIII (April, 1949), 287–300.

TRYTTEN, JOHN M., and WALTER E. HESS. "Extra Curricular Activity Funds," *Bulletin of the N.A.S.S.P.,* XXXVI (February, 1952), 204–29.

PART IV

MANAGEMENT OF SPECIAL PROBLEMS
IN SCHOOL FINANCE

17

WELFARE OF EMPLOYEES

THE MANAGEMENT of personnel welfare in a school system involves many different activities of the total administrative force. The purpose of this chapter is to present those personnel problems which are often the direct concern of the business department of a school system. It is realized that some of the problems presented in this chapter may be assigned as part of the work of the division of personnel. However, there are many school systems, even in cities of over 100,000 population, which do not maintain a personnel department. Regardless of which division of the administrative organization is assigned to carry out the work, there are certain problems to be solved that have financial implications and are essential for good morale of the employed personnel. Among these problems are (1) contracts, (2) retirement, (3) salary, (4) leaves, (5) records, and (6) liability of school employees.

I. CONTRACTS

A contract pertaining to personnel is an agreement between the board of education and the employee and it is enforceable by law. A contract may be verbal unless the statutes of the state require it to be in writing. In most school systems the verbal contract is used for the nonteaching personnel and the written contract for the professional personnel. In fact, in thirty-two states the state departments of education prepare the teachers' contract form for use, and boards of education are required by law to use the prepared contracts in sixteen of those states.

Form of contract

While a form of a contract used in one state may not include the essential elements in another state, there are some common safeguards provided by the better contract forms. Figure 61 shows a form of contract used in a midwestern city. It is to be noted that the contract form provides for (1) statement of the legal capacity of both parties, (2) salary to be paid based upon a salary schedule adjusted to the cost-of-living, (3) designation of date of contract, (4) duration of service, (5) date when services begin, (6) statement of legal capacity of parties making the agreement, and (7) execution in duplicate.

The contract presented in Figure 61 seems rather long due to the fact that there is a full explanation of the method used in determining the exact salary. There is a general tendency to make shorter contracts and include only those elements required by law. If the laws of the state require a definite contract form, nothing may be written in to supersede the material in the printed form. However, if the printed contract is only recommended by the state department of education, the local board of education may legally write in additional stipulations relative to employment. Such written words will prevail although they may be in conflict with the printed contract.

Responsibilities of business department

The business office has the responsibility to see that all contracts are executed properly, that is, to meet the requirements of the state laws and also those special requirements of the local board of education as set forth in the rules and regulations. After contracts have been signed they must be filed. The business office should maintain a folder on each employee and include the contract as a part of the employee's record. Any changes in salary should be reported in writing to the proper payroll officer.

2. RETIREMENT AND DISABILITY

Probably nothing will tend to make a person feel more secure and happier in his work than the fact that he and his family will have the necessities of life in old age or a livelihood in case of a severe illness or accident. Teacher retirement acts have gone a long way toward giving this feeling of security to the teachers of this country. The earning power of teachers has been none too good in the past and, as a class, they have not been able to maintain the standard of living expected of them or accumulate sufficient funds to retire and live as professional people should live in old age.

TEACHER'S CONTRACT
Arkansas City Schools

THIS AGREEMENT made --, 19------,
between the Board of Education of the City of Arkansas City, Kansas, party of the
first part, hereinafter designated "Employer" and --------------------------------
of --------------------------------, party of the second part, hereinafter designated "Employee," WITNESSETH:

The Employer, does hereby employ the Employee, and the Employee agrees to
teach in the public schools of Arkansas City for the school year of 19---- and 19----.

The Employer agrees to pay and the Employee agrees to accept the salary specified
in the salary schedule now in force or hereafter adopted by the Employer, and the
base salary hereunder, for the period above, shall be --------------------------------
---------------------------- DOLLARS for nine months teaching service, beginning
on or about September 1, 19------, payable in twelve equal installments, beginning
October 1, 19------, and a like sum on the first day of each succeeding month,
until the full sum last above specified is paid.

The annual remuneration of said Employee shall be adjusted and fixed in accord
with the Bureau of Labor Statistics cost-of-living index for February, 1948 (said index
being 170) to the extent that said cost-of-living index is applicable to $1700.00 of each
male Employee's salary, and to $1100.00 of each female Employee's salary, and said
revision and adjustment shall be calculated and put in effect in September and March
of each year as based on the August 15 and February 15 figure computed as above,
provided, that no revision shall be made unless the change under said cost-of-living
index shall be 5 or more points, and, provided, further, that each and every Employee
shall at all times maintain his relative step or point on said sliding scale schedule and
his increment or decrement, as the case may be, shall be computed from his said relative step or point.

The Employee shall abide by all rules and regulations set forth in the Manual of Operations, or elsewhere, made by the Employer for said schools, and said rules and regulations, now in effect or hereafter a d o p t e d, are made a part of this contract by·
reference.

The Employer reserves the right to make any change in length of time of employment or in the amount and payment of salaries that may become necessary by the
application of the laws of the state of Kansas in force and effect at the date hereof,
and the right and authority to do any act or acts which may be authorized or required by or of it by the laws or regulations governing such body in the state of Kansas
and said laws and regulations, now in force or hereafter enacted or promulgated,
are made a part of this contract by reference.

EXECUTED in duplicate the day and year first above written.

BOARD OF EDUCATION, ARKANSAS CITY, KANSAS

By --------------------------------------President

--------------------------------------Clerk
Party of the first part

Party of the second part

Fig. 61. Contract for teachers.

New Jersey, in 1896, was the first state to establish a state-wide system of teacher retirement. During the decade of the 1940's, over half of the states either enacted new retirement laws or revised the existing laws. Today, all forty-eight states have adopted some type of retirement plan.

Financing

Forty-six of the state retirement systems are financed by public and membership contributions. Contributions made by the state and the membership are fixed by actuarial estimates in eleven of the states and by laws in twenty-nine. In eleven of the twenty-nine states where membership contributions are fixed by law, the contributions by the states are based upon actuarial estimates. In three of these states the amounts contributed from public funds are fixed by law and the contributions by the membership are based on actuarial estimates. There are two states, Delaware and New Mexico, which have the retirement systems supported entirely by public funds without contributions from the members. The systems in these two states are more like the pension-type retirement plan. Table 14 shows the sources of public funds used to support the forty-eight state-wide retirement systems. It may be seen from this table that a vast majority of the retirement systems are supported from the general revenues of the states or districts. Earmarking of taxes to support a retirement system is used in only five states. Most authorities in the field of public finance will agree that earmarking of taxes for special funds is not a good practice.

Benefits in normal retirement

The qualifications for nondisability or normal retirement benefits are based on years of service, age, or a combination of the two factors. In more than half of the states it is possible for one to retire on years of service, regardless of age. This period of service ranges from twenty to thirty-six years. In some of these states, however, there are minimum ages at which payment begins. For example, in North Carolina one may retire after twenty years of service, but the retirement payments will not begin until the member is sixty years of age. A member may retire on the basis of age alone in a number of states. The ages vary from fifty-five in Massachusetts and Minnesota to seventy in New York. The above-mentioned factors are minimum requirements; therefore, the benefits will be the minimum. For a member to receive greater benefits, he will need a longer period of service or he must continue to work after reaching the minimum age

TABLE 14. Number and sources of public funds for the support of state-wide retirement systems

Sources of Funds	Number of State-wide Systems
1. State funds only:	
A. General revenue or general school fund of the state	26
B. Earmarked state taxes	2
C. Special state tax for retirement system	1
State and local funds:	
A. General revenue	7
B. General fund of state plus special local tax	3
Local funds only:	
A. General revenues or general school funds of the local district	8
B. Special local tax for retirement system	1
Total	48

Adapted from National Education Association, Research Division, "Public School Retirement at the Half-Century," *Research Bulletin,* XXVIII, No. 4 (December, 1950), p. 123.

for retirement. Minimum and maximum retirement remuneration varies widely in the several states. There are many variable factors which determine the benefits received by a member.

Disability benefits

All state-wide systems with the possible exception of Iowa have some arrangements for permanent disability allowance. Only a few states, however, provide for temporary disability. There does not seem to be any set pattern for calculating disability allowance. Some states use the same method for calculating disability allowance as is used for regular retirement allowance; others use a different formula. In most of the states a period of service ranging from ten to fifteen years is required before a member is eligible for disability allowance.

Survivor's benefits

In most of the states, if a member dies while in active service, his contributions plus interest are paid to his beneficiaries. In such cases the survivors will really not obtain any benefits beyond that of a savings account. A few of the systems provide for the payment of a lump sum of money to the survivor in case a member dies before retirement.

Most of the state systems have options from which a member may make a selection upon retirement. The option selected will determine the benefits the survivor will receive at the death of the person retiring. In general, if the retirer takes a smaller amount of pay, the survivor will receive greater benefits.

Members withdrawing before eligible for retirement

Most of the states provide for members to withdraw from the retirement system if they leave the service of the state before being eligible for retirement. The common practice is to refund the contribution made by the member plus certain interest the retirement board may allow. Some states provide that under certain conditions deferred allowances be made to those who leave the service before eligible for retirement. Only three states, Colorado, Kentucky, and West Virginia permit members to continue their contributions to the funds after they withdraw from the services of the state.

Some needed improvements in retirement laws

Although there has been more legislative action since 1940 relative to teacher retirement than in any other fifteen-year period in the history of the public school system, there are some improvements which should be made.

The great decrease in the value of the dollar has caused a hardship on the persons who retired some ten to fifteen years ago. Retirement usually bears a direct relationship to salaries earned, and those persons who have retired are not receiving adequate benefits. The authors realize that the retirement systems are based upon certain facts found to be sound by actuaries and they do not desire to weaken any system. However, there is no sound reason why the legislatures cannot appropriate sufficient funds to care for those persons who have been caught in a period of inflation.

A second problem which needs serious consideration is a satisfactory reciprocal relation between states. Each year there are a great number of teachers who, for some reason, cross state lines and lose all or a substantial part of their retirement benefits. There are administrators and teachers who have opportunities in another state but cannot afford to move because of retirement benefits. This fact not only handicaps individuals but also many schools. The solution of the reciprocity problem is not simple; however, one must be found. The application of social security to school employees may be the solution.

The third program which needs attention is closely related to the two preceding. The average monthly allowance for normal retirement paid through teacher retirement systems is approximately $100. Teachers' salaries have been and still are low; therefore little opportunity is offered to build up a satisfactory retirement. Some means will have to be found whereby teachers can retire at a reasonable age and be assured of the necessities of life in old age. Also more liberal benefits must be secured for survivors. Social security provides better benefits to a man and wife than most teacher retirement systems. Certainly a widow whose husband was protected by social security has better benefits than the widow of a retired school teacher. Such a situation does not offer much encouragement for a young man to enter the teaching profession as a classroom teacher.

Suggested plans for improving teacher retirement systems

It was pointed out in the preceding paragraph that one of the improvements needed in teacher retirement systems was a satisfactory reciprocal relation between states. The National Council on Teacher Retirement has recognized the importance of this problem and has recommended that each state adopt the following plan:

1. An optional deferred benefit should be provided for members of publicly supported teacher retirement systems who terminate contributions after five or more years of credit for services rendered as a member of a system.[1]
2. Members should be permitted to purchase credit for teaching service in other states, provided they are ineligible for deferred benefits for such services.
   a. The total out-of-state service creditable should not exceed the total service in the state prior to eligibility for superannuation retirement.
   b. The following qualifications of eligibility for purchase of out-of-state service credit should be imposed:
      (1) A teacher must serve a minimum number of years in the new state, preferably five years.
      (2) A teacher must declare in writing his intention to purchase out-of-state service credit within a specified period after migration, such as three years.

[1] Such benefits would be based upon the contribution made by state and member. This would enable one to leave the service and receive retirement benefits at the required age.

(3) Benefits from the purchase of out-of-state service should be the same as though the service and contributions had been rendered in the new state.[2]

In 1954 Congress amended the Social Security law which enabled teacher or state retirement systems to become a part of the federal system. Several states have taken advantage of this amendment. Probably this is one of the best means of obtaining increased retirement benefits.

3. SALARIES AND SALARY SCHEDULING

The story of the improvement in the status of teachers in the past twenty years is encouraging. Although the economic gains have not been as great as one would desire, the value and importance of the public school system and its dependence upon a well-trained and capable teaching staff have received considerable recognition. Educational and lay leadership, which has presented a concise and understandable plan of action for the improvement of education, has elicited more enthusiastic community support than ever before. Moved by the shortage of qualified personnel, particularly in the past decade, boards of education and legislatures have acted decisively to raise the level of income for all school personnel.

Conditions which affect salaries

The very nature of the educational system makes it hard to obtain an adequate wage for teachers. The structure of education is different from that of business. Business is carried on for profit, while education is maintained so that the product may be given away.[3] Business is conducted as a private enterprise, the public school as a community or state product. The wages of teachers come from the money of citizens while wages paid in industry come from profit. The school system and industry are so different in every respect that it is hard to make people realize the need for adequate salaries for teachers.

Again, it is difficult for the average layman to see how the school creates wealth. The wealth created by the school is more or less hidden; it is wealth that will produce a return ten to twenty years hence. In business, however, a monetary value is placed upon the product immediately. A manufacturer can produce a commodity

[2] *How To Provide Reciprocity in Teacher Retirement* (Washington, D.C.: National Education Association Research Division and National Council on Teacher Retirement, 1951), p. 9.

[3] Willard S. Elsbree and E. Edmund Reutter, Jr., *Staff Personnel in the Public Schools* (Englewood Cliffs, N.J.: Prentice-Hall, Inc., 1954), p. 125.

and sell it at once for a certain value and see the wealth produced, while in teaching the value of the product is delayed.

Although the law of supply and demand does have some effect upon salaries of teachers, it does not have the same effect upon the schools as it does in industry. When there is a scarcity of labor in industry, many teachers or would-be teachers go there for work. Again, the salaries paid in the school cannot change as quickly as those paid in private industry. Salaries are set for a year and often two years in advance because of the financial structure based on a system of taxation.

Other factors such as character, personality, and intelligence are valued highly in both private enterprise and education. Private enterprise will recognize these qualities and pay accordingly. There are, however, many school boards that are satisfied to secure an individual who meets the technical requirements regardless of other traits.

Teaching is supposed to be a profession. It requires special training of the individuals as do other professions. However, the doctor, the lawyer, the accountant, and other professionals can set their salaries through fees, while teachers must accept the prevailing salaries paid at the particular place.

There are many women in the teaching profession. In general, they can accept smaller wages than men who must support families. It is realized that there are a great number of women teachers who have dependents, but there are thousands of women teaching who are married and whose husbands are also earning incomes. This fact should not influence teachers' salaries but *it does*.

Many other conditions and factors besides those mentioned have great influence upon the salaries paid to teachers. It has been and will continue to be a long hard pull to get the citizens of this country to realize the value and need for paying school teachers salaries that will attract the best youth of our land. The salary paid to the teachers is not the only determining factor which makes a good school, but it is a very important one.

State salary schedules

Although more than half the states have minimum salary laws, making the salary schedule in nearly all states is a local responsibility. Most of the minimum salary laws provide that no teacher be paid less than a stipulated amount. Often these minimum amounts are so low that the laws have little meaning. There are a few states such as North Carolina and Delaware that have state-wide salary schedules paid by the state. The local administrative unit may supplement the salaries but in many cases the state schedule prevails. In too many instances the state minimum salary tends to become the maximum salary paid by the local school. There is a tendency for state schedules to kill local initiative not only in salaries paid to teachers but also in other items of school support. The state schedule does guarantee a certain wage to teachers and it also makes it possible for rural areas to pay salaries that will tend to attract better teachers than they might otherwise get.[4]

Local salary schedules

Traditionally, the employment of teachers was an individual matter between the teacher and the board of education. Although considerable discretionary power as to what salary a teacher is to receive rests with the board of education, a great majority of the city school systems now pay salaries according to some kind of definite salary schedule. A salary schedule is not only beneficial to the teachers but also to the school district. It is the only means of getting accurate information for making the budget. About 70 per cent of the current school budget goes for teachers' salaries and if the administrator does not have some means of calculating this amount, the budget would likely be of little value. Unjust differentials in salaries will cause much unrest and poor morale among the teaching force. The salary schedule tends to make teaching more professional because individual bargaining practices will be eliminated. The community should profit through a better instructional program for the boys and girls.

The modern salary schedule

The salary schedule being used in a vast majority of the school systems today may be classed as the preparation type or the single salary schedule. This type of a salary schedule makes provision for classifying the teachers in terms of professional training. The college graduate receives the salary scheduled for college graduates, whether a teacher of first-grade children or high school seniors. Such a schedule also stresses the principle that successful teaching contributes to the ability of a teacher to render more valuable service.

The single salary schedule permits the administrator to assign teachers where they are best suited to work. It encourages young

[4] Calvin Grieder and William E. Rosenstengel, *Public School Administration* (New York: The Ronald Press Co., 1954), pp. 208–10.

people to prepare to teach in the division of the school in which they feel best suited. Some people prefer working with very young children while others prefer older pupils. If there is not a differential in pay to influence a person's selection of a particular group to work with, there is a likelihood that interests will be the controlling factor. This should make better teachers.

When teachers are paid on the bases of training and experience there is likely to be better morale among the teachers. One of the best methods of building morale is for the employees to have the feeling that they are being treated fairly and that they are receiving a just amount for their services.

There are some issues pertaining to the single salary schedule on which school authorities are not in complete agreement.[5] Some of these issues are (1) prior service, (2) nonteaching experience, (3) extra pay for extra services, (4) equivalency credit, and (5) recognition of dependents. Although each or all of these may be considered differently in several different cities, it is possible for the teachers and officials of a particular school system to agree on how these issues will be treated. If it is found that the method of handling one or all of these problems in a particular school system is handicapping the educational program, changes may be made. As a general rule low salaries will cause much dissatisfaction among the personnel and often will bring forth many of the issues that have been mentioned. When teachers' salaries are sufficiently high to make one feel that he can afford some of the better things of life—own a home, take vacations, save some money, and the like—many of the issues will no longer be problems. It is when salaries are so low and teachers are having a hard time making "ends meet" that the many salary schedule problems become acute.

Organization for study of local schedule

The development of a salary schedule for a local school system should be a cooperative project. There was a time in the history of the public school system when the administrator made or revised the salary schedule at the request of the board of education. Today, however, salary schedules are developed through group study and discussion and are designed to more nearly meet the needs of the employees according to the ability of the community to pay for their services. Representatives of the teaching force, administrators, central office staff, and interested lay citizens are formed into a special

[5] See Elsbree and Reutter, *op. cit.*, pp. 146–57 for a discussion on salary schedule issues.

committee to study the salary schedule problem and make recommendations to the chief administrator and the board of education for consideration. Many school systems are finding that the employment of competent consultants to advise and consult with the committees is well worth the expense involved.

The schedule committee should be given ample time to study the whole problem and also keep the teaching staff informed of the progress being made. The administration will need to assist the committee by making available all necessary information and by providing funds for the study. A free hand should be given to the committee to study thoroughly the whole problem.

Some of the information which the committee will need to have and study includes:[6]

1. Pay received by each teacher
2. Present schedule
3. Experience of teaching personnel
4. Qualifications of personnel
5. Cost of living in community
6. Salaries paid by similar schools
7. Ages of teaching personnel
8. Tenure of personnel
9. Policies of board pertaining to sick and professional leaves
10. Teaching load
11. Minimum and maximum salaries
12. Number and size of increments
13. Extra pay for extra work
14. Prior service
15. Advancement through the schedule
16. Different classifications
17. Equivalency credit
18. Salaries paid to persons in other local occupations requiring similar training
19. Ability of district to pay

The committee should study and discuss any and all problems pertaining to salary scheduling which may be presented by any teacher or citizen of the community. The committee should be charged with the responsibility of making a schedule which the district could finance not only at the current time but also for several years hence.

Minimum and maximum salaries

The determination of the minimum or base salary in the salary schedule is an important feature. This is the minimum that may be

[6] Grieder and Rosenstengel, *op. cit.*, p. 213.

paid to a teacher at the beginning of employment. Since the salary schedule should be tailor-made for a particular community, there are several factors that should be considered in establishing the base pay. Among these factors are the cost of living per year for a beginning teacher, provisions for saving and advancement, returns upon investment cost, and the base pay in similar communities. The base pay should be sufficiently high to attract capable, alert young people to accept employment. If the base pay is too low, many of the better prospects will not accept employment.

The upper level or the maximum of the salary schedule may depend on both the willingness and the ability of the community to support education.[7] The maximum salary should be sufficiently high to encourage a young person to remain in the teaching profession. It should be of such an amount that a person of maturity would be able to support a family, educate children, maintain a home, pay life insurance and taxes, take vacations, travel, study, and save a reasonable amount each year. Certainly the maximum salary should be at least two to three times the minimum or base pay. It is only through an adequate salary schedule that a community will be able to attract and hold good people in the classrooms.

Increments

The size and number of increments in the salary schedule will depend upon the difference between the minimum and maximum salaries. The Research Division of the National Education Association[8] reporting on salary schedules showed that the median number of increments was approximately twelve, and the range from five to over twenty-three. The number of increments should not be so many that the young teacher will become discouraged before reaching the maximum, and at the same time the number should not be so few that he may reach the top salary too early in life and feel that there is no further inducement to stay in the position. Probably twelve to fifteen increments of $250 to $350 each is a good recommended practice. The top salary must not be too low to attract career people.

Some school systems have salary schedules with "stops" or "hurdles" which make it necessary for teachers to do certain professional study before advancing to higher positions on the schedule. For example, a teacher may advance automatically for the first five increments and then be required to have completed a minimum amount of

[7] William A. Yeager, *Administration and the Teacher* (New York: Harper & Bros., 1950), p. 352.
[8] National Education Association, "Salaries and Salary Schedules of City School Employees, 1950–51," *Research Bulletin*, XXIX (April, 1951), 80.

college credit before advancing to the sixth increment.   Certainly this method will encourage and stimulate teacher growth.

Salary classes

The distinguishing characteristic of the single salary schedule is that there may be several different classes based upon preparation and not upon position.   The number of different classifications will depend upon the philosophy held by the administration as to the value of extended training of teachers.   Certainly a teacher who holds a master's degree should be in a different class than a teacher who has not finished college.   Some of the more common classes are:[9]

Class 1. Teachers without degrees
Class 2. Teachers with bachelor's degrees
Class 3. Teachers with master's degrees
Class 4. Teachers with master's degrees plus thirty semester hours of additional graduate study

The salary schedule should make provisions for a teacher to advance from one class to another.   Some school systems will construct the different classes on the basis of fifteen semester hours graduate credit.   No doubt where salaries are sufficiently high to attract people who receive the doctorate degree, provision must be made for classifications for such training.

Merit rating

Today, there is much discussion on the use of merit rating as a basis for pay.   Most school authorities will agree that paying teachers according to the quality of their performance is good, but they will not agree on how this appraising may be done.   At this time, research has not revealed a reliable method of measuring teacher merit.   A very small percentage of the school systems of America use merit as a basis for teachers' pay.

Some of the arguments for merit rating are:

1. Higher salary schedules may be provided because fewer teachers will reach the top brackets.
2. Teachers will be more alert so that they may receive more pay.
3. Teachers are paid on the basis of what they do and they do not advance unless they deserve it.
4. Industry and government use merit as the basis for paying employees.

The authors recognize the above arguments and feel that they are sound.   The knowledge of measuring merit possessed by professional

[9] Grieder and Rosenstengel, *op. cit.*, p. 215.

school people, however, is not sufficient to rely upon. Merit rating fails to improve the instructional program because:

1. Rating plans fail to respect the individual personality.
2. Rating plans encourage conformity rather than an action program on the part of the individual teacher.
3. Rating plans rely upon individual evaluation which is not always sound.
4. Rating plans do not always consider the hidden or delayed results of teaching.
5. Rating plans are very subjective.
6. Rating plans make for poor morale among teachers.
7. Rating plans, at this time, do not use all the elements essential for good teaching.

The single salary schedule recognizes training and experience of teachers and at present these two elements are about the most objective evidence of measuring merit. A teacher who continues his training and experience should improve from year to year.

Extra pay for extra work

In theory, perhaps, teaching load should be equalized and teachers should be paid salaries according to schedules. However, there are a great number of school systems which are understaffed and complete equalization of load is almost impossible. Therefore, the administrator must assign extra duties to some members of the teaching staff. In 1951, 83 per cent of 1,615 cities reporting to the Research Division of the N.E.A. gave extra pay for extra assignments.[10]

The extra assignments for which extra pay is most often provided are (1) coaching athletics, (2) coaching dramatics, (3) directing music, and (4) sponsoring publications. The amount of extra pay will vary from school to school.

Although the authors are opposed to the principle of extra pay for extra work, they realize that the practice should continue until the time when the schools are able to employ a sufficient number of personnel to equalize the loads and yet be able to pay salaries which are adequate and just for professional employees.

Format of the schedule

The salary schedule should be published and made available to all persons concerned including lay citizens. It needs to be in such a form that it is easily understood. The employee must be able to

[10] "Teacher Personnel Procedures, 1950–51: Employment Conditions in Service," National Education Association, *Research Bulletin,* XXX (April, 1952), 43.

study the schedule and understand how he will progress year after year.[11]

An adopted schedule should not be considered a schedule to be used for ever. It should be reviewed from time to time and adjusted to meet the current needs. The form, however, can be so designed that a revision will not necessarily destroy the whole make-up. A simple, concise, and clearly presented schedule will aid in developing good morale among the teachers and should aid the instructional program as well.

Salary schedules for nonteaching personnel

Most school systems provide salary schedules for classroom teachers, but there are few in comparison that provide them for principals, supervisors, superintendents, or noncertified personnel. The teachers as a group fall into one major classification, and they constitute a large proportion of the employed personnel; therefore, attention has been given to working out a satisfactory plan for payment of their salaries. On the other hand, the administrators, supervisors, and noncertified personnel have been paid on a hit-or-miss basis. The fundamental principles of salary scheduling which apply to the teaching group will also apply to these other groups. The several different jobs should be thoroughly studied with a view to establishing a satisfactory salary schedule for each class of workers. Salary schedules for the different groups of nonteaching personnel will not only be beneficial to these employees but also to the administration. If for no other reason, salary schedules for different groups of employees are essential for good budgetary procedures.

4. LEAVES OF ABSENCE

An integral part of a good personnel program for all certified and noncertified employees is adequate provision for absences. Leaves of absence are often classified as (1) sick leave for reasons of personal health, (2) illness or death in the immediate family, (3) professional leave for short or long periods of time, and (4) other personal reasons. The first three are classified as justifiable excused absences and the latter as unexcused.

The board of education should develop (cooperatively) policies or rules and regulations governing all leaves. The policies should consider not only the welfare of the pupils and employees but also the financial ability of the school district to support the program. The

[11] See Grieder and Rosenstengel, *op. cit.*, p. 216 for the information which should be included in the published schedule.

policies pertaining to leaves should be in writing. They should be so stated that all employees will be able to clearly understand them so that there will be no misunderstandings. The policies should be administered in an impersonal and objective manner becoming to the school system. An adequate and complete record of each employee's leave status should be maintained at all times.

5. PERSONNEL RECORDS

Each school system should provide and keep up-to-date an adequate personnel record for all employees. There is no uniform record used throughout the country and few of the states make it mandatory for the administration to keep such records. The time has come, however, when a good record system for all personnel is essential in the administration of a school system.

Functions of personnel record

It is a known fact that administrators change positions rather frequently. If for no other reason, this changing of administrators makes it essential for a complete record of each employee to be kept. The personnel record is a written means of keeping an accurate record of each employee's status and activities up to date at all times.

The personnel record provides a means for the administration and the board of education to carry out the business affairs of the school. The position of the employee on the salary schedule, number of days accumulated for sick leave, number of years of experience in the school system, in-service education requirements met, interests, special accomplishments, and numerous other kinds of data pertaining to each employee are essential for the efficient administration of a school system.

Research is an essential in the administration of a school system. It is only by having an adequate personnel record system that the research department will be able to study and analyze specific personnel problems. Such studies may require information over a number of years and unless it is possible to secure the data they cannot be made. Some of the research studies which may be of value are:

1. The cost for sick leave
2. The extent of turnover of teachers, custodians, and other groups of employees
3. The tenure of teachers
4. The qualifications of teachers over a period of time
5. The amount of time lost by teachers and other employees for unexcused or unpaid absences

PERSONNEL RECORD

BLANKBORO SCHOOLS

1. Name_____Date of Birth_____

2. Place of Birth_____Home Address_____   PICTURE

3. Kind of Certificate_____

4. Educational Experience Outside of Local School

Date	Place	Grade or Subject Taught	Extra Responsibilities	Annual Salary

5. Work Experience Other Than Teaching

Date		Place	Position	Salary
From	To			

6. Educational Preparation

Kind of School	Dates Attended	Name and Location	Honors, Etc.,	Year Graduated	Degree
Elementary High School College University					

Fig. 62. Personnel record, part 1. Data obtained at time of employment.

6. The cost of substitute services
7. The community activities in which teachers participate
8. The nonprofessional experience of teachers
9. The professional activities of teachers in the state and nation
10. The professional history of certain individuals

The personnel record

A folder type of a personnel record is probably the most satisfactory. It affords an opportunity to file in one place all letters, anec-

PERSONNEL RECORD

BLANKBORO SCHOOL

1. Name_____ Sex _____Home Address _____
2. Social Security No._____ Retirement No. _____
3. Date First Employed_____ Kind of Work _____
4. Date Left Employment of Board_____ Reason _____
5. Educational Experience in Local Schools

Year	Building Assigned	Position	Yearly Salary	Position on Schedule	No. Days Absent	Local Address	Telephone

6. In-Service Development

Date	Summer Schools or other type Name of Institution or Explain other type	Credit	Degrees Earned

7. Publications
8. Other Accomplishments
9. Sick Leave Record

Year	Number Days Due End of Last Year	Days Allowed This Year	Cumulative Total Days	Days Used This Year	Balance Unused

10. Supplementary Data

Fig. 63. Personnel record, part 2. Data obtained during employment.

dotal notes, and other inserts pertaining to each employee. A single folder containing all information on each employee will certainly aid the person who, for any reason, desires to study some personnel problem. Figures 62 and 63 show a personnel record in two parts which may be printed on a folder. If for any reason a folder is not desired, similar information may be printed on cards or paper and filed in a folder. If the record is to be on cards or paper it should probably consist of two parts. Part one would be the personal data and information secured at the time of employment, and part two would be the data collected after the candidate was appointed to a position in the school system.

6. LIABILITY OF SCHOOL EMPLOYEES

Personal liability of school employees usually comes from negligence resulting in bodily injury or charges arising from punishment.

Negligence of employees

Negligence is often defined as the failure "to act as a reasonably prudent and careful person would under circumstances involved."[12] Thus it is apparent that any person at fault must owe a duty to another and be aware of this duty and responsibility. Teachers are held more accountable for injuries to pupils than the ordinary person because the pupils are under the care of the teachers. If negligence can be proven in a case of an injury to a pupil, the employee can be held for damages. Since there are many accidents to pupils in schools and on the playgrounds and teachers are often sued because of these accidents, some of the states are enacting laws protecting school employees from financial losses arising out of any claim, demand, suit, or judgment by reason of alleged negligence.[13] All employees of a school system should take more than ordinary care so that pupils will not be injured as the result of an accident—for children are often indiscreet, careless, and indifferent in the face of danger.

Charges arising from punishment

Pupils are under the supervision of the public school authorities and are subject to their control. The school laws and the rules and regulations of the state and local boards of education give the teachers the authority over the pupils. All the states except New Jersey permit the school personnel to inflict punishment, if necessary, for the control of the pupils. The local boards of education, however, may determine through their rules and regulations the nature and extent of the punishment which may be inflicted by the teaching personnel. In the absence of laws or rules and regulations prohibiting corporal punishment, the teacher is privileged to take disciplinary steps under certain circumstances and for certain purposes. There are, however, certain common-law principles which must be obeyed. The punishment must not be unreasonable nor excessive in view of the age and sex of the pupil. Also the punishment must not be administered maliciously nor be excessive in light of the offense. Cruelty to children is prohibited in all the states.

[12] Harry N. Rosenfield, *Liability for School Accidents* (New York: Harper & Bros., 1940), p. 3.
[13] New York Education Law, Sec. 3023.

Those who administer punishment should be careful. Although the courts are favorable to the teachers, it is easy for one to inflict punishment which may cause injury to a child or provoke a parent to the extent that he will take the case to court. Such a case will be subject to a jury decision and it will be based upon the case before the court. There is a trend for the jury to determine what is reasonable and moderate punishment regardless of the teacher's judgment. Non-certified personnel should not administer corporal punishment unless authority is given by law.

TOPICS FOR STUDY AND DISCUSSION

1. What are the essential parts of a contract?
2. Evaluate the retirement law under which your school system operates.
3. What are some of the factors which affect teachers' salaries?
4. What are the advantages and disadvantages of state salary schedules?
5. Who should participate in preparing a local salary schedule for teachers? for custodians?
6. What procedures would you follow in setting up a committee to study the local salary schedule?
7. Evaluate the salary schedule of your school system.
8. Does your salary schedule provide for merit rating? How?
9. Who should receive extra pay for extra work in your school system? Why?
10. Evaluate the provisions made in your school for leaves of absence.
11. When should a person be granted a professional leave?
12. Should custodians and secretaries be granted leaves? If so, what kind and why?
13. What personnel records are kept in your school? Are they adequate? If not, why?

SELECTED REFERENCES

AKER, HOWARD M. "Working with a Preparation-Type Salary Schedule," *American School Board Journal*, CXXIV (May, 1952), 31.

CLIFFORD, JOHN M. "Critical Years Ahead for Retirement Systems," *Nation's Schools*, LIV (October, 1953), 43–46.

——. "Some Proposed Changes in Retirement Plans," *Nation's Schools*, LIV (November, 1953), 79.

——. "Legislatures and Liberalizing Retirement Systems," *Nation's Schools*, LIV (December, 1953), 67–70.

ELSBREE, WILLARD S., and E. EDMUND REUTTER, JR., *Staff Personnel in the Public Schools*. Englewood Cliffs, N. J.: Prentice-Hall, Inc., 1954, chaps. VI, VII, VIII, and XIII.

GRIEDER, CALVIN, and WILLIAM E. ROSENSTENGEL. *Public School Administration*. New York: The Ronald Press Co., 1954, chaps. VIII–IX.

HAGMAN, HARLAN L. *The Administration of American Public Schools*. New York: McGraw-Hill Book Co., Inc., 1951, chap. XII.

HAISLEY, OTTO W. "The Formula in Determining Salaries of School Executives and Supervisors," *American School Board Journal*, CXXIII (December, 1951), 45.

LINN, HENRY H. *School Business Administration*. New York: The Ronald Press Co., 1956, chap. III.

National Education Association. "Public-School Retirement at the Half Century," *Research Bulletin*, XXVIII (December, 1950).

——. "Salaries and Salary Schedules of City-School Employees, 1950–51," *Research Bulletin*, XXIX (April, 1951).

——. "Salaries and Salary Schedules of Urban School Employees, 1952–53," *Research Bulletin*, XXXI (April, 1953).

——. "Teacher Personnel Practices, 1950–51: Appointment and Termination of Service," *Research Bulletin*, XXX (February, 1952).

——. "Teacher Personnel Procedures, 1950–1951: Employment Conditions in Service," *Research Bulletin*, XXX (April, 1952).

REMMLEIN, MADALINE K. *The Law of Local Public School Administration*. New York: McGraw-Hill Book Co., Inc., 1953, chap. VI.

WERF, LESTER VANDER. "The Trouble with Merit Systems," *American School Board Journal*, CXXV (August, 1952), 17.

WEST, ALLAN M. "The Case For and Against Merit Systems," *School Executive*, LXIX (June, 1950), 48.

YEAGER, WILLIAM A. *Administration and the Teacher*. New York: Harper & Bros., 1954, chaps. IX, XVI, XVIII, and XXI.

18

SCHOOL PLANT INSURANCE

BOARDS OF EDUCATION are legally charged with the supervision and care of the school property. The financial investment in the school plant and equipment in many communities constitutes the largest single outlay of funds which affects all the people. In many of these small communities a single fire might destroy the only school plant and leave the board of education without any financial means for rebuilding. The protection of the *community's investment* against losses from fires and other accidents through insurance coverage is a responsibility of the board of education.

I. PURPOSES OF SCHOOL PLANT INSURANCE

Three main purposes of the board of education for carrying insurance on school property are (1) protection of the community investment, (2) protection of human lives, and (3) a guarantee of funds to provide housing facilities for the educational program of the community.

Protection of community investment

The protection of the school district against a financial loss due to a fire or any other type of a misfortune is good management. A school plant represents thousands of dollars invested by the community in material and equipment and in case of a disaster this investment would be a loss unless it is insured. In spite of every precaution which may be taken by the school officials and employees, fires or some other type of disaster may occur. To protect a community from such an unforeseeable loss, insurance of some form must be provided. The laws of the several states authorize the boards to carry insurance on school property; and also the courts have ruled that the power to insure school property against fire losses is implied in the power which the board of education has in the management of school property.

Protection of human lives

As a general rule compulsory attendance laws require children to attend school. If our society makes it compulsory for a child to attend a school, it would seem that the child would have a right to expect the same society to protect him against undue hazards of fire while attending school. The authors have visited a great number of school plants during the past two decades for the purpose of helping the boards of education to determine building needs and have found a great deal of evidence to prove that children are not being protected as well as they should be against the hazards of fire. It is not uncommon to find storerooms under a combustible stairway; and to make it worse, these storage places are literally filled with highly combustible materials. Auditoriums in many of the older buildings are on the second floor, with inadequate exits for the pupils. If one observes school plants while driving through many of our cities and rural areas, he will see old buildings with the so-called fire escapes. If an investigation were made of many of these fire escapes, it would be found that they are hard to enter and are often near or over windows. Children should not be forced to attend school under such hazardous conditions. A good insurance program will help to eliminate many of the fire hazards through a system of inspection. The State Board of Education in North Carolina is authorized and empowered by the state school insurance law to maintain an inspection and engineering service for the schools of the state with the purpose of eliminating fire hazards.

A guarantee of funds for buildings

Although school buildings as a class of public property have not suffered the losses that other public buildings have, it is a known fact that losses do occur and that some districts have losses which they would be financially unable to rebuild without the insurance money. A number of the smaller administrative units have limited valuation and cannot secure funds for school buildings except through bonded indebtedness. Bonding capacity in most districts is related to the assessed valuation of the property. It is not uncommon for a district to be bonded to the constitutional limitation, and should the building be destroyed by fire there would be no funds for rebuilding unless it is from insurance. A good insurance program is a guarantee to the community that a school plant will be provided.

2. METHODS OF INSURING

There are three distinct methods of insuring school buildings used by boards of education. They are (1) commercial insurance, (2) state insurance, and (3) self-insurance.

Commercial insurance

By far the majority of the school districts carry their insurance with commercial companies. These commercial companies fall into two groups, either stock companies or mutuals.

Stock companies are corporations or companies which are organized on a capital stock basis. When the corporation or company was organized, the persons in control set up so much capital stock as being available to pay losses in the event that the premiums collected were insufficient to pay the losses. The stockholders are the owners of the company and elect officers from the group. The capital stock may be increased from time to time. If a small company has exceptionally large losses at one time the stockholders may be liable for at least the amount of the stock. The insurance laws of each of the states set up the ratio of capital and other assets to liabilities necessary for the company to do business within the state. These stock companies are often referred to as "Old Line Companies."

Cooperatives or mutuals include insurance companies or associations which do not have stock for capital assets. The policyholders take the place of the stockholders found in stock companies. Each policyholder is liable to assessment if the losses are greater than premiums. The profits of the company are returned to the policyholders in form of reduced rates. The company, however, usually sets aside some of the profit as a reserve or surplus to protect the policyholders from assessments.

Because of the method of assessing policyholders to pay losses, some states have ruled that school boards cannot insure school plants with mutuals. This is based upon the fact that a board of education cannot legally incur an indeterminate liability. There are, however, some mutual companies that sell nonassessable policies to boards of education. In most of the states, school boards may insure with a mutual company if the amount of liability or assessment is stipulated. The administrator needs to know the laws of the state in which he works so that he may be able to advise the board of education concerning insurance problems.

State insurance

More and more each year the states are assuming a greater share of the cost of new buildings. But there are only four states which have assumed the risk for losses of school property. One of these, North Carolina, has an optional plan of state insurance. In 1949 the State Legislature passed a law which permitted the local districts to carry insurance with the state. The State Board of Education was given control of the program. The state established a $2,000,000 reserve fund. The following gives some of the more important aspects of the program:

1. The fire and lightning rates will be not less than 83 nor more than 86 per cent of the published rates in effect prior to May 31, 1948. On June 1, 1948, the commercial rates were increased 25 per cent.
2. Extended coverage rates are 5 cents per hundred dollars. This coverage provides the same protection as the standard extended coverage endorsement used by commercial companies, plus boiler explosion protection. The boiler explosion does not cover personal injury. The extended coverage is optional with the local unit.
3. Credits are allowed from the basic fire rate as follows:
    a. A 10 per cent reduction on unprotected and 5 per cent on protected property for self-inspection.
    b. A 6 per cent reduction for 90 per cent coinsurance.
    c. A 12 per cent reduction for 100 per cent coinsurance.
4. Buildings must be insured up to 75 per cent of the present value. The local boards determine the value of the plant until the officials of the local and state boards have opportunity to review jointly the values.
5. Policies are issued and paid on an annual basis. The local unit may withdraw at the end of any year.
6. When the premium receipts in excess of losses reach 5 per cent of the total insurance in force, annually thereafter the premium rates are decreased sufficiently to maintain the 5 per cent; and, if funds are sufficient, no premiums are charged for the ensuing year.
7. The State Board maintains an inspection and engineering service to help the local units reduce fire hazards.

Although the program had been in operation only seven years, in 1955, 91 of the 174 administrative units were taking advantage of the state program. The last financial statement showed that the fund had an earned surplus of over $640,000 after paying all losses and the administration cost of the program.

The other states which have a state plan of insurance are South Carolina since 1900, Wisconsin since 1903, and North Dakota since 1919. All of these states have good records, and a very substantial savings in the cost of insurance to the local administrative unit. The authors believe that more states could well afford to consider a state plan of insurance. This is stated with the realization that commercial companies will be in opposition to such a plan.

Self-insurance

Under the self-insurance plan the administrative unit or district assumes all risk of loss. On first thought this plan seems very attractive because of the apparent economy, and large cities such as Philadelphia show tremendous savings. Over a seventeen-year period Philadelphia fire losses amounted to $406,000, while the premiums would have amounted to $1,250,000. A large city system can well afford to assume the risk while thousands of the smaller units of administration cannot.

Self-insurance is of two types. In one plan the district does not carry any insurance, and if a loss occurs the district levies sufficient taxes to replace the loss. In the other plan the district sets aside a reserve fund each year until a sufficient amount of money has been accumulated to finance the replacement of any loss which might occur. The reserve fund is usually invested in high grade securities.

3. STATE REGULATIONS OF INSURANCE

Insurance is not considered a commodity; therefore, the local district is not required to take bids when purchasing insurance. Most of the states have laws which require the state insurance commissioner to approve the commercial companies before they can sell insurance within the state. Since the insurance commissioner must approve all companies before they can operate, the boards of education are fairly safe in dealing with local agents. The statutes will vary in the several states as to the requirements which must be met by a company before it can do business. In general the following are some of the requirements:

1. The company must file policy forms with the commissioner of insurance and the policies must meet certain standards.
2. The company must pay certain fees and taxes to the state.
3. The company must meet the standards of solvency required by state laws.

The local school officials should also make a study of the companies doing business within the district. The simplest rating system and the one most generally used is that of the A. M. Best Company. An A:AA financial rating of the company is very satisfactory. It is important to know something of the company's local representatives and also how prompt the company is in making settlement of claims.

4. TYPES OF INSURANCE

Types of insurance may be classified several different ways. For the purpose of this book the classifications are listed as (1) flat-rate, (2) coinsurance, and (3) extended coverage.

Flat-rate

This type of insurance requires a payment of a fixed rate for a certain per cent of the value of the property. The building may be insured for any per cent of the value and if there is a loss the company will pay up to the amount of the policy. If a building is valued at $500,000 and the board of education decides to carry only $200,000 insurance, the company will pay all losses amounting to $200,000 or less. If the building is completely destroyed the company would pay the face value of the policy which in this case would be $200,000. If there were damages amounting to $175,000 the company would pay that amount. A word of caution should be given. In many of the states the laws are such that a company will not pay more than the building is worth, regardless of the amount of insurance carried. For example, a building worth $100,000 is insured for $125,000 and it is destroyed by fire; the company will pay only $100,000, the value of the building. However, some states have a law under which the amount of insurance on a building is considered to be the value regardless of what its real value may be.

Coinsurance

This type of insurance has come into much prominence in recent years and it seems to be supplanting the traditional flat-rate type. The premium rates for coinsurance are much less than flat-rate policies because the owner agrees to carry, at all times, a stipulated percentage of the property value. Under insurance is more prevalent than over insurance with those who use coinsurance. No doubt this practice is followed because the school officials are attempting to save through small premium payments. Experience has shown that such practices are treacherous.

Because of the requirements imposed on the owner by coinsurance better insurance practices are automatically received. In the first place, a determination of insurable value must be made and should be kept up to date year by year. Secondly, an inventory of buildings and contents—a document which every district should have but which many, unfortunately, do not possess—evolves from the appraisal of value. Thirdly, the insured is required to maintain coverage at a stipulated percentage (stated in the coinsurance clause of the policy) of sound value. Lastly, in return for the owner's agreement to carry a stipulated percentage of coverage, a large reduction from the flat rate is granted on buildings and contents (and usually, also, on extended coverage if 80 per cent or more is carried). However, if the owner fails to meet his part of the bargain, much of the advantage of coinsurance is lost.[1]

The following formula indicates the operation of the coinsurance clause in case of a loss:

$$\frac{\text{Amount of Policy}}{\text{Amount Required by Policy}} \times \text{Loss} = \begin{array}{l}\text{Amount Collectible}\\ \text{up to Face of the}\\ \text{Policy.}\end{array}$$

As an application to this formula, District #1 has a school building valued at $200,000. The property is insured under 90 per cent clause. The district should purchase $180,000 of insurance. If a loss of $60,000 should occur, the formula would apply as follows:

$$\frac{\$180,000}{\$180,000} \times \$60,000 = \$60,000.$$

Amount of Policy	$180,000.
90 per cent of value of property	$180,000.
Loss	$60,000.
Amount Collectible	$60,000.

To illustrate further how coinsurance works the following examples using the 90 per cent clause are given:

Example #1. The coinsurance clause does not penalize the insured when the amount of insurance carried is 90 per cent of the value of the property. The entire loss is paid by the insured up to 90 per cent (amount of policy) of the value of the property. The company will never pay an amount in excess of the amount of the policy.

Case	Value of Property	90 Per Cent of Value	Amount of Insurance Carried	Loss	Amount Collectible from Insurer	Amount of Loss by District
1	$100,000	$90,000	$90,000	$ 45,000	$45,000	Nil
2	100,000	90,000	90,000	90,000	90,000	Nil
3	100,000	90,000	90,000	100,000	90,000	$10,000

In all three cases the amount of insurance carried was 90 per cent of the value of the property. In cases 1 and 2 the losses were less or equal to the amount of the policies; therefore the company paid the whole loss. In case 3 the loss was more than the amount of the policy;

[1] Calvin Grieder and William E. Rosenstengel, *Public School Administration* (New York: The Ronald Press Co., 1954), pp. 551–52.

therefore the insurer paid the amount of the policy which was $90,-000 and the district lost $10,000. The district and the insurer shared in the total loss.

Example #2. The coinsurance clause does penalize the insured if the amount of insurance carried does not equal the stipulated percentage.

Case	Value of Property	90 Per Cent of Value	Amount of Insurance Carried	Loss	Amount Collectible from Insurer	Amount of Loss by District
1	$100,000	$90,000	$80,000	$45,000	$40,000	$ 5,000
2	100,000	90,000	80,000	90,000	80,000	10,000
3	100,000	90,000	80,000	99,000	80,000	19,000

It is to be noted that in each of the three cases the amount of insurance carried was less than 90 per cent of the value of the property. Therefore the districts received only part of the losses. Had the district carried the 90 per cent of the value of the property in cases 1 and 2, the total losses would have been collectible. In case 3 the district would have collected $90,000 instead of $80,000.

Extended coverage

Ordinary fire insurance policies do not include extended coverage. Extended coverage pertains to losses sustained through causes other than fire. Among these causes are windstorm, hail, explosion, smoke, vehicles, aircraft, and riot. The extended coverage may be secured by the payment of a small additional premium. This plan of protection is relatively new and is obtained by an endorsement to the fire insurance policy. It is a plan to give more nearly complete protection from all risks. The endorsement should be carefully studied to see if the board of education is getting the desired protection. The authors are of the opinion that extended coverage is well worth the cost.

5. KINDS OF POLICIES

The three kinds of policies in common use among school districts are (1) specific, (2) specific schedule, and (3) blanket. Boiler insurance will also be considered in this section.

Specific

Specific coverage applies to insuring one kind of property in one definite location. For example, a school board has a school building located at a particular number on Y street. The policy would be written to cover the building at that particular location. A second policy may be written to cover the contents of the particular building, or the building and contents may be covered by one policy. This may be done by listing the definite amounts of insurance carried on the building and on the contents. This type of policy is satisfactory for a small administrative unit with one or two buildings. In a large district with a number of buildings there will be many policies to look after.

Specific schedule coverage

Under this type of policy all the buildings and contents may be grouped on a single form instead of written as specific insurance on separate policies. The specific schedule states the amount of insurance carried on each building and also the contents. The premium costs are determined by multiplying the amount of coverage on each building or content by the appropriate rate. The sum of the premiums is divided by the total amount of coverage. This will give the average rate for all the buildings and their contents. All policies are written at this average rate. The board of education usually has this information worked out on a form which is attached to the standard policy. Such a plan has value in that it reduces the number of policies and permits better supervision.

Blanket policy

Although there is no saving in the use of the blanket policy it is becoming more popular. The blanket policy covers all property and contents with separate items insured being specified. It may cover property at different locations or building and contents at a single location. This type of policy requires that 90 per cent coinsurance must be carried with an 80 per cent rate. The rates for each building and contents are used to get the average rates for all property. In case of a loss at one building the insured would have to prove that coverage at the site of the loss was 90 per cent of the value. There are several advantages to the blanket policy:

1. The equipment moved from one building to another is always insured.
2. The district has an average rate to use throughout the city.
3. The policies are more easily checked since one rate prevails.
4. The insurance program is more easily supervised.
5. There is less danger of property not being insured as there may be in the specific policy.

Boiler insurance

Extended coverage insurance discussed in this chapter does not include boiler insurance. Boiler insurance covers such damage as may result from the explosion or rupture of a boiler, hot water heater, compressors, and so forth. However, most schools insure only the boilers. If a school system has high pressure boilers, careful consideration should be given to boiler insurance. Most schools now use low pressure boilers and explosions are not so likely to occur. However, something may go wrong with a low pressure plant that might cause an explosion. Probably the greatest value derived from boiler insurance is the systematic inspectional services given by the insurance company. Through these inspections defects may be found and corrections made that will save much more than the price of the insurance, not considering the damage which might occur if the corrections had not been made. In purchasing boiler insurance extreme caution should be taken to see that the district gets the services and protection for which it pays.

6. ADMINISTRATION OF THE INSURANCE PROGRAM

The administration of an insurance program for a school system requires several steps to insure adequate coverage at the least possible cost. These steps may be listed as follows:

1. Place responsibility for handling the program
2. Ascertain the coverage needed through reliable appraisal of property
3. Set up long-range program
4. Distribute the school insurance business
5. Maintain adequate records
6. See that correct adjustments are made if losses occur

Place responsibility for handling program

The handling of the insurance program of a school system is an administrative responsibility. The board of education is a policy-making body and should not carry out administrative responsibilities. The board should make the policies, in council with the administration, which are necessary for the execution of the insurance program and then leave the work to the administration. Some of the policies which the board may make are:

1. How appraisal of property is to be made.
2. What amount of coverage will the district purchase.

3. What type of insurance and kind of policies will be used.

4. How the insurance will be distributed to companies and agents.

The above policies will be passed upon the recommendation of the administration after the necessary facts have been presented. After the policies have been passed by the board then the administration can proceed to carry out the program, year after year, or until a policy should be changed. The administration should report to the board, from time to time, facts concerning the insurance program so that the members may be informed.

A study made by the School Business Officials Association shows that there are several methods of handling the insurance programs used by boards of education throughout the United States. They are:

1. The Board of Education as a whole or a committee of the Board handles and distributes the insurance.

2. The Superintendent, Business Manager, or other district officer is held responsible for the function.

3. Authority is given to an insurance advisor, usually a local insurance agent or broker, who receives a larger proportion of the premiums in return for his services.

4. A local agents' association, as a unit, handles all the fire insurance of the school district. This method is used quite widely. Under this plan the distribution of commissions is made by the local association to its members. Membership in the local unit is open to all representative agents.[2]

The authors believe that the only sound practice is given in number 2. Number 4 may be used for distributing the insurance; however, the program should be worked out by the administration and approved by the board of education. If business managers are employed by schools, the management of insurance should be assigned to them.

Ascertain coverage needed

The insurance companies will accept the statement of the school officials as to the value of the property to be insured, but if a loss occurs, the insurance adjustors always check on the insurable value and make the payment accordingly. It is necessary for the school officials to ascertain the true value of the property so that the district will not be paying premiums on more insurance than is collectible and, at the same time, that it will be carrying sufficient amounts to make replacements in case of loss. To determine the replacement

[2] The Association of School Business Officials, "Insurance Committee Report on School Fire Insurance, 1938–45," *Bulletin No. 11* (Kalamazoo, Mich.: The Association, 1948), p. 8.

Date of Acquisition	Building or Fixture	Original Cost	Estimated Value at Beginning of Year	Cost of Additions	Deduction or Losses	Depreci- ation	Value at End of Year

Fig. 64. General property inventory ledger.

cost of a building and equipment an accurate appraisal must be made.

There are several methods used for obtaining an accurate appraisal of the value of property.

1. Fire insurance companies will provide, without charge, appraisal services through the local agent. Some might feel that such a procedure might not be best because there may be a tendency to appraise the property too high.

2. Competent local contractors, architects, and/or state school plant specialists, who are familiar with current costs, may be used. The method used by such a person is usually based upon current cost price per square or cubic foot. Since buildings vary so much in every way and bids on a new building vary in amount by different contractors, this method may be considered questionable by many people.

3. Professional appraising agents may be employed. From the standpoint of expert and impartial appraisal, this method is probably the best procedure but it is also the most expensive. The fees are usually based upon the valuation of the property. If the same company is used year after year for such work the cost is much less.

4. Business managers of some school systems make the appraisal of property. In a recent study of 114 cities it was found that more than half of the business managers made appraisals.[3]

Unless these business managers have the technical competence for such work it is doubtful if this method should be used.

Appraisals of school property are aided if the school district maintains adequate records of all property. A continuing account, such as is shown in Figure 64, will give the value of the school property at a given time.

[3] William E. Rosenstengel and Willard S. Swiers, "Business Administration in City Schools—IV," *American School Board Journal*, CXIV (June, 1947), 31–32.

Regardless of how the appraisal of property is made it is essential to determine the insurable value. *Insurable value equals replacement cost minus deductions for value of certain nonburnable items minus depreciation.*

Replacement cost is the amount of money necessary to construct a new building at the present-day prices. This may be based upon square or cubic foot prices. The type and design of the building will also enter into the cost price. Another method of determining replacement cost is through index figures on construction. These index numbers are based upon date of original construction and cost of labor and materials. The School Housing Section of the U.S. Office of Education will furnish such indices.

Nonburnable items of a school building are those parts which are less likely to be damaged by fire and would not have to be replaced if the insurance company should elect to replace the building if destroyed by fire. The following are often classed as nonburnable: architects' fees, excavations, footings and foundations below the surface, and plumbing or piping below the surface inside the foundation walls.[4]

Depreciation represents the loss in building value because of use and age. There is no one method of calculating depreciation which is applicable to all buildings and under all conditions. In financial accounting, distinction is made between general and normal depreciation. In normal depreciation the building is being operated and maintained, while in general depreciation the maintenance cost is considered as part of the depreciation. For the purpose of school accounting, general depreciation is the usual accepted practice. Probably the most satisfactory method of determining the depreciation of school property is known as the *straight line method*. Such a method assumes there will be a uniform change over a fixed period of time. There are three factors to be considered in calculation by the straight line method. They are (1) original cost, (2) years of useful service, and (3) the salvage value at the end of the period of usefulness. The first factor (original cost) may be obtained accurately while the latter two factors are variable and must be estimated. Thus annual depreciation may be determined by the following formula:

$$\text{Annual Depreciation} = \frac{\text{Cost} - \text{Salvage Value}}{\text{Life of Building or Item}}$$

Should a school plant cost $510,000 and have a salvage value of $10,000 and the life of the plant was estimated to be 50 years, the

[4] American Association of School Administrators, *Managing the School District Insurance Program* (Washington, D.C.: The Association, 1953), p. 9.

annual depreciation would be $10,000. This same formula may be used for calculating depreciation on equipment.

Set up long-range program

It is most desirable for the school administrator to work out a long-range program of insurance for the school district. Such a plan would involve (1) a budget plan, (2) expiration schedule, (3) rate reduction, and (4) distribution of coverage among different companies.

The budget plan of an insurance program is set up so that approximately equal amounts of coverage will expire each year. Therefore the amount of premiums to be paid will be approximately equal each year. On a three-year program one-third of the insurance will expire each year; likewise, on a five-year program one-fifth will expire each year. Most companies will help the district to establish such a program by cancelling certain policies and rewriting them without penalties for shorter terms.

An expiration schedule should be set up so that all policies expiring each year will be on the same day. It is preferable that this expiration date be the same for each year. The administration should set the expiration date for a time when the board will have ample funds to pay the premiums when due. In those districts which rely heavily upon local taxes for income the expiration date should be set after taxes are collected. The management of the insurance program is made much easier if all policies expire at the same time. Policies expiring throughout the year require constant checking by the person in charge.

Insurance costs can be a burden upon a school district. Too often the administrator assumes that the cost of insurance is a fixed item of expenditure and little or no effort is made to reduce the rates which are being paid. A careful inspection of all buildings by the Rating Bureaus should be made at periodic intervals to see what credits are possible. Some rating bureaus have a standard rate for each public building and to this rate are added debits and credits according to the presence or lack of hazards found. Many times relatively simple actions result in a savings. For example, an added penalty may be placed upon a building because of broken plaster. If this is repaired the penalty will be removed. Again, by purchasing a few fire extinguishers, the rate on a building may be reduced.

Many structural penalties are not always practical to remove. The replacement cost of a roof made of combustible material would be so great that the savings would not justify the expenditure. On the other hand a building may have a structural penalty because the stairways which lead from one floor to another are open. If these are closed from the halls by fireproof doors and are housed in fireproof walls no penalty will be assessed.

Rate reductions may be obtained by purchasing on a three- or five-year term. In most cases a three-year term rate is two-and-one-half times the one-year rate. The five-year rate is four times the one-year rate. There is a 16 2/3 per cent saving by using the three-year rate over the one-year and a 20 per cent saving of the five-year rate over the one-year rate. The five-year rate gives a 4 per cent saving over the three-year rate.

Coinsurance offers a considerable savings over a flat-rate insurance. A school district may obtain much more coverage at much less cost by using coinsurance. This is especially true when a great majority of the buildings are of the better type. The amount of reduction will vary according to the contract percentage, the type of building, and local fire protection. Such rate reductions are fixed according to the published schedule. Linn and Joyner[5] bring out the fact that school property should be considered by rating bureaus as a separate class of risk. This statement is made because of the wide disproportion shown in reports between the amount paid for premiums and the return in payment for losses. The statutes relative to establishing rates are not the same in all states. "The actual business of rate-making or setting up of rate schedules, however, is carried on by central rating organizations or general inspection bureaus which are strictly private agencies. Such rating organizations offer many advantages to the insurance business and are directly sponsored by the insurance companies."[6] If schools are to be considered for special rates, it would be necessary to consider them on a state-wide basis. The school people of each state should obtain the necessary data, amount paid in premiums and losses over a period of years, and present these findings to the state insurance commissioner for consideration. There is a breaking point in insurance rates and a careful study of the problem is necessary.

A sound policy for a long-range insurance program is to distribute the coverage among a number of companies. By such a plan the risk will be less. No one company should have all the insurance.

Placement plan of insurance business

How to distribute school insurance business among the local agents is a very touchy problem. The pressure of the local agents to get a

[5] Henry H. Linn and Schuyler C. Joyner, *Insurance Practices in School Administration* (New York: The Ronald Press Co., 1952), pp. 117–19.
[6] *Ibid.*, p. 118.

part of the business is very strong especially in the smaller cities and towns.   Unless there is some systematic method worked out and adopted by the board of education, the administration will be faced with the problem of trying to satisfy a number of the local agents. This may result in dozens of policies and a poor insurance program. Smaller administrative units should follow the plan which is often called the Local Board Placement Plan used in many large cities.[7]   In such a plan the administrator is instructed to deal with a committee or a representative of the local association of insurance agents.   The committee agrees to scatter the insurance business among the association members.   This plan will limit the number of policies, reduce the pressure upon the board members, and help develop a coordinated insurance program.

Insurance records

Good management of the school insurance program requires the keeping of adequate records.   They should be simple, easily maintained, and provide reliable information when needed.   One of the essential records is the insurance register.   It should be the size of the regular accounting books so that it may be filed with the accounting records.   Figure 65 shows an insurance register.[8]

Adjustment on fire losses

Insurance is carried on a building to protect the district from a financial loss in case of fire or other hazards which are covered by the policy.   Should a loss occur, the administration is required to perform certain duties.   Among the duties which are usually required are:[9]

1. Report the loss to the insurance company or companies by a written notice.   This notification should be prepared in duplicate and the duplicate copy should be retained in the file of the school system.
2. Guard the property so that further damage will not occur from any source.
3. Salvage all undamaged property and place in order for checking. This is especially essential in case of a partial loss.

[7] *An Insurance Program for Guidance of School Boards* (Albany, N.Y.: New York State School Boards Associations, Inc., 1951), pp. 39–40; Oklahoma City School Insurance Committee, *A Guide to Boards of Education for Planned Insurance Program* (Oklahoma City, Okla.: Oklahoma City Board of Education, 1951); and C. L. Suffield, "An Agreement for a One-Client Association of Insurance Agents," *American School Board Journal,* CII (June, 1941), 50–51.

[8] See Chapter 19 for additional property records.

[9] Adapted from *Insurance Practices in School Administration, op. cit.* pp. 134–35.

Date of Issue	Name and Address of Company	Name and Address of Local Agent	Policy Number	Property Insured	Amount of Policy	Premium	Term of Policy	Rate	Expiration Date

Fig. 65. Insurance register.

4. Prepare an inventory of property destroyed. All items destroyed and cost of each should be included in the inventory. Property records as presented in Chapter 12 will be of untold value in preparing such an inventory.
5. Furnish, when requested by company, plans and specifications of building and all equipment which were destroyed.
6. Show company officials the remains of the property after fire or other disaster covered by the policy.
7. Produce for company all books of accounts pertaining to the loss. This makes it very important to keep accurate records of all buildings and equipment.

Insurance companies are usually eager to make settlements in case of a loss with a school district. A quick, satisfactory settlement is a good form of advertisement for the company. However, if the company feels that the district is asking for a greater amount of money than is due, protests will be made. If the company and the officials of the school cannot come to an agreement upon the amount of loss, the company will demand an appraisement. The appraisement will be made by three competent persons. The insurance company and the board of education will each appoint an appraiser and these two appraisers will appoint the third person. The amount of loss agreed upon by any two of the appraisers will be the sum that the company will pay. It is much more satisfactory if the board of education and the insurance company can agree upon the settlement. Usually a cash settlement over replacement is more advantageous to both parties.

7. FIRE PREVENTION

No insurance program is complete without a good fire prevention program. A successful fire insurance program will help reduce school fires. Prevention of fires not only protects the insurance company but also protects the school district.

Fire prevention aids the school

Should a fire occur during the time school is in operation, there is a great danger of loss of life. During the past 50 years there have been approximately 850 lives lost in school fires and of this number nearly 700 were school children. Not many school districts have fires without financial losses. Even though the building is insured the settlement will not amount to 100 per cent of the loss. In addition to destruction of materials whenever a fire occurs, the educational program is likely to be disrupted. Children may have to be housed in

TABLE 15. Cause of 1,116 school fires

Cause	Per Cent
Heating defects	
Faulty equipment or improper operation	10.0
Defective or poorly installed chimneys or flues	6.4
Careless disposal of hot ashes or coals	1.6
Misuse of electricity	17.0
Smoking and matches	12.1
Spontaneous ignition of oily rags or material	10.3
Incendiary	8.8
Improper rubbish disposal methods	5.0
Careless handling of flammable liquids	4.9
Special hazards associated with manual training	4.6
Open flame devices in laboratories and kitchens igniting combustible materials	4.4
Explosions (gas heating, chemical, and flammable vapors)	3.0
Lightning	3.0
Exposure	2.7
Miscellaneous	6.2
Total	100.0

temporary quarters until the plant is rebuilt. This oftentimes means that a year or more will pass before adequate facilities have been replaced. Children who attend school under makeshift conditions for one or two years lose something that cannot be measured in terms of money. Therefore, school officials should carry out a good fire prevention program that will hold fires to the very minimum.

Causes of school fires

One of the first steps toward the elimination of school fires is to know some of the causes. The National Fire Protection Association lists the causes of 1,116 school fires (see Table 15).[10]

The Association also states that almost three-fourths of all fires start in the service and student areas. Boiler rooms, storerooms, and closets are extremely hazardous according to all reports. Probably poor housekeeping may be said to be the greatest single cause of fires.

Self-inspection a means of eliminating fires

One of the best ways for a school system to help carry out a fire prevention program is through the use of self-inspection with a view to the elimination of fire hazards. The National Board of Fire Under-

[10] National Fire Protection Association, *Handbook of Fire Protection* (Boston: The Association, 1953), p. 1385.

SELF-INSPECTION BLANK FOR SCHOOLS
Prepared by
THE NATIONAL BOARD OF FIRE UNDERWRITERS
Chicago   New York   San Francisco

Approvéd and Adopted by
The National Association of Public School Business Officials
Endorsed by the
International Association of Fire Chiefs

If precautions are taken to minimize the danger of fire and to provide for safety in case fire occurs, real progress will be made in safeguarding life and protecting property. Intelligent thought and care in practice can eliminate practically all fires within schools.

INSTRUCTIONS

Inspection to be made each month by the custodian and a member of the faculty at which inspection only Items 1 to 20 need be reported. At the quarterly inspection, a member of the fire department should accompany the above inspectors, and the complete blank should be filled out. The report of each inspection (monthly and quarterly) is to be filed with the Board of Education or School Commissioners.

Questions are so worded that a negative answer will indicate an unsatisfactory condition.

Date...

Name of School .... City..

Class: Elementary................... Junior High................... Senior High ....

Capacity of School?........................... Number now enrolled ....

1. Are all exit doors equipped with panic locks?........................... Are these locks tested each week to insure ease of operation?........................... Do these lock securely so that additional locks, bolts or chains are not necessary?........................... Are such additional locks open whenever building is in use? ....

2. Are all outside fire escapes free from obstructions and in good working order?........................... Are they used for fire drills? ....

3. Is all heating equipment, including flues, pipes and steam lines:—
   (a) in good serviceable condition and well maintained? ....
   (b) properly insulated and separated from all combustible material by a safe distance? ....

4. Is coal pile inspected periodically for evidences of heating? ....

5. Are ashes placed in *metal* containers used for that purpose *only?* ....

6. Is remote control provided whereby oil supply line may be shut off in emergency? ....

7. Where is outside shut-off valve on gas supply line?...................

8. Check any of the following locations where there are accumulations of waste paper, rubbish, old furniture, stage scenery, etc., and explain under remarks:— attic,   basement,   furnace room,   stage, dressing rooms in connection with stage,   other locations ....

9. Is the space beneath stairs free from accumulations or storage of any materials? ....

10. What material or preparation is used for cleaning or polishing floors? ....
    Quantity on hand? ....Where stored? ....

11. Are approved metal cans, with self-closing covers or lids, used for the storage of *all* oily waste, polishing cloths, etc.? ....

12. Are approved metal containers with vapor-tight covers used for all kerosene, gasoline, etc., on the premises? ....Why are such hazardous materials kept on the premises?

13. Are premises free from electrical wiring or equipment which is defective? ....
    (If answer is *No*, explain under Remarks.)

14. Are only approved extension or portable cords used?...................

15. Are all fuses on lighting or small appliance circuits of 15 amperes or less capacity? ....
    (Continued on reverse side).

Fig. 66. Self-inspection blank for schools.

writers has prepared a *Self-Inspection Blank for Schools* which may be used by any school system. Some school systems have designed their own forms which more or less follow the one prepared by the National Board of Fire Underwriters. The great value derived from the use of such a method is to make those persons who inhabit a building conscious of the many hazards which may be eliminated.

16. Are electric pressing irons equipped with automatic heat control or signal and provided with metal stand? ....

17. Are sufficient fire extinguishers provided on each floor so that not over 100 feet travel is required to reach the nearest unit? ....
In manual training shops and on stage, 50 feet? ....

18. Have chemical extinguishers been recharged within a year? ....
Is date of recharge shown on tag attached to extinguisher? ....

19. Is building equipped with standpipe and hose having nozzle attached? ....
Is hose in good serviceable condition? ....

20. Is a large woolen blanket readily available in the domestic science laboratory for use in case clothing is ignited? ....

Remarks (Note any changes since last inspection)

The following items to be included in each quarterly inspection:—

21. Building construction: Walls.......................... Floors,.......................... Roof..........................
No. stories .... No, class rooms ....

22. Which sections of buildings are equipped with automatic sprinklers? ....

23. Are there at least two means of egress from each floor of the building? ....
Are these so located that the distance measured along the line of travel does not exceed
From the door of any classroom, 125 feet? ....
From any point in auditorium, assembly hall or gymnasium, 100 feet? ....

24. Are all windows free from heavy screens or bars?..........................

25. Do all exit doors open outward? ....

26. Are all interior stairways enclosed? ....
Are doors to these enclosures of self-closing type?..........................

27. Are windows within 10 feet of fire escapes glazed with wire glass? ....

28. Are manual training, domestic science, other laboratories and the cafeteria so located that a fire in one will not cut off any exit from the building? ....

29. Is a smoke-tight projection booth, built of incombustible materials, and vented to the outside, provided for the motion picture machine? ....

30. Are heating plant and fuel supply rooms cut-off from the main corridors by fire-resistant walls, ceiling and doors? ....

31. Do all ventilating ducts terminate outside of building? ....

32. State type of construction of any temporary buildings in school yard ....

33. Is nearest temporary building at least 50 feet from main building? ....

34. How often are fire drills held?..........................Average time of exit? ....

35. Are provisions made for sounding alarm of fire from any floor of building? ....
Is sounding device accessible? .... Plainly marked? ....

36. Give location of nearest city fire alarm box ....

How far distant from the premises? ....

Remarks

Inspector.......................... Title..........................
Inspector.......................... Title..........................
Inspector.......................... Title..........................

The use of the Self Survey Blank by the children is an excellent teaching device and all teachers should welcome the opportunity to use it in connection with the study of safety and health. Such a study made by the custodians will also bring to their attention the need of better housekeeping standards. A school principal should consider such a program as one with many opportunities and not a duty imposed upon him by the board of education. A copy of the Self-Inspection Blank prepared by the National Board of Fire Under-writers is presented in Figure 66.

New buildings and fire prevention

In planning and constructing new buildings consideration should be given to fire prevention. Most of the states have certain laws to be observed in construction of school buildings. The plans and specifications should be approved by the state authority responsible for the enforcement of such state laws. There are, however, many simple but important matters pertaining to fire protection in new plants which are not mentioned in the state laws. The administrator who is really interested in constructing new plants with a minimum of fire hazards should prepare a check list to guide him in checking the plans and specifications for fire prevention. Such a check list may include the following:

1. Is the building constructed of fire-resistive material?
2. Is the furnace room located in a separate building? (It is not essential for a furnace room to be in the basement. In fact, a school plant should not have a basement. If there are rooms in the basement there is a tendency to house children in them. A basement is one of the most hazardous areas in a school building from the standpoint of origin of fires.)
3. Is the furnace room constructed out of fire-resistive materials?
4. Are all openings leading from furnace room to main building equipped with automatic closing fire doors approved by the Underwriters Laboratories?
5. Is there adequate fire-safe storage for fuel?
6. Do all fuel-oil or gas-burner installations comply with the standards set up by the Board of Fire Underwriters?
7. Is there at least one egress from furnace room which leads directly to the outside?
8. Do all electric wiring and connections comply with the Underwriters Code?
9. Are pilot-light indicators provided for irons and other heating units?
10. Is it essential to have a multistory building? (Today, single-story plants may be constructed about as economically as multistory plants. In some situations it is necessary to construct multistory buildings because of the limited amount of playground area.)
11. Are all multistory buildings provided with at least two main stairways remote from each other?

12. Are all classroom doors within 125 feet of a main stairway?
13. Are all stairways fireproof and placed at right angles to the hall?
14. Are the windows in the fire well made of wired glass and metal frames?
15. Are there fireproof doors leading to the stairs?
16. Are all exit doors equipped with panic bolts?
17. Do all exit doors open outward?
18. Are there illuminated exit signs in all auditoriums, gymnasiums, corridors, and stairways?
19. Is there a fire alarm system?
20. Is the building equipped with adequate fire fighting equipment which meets the standards of the National Board of Fire Underwriters?
21. Is there a sprinkler system provided for the stage and dressing rooms?
22. Is there an automatic-drop, fire-resistive front curtain?
23. Is there adequate water supply to the building?
24. Are all storage rooms fireproof?
25. Are all auditoriums, assembly halls, cafeterias, libraries, gymnasiums, and shops located on the ground floor? (A great number of schools are considering the campus-type construction more satisfactory.)

Good housekeeping aids fire prevention

Probably one of the most practical means of preventing fires is through good housekeeping standards. The administration is directly responsible for the housekeeping in the schools and should strive for the very best. There have been many fires started from unknown sources which could probably be traced to poor housekeeping. Closets which are not fireproof are often used to store all types of highly inflammable materials. These same closets probably have not been cleaned for long periods of time and are filled with dust and litter. Too often these closets are found under wooden stairs which have been oiled time after time. Storage of rubbish in attics, basements, and on stages or dressing rooms is not an uncommon practice in many schools, especially in the old buildings which do not provide for adequate storage facilities. Ashes dumped into wooden containers which may be near a pile of rubbish offers a good opportunity for a fire to start. Old rags saturated with oil are often allowed to accumulate in unventilated places and may start a fire by spontaneous combustion. These and numerous other bad housekeeping practices are often the causes of school fires, and may be eliminated by good housekeeping standards.

TOPICS FOR STUDY AND DISCUSSION

1. Why should a school district carry fire insurance?
2. What method do the boards of education use to insure school build‹ ings in your state?
3. What are the advantages and disadvantages of state insurance?
4. What school districts should consider self-insurance? Why?
5. What are some advantages of coinsurance?
6. A school building valued at $800,000 is destroyed by fire. The board of education carried $500,000 insurance with an old Line Company and had 90 per cent coinsurance. How much would the board collect?
7. Prepare a short research paper on the subject "Boiler Insurance."
8. Outline the steps you would advise a board of education to follow in administering the insurance program.
9. How may the insurance rate on a particular building be reduced? How would you go about trying to get a reduced rate for your buildings?
10. How may fire hazards be reduced in your school plant?
11. What are the advantages of using self-inspection blanks?
12. Make up a list of fire prevention suggestions you would hand to a group of custodians.
13. What material would you include in a course of study pertaining to fire prevention for school custodians?
14. Analyze a fire insurance policy and present your findings to the class.

SELECTED REFERENCES

American Association of School Administrators. *Managing the School District Insurance Program.* Washington, D.C.: The Association, 1953.

Association of School Business Officials, Insurance Committee. *Insurance Committee Report on School Fire Insurance, 1938–45.* Kalamazoo, Mich.: The Association, 1948.

EICHLER, GEORGE A. "Planning an Insurance Program," *American School Board Journal,* CXVIII (May, 1949), 39–40.

ENGELHARDT, N. L., SR. "Safeguarding Schools against Fire Dangers," *American School Board Journal,* CXXVIII (February, 1954), 65–67.

GRIEDER, CALVIN, and WILLIAM E. ROSENSTENGEL. *Public School Administration.* New York: The Ronald Press Co., 1954, chap. XXIV.

LINN, HENRY H., and SCHUYLER C. JOYNER. *Insurance Practices in School Administration.* New York: The Ronald Press Co., 1952, chaps. I–IV.

REMMLEIN, MADALINE K. *The Law of Local Public School Administration.* New York: McGraw-Hill Book Co., Inc., 1953. pp. 131–32.

State Federation of District Boards of Education of New Jersey. *School Insurance Facts for School Board Members Part 1.* Trenton, N.J.: The Federation, 1952.

VILES, N. E. *School Fire Safety.* U.S. Office of Education, Bulletin 1951, No. 13. Washington, D.C.: Government Printing Office, 1951.

Washington State School Directors' Association. *School Insurance Economies.* Olympia, Wash.: The Association, 1950.

19

SCHOOL PLANT RECORDS

PERHAPS NO OTHER ASPECT of business management has received less attention than that of accounting for school property. The reasons for such apathy on the part of boards of education and administrations probably have been due to the fact that (1) the schools do not operate for profit, (2) the districts do not pay taxes on property,[1] (3) the school districts have not followed the practice of setting aside reserve funds to take care of depreciation, and (4) the shortage of money prevents the employment of sufficient help to do all the necessary work essential for a school system.

During the depression years when the Federal Government was making grants for schoolhouse construction it was necessary for the district to show a clear title to the land before a grant was made. This pointed out the need for adequate plant records. During World War II little was done in school plant construction. In the past few years, however, when the great need for school buildings was brought forth and state monies appropriated for school buildings, the needs for school plant records have been made apparent. Although the problems associated with property management in a large city will be different in degree from those confronting the administration in the smaller units, the fundamental principles are the same. The basic records necessary for an adequate system of accounting for school property will be presented in this chapter.

The plot and plan book

Today many boards of education are faced with ever increasing problems of providing more adequate school sites for old buildings,

[1] School districts, however, are liable for assessment such as street improvements, sidewalks, etc.

TABLE OF CONTENTS

Sheet	School	Location	Sheet	School	Location
1	Spartanburg Sr. High	South Dean St.	11	Drayton	Drayton, S.C.
2	Cleveland Jr. High	Howard St.	12	Whitney	Whitney, S.C.
3	Jenkins Jr. High	So. Church St.	13	Carver High	So. Liberty St.
4	Pine Street	Pine St.	14	Mary H. Wright	Caulder Ave.
5	Oakland	Oakland Ave.	15	Highland	W. Henry St.
6	Fremont	Fremont Ave.	16	Cumming	Cumming St.
7	West End	Forest St.	17	Alexander	N. Dean St.
8	Southside	S. Spring St.	18	Administration Bldg.	So. Church St.
9	Cooperative	Rt. 4 Sptg., S.C.	19	Voc. Bld'g Warehouse	Oil St.
10	Zion Hill	Rt. 1 Sptg., S.C.			

Fig. 67. Table of contents—plot and plan book.

purchasing new sites, and building additional classrooms and other plant facilities on old sites. It is almost impossible for the average board member to keep in his mind the many details relative to the school property when he gives his attention to future planning. By our modern methods of reproducing drawings and written materials, the individual board member may be provided with a *plot* and *plan* book giving information on all school property. Such a book is not only valuable for board members to use but also is a means of providing an accurate record of school property which may be kept up to date at all times.

The plot and plan book should be in a loose-leaf binder and at least 15″ × 24″ in size. The covers should be durable and marked *Plot and Plan Book of (Blank) School District.* The first page should be the table of contents. In the table of contents each piece of property is designated by a number, the name, and the location in the city. The first piece of property listed would be designated by 1., the second by 2., and so forth. The pages of the book should have tabs with numbers corresponding to those assigned each piece of property. Figure 67 shows the Table of Contents of the plot and plan of Spartanburg, South Carolina, City Schools.

Following the table of contents would be a map of the entire district showing the locations of all school properties. A symbol should be used to show the type of school at each location. The remainder of the book will be divided into sections. Section 1 will be for property designated as number 1, section 2 for property number 2, and so forth. The first page under section 1 should show the boundary survey of school site No. 1 with bench marks or stakes indicated. The drawing should give the dimensions of the property, the streets surrounding the site, an outline of the building, sidewalks, direction arrow, and the scale of the drawing. Figure 68 shows plot-plan as used for page 1. Page 2 of section 1 should give a contour drawing of the site and the utility services (water, sewers, gas, and lights) accurately located. This drawing should also give the scale used and the direction arrow. Page 3 of section 1 should be a large photograph of the school building. If there is more than one building on the site, a photograph of each building should be on this page. Page 4 of section 1 should be a drawing of the first-floor plan of the school plant showing the dimensions of all areas and use of spaces. If the building is a two-story plant, page 5 should show the second-floor plan.

The plot and plan book should be kept up to date at all times. If additional property adjacent to a site should be purchased, a new drawing should be inserted or an additional sheet inserted and numbered 1A. Should the building be altered or additions constructed,

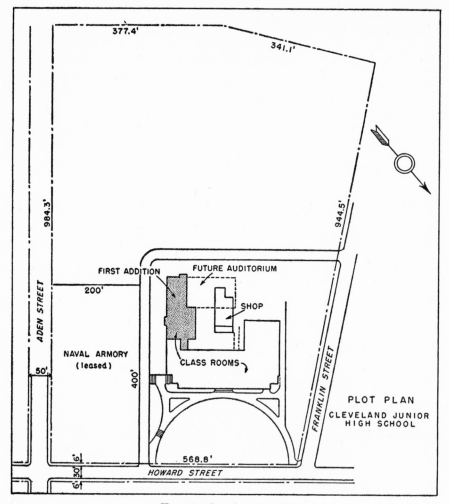

Fig. 68. Plot-plan record.

a new sheet properly numbered should be inserted. If a plot of land should be sold, all information should be noted on the plot drawing and the section removed from the book and filed. Make all changes in the plot and plan book as they occur.

Deeds and abstracts records

There should be a loose-leaf book or a file for all deeds and abstracts. These should be placed in the loose-leaf binder or filed in alphabetical order. The deeds and abstracts will also be recorded in the official books of the County Recorder. The administration should see that the titles to school properties are clear. School property has usually been secured through an easement or fee simple. There is no question about the fee simple since it gives the owner absolute and unqualified title with unconditional power of disposition. An easement is different. If the deed conveying a school site to the school district contains a clause to the effect that the property shall be used for school purposes or for school purposes only, it cannot be called a clear title. The administration should try to clear up all titles so that the question of ownership will never come up.

The property ledger

Most financial accounting systems used in the several states will provide for a property ledger. The size of the sheet is the same as that of the accounting forms. The ledger is a record of each item, usually by some standard classification made by the state, year when purchased, total cost, annual depreciation, additions, and estimated value at end of year. Figures 69 and 70 give two different kinds of property ledgers.

The school system may design a form which would meet the local needs better than some standard form. It is essential, however, that the property ledger be kept up to date each year. Keeping of the ledger does not involve much work, since the entries are made once a year.

Inventory records

There is no way to set up a system for keeping accurate and up-to-date records on value of buildings and equipment. It is recognized, however, that some system must be used. An accurate inventory of all physical property owned by the district is the only means of keeping track of the numerous items of furniture, buses, typewriters, adding machines, etc. Changes in personnel and moving of equip-

Building or Equipment Items	Code	Date of Acquisition	Original Cost	Estimated Value at Beginning of Year	Additions	Replacement and Repairs	Deductions or Losses	Depreciation	Estimated Value at End of Year

Fig. 69. Property record: 1.

Kind or Location of Property	School Invoice Number	Value Beginning of School Year	INCREASE DURING YEAR			DECREASES DURING YEAR			Value End of School Year
			Capital Outlay	Mainte-nance	Total	Loss or Sale	Depreci-ation	Total	
1									1
2									2

Fig. 70. Property record: 2.

ment from one school to another make it necessary to have some standard procedure so that property will not be lost. It is not only necessary to keep track of all equipment but also to be able to figure the value so that accurate information may be had for insurance purposes.

Figure 71 gives an illustration of a form which may be used for buildings. Such a form could be on a card or sheets of paper for a loose-leaf binder.

1. **Building** ____________________ **Location** ________
2. **Use** ______________________________
3. **Date of original construction** ________________
4. **Name of architect** ______________________
5. **Name of contractors: (1) general** ________________

   (2) Sub contractors ____________________
6. **Original cost complete $** __________________
7. **Additions**

Additions	Date	Description	Cost
______	____	________	$______
______	____	________	______
______	____	________	______

Fig. 71. Individual building record.

Fig. 72 shows a property inventory record which is of value in keeping account of all equipment. These should be filled out in duplicate yearly for each building. One copy will be retained by the principal and the other filed in the business office.

Description of Article	Date of Purchase	Unit Cost	Number on Hand and Location									
			1955–56		1956–57		1957–58		1958–59		1959–60	
			No.	Place	No.	Place	No.	Place	No.	Place	No.	Place

Fig. 72. Property inventory.

The business office should keep a depreciation record of all buildings and items of equipment. Fig. 73 shows such a form. This form may be used on a card or a sheet of paper for a loose-leaf binder.

Name of Building _____ Location _____

Name of Item _____ Number (Local School Assigned No.)_____

Normal depreciation rate_____ Estimated life_____

Salvage Value_____Other_____

Date	Description	Year Built or Installed	Total Cost	Amount Annual Depreciation	Total Amount Depreciated

Fig. 73. Depreciation record.

Building records for insurance purposes should be kept up to date year by year. The importance of having accurate appraisal records in case of a loss was pointed out in Chapter 18. Fig. 74 gives a simple form which would be of much value.

Name and Location	Cost or Appraisal Value	Building		Contents	
		Insurable Value	Amount of Insurance	Insurable Value	Amount of Insurance

Fig. 74. Building insurance record.

Blueprint records of buildings

A complete copy of all the blueprints of the school plants should be on file in the administrative office. If there is a special building department they would be filed there. In any event, the records should be complete. The filing case should be the drawer type. Single drawers for the blueprints of each building are more satisfactory than large drawers holding blueprints of several plants. At the time the architect makes the final drawings and specification, extra copies should be made for file purposes. Used copies are so badly worn that they are not satisfactory for filing. There will be need to refer to the blueprints of a building many times after it is in use. If the administrators had copies of the blueprints of all the present plants that were constructed years ago, much time, energy, and money could be saved in a number of the remodeling programs which are being made today.

TOPICS FOR STUDY AND DISCUSSION

1. Who is responsible for setting up an adequate system of school plant records?
2. How would you get the material together for a plot and plan book?
3. List the persons connected with your school who should have a copy of the plot and plan book.
4. What property records are kept in your school system?
5. What records would you use in your school system for setting up complete property accounts?

SELECTED REFERENCES

DeFrain, Frank J. "Accounting for School Properties," *American School Board Journal*, CVI (March, 1943), 20.

George, Norvil L. "The Importance of the School Property Inventory," *School Management*, XV (January, 1946), 240.

Grieder, Calvin, and William E. Rosenstengel. *Public School Administration.* New York: The Ronald Press Co., 1954, chap. XX.

Mort, Paul and Walter C. Reusser. *Public School Finance.* 2d ed. New York: McGraw-Hill Book Co., Inc., 1951, pp. 337–42.

Smith, Homer L. "Equipment Inventory and Inventory Records for a Small High School System," *American School Board Journal*, CXII (September, 1946), 45.

20

SUPPLIES AND EQUIPMENT

IN THE EARLY HISTORY of the public schools the management of equipment, supplies, and books was relatively simple. The equipment was meager, a small amount of supplies was used, the library contained few books, and the parents purchased the textbooks. Today, however, the problem is much different. Services of the schools have been expanded, different types of educational programs have been instituted, and the methods of teaching have changed. These changes, together with the changing concept of what the public schools should furnish free to all children, have brought about the use of a countless number of different items of supplies, equipment, and books.

Although the expenditure for material in the schools represents a relatively small per cent of the total costs of public education, it is of sufficient importance to require efficient management. Waste due to poor selecting and purchasing procedures cannot be justified. Moreover, public attention is easily attracted to physical and tangible objects. Visible waste may weaken the public confidence and thereby handicap the total financial support for public education.

I. SELECTION OF MATERIAL

Selection of supplies, books, and equipment is an important phase of school administration only as it aids the effectiveness of the instructional program. The amount of money appropriated for material is usually small in comparison with other items of the budget, therefore every possible effort should be made to get the best and most suitable material for the amount of money available. The work of many teachers and nonteaching personnel is often handicapped because of the lack of adequate supplies, books, or equipment.

Classification of materials

There is a wide range of supplies and equipment used in the instructional program and in the operation and maintenance of the school plant. There always seems to be some question in the minds of most people as to the distinction between supplies and equipment. Books are more easily classified. Those books not used as textbooks are classed as library books. The distinction between supplies and equipment is not so easily made. In some of the states the handbook of instruction for the accounting system sets up an arbitrary list of items classified as supplies and another list classified as equipment. In some situations the cost of the item determines whether it is classified as supplies or equipment. For example, an item costing less than five dollars would be classified as a supply, while an item costing more than five dollars would be equipment. A reasonable distinction would seem to be one that considered the period of usefulness. Those materials which are consumed or destroyed when they are used, such as paper, ink, soap, fuel, scotch tape, glue, test tubes, etc., would be classed as supplies. Some supplies may last a year or more. Items which would be more permanent and are not consumed or destroyed from use, such as scales, desks, chairs, refrigerators, band saws, etc., would be classed as equipment. The greatest value in making any distinction between the two is for accounting purposes. Those items which have more permanent value should be considered as equipment for getting a true value of property for insurance purposes.

Selection policies

Whether the material[1] is a library book, a textbook, an item of equipment or supply, there should be some general administrative policies concerning its selection. The main function of all material is to aid in the teaching or learning process. If this function is to be realized, some general policies such as the following should be considered.

1. Those who use the material should help select it.
2. Select those materials that will be used by the greatest number of persons.
3. Select those materials that will meet the demands of the curriculum.
4. Select those materials that will be of interest to the pupils.
5. Select those materials that will help the teacher to individualize the instruction.

[1] The word "material" will be used from time to time to mean equipment, supplies, or books.

6. Select those materials that will give the best results. If a less expensive item will give as good or better results than the more expensive, the former should be chosen.
7. Select those materials that can be used in the situation at hand. For example, if there is only play space for "soft" baseball do not select a regulation "hard" baseball for use. Do not select a book written on the eighth-grade level for pupils reading on the third-grade level.
8. Select new and untried material only after experimental use.
9. Select material on quality or specifications and not by brand name.
10. Give adequate time for users to make choices in selection.

The above list is given as an example of general policies which the administration may consider. Each administrative unit should develop a set of policies to meet the particular need.

Standard lists

There is much debate concerning the use of a standard list of supplies and equipment. As a general rule a school system will use certain adopted textbooks, although there may be several different sets used by the same teacher in a particular class or subject. There seems to be no need for standard lists of library books beyond a very minimum. Supplies and equipment, however, are somewhat different. Because of the great number and variety, it would seem advisable for an administrative unit to consider a standard list. This standard list should be revised each year and there should always be means of securing items which may not be included.

A standard list will be of much assistance in making up the needs of the individual school as well as the whole school system. It will reduce labor, space, and energy in the management of supply storage. It is also much easier to draw up specifications for certain material by use of a standard list. The use of such a list is more practical from the administrative point of view. However, it is realized that some individuals will not be satisfied by the use of standard lists. Figure 75 shows, in part, an example of a standard list.

Specifications

It is to be noted that the descriptions of the items given in Figure 75 are not specifications. A great number of purchasers base their contracts on certain trade-brand articles "or their equal," ignoring the fact that it is very difficult to determine equality. Trade names or brands alone cannot be depended upon when more than one firm is asked to bid on the supplies. Specifications may be developed through laboratory tests, through use, and through expert opinion. Most schools do not have the facilities to make the necessary laboratory tests and fail to secure the necessary expert opinion for writing out detailed specifications. The National Bureau of Standards[2] has specifications on a great number of items. These will be of much value to the person who has the responsibility of preparing specifications. There are many items which do not need detailed specifications, while many others do. For example, some items are purchased in a very limited number and at a low unit cost. It would probably be of greater expense to the district (than the cost of the items) to set up specifications. There are others, however, that would require complete specifications for bids, as well as test samples of the purchased items, to see if specifications are being fulfilled. A good example of an item which should have complete specifications is stoker coal.

In setting forth specifications of qualities, workmanship, and finish of an article, care should be given to see that the definitions are explicit and understandable. Both the purchaser and vendor should have a common understanding of the article to be supplied. The purchaser must make provisions to check all purchases to see that the specifications as given have been fulfilled by the vendor. If no check is made, specifications become worthless. Manufacturers in general are anxious to serve the schools and are usually willing to certify that their products comply with federal specifications.

Quantity determination

The determination of the quantity of supplies to be appropriated to each school creates a problem for most administrators. Some administrators arbitrarily assign fixed quantities of supplies to individual schools for a given period of time. Others appropriate a certain amount of money per pupil in average daily attendance or per teaching unit. There is a decided disadvantage to allotting supplies in quantity. There may be certain supplies allotted to a school that will never be used. On the other hand, one school may need more of some particular item than was allotted. If the appropriation is made on the money basis, the principal with the aid of the teaching and nonteaching personnel will be able to select those items which will be used. The amount of money appropriated for supplies will vary from school to school as will the cost of material.

Every effort should be made to anticipate the quantity of each material needed during the fiscal period. Since the quantity needed

[2] A catalog of specifications, *National Directory of Commodity Specification*, may be purchased from Superintendent of Documents, Washington, D.C.

must be obtained through estimates, every precaution possible should be taken to secure the exact amount. Consideration must be given to material on hand and the amount used the preceding year. Attention should also be given to any unusual circumstances which might arise during the ensuing year. Extra time and energy used in making estimates more accurate will be to the teacher's advantage since this will provide an adequate amount of supplies at the same time money is being saved for other needed expenditures.

2. PURCHASING MATERIAL

A good purchasing department buys the best supplies and equipment for a given purpose at the lowest cost. Good purchasing means buy-

Item	Description	Unit	Approx. Unit Cost
Paper, Construction	White 9" x 12"	50 Sheets	.20
	Assorted 9" x 12"	50 Sheets	.23
	Gray 9" x 12"	50 Sheets	.20
Paper, Construction	Red 12" x 18"	50 Sheets	.45
	Yellow 12" x 18"	50 Sheets	.40
	Green 12" x 18"	50 Sheets	.40
	Orange 12" x 18"	50 Sheets	.40
	Blue 12" x 18"	50 Sheets	.40
	Black 12" x 18"	50 Sheets	.43
	White 12" x 18"	50 Sheets	.40
	Assorted 12" x 18"	50 Sheets	.45
Paper, Finger Paint	16" x 22" — Shaw	100 Sheets	2.50
Paper, Fluid Duplicator Masters	8 1/2 x 11 Standard #24	Ream	1.65
	8 1/2 x 14 Standard #24	Ream	2.08
	8 1/2 x 11 Rex-O-Graph	250 to Pkg.	2.00
Paper, Fluid Duplicator Copy	8 1/2 x 11 #20	Ream	1.00
	8 1/2 x 14 #20	Ream	1.30
Paper, Hektograph	8 1/2 x 11 #16 stock	Ream	.60
Paper, Kraft Wrapping	Rolls: 36" wide, 9" diameter #40	Roll	9.06
Paper, Manila Drawing	Cream 9" x 12"	Ream	.88
	Cream 12" x 18"	Ream	1.76
	Cream 18" x 24"	Ream	3.50
Paper, Mimeograph	#16 wt. Craftsman 8 1/2 x 11	Ream	.61
	#16 wt. Craftsman 8 1/2 x 14	Ream	.77
Paper, Music	Std. Scale-both sides 7" x 8 1/2"	Ream	.48
Paper, Onion Skin	Myriad-White Cockle 8 1/2" x 11"	Ream	1.45
Paper, Practice Writing	Palmer Ruled with Red Headline 8" x 10 1/2"	Ream	.61
	Ruling long way 5/8" 7" x 8 1/2"	Ream	.46
Paper, Newsprint, Ruled	Alternating heavy & light lines 8" x 10 1/2"	Ream	.32
Paper, Newsprint, Plain	9" x 12"	Ream	.43
	18" x 24"	Ream	1.30

Fig. 75. Example of a standard list of instructional supplies. This is a partial list.

ing early enough to assure delivery by the time the materials are needed, and having them when they are needed and in proper quantities to meet overstocked or understocked conditions. Good purchasing requires a complete understanding of the school system and its needs as well as a thorough knowledge of the market. The purchase of supplies and equipment provides an excellent opportunity for the business department to render an important service for the efficient conduct of the schools.

Purchasing policies

The board of education should establish a series of written policies which should govern purchasing practices to be followed in the school

Units On Hand	Add'l Units Needed	Total Cost Add'l Units	Remarks

district. These policies should be well thought out and in a workable condition. The policies should deal with the broader aspects of purchasing and not with the details or the mechanics which will be executed by the business office. These policies, as all other general policies of the school, should be reviewed from time to time and changed as needed. In some of the states there are School Codes which set up certain legal limitations and requirements which must be followed. In these cases the policies of the board cannot conflict with the state codes. In those states where there are not state codes relative to purchasing, the policies should be more in detail.

Many schools have successful policies while others operate without any. The list which follows is not meant to be exhaustive, but merely suggestive of the type of policies which may be worked out by school employees and the board of education.

1. No member of the board of education or an employee of the board shall derive any financial gain or reward from the purchase of material or services for school use.
2. The best price for the quality of material or services desired by the school shall be obtained at all times.
3. All supplies and equipment shall be purchased only after careful consideration of needs and desires of the appropriate officials and users of the material.
4. Written quotations for supplies and equipment shall be obtained from two or more companies when the cost of the item or items is great enough to warrant the time and expenditure involved.
5. The purchasing division shall constantly search for items of supplies and equipment which may better fit the needs of the school system and make those items available for experimental purposes to those who may be interested.
6. All purchases shall be made in conformity with the legal requirements of the state.
7. The purchasing division shall work with principals, teachers, custodians, and other interested persons to modify or change the standard list from time to time in order that better materials may be supplied to the school system.
8. The purchasing division, with the aid of available help, shall draw up exact specifications for certain items of material used by the school system.
9. The purchasing division shall use bid forms which will meet the legal requirements of the state.
10. A firm which has been found to be unreliable in making deliveries according to specifications shall not be allowed to receive another contract until the company can prove to the board of education that it will be reliable.

11. Material shall be purchased in as large a quantity as possible in order that advantage may be taken of quantity discounts.
12. The board of education shall take advantage of all discounts offered by firms for paying bills promptly.

The above suggestions for policies represent only a few of the many problems connected with purchasing supplies, equipment, and books for a school system. The administration and the board of education should give serious thought to the whole problem and adopt a set of policies which would give the school system the needed material, both in quantity and quality, for the least amount of money.

State contract prices

Some of the states have laws which require all institutions, including the public schools, to purchase all material at state contract prices. Other states provide such services but the laws do not require the schools to purchase from the contract price list. In those states which offer such services there is a department which works out specifications and receives bids for all items. Each purchasing unit is furnished with a list of items, specifications, name of firm or firms which gave the low bid, and the price of each item. The list is kept up to date at all times.

Cooperative purchasing for small schools

There are a great number of small administrative units operating in the several states. In a great number of these, provisions are not made for state contract prices. Therefore the administrator in the small unit is unable to take advantage of quantity purchasing because of his limited needs. In some sections of the country, superintendents of several schools are cooperating in purchasing. They are working out standard lists and pooling their needs so that they will be able to buy larger quantities. One county in Texas reported a saving of 43.5 per cent over advertised school catalog prices on supplies for 1953–54 as a result of a successful cooperative purchasing plan.[3]

Time to purchase

It is a difficult problem to state the exact time of the year when material should be purchased for a school system. There are several factors to consider relative to the best time of the year to make purchases. An important factor is the provision the school system has for

[3] "Cooperative Buying for Schools," *American School Board Journal*, CXXVI (October, 1953), 76.

storage and distribution of supplies. Certainly the season of the year when the prices are lowest is the most economical time to buy. In general it may be said that most supplies, equipment, books, fuel, etc., should be on hand when the school opens.

A number of schools find that a purchase calendar is of considerable assistance in the administration of the supplies of a school system. The following is an example of a purchase calendar.

December 1	Guide sheets sent to principals.
January 1–20	Supply lists made by principals, teachers, and other users of supplies.
January 20	Requisition estimates due from all schools and independent departments.
January 20- February 5	Estimates checked with budget, with amount used during preceding year, etc.
	Principals and department heads contacted with respect to possible discrepancies.
	Tabulations made.
	Bids advertised by (1) local newspapers and (2) letters to prospective bidders.
February 5–20	Bid forms prepared.
February 20	Bid forms mailed to interested vendors.
March 20	Deadline for receiving bids.
March 25	Bids opened by the Board of Education.
	Record made in minutes.
March 25- April 10	Specifications, bids, and samples examined.
April 10	Bids reviewed for Board of Education by the Superintendent and the Purchasing Agent.
	Recommendations made by the Superintendent.
April 10–25	Purchase orders prepared.
April 25	Purchase orders mailed to successful bidders.
	Unsuccessful bidders notified.

Obtaining bids

After complete specifications have been prepared for all items to be purchased, the purchasing department should get bids from those companies which are interested in furnishing the material. The purchasing division should have a file of all agents who have bid in the past, those who have expressed an interest in bidding, and also those who might be interested. In case the files are not complete the public should be informed through a newspaper advertisement. In some of the states the laws require the board to advertise for bids. Specific conditions and regulations governing bids should be given in the advertisement or "call." To comply with the laws of some states, the call or advertisement must be inserted in a newspaper several weeks in advance of the date for filing bids; careful consideration should be given that the requirements of the law are observed. The following suggested form is an illustration of a call for bids:

Call for Bids by the Board of Education

Sealed proposals will be received by the Board of Education of (*official name*) at (*place*) until (*hour*) date 19 , for (*State here the nature of material to be purchased*).

1. All bids must be submitted in accordance with specifications to bidders on file in the office of the (*name office*) at (*address*), copies of which will be furnished to prospective bidders on request.
2. Payment for material will be made on or before (*number*) days after contract is completed.
3. No bid will be accepted unless accompanied by a certified check equal to (*state per cent or amount of check*), conditioned that the bidder will enter into and perform contract in accordance with his bid, if accepted by the board of education.
4. No bid may be withdrawn for a period of fifteen days after scheduled closing time of the receipt of bid.
5. The board reserves the right to reject any and all bids.

> The Board of Education of (*name*)
> by (*name of authorized person*)

Date_____

Instructions to bidders should be complete and given on the bid blank which lists the material needed. These instructions should include such points as the following:

1. Requirements as to bond
2. Requirements as to bid form (Usually made on the blank supplied by the board of education)
3. Terms of payment
4. Conditions under which substitutions are permitted
5. Requirements as to unit and quantity prices
6. Requirements as to samples
7. Requirements as to delivery
8. Certification of quality

The form used for securing bids will vary in accordance with the state laws and the requirements of the local administrative unit. However, every condition to be agreed to in connection with the proposed purchase should be set forth on the bid blank. Figure 76 is an illustration of a bid blank. It is to be noted that the conditions for bids, the bid, the acceptance, and the instructions to bidders are given on the back of the bid blank.

Evaluating the bids received

Bids should be opened publicly. Any bid which is not in accordance with the proposed form, instructions, or specifications should be rejected. The bids should then be tabulated on a proper form which would afford an analysis and comparison in the light of the specifications. The contract should be awarded as soon as possible after opening the bids. When the contract is awarded and the required bond

HIGH POINT CITY SCHOOLS
900 ENGLISH STREET — TEL. 6912
HIGH POINT, NORTH CAROLINA

TO:...   Date..............................19.......

Request For Bids on

Bids in writing, subject to the conditions on the reverse hereof, will be received at this office until 2 o'clock P. M.
....for furnishing the supplies, materials or services as described below delivered

HIGH POINT CITY SCHOOLS

By:...

QUANTITY	ARTICLE - DESCRIPTION	UNIT PRICE	AMOUNT DOLLARS CENTS
		LESS........PERCENT DISCOUNT	
		NET	

NO SALES TAX NOR EXCISE TAX IS PAYABLE BY HIGH POINT CITY SCHOOLS.

Fig. 76. Bid blank, front. (Courtesy High Point Superintendent of Schools)

is posted by the successful bidder, the board of education should return all certified checks to the proper persons.

The purchase order

When the successful bidders have been selected, the purchasing officer will fill out the purchase orders. Purchase orders are often

CONDITIONS

1. The High Point City Schools reserves the right to reject any and all bids, to waive any informality in bids and, unless otherwise specified by the bidder, to accept any item in the bid. In case of error in the extension of prices in the bid, the unit price will govern.

2. Time, in connection with discount offered, will be computed from date of delivery of the supplies or materials to carrier when final inspection and acceptance are at point of origin, or from date of delivery at destination when final inspection and acceptance are at those points, or from date correct invoice is received if latter is later than the date of delivery.

3. Unless otherwise indicated on face of this form, it is understood and agreed that any item offered or shipped on this bid shall be new and in first class condition, and that all containers shall be new and suitable for storage or shipment.

BID

Date _____19_____

In compliance with the above request for bids, and subject to all the conditions thereof, the undersigned offers and agrees, if this bid be accepted within _____days from the date of the opening, to furnish any or all of the items upon which prices are quoted, at the price set opposite each item, and unless otherwise specified, within _____ days after receipt of order, delivered _____

Discounts will be allowed for prompt payments as follows: 10 calendar days, _____ per cent; 15 calendar days, _____ per cent; 20 calendar days, _____ per cent; 30 calendar days, _____ per cent.

Bidder _____, Address _____

By _____, Title _____
(Members of firms or person authorized to sign bids for corporations)   Telephone Number _____

ACCEPTANCE

Date _____19_____

Accepted as to items numbered _____

HIGH POINT CITY SCHOOLS

By _____

Title _____

INSTRUCTIONS TO BIDDERS

1. Unless otherwise requested, only one copy of Bid Form need be submitted.
2. Prices should be stated in units of quality specified with packing included.
3. Attach complete specifications for any substitution offered, or when amplification is desirable or necessary.
4. If descriptive matter is attached to bid, bidder's name must be on each separate sheet.
5. Where a brand or trade name appears in the specifications it is understood that it refers to that material or its equivalt
6. If the item bid upon has a trade name or brand, such trade name or brand must be stated in the bid.
7. Samples of items, when required, must be furnished free of expense, prior to the opening of bids, and if not destroyed, will upon request, be returned at the bidder's expense. Request for the return of samples must be made within 10 days following opening of bids. Each individual sample must be labeled with the bidder's name and item number.

Fig. 77. Bid blank, reverse.

issued without having bids when the amount purchased is in a small quantity or when the prices of the items are known.

It has been found advantageous to prepare the purchase order in quadruplicate, each of the four copies in a different color. The original copy is sent to the vendor, the second is filed as an unpaid

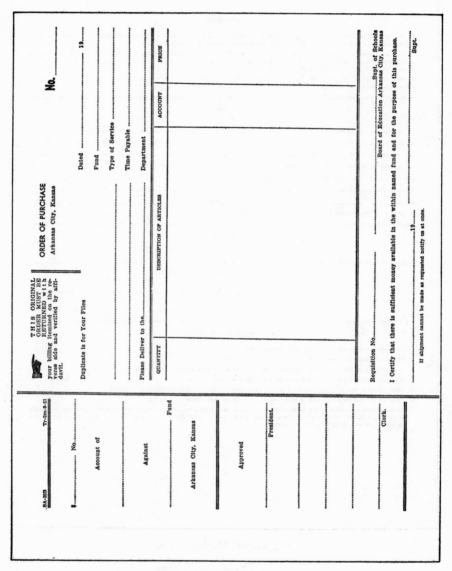

Fig. 78. Purchase order: 1.

BOARD OF EDUCATION

———————————— School District No. ————————

——————————————————,

PURCHASE ORDER

To ————————————————————

Ship to ——————————————————

Via ———————————————————

Order No. ——————————————
(Your invoice must show
this order No.)

Date Issued ————————————————

Date Wanted ————————————————

Quotation No. ——————————————.

Quantity	Description	Unit Price	Total Amount	Checked	Code

Conditions:

1. Please acknowledge receipt of this order by mail.
2. Make invoices in duplicate.
3. Right is reserved to cancel this order if it is not filled in contract time.
4. No modifications by verbal understanding.
5. Invoices and packages must bear this order No.

——————————————————————
Superintendent of Schools

Fig. 79. Purchase order: 2.

bill, the third is forwarded to the warehouse or to the school where the material is to be delivered, and the fourth is filed in the purchasing department according to serial number for reference use.

When the material which has been ordered is delivered to the warehouse or school, the shipment should be checked against the third copy of the purchase order. If all the material has been received, the third copy is so marked and returned to the purchasing officer who then fastens the vendor's bill to the second copy of purchase order and marks the bill ready for payment. The purchasing agent may destroy the third copy which was returned from the warehouse, as its usefulness has been fulfilled. The bill which has been marked ready for payment and attached to the second copy of the purchase order is placed in the voucher jacket.

Voucher jacket

The voucher jacket is a folder or an envelope in which vouchers (bills marked for payment) are filed. The face of the jacket is shown in Figure 80. It is to be noted that the face of the jacket carries the necessary spaces for coding the expenditures covered by the voucher. In addition to a copy of the purchase order and the invoice or bill, other information relative to the order such as any correspondence about the order and also the canceled check is filed in the jacket. Such an arrangement will facilitate accounting procedures and also auditing. Voucher jackets and contents should be filed in serial order as recorded in the voucher register of the accounting records.

Centralization of purchases

The purchasing of school supplies, equipment, and books should be in the hands of a centralized purchasing department. In the small schools where the superintendent carries out the functions of the business department, as well as the instructional program, one clerk should be assigned to do the work of purchasing, under the direction of the superintendent. In the larger school systems which have business managers, a purchasing department should be under his immediate supervision. In the very large schools there will be several assistants in the department such as bookkeepers, accountants, filing clerks, typists, and others as needed.

Purchasing of materials is closely connected with budgeting. The preparation and execution of the individual school and department budgets are important phases of supply administration. After the individual school budgets have been prepared they must be consolidated into one single budget for the school system, thus making it possible for quantity purchasing. Appropriations for individual schools and departments must be checked or some individuals will be extravagant while others will not receive their share. Making and controlling the budget for materials and purchasing are closely related and should be centralized for efficient administration.

3. STORAGE OF MATERIAL

The storage of material is just as important in a small school as it is in a large one, for about the same percentage of the budget goes for material in most schools, regardless of size. A fundamental princi-

VOUCHER JACKET

_____ Public Schools

Number _____

Creditor _____

Address _____

Purchase Order Number _____

Fund _____ Check No. _____ Amount Paid _____

General Control		Operation of Plant		Capital Outlay	
Code	Amount	Code	Amount	Code	Amount
Total		Total		Total	
Instruction		Maintenance of Plant		Debt Service	
Code	Amount	Code	Amount	Code	Amount
Total		Total		Total	
Auxiliary Services		Fixed Charges		Miscellaneous	
Code	Amount	Code	Amount	Code	Amount
Total		Total		Total	

Remarks:

_____

Approved By

Fig. 80. Voucher jacket.

ple of good supply management is to furnish the classroom teachers and users the material when needed and in the quantity and quality which will facilitate the educational program. In order to carry out this principle it is necessary to have a system of storage which will make the material available and relieve the staff members of unnecessary clerical work.   There are three different plans used for storage of materials—a centralized, a decentralized, and a combination centralized-decentralized plan.

Centralized storage

Centralized storage is used in the larger units of county or city administrative units.   This system provides for a central storeroom where all supplies are delivered and distributed to the several schools at a later date.   This system requires the services of adequate help in the storeroom.   It is essential to have a head clerk or manager and assistants depending upon the size of the system and the work assigned.

Material should be delivered to the central storeroom early enough to permit the personnel to make the proper checks before the supplies are needed in the several schools.   Some of the items to be checked are:

1. Compare the invoice with the purchase order to ascertain if quantity and quality are the same.
2. Compare the invoice with goods received as to quantity and quality.
3. Compare invoice with purchase order to ascertain whether any items have been back-ordered.
4. Check for damaged or broken materials.
5. Make the necessary storeroom records.
6. Place items in the proper storage places.

In those cases where items are damaged, broken, or of a kind different from that ordered, the manager should communicate with the purchasing agent or vendor asking for the proper adjustment.[4]   If facilities are provided for testing certain materials, the tests should be made immediately upon receipt of goods.   There are certain advantages in each type of storage plan.   Some of the advantages of centralized storage are:

1. A careful check is kept on each unit of material so that waste or loss from theft is reduced.
2. A perpetual inventory is easily maintained.
3. Depleted stocks are readily detected and replenished.
4. Principals, teachers, and other employees are relieved of much clerical work.

[4] The procedure to follow in dealing with such problems should be worked out by the business manager so there will not be a loss of time.   There should be a uniform practice so the manager of the storeroom will be able to report promptly.

5. Accurate records of receipts and distribution are more easily maintained.
6. Quantity purchasing is made possible.
7. Materials are kept in better condition, since adequate facilities are provided.
8. Budgetary procedures are more likely to be improved because of better records.
9. Materials needed for an emergency can be secured more quickly.
10. Qualified personnel are more likely to be employed.

The storeroom

The size of the storage space will depend upon the size of the school system. The storeroom or warehouse should be centrally located and reasonably near the general administration offices. There should be ample room on the site for parking the delivery trucks and several cars. A platform for loading and unloading should be accessible but where it will not cause a traffic hazard. The storeroom should be dry, fireproof, well lighted, heated, ventilated, properly equipped, and easily cleaned. There should be an office for the supply clerk in the storeroom. A number of schools are also providing, in connection with the central warehouse, a repair shop for machines such as radios, typewriters, and the like. In some of the county systems which have transportation the garage is located near the central storeroom. In this way the supplies used for automobile repairs may be handled through the regular storage room. The concentration of all supplies and repairs in a central unit facilitates better management and reduces costs.

The storeroom should be arranged with shelves and bins which are properly tagged in some systematic manner. Code numbers on the bins and shelves should correspond with code numbers used on the standard supply list. If such a system were used, it would be relatively simple for the person in charge of supplies to fill a requisition for an individual school. Figure 81 shows a form of a tag which could be placed on the bin or shelf.

```
Code:     666.27

Article:  Paper-Railroad
          Board

Unit:     Ream
```

Fig. 81. Bin or shelf tag.

It is entirely possible that some supplies will require special facilities. This is especially true of inflammables, poisons, and perishables. Special rooms for paints, gasoline, and other inflammables should be provided. These rooms should be fireproof, well ventilated and, if possible, well away from other supplies. Today, when there is an extensive cafeteria service in the schools and when the Federal Government supplies many perishable commodities, cold storage facilities should be provided.

Storeroom Records. Accurate record keeping is tantamount to good supply management. The supply manager should be responsible for all records pertaining to the storeroom. The supply manager's duties will be easier and more accurate if adequate record forms are provided. These records will fall into three main categories: receipt, inventory distribution, and budget control record.

When materials are received by the storeroom their receipts should be duly noted. A copy of the purchase order is sent to the storeroom clerk and when material is received and the necessary entries are made the copy is returned to the purchase department. Another method, which is often used, would be for the supply clerk to fill out a receipt for the material in duplicate. One copy is sent to the purchasing department and the duplicate copy is retained by the supply

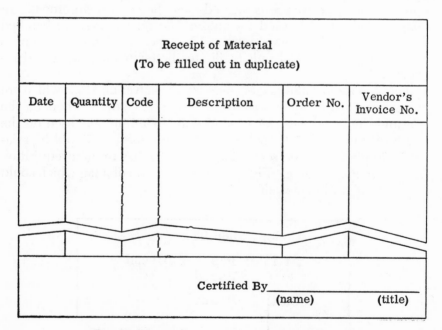

Fig. 82. Receipt for material received by storeroom.

Date	On Hand	Received	Receipt No.	Disbursed	Requisi- tion No.	School	Balance on Hand

Unit_____.   Unit Cost_____,_____,_____,_____.

Item_____   C ode Number_____.

Fig. 83. Perpetual inventory visible file card.

clerk for use in checking invoices and making entries on inventory form.   Such a receipt is shown in Figure 82.

After the goods have been receipted, entries should be made on the inventory record.   There are two types of inventory, the perpetual and the periodic.   The perpetual inventory enables the supply clerk to keep a running account of the amount of supplies ordered, the rate of use, and the amount on hand.   The perpetual inventory should be used with an occasional periodic item count.   An accurate inventory will facilitate long-range planning by the administration.

Several different types of perpetual inventory forms, such as the loose-leaf, the bin card, or a card file system are used.   A visible card file system is preferred.   Its advantages are:

1. The cards are kept in one central place thus saving time for the supply clerk.
2. The size of the card (5″ × 7″) effects a saving in the cost of forms.
3. The cards are less bulky to file.
4. The visible card is easily used.
5. The cards are less easily lost than loose-leaf forms.

A sample form of such a card is presented in Figure 83.   This card provides for entries of both receipts and disbursements.   Entries should be made on this card as soon as possible after each transaction.   Promptness is essential for accuracy and correct information.

Some organized plan of requisitioning material is essential if the storeroom clerk is to keep an accurate record of materials.   A plan which has proven satisfactory is the use of a requisition blank such as is shown in Figure 84.   This form contains space for unit and total

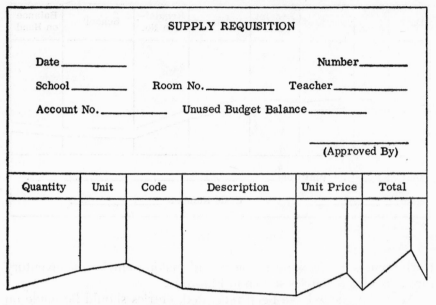

Fig. 84. Supply requisition.

price. The advantage of including these two items is twofold: (1) the teacher is made aware of the cost of supplies and hence will tend to be prudent in the use of them, and (2) in case the item is not on hand and must be ordered, some bookkeeping work is saved for the purchasing department.

The requisition is filled out by the teacher, who secures the needed information from the standard list supplied all employees. The teacher should also check the total amount of the requisition against the budget allotment to see if there are adequate funds. The original and duplicate copy are forwarded to the principal who should also check the budget. If adequate funds are available the principal will forward the original copy to the central storeroom. The storeroom clerk should also check the budget appropriations, and if there are adequate funds to cover the requisition the material should be delivered to the school and the necessary entries made on the inventory card and budget allotment card.

The budget control record is essential, if good budgetary procedures are to be followed. There is nothing to be gained by making a budget if those who have control over allotments are permitted to overdraw their accounts. A good form to use for budget control account is a visible card system shown in Figure 85.[5]

[5] See also Chapter 10, Encumbrance Record.

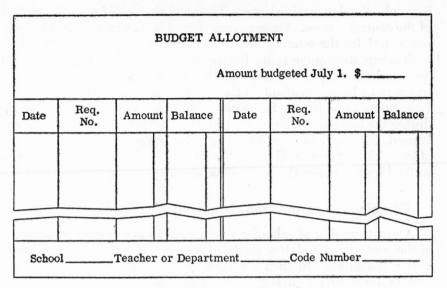

Fig. 85. Budget control record.

Decentralized storage

A great number of the smaller school systems do not have a central storeroom but deliver all materials directly to the individual schools. Although such a system does not seem to be as efficient, there are certain advantages. Some of the advantages which are often given by school administrators are:

1. Overhead costs are reduced through elimination of deliveries, original cost and upkeep of storeroom, and storeroom clerks.
2. Employees in each building are aware of the supplies they have to use, therefore they are more economical in consumption of materials.
3. Materials are always in the building and are available for use when needed.
4. Time is saved by employees since supplies are checked only at the time they are delivered.
5. Red tape is eliminated because of the requisitions required by central storeroom manager.

As it may be seen, some of the purported advantages may turn out to be disadvantages. For example, if there is not a central storeroom, requisitions will have to be sent to the purchasing agent from time to time when certain supplies are not on hand. It is almost impossible to buy all the needed supplies at one time and keep them in the individual schools. If there is not a central storeroom, it will be necessary for each school to establish one. The work then will be similar to that of the central system. Some person should be designated as the storeroom clerk for the school. Most individual schools are not equipped with adequate storage space for the many different supplies needed. Some administrators have found that there is a tendency for some teachers to be extravagant in the use of supplies when they have a large quantity on hand. Some persons would use the year's allotment during the first half of the year. If the decentralized system of storage is used, certain records must be kept by the general administrative office. The records will probably be about the same as those described for use under the centralized storage system.

Combination centralized-decentralized system

A great number of school systems have found that a combination of the centralized and decentralized methods of handling materials is very satisfactory. In such a system, provisions are made to deliver certain items directly to the schools and others to the storeroom. No attempt would be made to store items which were to be delivered to the individual schools. A good example of such material would be all types of furniture. Also such items as free textbooks would be delivered by the vendor to the buildings. Only a few extras would be stored in the central storeroom. If such a system is used, less storage space and less elaborate storage facilities will be needed. The records needed will be about the same as described under the centralized system.

4. DISTRIBUTION OF MATERIAL

Efficient supply management is not an end in itself, but a means of securing an adequate educational program for the pupils of the school. To this end, no matter what form of storage is provided, no matter how accurate and complete are the supply records, they are of no avail if the supplies are not in the hands of the teachers and pupils when they are needed.

Withdrawals

Supplies should never be issued from the storeroom without a formal requisition. A type of requisition to be used for withdrawal of supplies from the storage room has been described in this chapter under the heading of Storeroom Records. Whatever system may be used there should always be a signed request by some person in authority. The business manager and others who are concerned should draw up definite rules and regulations on how materials will be issued by the storeroom clerk.

Delivery

There are at least three factors which influence the delivery of material. They are: (1) the type of supply, (2) the facilities for delivery, and (3) the facilities for storage in the individual schools. Some supplies which may deteriorate easily or others which may cause extravagant use should be delivered in small quantities. Those materials which are bulky and hard to store or those which will not be wasted or deteriorate should be delivered in greater quantity. Judgment must be used in all cases. However, a complete understanding with those concerned should be maintained at all times.

Delivery from the central warehouse may be on a periodic basis. The number of deliveries per month should depend upon the storage facilities in each school and the cost of delivery. If the school district owns a light truck, which has been found to be advisable, delivery may be made weekly. In county systems which have a large number of buses it has been found profitable for the district to own a regular gasoline truck. This makes the rounds to the schools regularly and fills the tanks of the buses, thus eliminating the maintenance of gas pumps at each school.

Each principal should know the exact day delivery trucks will be at his school so that requests will be made on time. The storeroom clerk must be given ample time to fill all requisitions. In all school systems there are emergencies which will arise, and must be met. An understanding must be reached on how emergencies are to be handled. A complete understanding on the part of all persons concerning the delivery of supplies is essential for efficient management.

5. BOOK MANAGEMENT

The principles which have been presented in this chapter relative to supplies and equipment hold in the main for the management of textbooks, supplementary books, and library books. The selection of books is made more from the professional point of view. Prices are usually uniform and bids are not considered necessary. When books are presented for consideration the regular purchase prices are quoted. This serves as a bid.

Supplementary or library books are not stored. If it is the policy of the school system for all material to clear through the central storeroom, supplementary and library books should be checked and de-

	PRINCIPAL'S RECORD OF TEXTBOOKS Blankboro School Date_____				
	Title of Book	Total Number Received	Number Lost	Number Unfit	Number Usable
1					
2					
3					
4					
5					
6					

Fig. 86. Principal's record of textbooks.

livered as soon as possible to the specific schools according to the requests made. The same practice is often followed with textbooks. It is essential, however, to have some textbooks in the storeroom at all times for replacements and new students. Special racks should be provided for the storage of textbooks. Caution must be taken not to overstock on textbooks, especially if there is a possibility of readoption within a short span of time. Most school systems design certain forms to be used by the principal in accounting for books on hand at the close of the year (Figure 86). The storeroom clerk may use his regular forms in accounting for textbooks.

6. FUEL SUPPLY MANAGEMENT

Management of fuel supply is somewhat different from that of all other supplies. Whether coal or oil is used, the supply will be delivered directly to the schools. Every safeguard should be taken to see that the school district receives what it contracts and pays for. In the purchase of coal, the common practice is to have the coal weighed on registered scales. Samples of the coal should be taken and tests run to ascertain if the coal being delivered meets the specifications stipulated in the contract. The contract usually provides for certain penalties in price for coal not measuring up to the specifications. Those districts using oil should have contracts with reliable firms to deliver certain grade oil. A spot check should be made by a regular employee on the amount and kind delivered to the school and verified to the business office. Some schools use gas or electricity for heating. In such cases the amount used is measured by a meter. The meter should be checked from time to time as to accuracy.

7. BONDS ON PURCHASE AND SERVICE CONTRACTS

Many school districts require a performance bond of persons who contract to furnish certain supplies or equipment. This is particularly so when the contract is for a large outlay of funds. Most school authorities require a performance bond from a person who contracts to furnish fuel for the school system. The contractor furnishes the bond and it is usually in the nature of a surety bond. The board of education should be certain that the surety bond which the contractor or vendor furnishes will protect the school district in case the contract is not fulfilled. The demands made on the contractor or vendor for performance bonds by the board of education should be made known in the bid. Although the cost of surety bonds is relatively small, it is an item of expenditure which must be considered by the bidder. The board of education should have all contracts and bonds checked by its legal personnel at the time the bond is presented.

A surety bond eliminates all risks and uncertainty on contracts. It is simply a good business practice to require such bonds. The bond assures the board of education that the materials will be received as contracted. Not only is it a protection against a financial loss, but it is also a guarantee that the educational program may proceed as planned. The general public has a more secure feeling about the management of the school affairs if it knows that all precautionary measures possible are being practiced by the board of education. Board members are trustees of the school system and should protect the interests of the citizens of the community.

8. EVALUATION

There does not seem to be any one best method for doing any particular thing. Neither does a single individual always know what is the best plan of operation of a school system. The present plan of supply management for a school system may be working fairly satisfactorily, but is it the best plan that could be in operation for the schools? A change in an operational plan does not always improve the situation. Sometimes new methods are not as satisfactory as the older method. No school administrator, however, should continue a practice without having it evaluated from time to time.

The practices used in supply management should be evaluated from time to time. The policies which have been established by the board of education should be studied. Those people who use supplies have notions about the procedures and should be given an opportunity to carefully evaluate the present practices. Representatives from companies who sell the school materials will have many good suggestions to offer for improving local practices. Do the representatives of firms feel that they get a square and fair deal? Do the citizens of the community feel that adequate materials of the best quality are being furnished the schools? Do the custodians get those materials that they need for doing their work? Are the supplies reaching the schools on time? Do the students feel that they are being furnished adequate materials? These and many other questions could be raised about any system of selecting and purchasing materials for a school system. The administrator should recognize the fact that many people are affected by the supply system in use and should provide for a constant and systematic plan of evaluating supply management.

TOPICS FOR STUDY AND DISCUSSION

1. What per cent of the school dollar is spent for material in your school system?
2. What general policies does your board of education have relative to selecting and purchasing supplies?
3. Are the policies of your board made known to employees and citizens of your community?
4. Who selects the textbooks used in your classes?
5. Write out the plans you would use in your school system to develop a standard list of supplies.
6. When is the best time of year to purchase material in your city? Why?
7. Should bidders be permitted to attend the meeting of the board of education when bids are opened? Why?
8. Should all material be purchased through the process of bids? Why?
9. What are the advantages of a centralized purchasing department for a school system?
10. Write out a number of questions you would like to have answered if you were evaluating the supply management in your school system.
11. What improvements would you make in the storage and distribution of material in your school?
12. Describe the method used in your school system to keep account of the amount of money budgeted to a school.

SELECTED REFERENCES

BURKE, ARVID J. *Financing Public Schools in the United States*. New York: Harper & Bros., 1951, chap. XIX.

CRAWFORD, C. C. "Bidding Policies," *Nation's Schools*, LI (February, 1953), 100–2.

DAUM, HARRY F. "Better School Board Purchasing Policies," *American School Board Journal*, CVIII (July, 1953), 20–21.

GRIEDER, CALVIN, and WILLIAM E. ROSENSTENGEL. *Public School Administration*. New York: The Ronald Press Co., 1954, chap. XIX.

"Kalamazoo School Purchasing Policies," *American School Board Journal*, CXXVI (February, 1953), 52.

KRARUP, AGNES, "Pittsburgh Librarians Agree on School Policies for Curriculum Reference Materials," *Nation's Schools*, LII (October, 1953), 78–81.

LINN, HENRY H. *School Business Administration*, New York: The Ronald Press Co., 1956, chaps. IX–X.

LITTLE, T. C. "Measuring Efficiency in School Purchasing," *American School Board Journal*, CXVI (December, 1948), 25–28.

REDMOND, JAMES F., and ARTHUR G. PEARSON. "Purchasing School Supplies in a Big City System," *American School and University*, XXV (1953–54), 373–76.

21

PUPIL TRANSPORTATION

THE FREE TRANSPORTATION of pupils is not a recent development. The legal authorization for pupil transportation was first given by the Massachusetts Legislature on April 1, 1868. The following year, 1869, the Board of Education of Quincy, Massachusetts, began the first public transportation of pupils to the public schools and appropriated the sum of $521.12 for the payment of such services.

During the next twenty years only five states passed laws authorizing free transportation of pupils. By 1920, all the states had made transportation permissive and many of them provided some financial support. Today, pupil transportation has become big business. About seven and one-half million pupils are transported in approximately 135,000 buses daily. The annual expenditure for transportation is approximately $250 million. Approximately 5 per cent of current educational cost goes for transportation, and, in a few states, 15 per cent or more.[1] Transportation is not limited to rural communities. Many of the cities are spending thousands of dollars for pupil transportation on public carriers as well as operating school buses. It is a problem that must receive serious consideration from boards of education and administrators.

I. PLANNING THE TRANSPORTATION PROGRAM

Any part of school business that affects the lives of so many people and uses approximately 5 per cent of the current school dollar is worthy of a well thought out and planned program. The board of

[1] E. Glen Featherston, "Uniform Accounting Is the Crying Need in Pupil Transportation," *Nation's Schools*, XLV (April, 1950), 71.

education should give careful consideration to the adoption of policies which would help make the transportation system safe, economical, and efficient.

Policies of the board

The local board of education should adopt, upon recommendation of the superintendent of schools, certain policies for the guidance and direction of the transportation program. The policies or rules and regulations of the local board of education cannot be in conflict with the state laws or the state board of education policies. In some of the states there are very few state board rules and regulations, while in others there are many. The details of the rules and regulations made by the state board of education will be determined, to a great extent, by the state laws and the degree to which the state is financing local transportation. For example, the state of North Carolina finances current expense of all school transportation and also pays for replacement of buses. The state board has adopted a very complete set of rules and regulations governing school transportation. On the other hand, Virginia pays only a part of the transportation costs and the state board makes very few rules and regulations.

There are many decisions relative to transportation upon which the local board of education should decide if the laws of the state and the rules and regulations of the state board do not hand down mandates. Among the many decisions are:

1. Should transportation be provided through district-owned or contract buses? In a great number of states the school buses are owned by the local administrative unit or district and operated jointly by the district and state. In other states, the transportation is on the contract plan. There are arguments for each method. Those states which have district-owned buses claim more efficiency in the transportation system. The routes and time schedules may be changed to meet the changing school needs. Those school systems which use the contract plan find that such transportation consumes less time of administrators and costs little more. In making the final decision on the method to use, three factors should be kept in mind—safety, efficiency, and cost.
2. How far should a child live from school before he would be transported? The distances specified by the state laws will vary from one mile, in Louisiana, to four miles in South Dakota. The age of the pupil is a determining factor in some of the states. For example, in Florida, children seven to nine years of age are exempted from compulsory school attendance if they live over two miles from

school and transportation is not furnished, while children ten to sixteen years of age may be forced to walk up to three miles. The most commonly stated distance is 1½ to 2½ miles. Unless there is a law against transporting pupils who live less than a certain distance, the board of education should use its discretionary power and provide transportation where deemed advisable.

3. What should be the maximum time on the road for children who are transported? This is a problem that has been answered only in the beliefs held by individuals. One should be safe in saying that an elementary pupil should not be on the road over 45 minutes and the high school pupil not over one hour. In most of the states the roads are such that a child living twenty miles from school would not be required to ride over one hour.

4. How far should a child be expected to walk to the bus stop? In general, children should not be expected to walk over one-half mile to a bus stop unless the condition of the roads is such that it would be inadvisable for the bus to go closer. The bus stops should be set on each route not less than two-tenths of a mile apart. During periods of inclement weather, the bus should be permitted to stop at a safe point on the approved route nearest the child's home. Stops should not be made on blind curves, on steep grades, or near the crests of hills.

5. Should shelters be provided at bus stops? Although boards of education may not wish to become involved in the maintenance of such shelters, it would seem that encouragement should be given to interested parents to provide such facilities.

6. Should buses be used for the second or third trip? The practice of requiring a bus to make more than one trip is not desirable, although it is economical. With such schedules, some pupils leave home too early and have idle time in the morning and some pupils reach home very late after dismissal.

7. Should a bus serve more than one school? The problem of pupils having idle time in the morning and reaching home late at night arises when a bus serves more than one school. If the trips are short and the schools are near each other, it would be economical to use such a plan.

8. Who should be employed as drivers? This problem will be discussed fully in another section of this chapter.

These are only some of the many problems that must be solved by the board of education before an effective transportation system can be put into operation. If the rules and regulations are published and made known to all concerned, the general public will have a better understanding of the transportation system and at the same time administrators will be able to carry out the program more satisfactorily.

Financing the program

Financing the program of transportation is an important consideration of the board of education. In 1952 there were forty-one states appropriating monies for transportation of pupils. Two of the states, North Carolina and New Mexico, financed their entire transportation programs. The other thirty-nine used a variety of methods of appropriating state monies. Transportation, where needed, should be considered a part of the regular public educational program and financed in the same manner as all other parts of the educational program.

There are a number of factors that will affect the cost of transportation and that should be given careful consideration by the board of education. Among these factors are:

1. Size of the bus. The cost per pupil is less when larger buses are used. The conditions of the roads will be a factor to consider in deciding on the size of the bus.
2. The percentage of load carried by buses. In some states the laws permit buses to be overloaded as much as 20 per cent. This is not a sound practice.
3. The type or make of bus. The original and operating costs will vary with the type or make of the bus.
4. The length of routes and conditions of roads. Buses will last longer if they are driven over good roads.
5. The drivers. Some drivers are harder on buses than others; some get better gas mileage from the same type of bus. If students are used as drivers the cost will be less.
6. Program of bus maintenance. If the district owns a great number of buses, no doubt the cost of maintenance will be less by employing mechanics and making all repairs in a school-owned garage.
7. Plan of purchasing new buses. If the board purchases buses at the regular retail price, the cost will be much greater than purchasing them at fleet or state contract prices.

On the average, the current cost of transportation will be about 5 per cent of the current budget. This figure, however, cannot be relied upon for a specific school because of the many variables.

2. THE SCHOOL BUS

Whether the transportation of pupils be provided through district-owned or contracted buses, the board of education has a responsibility to see that the school buses are safe and meet the minimum standards.

Bus standards

The minimum standards for school bus construction were developed in 1938 by the National Conference on School Bus Standards and were revised in 1948 by the National Conference on School Transportation.[2] Although these standards were developed cooperatively by the directors and supervisors of transportation in the several states, their adoption was an individual state responsibility.   The main objectives of the committee which developed the minimum standards were safety and economy.   The members of the conference expressed a desire for each of the state legislatures to confer upon the proper regulatory agency the general obligation of setting up state-wide rules and regulations governing school bus chassis, body, and equipment. These standards must be adopted by a state to become legally effective within it.   The standards are made to apply to every type of school bus.   If the state has not adopted the minimum standards, a local board of education should consider them as a guide when purchasing new buses.

The bus record

The purchase of a school bus requires considerable outlay of money, and is considered a capital outlay expenditure.   If the administration desires to know something of the cost for operating and maintaining the school buses, a permanent record of the chassis and body of each bus should be kept. These records may be on either 8½″ × 11″ cards or a good grade of paper to fit a loose-leaf binder. Figures 87 and 88 are records for such purposes.[3]

Operation and maintenance of buses

The number of school buses operated by a school district will determine to a great extent the methods used for servicing and maintaining them.   If the school district is small and all of the buses come to a central school, the service and maintenance problems are rather simple.   A small garage of one or two stalls may be built at the central school and regular checks made on all the equipment.   The buses are maintained by private concerns when transportation is contracted. Some local school units which own their buses have the maintenance

[2] National Commission on Safety Education, *Minimum Standards for School Buses* (rev. ed.; Washington, D.C.: National Education Association, 1949).
[3] E. Glen Featherston and Andrew H. Gibbs, *Records and Reports for Pupil Transportation*, Special Series No. 2 (Washington, D.C.: U.S. Office of Education, 1949), pp. 22–23.

1. Bus number_____

2. Body serial number_____

3. Manufacturer's name_____

4. Length_____feet   5. Width_____in.

6. Inside height_____ in.   7. Overhang_____in.

8. Type of construction (check): (a) Steel_____

   (b) Wood and steel_____ (c) Wood_____

9. Weight of body_____lbs.

10. (a) Manufacturers rated   (b) Seating
        seating capacity_____   plan_____

    (c) Width of seats_____

    (d) Seat center spacing_____

11. Date purchased_____

12. Purchase price: (a) Cost of body .... $ _____

        (b) Trade-in value of old body   _____

        (c) Amount paid by school unit   _____

Maintenance Record	
Year	Total
First	$_____
Second	_____
Third	_____
Fourth	_____
Fifth	_____
Sixth...............	_____
Seventh	_____
Eighth	_____
Ninth	_____
Tenth	_____
Eleventh	_____
Twelfth	_____
Total	$_____

13. Equipment and body features:

Item	Yes	No	Item	Yes	No
Axe			Flags and Flares		
Book Racks			Reflectors — Side and Rear ...		
Defrosters			Stop-Signal Arm		
Emergency Door			Mirrors — Rear Vision		
Fire Extinguisher...................			(a) Inside		
First-Aid Kit			(b) Outside		
Heaters			Rub Rails (Applied)		
Auxiliary Heater			Ventilators — Roof................		
Extension Ducts			Windshield — Wipers		
Insulated			(a) Vacuum		
Clearance Lights....................			(b) Electric.....................		
Stop Lights — Flashing Type ...			(c) Air...........................		
Directional Signals			Safety Glass.......................		
Dome Lights					

Fig. 87. Permanent-body record of school bus.

work done at private garages, sometimes on contract prices but often at regular prices.

Those school systems, such as county units, which operate a great number of buses serving several schools, have somewhat different problems. A practice which is becoming very common in county units is to construct one large garage at a central point where all major repair work is done. The preventive maintenance program is carried out at the several schools. The county employs a mechanic who goes from school to school each week, sometimes more often, to inspect the buses and make many minor repairs. A light truck, equipped to carry numerous supplies such as bolts, spark plugs, and so forth, is used by the mechanic. Through experience the mechanic

1. Make_____ 2. Year Model_____ 3. Bus No._____

4. Motor serial number_____ 5. No. cylinders_____

6. Purchased: New____ Used_____ 7. Date purchased_____

8. Purchase price: (a) Cost of chassis .... $ _____

               (b) Trade-in allowance on old chassis .... $ _____

               (c) Amount paid by school unit .... $ _____

9. Number of wheels_____ 10. Wheelbase_____in.

11. Gross vehicle weight: As rated by manufacturer_____

12. Tire sizes: (a) Front_____ 13. Rated horsepower_____

          (b) Rear _____

14. Cumulative data

	Year of Service									
	1	2	3	4	5	6	7	8	9	Total
a. Speedometer reading at beginning of										
b. Cost of: (1) Operation[1]										
c. Total miles of service ...										
d. Cost per mile...............										

15. Equipment: (Check items applicable)
    a. Spare tire: 1 tire____; 2 tires____.
    b. Stop light, rear: One side____; both sides____.
    c. Exhaust to rear of body____.
    d. Type of brakes:
        (1) Two wheel _____
        (2) Four-wheel, mechanical _____
        (3) Four-wheel, hydraulic_____
        (4) Separate hand emergency_____
        (5) Booster brake____ Air_____
    e. Repair tools_____
    f. _____
    g. _____

[1]Include in cost of operation gas, oil, grease, anti-freeze, parts, labor, tires and tubes. Do not include driver's salary. If chassis and body costs are not kept separate list total operating costs of complete unit on Permanent Chassis Record.

Fig. 88. Permanent chassis record of school bus.

or the supervisor of transportation will be able to ascertain what parts will be needed. In addition to making the minor repairs, the mechanic will make a monthly or 1,000-mile bus inspection. Figure 89 shows an inspection report-blank used in the state of Virginia. Figure 90 shows a report which should be made by the driver, as needed, to the mechanic or principal.

The report should be made in duplicate. After the repairs have been made the driver should be given a copy which shows what repairs were made, and the mechanic will keep a copy for his files. The mechanic should make a report to the supervisor of transportation showing work done, time and parts used. Figure 91 gives a report

MONTHLY SCHOOL BUS INSPECTION REPORT TO DIVISION SUPERINTENDENT

Driver _____ Speedometer Reading _____ County_____

Month of_____ Bus No_____

Chassis Make _____ License Number _____

The Division Superintendent should instruct all mechanics authorized to make inspections to correct at once all items listed under Col. 3

	1 Good	2 Fair	3 Must be corrected	4 Corrections Made	5 Do brakes need relining?		1 Good	2 Fair	3 Must be corrected	4 Corrections Made
1. BRAKES						**8. DOORS**				
Master Cylinder						Front door condition				
Pedal Pressure						Rear door				
Lines and Hose						Ease of control				
Foot____ft. @ 20 M.P.H.						Fastening				
Hand____ft. @ 20 M.P.H.						Accessibility				
Equalization										
2. STEERING						**9. WINDOWS**				
Bushings, tie-rod, etc.						Condition (broken)				
Play in wheel						Condition of sash				
Springs and Shackles						Condition of guards				
Front end alignment						**10. WINDSHIELD**				
3. TIRES					Uneven or excessive tire wear	Condition				
Left front						**11. WINDSHIELD WIPER**				
Right front						Operation				
Left inside rear						Blade condition				
Left outside rear						**12. MIRRORS**				
Right inside rear						Inside				
Right outside rear						Outside				
Spare						**13. HORN**				
4. EXHAUST LINE						Condition				
Muffler						**14. MISCELLANEOUS**				
General condition					Do bulbs need replacing?	General cleanliness				
Fume leaks into body						Paint outside				
5. LIGHTS						Markings-front				
Headlights						Markings-rear				
Rear lights						Speedometer condition				
Clearance lights						Fender condition				
6. SIGNALS						Step condition				
Traffic lights						Bumper condition				
Rear directional signals						Engine condition				
Front directional signals						Battery condition				
Dir't'l S'g'l switch & pilot light						First Aid Kit Condition				
Stop light condition						Flags and flares				
7. BODY						Fire extinguisher condition				
Sides, sills and posts						**15. HEATER and DEFROSTER**				
Roof										
Condition of seats										
General condition										

I certify that the above report indicates to the best of my knowledge and ability the true condition of this school bus at this date.

_____ Name of Garage or Center

Date_____, 19____   _____ Inspector.

Fig. 89. Monthly or 1000-mile inspection report.

used by mechanics for repair work done at schools. These reports may be bound in a small book or they may be kept on cards.

In addition to the mechanics going to the several schools to make repairs, a service man with a gas and oil truck will visit all schools once a week, oftener if needed, to grease and to supply oil and gas for the several buses. The service man should make a report in dupli-

```
┌─────────────────────────────────────────────────────────────┐
│                    School Bus Driver's Report                 │
│                                                               │
│   School_____     Date _____       │
│   Bus Number_____     Driver_____       │
├─────────────────────────────────────────────────────────────┤
│   The following items should be repaired      If repaired by  │
│                                               mechanic initial│
│                                               here            │
├─────────────────────────────────────────────────────────────┤
│   Accessories_____        _____ │
│   Cooling System_____         _____ │
│   Ignition_____         _____ │
│   Fuel System_____         _____ │
│   Motor_____         _____ │
│   Lights_____         _____ │
│   Tires_____         _____ │
│   Brakes_____         _____ │
│   Others_____         _____ │
│                                                               │
│   _____        _____ │
└─────────────────────────────────────────────────────────────┘
```

Fig. 90. Driver's report on needed repairs.

cate, one copy to the school and the other to the supervisor. In smaller units of administration the work of the mechanic and serviceman may be combined and taken care of by only one person. Figure 92 shows a simple report made by the service man.

All school buses should be taken to the central garage and stored during the summer months. Each bus should be thoroughly inspected and repaired. Figure 93 gives a form to use for such inspection.

3. SCHOOL BUS DRIVERS

An important factor in securing safety, economy, and efficiency in pupil transportation is the school bus driver. He has the safety of the pupils in his care from the time they get on the bus until they are unloaded. His skill in driving and knowledge of the automobile determine, to a great extent, the economy in the bus operation. The driver's training, of course, largely determines the efficiency of the transportation.

Report of Mechanic				
School_____ Bus No._____Date_____				
The following repairs were made.				
List repairs Time				
1.				
2.				
3.				
Parts Used:				
Quantity	Description	Part No.	Cost	
1.				
2.				
3.				
Signature of Mechanic_____				

Fig. 91. Report of mechanic on work completed.

Service Report on Bus			
School_____ Bus No._____Date_____			
Quantity	Description	Price	
	Gal. Gas		
	Qts. Oil		
	Lbs. Grease		
Signature of Service Man_____			

Fig. 92. Service report on bus.

School Unit _____ County _____ Bus Number _____
Make _____ Year Model _____ Speedometer Reading _____

Item[1]	Check-O.K.	Cleaned	Adjusted	Repaired[2]	Replaced
BODY					
Driver's Compartment					
Speedometer-lubricate cable					
Ammeter					
Oil and gasoline gauges					
Temperature gauge					
Choke and throttle controls					
Lights-horn-signals-fuses					
Transmission shift lever and cover					
Windshield wipers					
Flags and flares					
Fire extinguishers-axe					
Mirrors-first aid kit					
Heater-defroster					
Steering wheel-column					
Clutch and brake pedals					
Floor boards-mat-stanchions					
Driver's seat					
Cowl-to-dash bolts					
Body-Fenders-Grille					
Glass: windows-windshields					
Window frames-fasteners					
Seats: frames-upholstery					
Floor: covering-wheelhousings					
Body bolts					
Service door: controls-steps					
Emergency door: release					

Item[1]	Check-O.K.	Cleaned	Adjusted	Repaired[2]	Replaced
Engine (Cont'd.)					
Main bearings-connecting rod inserts					
Fly wheel-ring gear					
Timing gears or chain					
Motor supports: front-rear					
Oil filter lines-filler pipe					
Manifold and exhaust line-gaskets					
Distributor-condenser-spark plugs-coils					
Generator-starter-wiring					
Battery: electrolyte-cables-holddown clamps					
Fan-fan belt-water pump					
Radiator-supports-thermostat					
Hose-hose clamps					
Fuel system-gas tank-supports					
Gas line-fuel pump-carburetor gaskets					
Governor tested and set					
Air filter or oil bath air cleaner					
Brakes					
Drums: front-rear					
Lining: front-rear-parking (hand)					

Side panels-posts-roof....
Paint: body-chassis-under floor and fenders....
Lettering....
Bumpers-fenders-braces....
Hood-fastening device....
Head and other lights....

CHASSIS

Front End Assembly

King pins-bushings....
Spindle and pitman arms....
Tie rod ends and drag links....
Front springs-u bolts and shackles....
Front wheel bearings....
Steering: sector-gear box tight to frame....
Wheel alignment....

Engine

Block-cylinder head-gasket....
Crank and cam shafts-valves....
Pistons-rings-pins....

Cylinders: master-wheel....
Fluid lines and hose....
Adjust: service-parking (hand)....

Clutch-Transmission-Driveline

Clutch....
Universal joints-D.S. bearings....

Rear Axle Assembly

Ring gear-pinion-carrier bearings....
Axle-spider-spider gears....
Rear springs-clamps-shackles....
Axle flange nuts-lug and wheel nuts....

Tires

Cuts-bruises-uneven wear....
Inner tubes....
Matched duals....
Air pressure....

CHANGE OIL AND GREASE
LUBRICATE ACCORDING TO
MANUFACTURER'S CHART....

[1] When check applies only to one item on a line circle the appropriate item.

[2] The nature of a repair may be indicated by the side of the item. For example, "Rebored" might be written by the side of "Block" when it has been checked as repaired.

Remarks:

I certify that I have completed the annual overhaul of this bus as indicated above.

Date _____   Signed _____

Mechanic

Fig. 93. Annual school bus inspection report.

The driver influence

The school bus driver has a definite responsibility in dealing with pupils and parents. He must exercise control over the pupils while they are on the bus and his conduct must be such that parents will feel that the safety of their children is secure. Through his actions and conduct he exercises a tremendous influence over the morals of the children. A school bus driver, either a high school youth or an adult, will be imitated by the children, therefore at all times he must be and act the part of a gentleman in every respect.

Qualifications of bus drivers

In all too many cases, school bus driving has been considered a part-time job. States have been very slow in setting up standards for drivers and many undesirable persons have been employed. In some of the states there are no requirements except a license to drive a car, in others there are only minimum age requirements, and in a few there are other qualifications such as physical health and moral fitness.

Adult drivers are used in many of the states, while in others, high school youth are used. In North Carolina approximately 90 per cent of the bus drivers are high school boys and girls. That state has an excellent record for safety, economy, and efficiency.

The National Conference on School Transportation in 1948 studied the job of the school bus driver and made some specific recommendations which should be followed by all states in licensing drivers for school buses. These requirements may be summarized as follows:[4]

1. The driver should be at least sixteen years of age.
2. The driver should be of good moral character. Among the elements to consider in character are (1) reliability, (2) initiative, (3) self-reliance, (4) leadership, (5) ability to get along with others, (6) freedom from use of undesirable language, (7) honesty, and (8) freedom from use of alcoholic beverages and narcotics.
3. The driver should be emotionally stable.
4. The driver should be trained and skilled in driving a bus and should have a license.

There is a feeling on the part of some persons who have charge of pupil transportation that a training program should be tied in with the granting of a school bus driver's license. Some states are using the training programs where high school students are bus drivers.

[4] National Commission on Safety Education, "Standards and Training Programs for School Bus Drivers," in *Recommendations of National Conference on School Transportation* (Washington, D.C.: National Education Association, 1949).

Each trainee must receive at least five hours of classroom instruction and pass a written or oral test on the material included in the instruction as well as a performance test by driving a school bus.

In-service training

"The driving of a school bus involves the safety of so many pupils, relations between so many people, and the handling of equipment of such considerable value that the lack of any sort of training for doing the job well is difficult to justify."[5] The state department of education, in cooperation with the local administrator, should accept the responsibility for planning and carrying out an in-service training program for all school bus drivers. The content of the program should be planned to meet the needs found in the local community and state. Some of the general topics of instruction may well include (1) state laws and other rules and regulations of agencies governing school bus operation, (2) personal qualifications of bus drivers, (3) responsibilities of bus drivers, (4) operational procedures on local level, (5) first aid, and (6) bus maintenance. It would be most desirable if such a training program came near or before the opening date of school.

Compensation

Pay for school bus drivers is almost always a problem. If high school pupils are used, the problem may be solved rather easily since the pupils would consider doing a part-time job. If adults are used, it is a different situation. The driving of the bus requires only two or three hours a day; hence full-time pay is out of the question. Some schools have found that using bus drivers for part-time school plant maintenance work or school bus maintenance will solve the problem. The practice of using teachers as bus drivers is not educationally sound. Teachers should be at the school before pupils arrive and when they leave. In any case the compensation should be sufficient to encourage able persons to do the job. Driving a school bus is important and only competent drivers should be employed.

Supervision of drivers

School bus drivers should be supervised. The employment of well-trained drivers will not insure safe, efficient, and economical transportation. There should be someone to assume the responsibility of

[5] *School Bus Drivers—Current Practices in Selection and Training*, U. S. Office of Education Pamphlet No. 100 (Washington, D.C.: Government Printing Office, 1946), p. 38.

PRINCIPAL'S MONTHLY BUS REPORT

_____ COUNTY _____ SCHOOL

Record for_____Month, Beginning_____ 19____, Ending_____19____

1 BUS NO.	2 DRIVER'S NAME	3 AVERAGE NO. PUPILS TRANSPORTED DAILY BY TRIP FOR MONTH								4 TOTAL NO. PUPILS TRANSPORTED DAILY		5 MILES TRAVELED THIS MONTH
		1st Trip		2nd Trip		3rd Trip		4th Trip				
		Elem.	H. S.	Elem.	H. S.	Elem.	H. S.	Elem.	H. S.	Elem.	H. S.	

LIST BELOW BUSES ARRIVING TARDY

Bus No.	Times Tardy	Bus No.	Times Tardy

REMARKS: _____

_____

Principal

Fig. 94. Principal's monthly bus report. (Courtesy State Board of Education, Richmond, Virginia)

seeing that drivers are obeying the state laws and the rules and regulations of the board of education. Some driver may become negligent in his duties and cause a serious accident. The supervisor should accompany the driver over the route at stated intervals and give close attention to all phases of the program. A good supervisor should have as a goal the improvement of the transportation system and not mere checking with a view to catching someone derelict in his duties. The principal of the school usually is the supervisor of the drivers. Figure 94 gives a form used in reporting monthly transportation.

4. PLANNING SCHOOL BUS ROUTES

In light of the policies or standards set up by the local board of education, the rules and regulations of the state board of education, and the laws of the state, the local administrator must establish the regular bus routes.

The transportation map

One of the first steps in planning the bus route is to locate the pupils eligible for transportation. Those eligible should be spotted on a map which corresponds to the school organization. The map should be sufficiently large to record the necessary information and it should also show all roads of varying types, and the hazards which exist. The children of different grade levels should be spotted by different colored pencils or pens. There is also value in giving other information on the map such as waiting stations, vacant homes, business establishments, and so forth.

Trial routes

With the data given on the transportation map, the next step becomes one of making trial routes. In making the trial routes, one must consider the size of the bus, length of route, type of routes, "circular" or "shoestring," and the location of the bus driver. The size of the bus will, to a great extent, be determined by the conditions of the roads and the number of pupils to be served. The length of the route will usually depend upon the density of population and the maximum time pupils may be required to ride a bus. There is much criticism on the circular or "loop" route because those pupils who live near the school are loaded first and are hauled a greater distance than those who live farthest from the school. Using the shoestring route, the pupils who live the greatest distance from school are loaded first and those living nearest the school will load last. If a driver is secured who lives near or at the end of the route, the bus may be stored overnight at the driver's home. Such procedure will cut down on the number of miles the bus will travel before loading pupils.

It may be necessary to try several trial routes before the problem is solved. This is especially true if the routes must be adjusted to fit the transportation equipment on hand.

Bus schedule

After the trial route has been worked out the next step is one of determining the stops on the trial route. The minimum distance be-

1. Driver_____   Bus No._____

2. Administrative Unit_____

3. Bus seating capacity[1]_____   4. Total miles to cover this schedule in a.m.:

(a) Distance from initial starting point of bus to point where pupils are first picked up:_____ miles (unloaded mileage)

(b) Distance from point where pupils are first picked up to point where pupils are last discharged:_____ miles (loaded mileage)

Time Bus Unloads at Each School	Time School Opens A.M.	Time School Closes P.M.

5. Schools[2] — Listed in order first served in morning:

School A_____

School B_____

School C_____

School D_____

6. Pupils to be transported:

Bus Stop No.	Time Scheduled for Stop A.M.	Name of Each Pupil Loaded in the morning	Miles from Home to Bus Stop	Miles Pupil Rides Bus to School	Grade	School Attended (checks)[2]				Time Scheduled for Pupil Unloading P.M.	Dates Pupil Transported	
						A	B	C	D		First Date	Last Date
1	2	3	4	5	6	7	8	9	10	11	12	13

(Continue this part of the form on the back of the sheet)

[1] According to State standards.

[2] Or buses served by this bus; e.g., if pupils are transferred to another bus instead of being taken to a given school, this schedule should be modified by writing in the number of the bus to which pupils are transferred.

Fig. 95. School bus schedule.

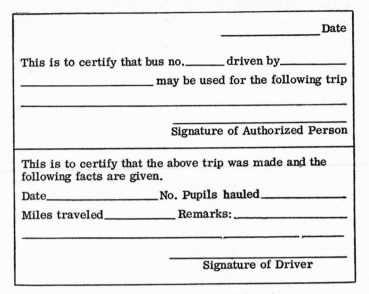

Fig. 96. Special trip authorization and driver's report.

tween stops is usually determined by the rules and regulations of the board of education. The exact stops will often be determined by traffic hazards, roads, and the terrain. After stops have been determined, a trial run should be made. In making the trial run all stops should be made, ample time given for loading or unloading, and normal operating speed should be observed. Any modifications found needed in the trial run should be made and then the schedule set up. The route schedule will show stops, length of stops, name of each pupil to be loaded, miles from child's home to bus stop, miles pupil rides on bus, and the time schedule for unloading pupils. Figure 95 gives the form recommended for such use by the Division of Transportation of the United States Office of Education.

A copy of the bus schedule should be sent to the home of each pupil who rides the bus and one copy each given the principal, the driver, and the director of transportation. Daily reports to the principal are usually required of the driver. Such a report should indicate time schedule, number of pupils hauled, new pupils, pupils who now ride the bus, and behavior report on pupils.

5. AUXILIARY USE OF SCHOOL BUSES

Some of the states prohibit the use of school buses for functions other than the regular transportation of pupils to and from school. Others permit the use of buses for extended educational purposes.

If buses are used for educational purposes, the board of education should establish rules and regulations for such use. The person who has the responsibility for granting permission for extra use should keep accurate records on each trip. Figure 96 shows a form which may be used.

It is recognized that the use of school buses must be carefully safeguarded to prevent abuse and avoid interference with maintaining the regular schedule. There are, however, many uses which may be made of school buses which will be an aid to the instructional program. More and more the citizens are realizing that all education is not obtained in the school building and demands will be made to use buses for educational purposes. It would seem that the use of school buses should not be directed by law but left to the discretion of the board of education.

6. SCHOOL TRANSPORTATION INSURANCE

The problem of school transportation insurance is a complicated one. There are several reasons why such conditions exist. In the first place, there is a vast difference among the states with respect to the authority and responsibility which has been conferred upon the boards of education. Secondly, pupil transportation is comparatively new and the judicial and legislative policies have not crystallized into a single pattern. In the third place, bus ownership is not the same in all states. Some schools use private buses, other uses publicly-owned buses, and still others use both private and publicly-owned buses. A fourth factor which complicates the problem is that some of the states may require insurance, others may authorize it, and still others prohibit it. All of the variances together with the different types of school transportation insurance create a complicated problem.

Types of school transportation insurance

There are at least four major types of insurance:

1. *Liability*—For compensation to pupils (and perhaps to other persons) who may be injured in school bus accidents.
2. *Property damage*—For the reimbursement of anyone whose car or other property is damaged by a school bus.
3. *Fire, theft, storm damage, etc.*—For specified losses incurred.
4. *Collision*—For the repair of damage to school buses themselves.[6]

[6] *School Transportation Insurance*, U. S. Office of Education Pamphlet No. 101 (Washington, D.C.: Government Printing Office, 1948), p. 2.

Liability insurance

The problem of liability of a school district for injury of a pupil while being transported varies from state to state. Traditionally, school districts have not been liable in tort action. The state and its political subdivisions could not be sued unless they consented, and then the consent must be in the form of enabling legislation. At this time, however, about ten states have removed the immunity of all governmental bodies and require publicly-owned school buses to be insured against injury to person; about twenty-five states authorize the purchase of liability insurance. In the other states the laws do not mention liability insurance.[7]

In three states there are state-wide plans of compensation or reimbursement for individuals injured in school bus accidents. Two of the three, North Carolina and Alabama, make the payments from state appropriations. The maximum allowable payments are $600 in North Carolina and $5,400 in Alabama. Delaware, a third state, carries a group accident insurance policy under which payments are made in cases of injuries resulting from bus accidents.[8]

In about twenty states liability insurance is required on privately-owned school buses, and in the others the school boards would have the implied rights to require liability insurance as a part of the contract for transportation with private owners. The laws seem to be much clearer concerning liability in event of injuries resulting from school bus accidents on privately-owned buses than on publicly-owned buses.

Property damage insurance

The reimbursement to anyone whose car or other property is damaged by a publicly-owned school bus is about in the same state of affairs as liability insurance. "Because of governmental immunity, school boards are powerless to assume any obligations for risks of harm to the property of others or to provide any form of insurance protection against property losses incurred by others in school bus accidents."[9]

Several states require owners of privately-owned school buses to carry property damage insurance. In some others, the states direct the boards to make property damage insurance a factor in the contract for privately-owned buses. The whole problem of liability and

---

[7] Madaline K. Remmlein, *The Laws of Local Public School Administration* (New York: McGraw-Hill Book Co., Inc., 1953), pp. 150–53.

[8] *School Transportation Insurance, op. cit.*, p. 13.

[9] Remmlein, *op. cit.*, p. 153.

property damage insurance needs attention from the lawmakers and courts. A uniform practice established throughout the whole country would make for a better situation. In the meantime administrators should know and understand the laws of their state in regard to pupil transportation insurance to prevent boards of education spending money from which no value will be derived.

Collision and fire-theft insurance

These types of insurance provide for the reimbursement to the district for losses or damages to a bus as a result of a wreck, fire, or theft. The legal principles are quite different concerning collision and fire-theft insurance from those concerning liability or property damage. Here the board's interest is in safeguarding the school property of the district. The school board in every state has the power, either expressed or implied, to care for and protect all school property.

7. PUPIL TRANSPORTATION IN CITIES

Pupil transportation has not been as extensive and important in cities as in rural areas even though transportation of certain groups in some cities antedates rural transportation. Probably the reason for this is that large cities which require pupils to travel distances greater than two miles have good systems of common carriers. Today, when many of the smaller cities are going out to the edge of town for larger school sites, transportation is becoming more of a problem.

Handicapped children make up the largest single group to be transported. More attention is being given to the education of the handicapped, and it is likely that more states will enact legislation which will require the transportation of certain pupils as part of the special education program.

The use of public service vehicles for pupil transportation is rather extensive in cities where transportation is needed. The school pupils usually get a reduced rate on the common carrier and the boards of education allow or pay for such services. Such a method relieves the board of education of many problems and doubtless is no more expensive than it would be to operate school buses. In those cases where boards of education own school buses the same principles and practices which have been mentioned in this chapter for rural transportation would apply to the cities. Cities are not likely to use publicly-owned buses for pupil transportation as long as they can use the common carriers.[10]

[10] See E. Glen Featherston, *Pupil Transportation in Cities,* U. S. Office of Education Pamphlet No. 111 (Washington, D.C.: Government Printing Office, 1951) for the status of transportation in the city.

TOPICS FOR STUDY AND DISCUSSION

1. Trace the development of school transportation in your local state.
2. What rules and regulations pertaining to pupil transportation do you have in your district? Evaluate these in light of best practices.
3. Who should be transported to and from school?
4. What are the bus standards used in your state?
5. Describe and evaluate the maintenance program used in your district.
6. What are the requirements for school bus drivers in your state?
7. Write out in detail how you would plan a bus route in your district.
8. What are the laws relative to insurance in your state?
9. When should a school bus be used for purposes other than transportation of pupils to and from school?
10. What records and reports are required in your school system?

SELECTED REFERENCES

American Association of School Administrators. *The American School Superintendency.* Washington, D.C.: The Association, 1952, pp. 188–95.

BELNAP, B. H. "State Aid for School Transportation," *School Executive,* LXX (February, 1951), 52.

BUTTERWORTH, JULIAN E., and HOWARD A. DAWSON. *The Modern Rural School.* New York: McGraw-Hill Book Co., Inc., 1952, chap. XXII.

FEATHERSTON, E. GLEN. "Uniform Accounting Is a Crying Need in Pupil Transportation," *Nation's Schools,* XLV (April, 1950), 71.

———. *School Bus Maintenance.* (Office of Education, Federal Security Agency, Bulletin 1948, No. 2.) Washington, D.C.: Government Printing Office, 1948.

FEATHERSTON, E. GLEN and ANDREW H. GIBBS. *Records and Reports for Pupil Transportation.* (Office of Education, Federal Security Agency, Special Series No. 2.) Washington, D.C.: Government Printing Office, 1949.

GARBER, LEE O. "Legal Responsibilities of School Bus Drivers," *Nation's Schools,* XLIV (January, 1952), 41.

GRIEDER, CALVIN, and WILLIAM E. ROSENSTENGEL. *Public School Administration.* New York: The Ronald Press Co., 1954, chap. XII.

LINN, HENRY H., and SCHUYLER C. JOYNER. *Insurance Practices in School Administration.* New York: The Ronald Press Co., 1952, chaps. VI–VII.

National Commission on Safety Education. *Standards and Training Programs for School Bus Drivers.* Washington, D.C.: National Education Association, 1949.

National Conference on School Transportation. *Minimum Standards for School Buses.* Washington, D.C.: National Education Association, 1949.

National Education Association. *Pupil Transportation* (Department of Rural Education, Yearbook, 1953). Washington, D.C.: The Association, 1953.

POPE, F. G. "Which System of Transportation, District-Owned or Contract, Is More Economical?" *American School Board Journal,* CXXI (August, 1950), 25.

REMMLEIN, MADALINE K. *The Law of Local Public School Administration.*
New York: McGraw-Hill Book Co., Inc., 1953, chap. V.

STACK, DORR. "School Transportation—A Look Ahead," *American School and University 1953–54.*   New York: American School Publishing Corp., 1953, pp. 387–90.

WALQUIST, JOHN T., *et al.* *The Administration of Public Education.* New York: The Ronald Press Co., 1953, chap. XIV.

NAME INDEX

SUBJECT INDEX

435